Eva Reichel
The Ho: Living in a World of Plenty

Eva Reichel

The Ho: Living in a World of Plenty

Of Social Cohesion and Ritual Friendship
on the Chota Nagpur Plateau

MANOHAR
2022

Library of Congress Control Number: 2020933302

Bibliographic information published by the Deutsche Nationalbibliothek
The Deutsche Nationalbibliothek lists this publication in the Deutsche Nationalbibliografie;
Detailed bibliographic data are available in the Internet at http://dnb.dnb.de.

First published in 2020 by
Walter de Gruyter GmbH, Berlin/Boston

Reprinted in India with permission of the original publisher 2022

© Walter de Gruyter GmbH, Berlin/Boston 2020, 2022

ISBN 978-93-91928-18-6

Published by
Ajay Kumar Jain *for*
Manohar Publishers & Distributors
4753/23 Ansari Road, Daryaganj
New Delhi 110 002

Printed at
Replika Press Pvt. Ltd.

In memory of
my *saki* in Ho country,
to my husband
and Georg Pfeffer

**Glimpses from
Ho Country I**

Abstract

Survey of fieldwork and region of research: The book is based on long-term research between 2005 and 2019. In participant observation fieldwork was done in Kolhan, a terrain in Central Eastern India transgressing the borders of the states of Odisha and Jharkhand and part of Middle India's tribal belt. This constitutes one of India's four tribal zones inhabited by altogether more than 100 million people administratively catalogued as Scheduled Tribes.

The study focusses on the Ho, a tribal community of approximately one million people. With members of other aboriginal (*adivasi*) communities and artisan nontribal categories they have shared cultural norms and the space of the hilly region and plateaux of the Chota Nagpur Plateau within an ordered multi-ethnic assemblage "for ages". Recognized in the region of research as first settlers and landowners Ho command a high status as they cultivate the land cleared by their forefathers and given to them as a gift by their creator god Sinbonga. Land is honoured by the Ho as Mother Earth.

Outline of the argument: The book explores the structured tapestry of Ho people's relations and interrelatedness within their culture-specific sociocosmic universe ensuring their social reproduction in the present and affording them the means for and the awareness of living in a world of plenty. This world of abundance – with the Ho ("a man; a Ho") as its conceptual centre – includes the Ho's dead, their spirit world and supreme deity, and their tribal and nontribal fellow humans.

The core of the book is an arrangement of chapters studying how social cohesion of specific Ho social categories and ordered coexistence of notionally distinct categories across tribal boundaries manifest themselves in the region of research in manifold ways: socially, ritually, economically, and linguistically.

Of course, the representation of the Ho's universe in the book is *my* representation as it has been filtered through *my* perception, *my* interpretation, and *my* understanding of it. Among other factors, this was certainly impacted by the ritual friendship relation *saki* that has accompanied me over the years almost since the very beginning of fieldwork. It has hence lent itself to being analysed as a resourceful focal point contributing to relatedness and social cohesion across tribal boundaries in its own right.

https://doi.org/10.1515/9783110666199-001

**Glimpses from
Ho Country II**

Contents

Acknowledgments

This book is about a fascinating world that I have been privileged to share over a period of more than a decade of my life. It is the world of the Ho people who inhabit India's interior as one of the numerous 'tribes' and who to this day claim to be living in a world of plenty – despite their being faced with all different kinds of pressure, discrimination, and state interventions.

Research during long-term stays and frequent return visits to Ho country resulted in a doctoral thesis handed in at the Johann Wolfgang Goethe-University Frankfurt/Main in 2018 which was then turned into this book. All of this would have been impossible without the commitment, guidance, and encouragement of many people, the incredible hospitality of all of my hosts in various parts of India and the generous help and support I have received over many years. I apologize that I will be unable to name all who have contributed in manifold ways – at home and in the field.

First, I must thank all the villagers who tolerated my alien presence in their midst and who welcomed me with an open mind in the various sites of Jharkhand and Northern Odisha where I conducted fieldwork. They invited me into their homes and into their lives, assisted me in coming to terms with the Ho language, and they offered me rice-beer. I am especially indebted to Santi Purty (late), the village head's wife of Pathan Sai, for asking me to become her *saki* or namesake on the eighth day of my stay in Ho country. That way a ritual relation came into being between the two of us and I became gradually transformed into a person, a social being. I am likewise indebted to Chumburu Purty, her husband and village head, for endless talks on Ho society. He patiently introduced me into his *miyad mandi chaturenko*, when I was still utterly ignorant of that key feature of Ho social organization. Gurucharan Hansda was so much more than my Santal assistant: he was my informant, my interpreter and confidant, and he became my son. He, his wife, and their two sons shared as much of their days with me as they possibly could. Sadurgon Kondangkel, village head of Gara Sai, became a close friend. He helped me in catching a glimpse of the Ho male ritual world and took me along at night, where women are usually denied access. He eventually introduced me to my *kaki-ma* and *kaka,* who would turn out to be my parents and who moved family members and things, so I could have a complete house quite to myself in 2009/2010. Thank you all for transforming my identity from that of an outsider into one of mother, daughter, elder sister, mother-in-law, sister-in-law, grandmother, elder brother's wife etc. My stay also became pleasant thanks to all the children around me. Their big, warm smiles encouraged me. They proved to be fantastic language teachers

https://doi.org/10.1515/9783110666199-002

and kept working on my pronunciation. In fact, my Ho (grand-) children, their social competence and self-confident growing into the world of the adults impressed me more than I can say. Just by their being the way they were they inspired me to learn more about Ho culture and become part of it myself.

In Chaibasa/Jharkhand I am most grateful to the Tribal Research and Training Centre (TRTC) of Lupungutu and to the staff of the St. Xavier's High School for Boys there. They repeatedly provided me with shelter and food. Eventually I was offered free access to their technical resources and wonderful library. They inspired me with their commitment, their open hearts, and their genuine respect of Ho culture. They guided my first steps into the interior. Especially Mike T. Raj, S.J., head of the TRTC in Guira, later director of the XLRI in Jamshedpur, today Rector at Vidyajyoti College of Theology in Delhi, proved extremely supportive and interested over the years; he took me to remote Ho villages in his jeep many times and helped me sort out the logistics of life in tribal Middle India. It was J. Deeney's (S.J., late) personality, his profound knowledge of the most intricate subtleties of the Ho's language, his admiration of Ho ways of constructing their world, his warm friendship and generous sharing of the results of his many years of work among the Ho that kept being a constant inspiration and obligation to me. Four days before his death we hugged farewell. Father Deeney, I owe you so much, I thank you so much! I am also grateful to Fr. Jerry Cutinha, S.J, who helped me in my struggle with the language and enabled me to eventually get in touch with Barbara Verardo from the LSE in London. I want to thank Fr. Tom Nelles, S.J., who as a lawyer introduced me into the legal situation of Ho women, and to Dhanur Singh Purty, Deeney's Ho scholar and assistant, who came on his bicycle many times in the blazing hot sun to see me and discuss my fieldwork data. In Jamshedpur I want to thank the staff of the XLRI, especially Fr. James and Fr. Paul, who helped and did not lose their heads as I did mine, when heavy floods had washed away the rails and I got stuck in the middle of nowhere – or so I thought.

In Sambalpur it was Prof. Deepak Behera, head of the Department of Social Anthropology, who welcomed me in his family, squeezed me into his busy days, and discussed my initially quite vague ideas. He helped me get in touch with Promod Mohanta, lecturer of anthropology at Rairanpur College. Without their initiative I would never have ended up where I finally did for my first fieldwork of four months in 2006. It is thanks to them that a suitable village, a home, and a research assistant were found. Sauna Majhi was such a charming young man with an extremely pleasant character. Looking back, I am afraid that I was often too impatient with him. In Ranchi my thanks go to Ganesh Murmu, who took me around the Tribal and Regional Languages Department of Ranchi University and introduced me into the projects of his institute and that of Gregory D.S. Anderson, director of the Living Tongues Institute for Endangered Languages.

In Delhi I am grateful to my friends Vikas and Prakash Mathur, in whose house I have always been welcome. Close friends with their parents Urmila (late) and Vishu (late) Mathur, I have accompanied their sons' lives for more than forty years by now. It is great to know you two out there and to enjoy the privilege of this cross-generational and cross-cultural long-lasting friendship. It is also thanks to you that I got lured into this Indian adventure!

From London I received constant enthusiasm for my Ho project and valuable information from Michael Yorke, Barbara Verardo and Alpa Shah. They generously shared with me insights from their fieldwork experience as well as their unpublished Ph.D. theses all of them based on long-term fieldwork in 1973, 1998 and 2000 respectively among the Ho and Munda people of Jharkhand.

Everything started in Berlin with Prof. Pfeffer, my supervisor. In his seminars he kept saying things that I did not understand, but that I wanted to understand. I am grateful for his sensitive guidance at home and in the field, his patience, his fine sense of humour, his encouraging mails, frequent discussions on an equal footing, the gift of his time that I had the privilege to receive over a substantial number of years, and his sincere respect for *Anthropos* – here and elsewhere.

My husband and my family mean more to this book than can be expressed here. My husband has been simply amazing in his sincere, unshaken and loving interest in my work, the people in the field, and me. He accompanied me to the field for a few months, while my grown-up daughters patiently stayed back wondering and a bit proud of what their elderly mother was doing 'out there' in the field for so long and so often.

Last, I want to extend my gratitude to the editors of De Gruyter's "Religion and Society" series for having my manuscript reviewed and accepting it for publication.

Berlin, February 2020

Annotations

Abbreviations

Relationship terms

M	mother	+nie	cross niece
F	father	e	older
Z	sister	y	younger
B	brother	(ws), ♀ sp.	woman/female speaking
D	daughter	(ms), ♂ sp.	man/male speaking
S	son	y +cou	younger cross cousin
W	wife	e +cou	older cross cousin
H	husband	y//cou	younger parallel cousin
P	parent	e//cou	older parallel cousin
Ch	child/children	+2, (+2)	grandparents' generation
sib	sibling	+1, (+1)	parents' generation
sp	spouse	0	*ego*'s generation
nep	nephew	-1, (-1)	children's generation
//nep	parallel nephew	-2, (-2)	grandchildren's generation
+nep	cross nephew	os	opposite sex
nie	niece	ss	same sex
//nie	parallel niece		

Combined relationship terms

eBW	older brother's wife
MBDy	mother's brother's daughter, younger than *ego*
spsibsp	spouse's sibling's spouse
sibspsib	sibling's spouse's sibling
HMeB	husband's mother's older brother

Abbreviations: social and political

mmc *miyad mandi chaturenko* – the people of one rice pot. This specific social Ho unit has been discussed in chapter 3. The abbreviation *mmc* is frequently recurred to throughout the book.

TRTC Tribal Research and Training Centre

BJP Bharatiya Janata Party (established in 1980; Narendra Modi has been Prime Minister since May 2014)

https://doi.org/10.1515/9783110666199-003

ST	Scheduled Tribe	OBC	Other Backward Classes
SC	Scheduled Caste	BPL	Below Poverty Line

Abbreviations: linguistic and other

pass.	passive voice	refl.	reflexive voice
tr.	transitive	Hi	Hindi
itr.	intransitive	U	Urdu

cf.	confer; reference to word or material related to topic under discussion with opposite or contrasting meaning
see also	reference to word or material related to topic under discussion with similar meaning
see	reference to other sources of information
E.M.	*Encyclopaedia Mundarica* by Hoffmann, John et al. 1990 [1950]. 16 volumes. New Delhi: Gian Publishers.
ALD	Crowther, Jonathan (ed.) 1995. *Oxford Advanced Learner's Dictionary* 1995. Oxford: Oxford University Press. 5th edition.

Notes on transliteration and formal remarks

Spelling and denotation of the Ho terms have been checked with Deeney's Ho-English Dictionary (one volume) from 2005 [1978]. In this Deeney has rendered Ho vocabulary in Roman script and a slightly modified Devanagari taking into account that Ho does not know aspirated consonants and is not identical with Mundari or Munda in terms of grammar and vocabulary despite a high degree of correspondence.

Ho terms and the very few Santali expressions that I make use of in this book are italicized. The names of persons (Lako Bodra), of geographical sites and localities (Chota Nagpur Plateau, Chaibasa), of communities (Gau, Pano), of clans (Purty, Kisku) and subclans (Doraiburu Bodra), of languages (Santali, Kui) and of Sinbonga are capitalized, but not italicized. Following Deeney (2005), the names of Ho deities/spirits (*desauli*) and of Ho/Gau/Santal festivals (*mage, gowa bonga, sohrae*) are italicized, but not capitalized.

The Roman script is used throughout for Ho words largely neglecting diacritic marks except where these are phonemic (*jati, jaṭi*). The colon (:) indicates a glottalized vowel. The check is always given, the length of a vowel only when it is phonemic (*goe:* versus *gōe:*). I refer to Ho and Santal people as Ho and Santal in the singular and plural without adding the English plural s-marker. Where necessary the Ho plural marker -ko is suffixed to a noun.

Single quotation marks indicate that the English expressions are considered culturally inadequate, misleading, or narrowing the meaning of the concepts indigenously implied in the terms (haga-'brother'). Double quotation marks come with quotations from oral communication or literary sources.

As a rule, the denotations of indigenous terms are given as they arise. This is repeated throughout the book to improve the readability of the text. Exceptions are frequently used Ho terms when the context allows to do so. This concerns especially the following terms:

adin	inner room of a house; abode of the forefathers' souls; during festivals meals are prepared inside	ham ho- dum hoko	old men/ sleeping men; the dead of the house whose spirits/ souls dwell in the adin
dewa	shaman	munda	village headman
diuri	ritual guide	bonga	a spirit; to sacrifice
diyan	rice-beer	haga	'brother', brother

In Glossary II the denotations of many Ho terms that have been used in the body of the text have been contextualized and complemented, where considered insightful, by term-related references to fieldwork and brief comments.

A separate glossary I with notes on Ho history concerns the situation on the Chota Nagpur Plateau during the colonial and precolonial period. It provides background information complementary to that given in the main body of the text. Browsing through the two annotated glossaries first before reading the book may be an idea for some to become preliminarily acquainted with a few notions, perspectives, and specifics of Ho people and the world they live in.

I have been given permission by all informants to make use of our conversations, their names, and the names of their villages. They also agreed to having the photos published.

Prologue

'They' versus 'we': J. Nehru's perspective

> *I am alarmed when I see – not only in this country but in other great countries, too – how anxious people are to shape others according to their own image or likeness, and to impose on them their particular way of living. We are welcome to our way of living, but why impose it on others? This applies equally to national and international fields. In fact, there would be more peace in the world if people were to desist from imposing their way of living on other people and countries. I am not at all sure which is the better way of living, the tribal or our own. In some respects, I am quite certain theirs is better. Therefore, it is grossly presumptuous on our part to approach them with an air of superiority, to tell them how to behave or what to do and what not to do. There is no point in trying to make of them a second-rate copy of ourselves.*
> (J. Nehru, quoted in M. Raza and A. Ahmad 1990: 64)

'They' versus 'we': the anthropologist's perspective

Plate 1: Before the harvest I.
Rice field in the village of Tarana, Mayurbhanj District, Odisha, India (October 2009)

https://doi.org/10.1515/9783110666199-004

Notes from a Ho village in Odisha

Village life begins early in tribal Middle India: occasionally at 4 a.m., seldom later than 5 a.m., women sometimes getting up a little earlier than men and children. Cows are led out of their sheds and fed. Other cattle will be taken care of later; there seems to be an order. In winter, when it is bitterly cold, fires are lit outside, often by young boys, and expertly fed with rice straw, never allowing flames to leap up and burn high. Neighbours – at least those who are on speaking terms, but in any case beyond the bounds of what in the West is considered a nuclear family, male and female, young and old, squat around the fires warming their hands and feet. Watching the dark transform into dawn, they talk each other into the day long before sunrise at around 6:15, by which time everybody is already busy. Carried along and safely seated on the hips of their elder siblings (an identity which is not to be understood in terms of blood relationship), infant boys and girls grow into social maturity, self-confidence, and the principle of seniority. Other daily chores, such as sweeping, fetching water from the well, doing the dishes, cleaning the sheds, purifying the courtyard and the adjoining footpaths with cow dung, and cutting up vegetables are seen to in known and separate ways by males, females, and also children. Whenever and wherever people see or meet others, while on their way to the well, across the rice fields, to the jungle, or to the market, they will speak to each other, even if only briefly and even if 'only' enquiring about the way. Almost never will anybody slow down for this. People never pass silently, wordlessly, and if they do, most certainly there is a reason.[1]

During the harvest as well, villagers are busy leading their individual lives collectively. Landowners may either work on their own fields or, especially if the land has not been divided among brothers and officially so registered, help each other. Also, while some villagers will work on someone else's land as part of an exchange of reciprocal assistance, others, as day labourers, will be paid in kind or in cash. After the harvest, which may stretch into the middle of January, but ends before *mokor sankranti*, hard work continues on the threshing floor until the rice is safely stored inside the houses in big rice-bundles. If sufficient rice is there and leisure time, women prepare and – proudly displaying their well-accomplished mastery as hosts – share their homemade rice-beer (*diyan*), but not indiscriminately with everybody. Very young children are also welcome to drink their portion, and most accept willingly, even demanding it,

---

1 I have often observed that silence in interaction has a purpose and social significance, e. g., in the case of unresolved quarrels and conflicts or as a kind of social punishment.

as a matter of fact. Kinsmen, though not invited, turn up for a break, and while enjoying amazing amounts – at least so it seems to the observing anthropologist – exchange their news and views, have a good laugh together, and discuss the agenda of the days to come. In groups, never individually, necessary items such as firewood, leaves, roots, fruit, and toothbrushes are collected from the jungle, which may take the major part of a day. For those who stay behind, life will mainly take place outside and around the house, except during the monsoon period between the months of July and September. The inside of a Ho house serves as a storage room for rice and other household items, the most valuable of which are kept inside the *adin*, the sacred space of every Ho household, which is separated by a wall. To sleep in this protected vicinity makes for good dreams, which are shared first thing in the morning. Children and their age mates in a hamlet and beyond consider each other siblings who grow up together, and the whole village keeps a responsible eye on them. Not all children attend school. Many do so irregularly, not infrequently running away from it. I have never observed a child being scolded for this, and this was surely not a sign of parental indifference or neglect. Then there are other children, male and female, slightly older, who are not Ho, who are from nontribal communities that have lived with the Ho for centuries, and who herd the Ho's cattle.

Beyond this kind of village life which is patterned and organized, though not by an outside administration or an outside political centre, and which is realised in face-to-face relationships that are active, public, collective, social, and visible, there is an invisible realm which is no less important, no less active, no less public, and for that matter no less real for the Ho.

Most activities are rice-related and in that way ancestor-oriented, as rice and ancestry are notionally closely interrelated for the Ho. Ancestors are an omnipresent category. The living are well aware that they owe everything to their ancestors, who cleared the jungle, who cultivated the land, who built the houses, who fought all different kinds of attempts at trespassing into their territory and their universe. Ho ancestors are known to be in constant interaction with the living as well as with the spiritual world and Sinbonga, their God who created the world and the Ho. Ancestors' bodies are buried close to the living, either right in the courtyards in front of the houses or behind them, under huge tamarind trees that offer shade to the big, flat burial stones and the people who sit on them seeking refuge from the heat. Ancestors' souls continue to stay with the living. They are given shelter within the *adin*, that protected part of the house where they are safe from any defiling gaze. Here rice is also stored, often complemented by an egg symbolically added. On specific occasions, meals are cooked here. It is an area that I was never allowed to enter, because entrance is strictly reserved for "the people of one rice pot" (*miyad mandi chaturenko*), as the Ho refer to their specific network of kin relations. Relatives by marriage are excluded as a matter of principle. Ancestors pass on their names to the newly born, who only after the naming ceremony acquire a social identity, a quality they lack before the ceremony. A woman after marriage may enter her husband's *adin* only after having been introduced to her husband's ancestors in a proper ritual. The Ho are convinced that ancestors insist on being properly taken care of. This includes the regular performance of animal sacrifices in the rice fields to ensure the continuous fertility of the land and to honour the dead. Commensality includes the ancestors of the household daily. However small the quantities they are offered may be, the ancestors are – as a generic category – invited and served first whenever someone is eating or drinking. In this way, every household actively and effectively contributes to the well-being of its members and that of the whole village. Epidemics, diseases, and other misfortunes are understood as the result of mistakes that living humans have made and that have angered the ancestors, usually imagined as protective, and need to be atoned for. In their specific ways, the dead in Ho country are as real and alive as the living.

Notes from a German village[2] in Brandenburg

The landscape is hilly and spectacularly beautiful, not too dissimilar from the area in Boja Sai described above, and the houses are surrounded by fields of enormous size, on which, however, maize and millet are grown. As far as village life is concerned, well, there is hardly any: a few old people are still there, leading their individual lives inside their houses most of the time. Young families and most young people have left. There are hardly any children or animals but for the occasional cat or dog, no job opportunities, no shops, no butcher, no baker, no school. The nearest larger town where people can do their shopping is fourteen kilometres away. Some houses are empty; some have been rented out to people from outside who show up irregularly on the weekends to enjoy the peaceful environment, especially during summer. The small church, a historic building dating from the fifteenth century, was utterly run down not long ago and only recently restored by a group of enthusiasts coming mainly from outside. In order to inject some life into an otherwise neglected area, perhaps once every

---

2 After returning from fieldwork I found a retreat in Kirchfelde, a small village 80 km north of Berlin to work on my thesis. The social and cultural differences between the two settings – the various villages which had been the sites of my fieldwork in Odisha, and the other one in the Uckermark/ Brandenburg/ Germany – are telling, despite some obviously striking similarities, not least those of the habitat.

two or three weeks some cultural event of fine quality in the church is advertised. People from outside will perform before a very small audience, mainly from outside, a highlight of two hours or so for some in the village. This was the only social interaction beyond the individual household that I was able to observe during the three weeks that I stayed there. Otherwise, communication with the outside world is mediated by television, with the villagers restricted to the passive receiving end; there are probably as many television sets as there are houses. Towards the end of September, the harvest is collected by a single man over the course of three full days, with the help of a gigantic tractor. It takes another two days to have the land ploughed by another machine and one more day to sow rape and have it worked into the soil by still another machine. The harvest will be used as pig fodder or biodiesel or maybe even for human consumption – villagers do not know exactly and are not particularly interested to find out, since land, harvest, and machinery alike are owned by people from outside.

Plate 2: Before the harvest II.
Cornfield in the village of Kirchfelde, Uckermark District, Brandenburg, Germany (September 2010)

In Kirchfelde there are more containers for household rubbish than there are households. In Boja Sai there are neither rubbish containers nor rubbish collection. But then – apart from organic refuse – there is no rubbish in the first place.

1 Introduction: Living in a world of plenty

This book is based on more than sixteen months of fieldwork in the states of Odisha[1] and Jharkhand, India. The main fieldwork was done in 2006 and 2009–10 and complemented by research on shorter return visits every year or two throughout the period between 2005 and 2019. The study focusses on the Ho, a tribal community whose lives I was welcomed to join and document in participant observation.

Plate 3: Honouring Mother Earth.
Inside the sacred grove (*desauli*) during *mage porob*, a Ho festival performed at the village level in Pathan Sai (February 15, 2006). On the left are the village's ritual guide (*diuri*) and one of his men (*jom sim*, assistant to the *diuri*) who is ritually entitled to blow a horn for the village feasts. The horns are those of either a jungle bison (*oron sakowa*), as shown in the photo, or a wild buffalo (*bir-dirin*). On the right are the village headman (*munda*) and one of his men. The blood of a black cock and a red-brown hen (see collage II, top left) has been offered to Mother Earth (*ote enga*) and the two guardian spirits of the village's sacred grove, *desauli* and his wife *jayer buri*.

---

1 The union state Orissa became Odisha in 2011. Consequently, in literature published before 2011 and quoted in the body of the text of this book, the previous form is employed, whereas I will use the present-day name whenever referring to the territory of the state within its current administrative boundaries or to literature published after 2011.

https://doi.org/10.1515/9783110666199-005

The book explores the tapestry of Ho people's relations and relatedness within their culture-specific universe including the Ho's tribal and nontribal fellow humans, their dead, their spirit world and supreme God. I will show how social cohesion and ritual friendship in that part of the Chota Nagpur Plateau express and contribute to the Ho's firm conviction of continuing a heritage entrusted to them by their deities and spirits, their forefathers and ancestors. As seen and represented from their perspective, these relations ensure their social reproduction in the present and afford them with the awareness and means to live in a world of plenty, of abundance (*sumuki*), and wealth (*punji*) – with the Ho as its conceptual centre. Ho people are embedded in a sophisticated sociocosmic order within which they claim to have been making a living "since ancient times" in a territory of which they consider themselves to be the autochthonous inhabitants, in any case the rightful and legitimate settlers. This claim applies especially to Kolhan (outlined in chapter 2), a region perhaps so called after the Ho, who are also known by exonyms including Kol and Larka Kol (Areeparampil 2002: 36; Dalton 1868: 3; Das Gupta 2011: 28; Majumdar 1950: 18; Hoffman and van Emelen 1990 [1950]: 1763).[2] The region overlaps modern India's administrative border between the states of Jharkhand and Odisha (see map 3).

The Ho's oral 'history'

Ho, as this people's language is called by others and by themselves, is a spoken language. In the absence of written texts, documents, and records produced by themselves about themselves, Ho maintain a strong sense of "oral history" (Assmann 2007: 51, 56, 66).[3] This encompasses their creation myths and, as will be shown in chapter 4, their spirit world, as well as their 'histories' of migration and land acquisition, their claim to the status of original settlers in large parts

---

2 For *Ho*, *Kol* and *Kolhan* see glossary I.

3 Leach is critical of the concept of oral history and calls it a misnomer. He opposes myths as transmitted by *oral tradition* and *written history* as based on fixed texts recording potentially datable events in the past (Leach 1990: 229). Assmann uses the concepts of oral history and oral tradition synonymously by referring to Vansina's book 'Oral Tradition as History' (1985) and by pointing out that also in literate societies the so-called communicative memory relates to a recent past of about 80 – 100 years. As in contemporary political discourses in India tribal societies are often characterized as primitive and backward and as to my understanding the classification as 'traditional' may carry such connotations and derogatory overtones I will avoid the term 'traditional' altogether and resort to oral 'history' instead.

The distinction of and relation between 'history' and myth in Leach's definition is taken up in the introduction to the myth of origin of the Holon Purty clan in chapter 4.

of Kolhan, and the battles of old that their ancestors fought against foreign intruders and against local inhabitants driven out by the Ho. Understandings of
Ho history are locally fed into Ho people's collective memory and actively kept
alive by being publicly negotiated, questioned, debated, and confirmed across
generations and orally passed on to the younger ones (*kaji-uju:*). Ho people
can be passionate storytellers and conversationalists indeed: in the course of
my fieldwork I found myself several times in formal and informal situations in
which Ho history, including the colonial encounter and tribal resistance, was
constructed and reconstructed and in which, by the same mechanism, the
Ho's cultural identity was reproduced and recreated.

As far as attempts to reconstruct population history or identify the aboriginal
inhabitants in the region of research, historians of the indigenous populations of
the Chota Nagpur Plateau deplore the fact that reliable pre-Aryan,[4] precolonial,
and colonial 'data' are either missing, biased, fragmentary, speculative, "purely
conjectural" (Das Gupta 2011: 31), or "guesswork" (Hoffman 2005: 7). Ho people,
however, find orientation and meaning in their oral 'history' – or rather, 'histories'. The oral accounts that I was given were usually grounded territorially in the
local environment and thus revealed regionally diverse centres of gravity.

The special long-term relationship between Ho and Munda, reflected in remembered intermarrying practices as well as in the knowledge that they used
to be one 'kind' (*jati*), was locally emphasized in the Porahat area (Verardo
2003b: 10, 13), in the Chaibasa area, and in Ranchi, according to Munda and
Ho informants there. However, this was not the case in the region of my fieldwork on the eastern fringes of Kolhan, in northwestern Mayurbhanj, where I
only once came across two Munda households in one village. Also, the concept
of status ranking between Ho and Munda and their self-identification as "paired
categories," with the Ho as "relative seniors" and the Munda as "relative juniors"
(Pfeffer 2002: 215; 2003: 71) or the other way around (Parkin 1992; Bouez 1985;
Pfeffer 1982),[5] was unknown to Ho informants in the region of research.

---

4 So-called 'pre-Aryan' data presuppose a what has been called Aryan invasion in India which
to this day finds its expression in the so-called Aryan Invasion Theory (AIT). This linguistically
based construct of long standing and high reputation has been convincingly and polemically
criticized by Leach (1990) and Tripathi (2015) who argues in favour of an alternative migration
theory called Out of India Theory (OIT). Recent genetic research published by Reich et al. in *Nature* (2009: 489–494) supports OIT in that genetic links between Aryans and North Indians are
disqualified instead of Ancestral North Indians (ANI) being linked with Ancestral South Indians
(ASI). In other words: most Indians today are genetically a mixture of ANI and ASI, and both
ancestral groups predate the arrival of Indo-Europeans in India.
5 Pfeffer (1982: 31,79) calls the Ho "the little Munda, their younger brothers" and so does Parkin
(1992: 25). Bouez writes: "Les Hos sont les cadets de Munda" (1985:43).

The status concept of relative seniority structuring relations *within* the Ho tribe and *within* the Ho clan and subclan system (see chapter 3), however, is known, though not as an abstract notion, and attributed authority by local(-ised)) myths. The notion of seniority was explained to me in the language of elder brother and younger brother by the local village headman (*munda*) in the research area and had become part of the Ho's oral 'history' in that region. Marriage rules are regionally qualified and modified by the fact that certain clans are classified as another clan's 'younger brothers'. For example, in the research area members of the Bari clan and the Alda clan are conceived of as the 'younger brothers' of the Purty clan, understood as their common 'elder brother', with the effect that intermarriage between these three clans is normatively proscribed (see chapter 4).

Another instance of the Ho's oral 'history' concerns local knowledge of the conflictual encounter between Ho and Dhurwa in the area. This was never a topic where I enquired about it in the Chaibasa area, but it definitely was in the Jamda area where I did fieldwork, and it was the ritual guide (*diuri*) of the dominant Bage clan there who was authorized by his co-villagers to tell it. According to his oral account, Ho do not deny their having settled in a territory that was originally inhabited by others, at least with regard to the region that used to be known as Lagra Pir and Lalgar Pir (Tuckey 1920), part of Odisha today. He mentioned the community of the Dhurwa as having been in the area when the Ho, along with their cattle, migrated there from the northern and northwestern regions of the Plateau. Other Ho elders also passed on to me a history of the Dhurwa's continuous fierce atrocities against the Ho, of their regularly seeking to capture Ho as human victims to be sacrificed at the time of *her mut*, the feast and sacrifice held by Ho people before the sowing of the main paddy crop.

Dhurwa are portrayed as having used the skin of sacrificed Ho persons for their drums (*dama duman*). Plate 4 shows a kettle drum (*dama*) which was captured from the Dhurwa by the Ho in one of the battles waged against them. Today it is kept in the house of the Ho *diuri* of Jamda and covered by the skin of a buffalo. A sacrifice of a red cock (*ara sandi*), two pigeons (*dudlumkin*), vermillion (*sinduri*), and *ganja* (hemp; Ho *ganjae*) is regularly offered by the *diuri* of Jamda to elicit the drum's hidden divine powers before it is used in the course of the Ho's annual village feasts in this area. On these occasions the drum becomes the material witness to the Ho's oral 'history' of the adverse relations between Ho and Dhurwa, which is then narrated and passed on.[6] Typically, Ho mention among the items offered in the sacrifice *ganja*, which as far as I know is not used in any other Ho ritual. This foreign (*diku*) element is referred to in Hindi, the notionally foreign (*diku*) language associated with the Dhurwa as a *diku* category.[7]

Plate 4: Dhurwa kettle drum.
This kettle drum (*dama*) is reported to have been captured by Ho from the Dhurwa (name spelt as indigenously pronounced: the aspirated 'd' indicates a non-Ho term and category). According to the Ho *diuri* of Jamda, the drum used to be beaten in the 'old days' before a fight to induce the Dhurwa's gods to fill the Dhurwa fighters with strength and to protect them.

An upright standing stone (*bid-diri*) more than two metres tall stands in the field of the *diuri* of Jamda. It is similar in shape to, though not quite as tall as, the one in plate 5 below (top left). It is said to have been erected by the Dhurwa to commemorate the site before they fled the country to escape the recalcitrant Ho. The stone is considered to belong to the Dhurwa and will as such not be removed. To the Ho it is a fearful reminder and material document of a troubled past. A *bid-*

---

6 Areeparampil confirms severe struggles between Ho and Dhurwa in the 18th century. According to him Dhurwa eventually fled to Seraikela district (2002: 116, 118).
7 The category *diku* is discussed in the following section.

diri may be erected in memory of a dead person, in memory of a person who has been missing for a long time or is assumed to be dead, or in commemoration of something of outstanding relevance, rarely with inscriptions in Devanagari, mostly without. While Ho acknowledge the Dhurwa's presence in the area preceding the advent of the Ho, they at the same time conceive of themselves as original inhabitants in the sense that it was the Ho, they say, who came to *settle* and stay: they felled the trees to cultivate the land by hoeing the soil, eventually by using the plough, and not the Dhurwa.

By felling trees Ho have initiated a relationship with the regionally rooted spirits of the land, since trees are known to be inhabited by the spirits and deities assigned to a specific region. Honouring these spirits and deities establishes lasting spiritual links among land, people, and spirit world. In this process, Ho say, they have acquired the right to land through an unwritten title deed, as well as the duty to ritually behave toward the newly acquired regional spirits and deities within a pattern of reciprocal gift exchange. Myths are passed on to explain how the spirits revealed themselves and their role of protecting men, cattle, and harvest while at the same time expecting to be served and sustained by men. The links among Ho people, land, and *ma:-nam chalu:-nam bongako*,[8] as these tutelary spirits are called, are encapsulated in the language. The designation can be translated as 'spirits committed/related to those who acquire land by cutting trees and hoeing the soil'. According to this cultural logic, Ho continue to be obliged to pay ritual attention to the spirits and deities of their original settlements even when they leave the area and migrate elsewhere. In such cases the spirits are invited to migrate along with the living, and they are given separate ritual attention every year on the eve of the village festivals (see chapter 4).

---

8 *ma:* denotes 'to cut, to slash', *chalu:* 'to hoe'; *nam* 'to receive, to get', *bongako* 'spirits'.

Plate 5: Oral 'history' as memory carved in stone
Top left and bottom left: *bid-diri*, standing memorial stones two to four metres in height, as distinct from *sasan diri*, large slabs of stone laid flat on the ground over a grave (top right). Centre right: the *diuri* of Jamda, R. Bage, in one of his fields next to a massive *sasan diri* put there in memory of one of his forefathers, S. Bage, who was the first *sadar* (head of a cluster of

villages, a term used by Ho people instead of *manki)* of the region. The stone has an extension of 350 cm x 200 cm x 30 cm and a weight of probably more than five tons. According to my calculations, about seventy men would be required to move it, each supporting a weight of roughly seventy kilograms or more. Bottom left and right: two of a total of four standing stones near Chakradharpur have inscriptions in Devanagari. One refers to 1891, the other, on which I could decipher the name Udai Purty, to 1904 and 1921. Bottom right: the titles *munda* (village headman) and *sadar* appear several times.

Stones of different shapes, sizes, and weights scattered purposefully over Ho country, alongside paths and roads and in fields, a few instances of which are illustrated in plate 5 above, are visible and eternal documents testifying to the Ho's oral 'history'. Often the stones were selected in the jungle and carried collectively by male villagers to their destinations. In addition to the tall standing stones (*bid-diri*) mentioned above, there are inconspicuously small standing stones (see plate 11), stone slabs (*sasan diri*) laid flat over a grave (see plate 5, top right, and plate 12), massive stones of more than five tons left somewhere for some remembered and narrated reason (see plate 5, centre right), and outwardly inconspicuous stones arranged in the Ho's sacred groves to accommodate their deities and spirits when invited to participate in a ritual there (see plate 13). Such stones in sociocultural context are meaningful in that they are linked with individual persons and/or past events. They bridge the worlds of the living, the dead and the divine. If one is lucky enough to meet a knowledgeable Ho – often an elderly person will be pointed out for this purpose – these stones will come alive and narrate stories of commemoration and precedence: oral 'history' as memory carved in stone.

Importantly, other communities indigenous to the area – tribal and nontribal – confirm the Ho's status as *adivasi*. This is the Hindi term for 'original inhabitants' and is used in much of the scholarly literature on the Ho and on the tribal population in general, by academics in the Chaibasa and Ranchi areas (P. Sen 2003, 2006; A. K. Sen 2012), and in international discourse on indigenous politics (Shah 2010), but to my knowledge not by my Ho informants. They prefer the Ho term *munurenko* (*munu* – origin, original, first beginning) – that is, if they make use of such generalizing and distant expressions at all. Deeney (2005: 217) gives the term *kunt-kati* ("of land, to belong to the family of an original settler of a village"), although I never heard it used among Ho people. *Kunt-kati* was explained to me as a term used by Munda people referring to Munda first settlers further north in the Ranchi area (see also Rothermund 2001: 2). As *munurenko* Ho people transform forest land into cultivable fields on the territory of Kolhan – a process under way possibly two thousand years ago and more (Dalton 1868: 11; Areeparampil 2002: 46). In any case, it seems largely acknowledged that by the nineteenth century the Kolhan area was populated predominantly but not exclusively by Ho people (Das Gupta 2006: 80; Tuckey 1920: 18; Tickell 1840; Dalton 1868). As a matter of anthropological principle, this study will consider the Ho's oral 'histories' rather than the published facts of Ho history written by colonial and post-colonial others. For this reason, it is irrelevant here that Ho claims of being autochthonous to all of Kolhan are contested, as are the location of their original homeland(s), their first entry into the district of Singhbhum, and the history and exact period of their migration (Verardo 2003b; Das Gupta 2006, 2011; Areeparampil 2002; Dalton 1868).

In the research area Ho people refer to Kolhan in their mother tongue as Ho country (*Ho disum*). Kolhan and Kol are Hindi designations and as such carry pejorative overtones as seen from the Ho's perspective. The notional antagonism is encapsulated in the language, as the Ho term *diku* implies the denotations 'to speak Hindi, to speak Odiya', along with the denotation 'foreign' given above. To my knowledge, Tickell was the only one of the colonial administrators and scholars writing on the Ho to acknowledge and recognize the Ho's terminology in this respect (Tickell 1840). Dalton once defines 'Colehan' in an aside as "Ho-desum" (1868: 11), but he then continues to write about Kolhan.

In contemporary administrative terms Kolhan has become one of Jharkhand's five divisions, along with Santal Pargana, North Chotanagpur, Palamau, and South Chotanagpur. The borders around today's Kolhan Division, however, are not identical with those of the Kolhan Government Estate that came into being in 1837 within Singhbhum District (see chapter 2).

Tribal society

That Ho people and other tribal categories have been living on the Chota Nagpur Plateau in splendid isolation to this day is an assumption which came into being long ago and which has been kept alive ever since for different reasons by different people, groups, and institutions, including British colonialists,[9] post-independence Indian governments in general, and nowadays the BJP. In addition, some anthropologists have contributed to this picture by focussing on and essentializing individual tribal communities as bounded entities, thus notionally iso-

---

9 According to Das Gupta (2006: 80; 2011: 63) the notion of the Ho's total isolation was conveniently spread by the British administration to legitimize their adopted paternalist policy of protectionism in the Kolhan Government Estate after 1837. This change of policy must be seen, says Das Gupta, as a response to the Ho's continuous resistance against *diku* attempts at interfering into tribal affairs such as implementing rent and tax obligations, and their determined refusing to co-operate with the regional chiefs or *rajas* as well as with the colonial powers.

lating them from their wider and encompassing sociocultural linkages and networks.

In their cultural memory, by contrast, Ho people have always lived on the Chota Nagpur Plateau alongside members of other aboriginal *(adivasi)* communities within a multi-ethnic assemblage. In the area of research the non-Ho living in villages otherwise predominantly inhabited by Ho are mostly Santal, with a small number of Munda families. At the same time, Ho say that they have established and lived in villages with and depended on members of artisan nontribal categories who themselves readily admit to having been invited to work as clients for their land-owning Ho patrons (see chapter 5). As such, they functioned as the Ho's middlemen in their trade exchanges with the outside world and as their interpreters and accountants when interacting with superior political authority (Das Gupta 2006: 80). Ho people have shared space and cultural norms with these nontribal communities or functional castes "for ages". Ho regard them as culturally distinct and do not interdine and intermarry with them – as a norm. Although they are nontribal, they are not classified and treated by the Ho as notional outsiders or foreigners *(diku)* (Moharana 2012: 113). Adverse relations between them are another myth that is conveyed in much of the colonial and post-colonial literature on the relations between the Ho and their nontribal clients. Amazingly few anthropologists have explored this ordered coexistence and the cultural complexity that it reveals from an anthropological perspective. Three who have, Pfeffer (1997), Das Gupta (2011), and Areeparampil (2002) argue that professional service groups such as blacksmiths, weavers, tailors, potters, and cowherds should – as nontribal caste categories – rather be considered part of the heterogeneous Middle Indian indigenous population of the plateaux and the hills, as Ho people and my non-Ho informants in the area themselves understand them.

The present study will explore the specific structure and interaction within the social tapestry of what has been called tribal *society* (Pfeffer 2002: 18, 208), of which the Ho form only one, albeit constitutive, community in the area of research.

Notional antagonism: the category 'outside', 'outsider' (*diku*)

In the course of their history Ho have been confronted by and have rejected continuous and diverse encroachments from outside since pre-colonial times. These encroachments are commonly classified as *diku* assaults on the tribal universe with its distinct tribal ideas and values. They are brought about by people who are identified by Ho as those typically living in or coming in from the plains – be they Mughals, British colonialists, members of mainstream India's caste system, economic entrepreneurs and industrialists, or any kind of officials and representatives of state and government, such as tax collectors, police officers, contractors, and teachers.[10] In his Ho-English Dictionary Deeney gives as denotations of *diku* "non-tribal; to speak Hindi; to act like a *diku*" (2005: 92). *Diku* is a descriptive as well as a judgmental category, implying behavioural elements. It is usually applied to nontribal, nonindigenous people or groups, making it a conceptual statement about notional otherness beyond the ethnic dimension. A Ho police officer – according to my Ho hosts a contradiction in terms – once came to my hosts' village and addressed them in their courtyard in quite a rude, intimidating manner. Afterwards my hosts referred to him as *diku* Ho, as someone who had become a stranger to his own people, who had alienated himself from his brothers, who had turned hostile towards them. Ho have experienced and keep experiencing *diku* people in their everyday lives as ignorant of, opposed to, disinterested in, and adverse to, altogether quite unsympathetic towards their ways of being in the world.

The classification of someone as *diku*, however, expresses not only a static state of being that Ho people characterize as distant from, conflicting with, and potentially endangering their sociocosmic universe. It is also a state of becoming that is reversible and hence dynamic. Ho people migrating for work outside Ho country are subject to this cultural logic. On returning home from outside they have to undergo a number of purification rituals in order to get rid of their acquired *diku*-ness and become Ho again. When I returned for fieldwork in 2012 after almost two years' absence from the area, I was addressed by a girl biologically much younger than I as "young 'foreign' girl" (*diku mai*), as 'one not belonging to us'.

As a concept, *diku* is a comprehensive term not only applying to people and their behaviour but classifying things, too. In the research area, people are aware of what to do and what to say in order to profit from government benefits for those registered as BPL (Below Poverty Line). As such, for example, they are entitled to receive rice from the local *panchayat* (village council) office. "What do you do with it?" I once asked my host, because their locally grown rice is so much better. "Do you eat it?" "Would you?" he replied, and he continued,

---

10 Most teachers in the region of research speak and teach in Odiya. Those that I communicated with neither speak nor understand Ho. Hence there is no alphabetization in the children's mother tongues Ho or Santali. Teachers usually do not live in the tribal villages but come from outside and return daily. Most of them are nontribals. Today there are, however, exceptions. Ho and Santal have begun to work as teachers. However, lessons are to be held in Odiya, as Ho is not recognized as a Scheduled Language and despite Santali being registered as Scheduled Language.

"This is *diku* rice. We give it to the pigs." In ritual performances also the distinction between things Ho and things *diku* becomes obvious. Although in everyday secular life plastic items and metal household wares from the markets are regularly in use and much appreciated, in ritual contexts they are excluded as a matter of principle. A higher value is attached to locally manufactured products.

Ho resistance: 'the tiger's den'

In pre-colonial and colonial times revenue collection was the main and one-way purpose of communicating with the tribal population of the Chota Nagpur Plateau in Bengal, Bihar,[11] and Odisha and of venturing into the "tiger's den" (Areeparampil 2002: 84) in the first place. Whereas in precolonial times Ho had found ways of defending their independence and escaping interference from outside, it was the British East India Company that made sure they really got the money they were determined to extract from the indigenous population. According to British colonial administrators who in their stocktaking efforts also produced written material on the conflictual encounter with the aboriginal population, the 'tiger's den' seemed the most apt metaphor through which to characterize the intensity of indigenous resistance, which turned the area into one of widespread unrest and turmoil in the nineteenth century. In line with their oral 'history', Ho informants in 2006 repeatedly reproduced instances of rebellion and resistance against British attempts at subjugating them. This awareness of resistance reigns superior over defeats, which are downplayed as occasional and preliminary.[12]

Colonial practices on the Chota Nagpur Plateau

Despite all later rhetoric about installing in the area a Pax Britannica advertised as a superior system of civilization, law, and order, the initial colonial focus was clearly on gaining control, including by military means, over a strategically important region, one that had also proved uncontrollable to its, some say self-styled, local *rajas* or indigenous chiefs. In a drawn-out process of entering the socioculturally complex tribal society of the Plateau over several decades, the

---

11 The union state Jharkhand was carved out of Bihar only in November 2000.
12 Assmann highlights this phenomenon by referring to Maurice Halbwachs' elaborations on the distinction between (collective) Memory versus History and the societies that Lévi-Strauss identifies as 'cold' (Assmann 2007 [1992]: 34–42, 68–70).

British colonial rulers employed their well-known policy of 'divide and rule'. They set out to administratively take apart what had belonged together for centuries, maybe millennia, by essentializing formerly fluid social compositions of tribes and nontribes into separate and named categories. These were reified as Ho, Munda, Santal, Oraon, Bhumij, Gond, Khond, Kharia, Juang, Birhor, Tamaria, and so on. Thus, British colonial administrators established an unambiguously defined catalogue of subjects and communities along ethnic lines. In most cases, they arbitrarily created exonyms that were neither used nor recognized by the people in question, who instead refer to themselves in their different mother tongues by designations all denoting 'man' in the singular form. To give two examples: Santal people refer to themselves as *hor*, Munda as *horo*. *Ho* also carries the meaning 'man', but as an exception, Ho is an ethnonym used in the Ho's mother tongue (*Ho kaji*). On the one hand, it connotes the social and empirical entirety of all Ho people as opposed to the more distant and abstract concept of *manwa* (mankind; human being); on the other hand, *ho* may be understood as encompassing males and females, since the Ho language does not have separate masculine and feminine forms.

By dividing the *adivasi* population into manageable units, the colonial power attempted to gain political control, an overall view of the rebellious population, and the economic upper hand. The Ho in particular gained a reputation of having ferociously, if not always successfully, refused to comply. It was only fifty years after 1765, when the British East India Company (hereafter: Company) was nominally granted administrative and *diwani* rights (the right to collect revenue) in a region including the territory of today's state of Jharkhand, that Company officials were able to effectively make their first appearance in the Kolhan area of Singhbhum. Except for several unsuccessful military expeditions against the 'tribal savages', the Ho, the densely forested terrain had remained inaccessible and *terra incognita* to them. In fact, probably in order to remain politically autonomous, the Ho had separated from the Munda,[13] to whom they are closely related culturally, and migrated to and settled in this part of the Plateau. They would not allow any nonindigenous outsiders (*diku*) to settle in, pass through, or trespass on their sacred landscape, including pilgrims on their way to Puri,

---

13 It is suggested that Ho and Munda were originally one tribe. While Ho elders pass on narrations of their having emigrated from the country of the Munda, but not of the Nagbansi dynasty, Munda people obviously retain a tradition of having elected their first Raja under the Nagbansi dynasty. It has been assumed for this reason by some that the Ho separated from the Munda before the Nagbansi Raja was installed (Areeparampil 2002: 36, 44, 84; S. C. Roy 1970: 71). The period when this split is supposed to have happened, is controversial.

as Dalton reports (1872: 178). They were the *Larka Kol* or Fighting Ho, a term that was attached from outside especially to the Ho of Southern Kolhan.

Wilkinson's Rules

In their self-perception Ho are a category with a noncentralized political organization. Consequently, according to several of my informants, Ho in the course of their history have never accepted being organized under or dominated by a central *diku* government and administration. Their resistance against British supremacy eventually contributed to the Kolhan being declared a Non-Regulation Area, where the Company's rules, jurisdiction, and regulations would not apply as they did in the rest of British India. It was decided instead that *adivasi* forms of self-government and of settling affairs and disputes were to be preserved and acknowledged by the Company government in Bengal. In the Ho's case this referred to locally existing indigenous institutions such as the village council (*panchayat*) and an intervillage council called *manki-munda*, made up of village headmen (*munda*) and headed by the headman of a confederation of villages (*manki*).[14] Thomas Wilkinson was appointed to work out new and modified rules and regulations for the Non-Regulation Area.[15] 'Wilkinson's Rules',[16] as they are known even today, were intended to guarantee revenue collection and a pacified region by recognizing the tribals' legitimate land rights and ensuring that land alienation became illegal. They were only to be applied in the newly annexed administrative unit named the Kolhan Government Estate, which was created in 1837 for this purpose and which brought the area under the direct management of the Company government (Areeparampil 2002: 120). This meant that the government acted as the direct landlord for all the land (Yorke 1976). In the Kolhan area of today's Jharkhand, but not in Odisha, the administration of civil justice and the law courts follow Wilkinson's Rules to this day. Pacification, however, did not come by itself, and an explosive situation characterized by hostility to Wilkinson's plans persisted, especially in southern Kolhan. The research area was very close to this region, and it is for this reason that this piece of history is given here. Wilkinson is a household name in both North and South Kolhan. But whereas I was instructed by some academically minded indig-

---

14 In Mayurbhanj/ Odisha the term *manki* is often replaced by *sadar* (see also plate 5, bottom right).

15 See glossary I for *South West Frontier Agency*, a terrain larger than and preceding the establishment of the Kolhan Government Estate.

16 See glossary I for *Wilkinson* and the concept of *landlord*.

enous scholars in the Chaibasa area about the farsightedness of Wilkinson's rules created for the protection of the Ho, most of my Ho informants in the region of research would instead recall the ruthlessness of Wilkinson's whirlwind campaign, in the course of which villages were burnt to the ground, grain looted, and Ho women and cattle abducted. Five Ho rebel leaders were publicly hanged – the first executions to take place in Singhbhum. My Ho informants also took pride in recalling that despite ongoing atrocities, Ho resistance could not be crushed but used to flare up time and time again. This is what stands out in their collective memory.

After Independence: Jharkhand, India, and the tribal population

In Jharkhand's contemporary governmental structure, tribal forms of local self-government such as the *panchayat* (village council) and the *manki-munda* system have become institutionalized and a constitutional reality, thus, it is officially claimed, empowering the tribal population of the state to voice their demands and needs directly and authentically. This is a bold statement indeed. In the case of the Munda, it has been evaluated by Shah (2010), who has critically highlighted indigenous politics as practiced by the state and against the state. From the perspective of action anthropology she has focussed on processes of transition, corruption, and exploitation that have had negative or at least quite controversial impacts on the indigenous population since Jharkhand's statehood in November 2000 (Shah 2010: 1ff, 66ff). In the case of the Ho of Singhbhum, Yorke (1976: 13) also has some critical remarks. Quite similarly, my Ho informants are deeply sceptical of the situation and question the commitment and independence of their representatives since the latter have agreed to become government employees: "How can they represent us, how can they be trusted to work for us if they agree to be paid by the government at the same time? Isn't it the case that they will represent the government's interests instead of ours if they accept government salaries?"

The Indian constitution has perpetuated the British cataloguing of social categories as bounded substances or "social isolates" (Leach 1977: 60), continuing to arbitrarily split the tribal *society* of the hill regions into separate administrative entities of so-called Scheduled Tribes (ST), Other Backward Classes (OBC), and Scheduled Castes (SC) (Skoda 2005: 49–60; Berger 2007: 18–21; Pfeffer 1997: 3–27). From this perspective, Ho people are classed as a Scheduled Tribe. They are listed in official government records and in the 2001 Indian census as one of a total of 461 tribal communities in India, whereas the 2011 census provides a list of 700 such communities. The government and the constitution define tribes as an "administrative and political concept" (K. S. Singh 1997: xiii), one that makes it possible to turn the anthropological category of 'tribe' (Sahlins 1968; Pfeffer 2002, 2004) into a quantifiable and reified entity within a given Scheduled Area. The Scheduled Tribes of India constitute over 8 percent of the total population or more than 100 million people according to the 2011 census of India. Where the Ho population is concerned, said to consist of more than one million individuals according to the 2001 Jharkhand census highlights, the situation is paradoxical: my fieldwork was primarily done among the Ho in the state of Odisha, where more than a third of the Ho population lives (Deeney 2002: ix; 2008: 67). However, while Ho are listed for Jharkhand in both the 2001 and 2011 Indian censuses, they do not appear at all in the state list of more than sixty-two officially registered tribes living in Odisha. My Ho informants are not too surprised at this, as according to their experience it fits in with other instances of the Indian state's intentional ignorance of things tribal.

Ram Dayal Munda gave me another example (personal communication, April 2009). On the census questionnaires filled out every ten years and in nationwide elections those eligible to vote have to tick one of the following categories to identify their religion: Hindu, Muslim, Sikh, Buddhist, Christian, Jain, or Other. "Now who wants to be relegated to the rank of anonymous 'Other'?" he said. "So tribals will tick 'Hindu', although they do not belong there. This is a huge problem in terms of tribal identity! Therefore the Census of India has become a major focus of the political movement.[17] Today 'Hindu' constitute the main section of Indian society, but 'Tribal', if officially recognized as a category, might become the second largest." Munda gave an estimate of 100 to 300 million people in India whom he considered to belong in the category 'tribal' as he defined it. In doing so he ignored the artificial boundary drawn by the census between the tribal and the 'caste' artisan communities of the hills and grouped them together, as outlined above for the tribal society as such. Thus, if considered together, with an understanding of their economic collaboration and the quality of their historically developed coexistence, Scheduled Tribes and Scheduled Castes amount to approximately 25 percent of the total population of India (ST: 8.6 percent or 104 million inhabitants; SC: 16.6 percent or 201 million).

---

17 He referred to *Adi Dharm* and his book of the same title that had just been published in Ho and Hindi in 2009. A shortened version was translated into English in 2014. For a contextualization of the above quotes see Munda (2014: IX, 2).

Encroachments on the tribal mind

Since Indian independence, interventions into tribal affairs by the Indian nation-state have officially and ideally been explained to this day as constitutionalized protective discrimination. 'Reforms' are advertised as 'advancing' those classified as Scheduled Tribes for their own good and 'integrating' them into the Indian nation. In theory, this approach follows the Nehruvian ideal of tribal development along the lines of the tribes' own genius, as suggested in the quotation that serves as the epigraph to the prologue, and is in accord with promises to avoid impositions of any kind. *De facto*, however, and in practice, governmental programmes and schemes have been criticized for continuing to aim at *assimilating* the world of the tribes into mainstream Indian (Hindu nationalist) ideology and society instead of *integrating* it (Mundu 2012: 7; Areeparampil 2002: 242; A. Roy 2012: 26).

In the research area the assimilationist approach takes clear material form in the educational sector. To highlight just one significant aspect: although there are school buildings, only a few of them operate regularly as schools. Teachers either are missing or often have duties outside of school. Most teachers neither understand nor speak Ho or Santali nor attempt to do so. There is no school in the area offering alphabetization in one of the tribal languages. Tribal history and culture are not part of the curriculum and are consequently not taught. Conversely, tribal children are introduced to Hindu culture. They are taught how to observe festivals such as *makar sankranti*, which Ho translate as 'foreign/foreigners' festival' (*diku porob*) and which they do not celebrate themselves.

In a globalizing contemporary India, encroachments on the tribal mind and terrain keep euphemistically coming their way locally in the guise of civilization, modernization, development, and progress, of Hinduization and Christianization. Jharkhand, about the size of Scotland, contains 40 percent of all of India's mineral resources. It is a state that legally disallows alienation of ancestral tribal land on behalf of its large number of tribal inhabitants. As development in modern India spells economic development, however, access by national and multinational companies to Jharkhand's subsoil resources has been given national priority. This is presented to the outside world as "bringing tribals into the mainstream" or giving them "the fruits of modern development" (A. Roy 2012: 43). The internal displacement and dispossession of several million people throughout India have been legalized for dams, irrigation projects, aluminium refineries, steel plants, and mines. A great majority of the displaced and dispossessed are tribal people. Thus, this mineral-rich terrain in Central India has become a much-contested and vulnerable region indeed. While the government speaks of improved tribal welfare due to improved job opportunities, for example, in the uranium mines, it is a public secret that nuclear waste is being dumped near Ho and Santal villages in the Jaduguda area of Dalbhum, but the Uranium Corporation of India Ltd. (UCIL) keeps denying any ill effects of radiation on people's health (Lourdusamy 1999: 105).

Determined to advance the tribals' lot, representatives of the state[18] are active in the hills, along with social and political rights activists[19] and the Naxalite Movement, which operates mainly in a forested belt which reaches from Bihar across Jharkhand and Chhattisgarh into Odisha and Andra Pradesh (Jaoul and Desquesnes 2011: 15).[20] All of them in their different ways claim to represent, act on behalf of, and be aware of the tribes' grievances. Even if formulated by nongovernmental institutions, these claims do not always reflect the desires of the *adivasi* people on whose behalf they are put forward. The Naxalites are engaged in an armed (class) struggle against the Indian state. They hide in tribal villages, as the state's presence there has always been weak. Kharia, Munda, and Ho informants in the Chaibasa area suggested to me that they had found a rather reluctant *modus vivendi* with Naxalites staying in and operating from their villages, but this seemed a matter of hesitantly tolerating them rather than actively siding with them.[21]

At the receiving end in the villages and against this background, *adivasi* often meet outside concerns with scepticism, distrust, suspicion, and cautious or open hostility – irrespective of the professed humanitarian ethos of those intent on improving their lives. For indigenous people, outside attempts at 'reform', however ideologically diverse they may be, are experienced as patronizing efforts to 'reform' their tribalness and sacral polity by distorting, redefining, and

---

18 Not denying her own activist inclinations and advocacy, Shah summarizes the Indian state's strategies and practices as follows: "For the greater part of Indian history, *adivasis* have experienced the state in its most exploitative form of police brutality, venality of forest guards, or the predation of tax collectors and other state officials" (Shah 2010: 477). This coincides to a large degree with J. Hoffman's remarks about eighty years ago concerning the Munda's perspective on state institutions: "The law courts are venal, the police are both brutal and venal" (Hoffman 2005: 16).

19 On behalf of Ho people these are especially active in the urban areas of far away Ranchi and Chaibasa in Jharkhand.

20 For a map showing the Naxalites' operating areas which was published by the International Institute for Strategic Studies (IISS) see *Le Monde diplomatique* (November 11th, 2011: 15).

21 Based on her long-term fieldwork among the Munda of Jharkhand and in Naxalite strongholds Shah (2003, 2010, 2013) draws a more positive picture of Maoists' integration in tribal villages and their alleged "sustained local support" (2013: 477). In addition, A. Roy in her role of investigative journalist documents local support for the Maoist rebel army in tribal villages (A. Roy 2012).

devaluing their specific tribal ways of being in the world. As such, these efforts spell hegemonization and internal colonization. Ho and Santal in the research area are rooted in tribal village life and cultivation of the land and are used to running their affairs by themselves, without any external leadership. Outside perspectives regularly culminate in the homogeneous, sanitized vision of an acculturated, secular *adivasi* person as a civil-rights bearing, formally educated, modern Indian national. Ho are regularly highly sensitive if they are not taken for who they are, if communication with and about them does not take place with an attitude of respect.

In modern India a paradoxical situation exists in which, on the one hand, highly educated, cosmopolitan Indian citizens in the urban centres may be utterly unaware of a large tribal population's existence within their country. On the other hand, there are intellectuals and political rights activists who, given the global spotlight on indigenous issues and the discourse of human rights, claim to internationally represent *adivasi's* best interests, including at various UN institutions.

In my research area in Mayurbhanj, I was present in situations in which people informed each other about sensitive matters in the closer vicinity and also in the wider area. This briefing about the latest news often happened while people enjoyed some rice-beer at the weekly markets. News concerned persons alien to the area or elephants roaming around and spotted in the jungle by women collecting firewood. The exchange of news also concerned newspaper reports about clashes in the Chaibasa and Jamshedpur areas between Naxalites and police, who regularly blame all atrocities and casualties on the Maoist guerrillas, unambiguously portrayed as terrorists. People are aware of Operation Green Hunt, which began in October 2009 and is still going on. At that time, more than 50,000 paramilitary forces were introduced into the forested tribal areas to collaborate with the local police in fighting the Maoist rebels. My impression was that people felt more intimidated by the local police in their villages than by the Naxalites. Ho would keep an eye out as a matter of principle, but the Naxalites' and political activists' issues on the whole were considered far away, academic, and almost unrelated to tribal lives and priorities, and as such, they were not debated among my informants. Although news concerning clashes between Naxalites and police is relevant to the general political climate in Jharkhand, it is a subject that will not be analysed further in this study, since it does not seem to have been at the centre of my informants' attention.

2 The Chota Nagpur Plateau: terrain and people

The region of research

The region of research is in the southeastern portion of the Chota Nagpur Plateau in India, which is connected with the Vindhyan ranges to the west by a continuous chain of hills and forests. Thus, in a wide sense, the Chota Nagpur Plateau can be said to extend across India's Peninsular Plateau.

In a narrower sense, as it is used here, it forms the northeastern extension of the central plateau of India, covering all of the territory of the present-day state of Jharkhand, touching upon eastern portions of Maharashtra, and reaching into Madhya Pradesh, Chhattisgarh, Uttar Pradesh, Bihar, West Bengal, and Odisha. *Jharkhand*, denoting 'forest region, dense forest' in Hindi, is a name recorded for and given to all – or part – of the Chota Nagpur Plateau that can be traced back to the thirteenth century. *Chota Nagpur* or *Chotanagpur* cannot be defined unambiguously, as it reveals a long history of naming and renaming, of partitioning and reorganization. It reflects a long political history of oppression and aggression against its multiethnic indigenous population, as well as several pacification schemes[22] and settlements. In the past Chota Nagpur referred to various administrative regions of different extension, whereas today North and South Chotanagpur constitute two of the five divisions of present-day Jharkhand state.

Geographically, the Chotanagpur Plateau is a vast tract of uneven uplands that lies between the Gangetic and the Mahanadi Plains. Most of the Plateau has an elevation between 1,000 feet, as in the area of research, and 2,300 feet above sea level, with its highest peaks, among others, in the Simlipal Massif, which exceeds 3,800 feet. Simlipal is mentioned here because Ho alliance relations extend into Simlipal in Odisha, as they do into Jharkhand. My informants refer to Simlipal when they want to emphasize that a new marital 'road' (*hora*) is being initiated, that is, when two individuals are about to marry whose clans (*kiliko*) are said to have had no marital interrelations so far. Simlipal in this sense is synonymous with a region far away. Otherwise and characteristically, the region consists of a succession of plateaux interspersed between undulating hills, dense forests as well as now-deforested areas, mountainous regions, and open valleys drained by several large rivers, some of which feed into rivers flowing into the Bay of Bengal.

---

22 See *Chota Nagpur* in glossary I.

https://doi.org/10.1515/9783110666199-006

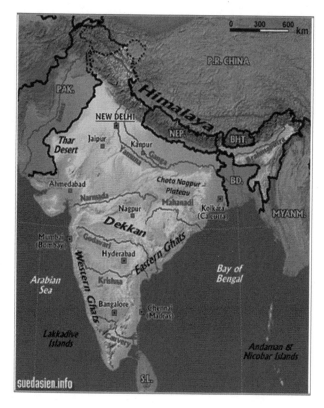

Map 1: Topographical India
The Chota Nagpur Plateau is the northeastern extension of the central plateau of India between the plains of the rivers Ganga and Mahanadi. Source: suedasien.info (retrieved November 2013; my adaptation)

People of the Plateau: statistics and the language situation

Generally speaking, a large share of India's tribal population of more than 104 million people (Census of India 2011) lives in the upland plateaux and mountain ranges of the Chota Nagpur Plateau – away from the coastal plains towards the east. Talking about topographical features in India is a sociocultural statement more than anything else (Pfeffer 1997; Verardo 2003b). They function as markers of status and identity construction beyond being natural givens or geographical asides. Living in a hilly forested region, despite its "genial climate and its fertilising streams" (Dalton 1868: 2), is often synonymous with being linked to the wilderness and the jungle, a phenomenon long considered pejorative by plains people and people from outside (*diku*) in India (Das Gupta 2006: 77) but not by the tribal population, for whom jungles, rivers, and hills are symbols of affluence and plenty (*sumuki, punji*), sustaining and providing them with their spirit world and everything they need for a living but salt.

The forested hilly upland regions of the Plateau are the homeland of almost 100 out of India's 461 tribes officially registered by the Survey of India (Areeparampil 2002: 18; K. S. Singh 1997: xiii; Mundu 2012: 8). These figures, however, constitute no more than vague estimates: the number of tribes in the 2011 Indian Census increased to 705, found in thirty states, due to "changes in the list of SCs, STs during the last decade" (Chandramonti 2013: 3), but these "changes" remain unexplained. The tribal population living on the Chota Nagpur Plateau constitutes the tribal belt of Middle India, which is one of India's four tribal zones. Here tribal people say they 'belong' to the Plateau (Verardo 2003b: 9). I was also told by Ho people that they 'belong' to their land(scape), and Ho women often sing songs about their beautiful country(side) (*esu chera disum*) when they go to collect firewood in the jungle – but they never refer to the arbitrarily invented and re-invented politico-administrative units created in colonial times or post-Independence India in this context. Whenever tribal people claim to be autochthonous to a certain region, they relate their claims to a given territory that links them to their ancestors and deities through the process of clearing the land.[23] When they claim relatedness to the jungle-covered hills, it is about relatedness to their spirit world, since all hills and mountains are known to be inhabited by distinct classes of spirits (*pat, bonga*). These spirits are no isolated or abstract category but are relevant to Ho lives, as they will be regularly called upon by shamans (*dewako*), for example, to help diagnose the cause of a disease or find out about some other irregularity empirical instances of which will be provided in chapter 4.

Compared to the 2001 census figures, there was an increase of 23.7 percent in India's tribal population according to the 2011 census. Whereas in Jharkhand and Odisha Scheduled Tribes constitute just below 10 percent of the overall population in each state on average, the ratio is significantly higher in the two districts of Mayurbhanj and West Singhbhum where fieldwork was done. In Mayurbhanj tribal communities officially account for over 58 percent of the population, in West Singhbhum for more than 50 percent. In the heart of the region of research, in the Jamda block of Mayurbhanj, the percentage is even higher – that is, if one is prepared to concede any validity to the 2001 census's report by the *Gram Panchayat* of the population of Jamda Block.

---

23 See also *The Ho's oral 'history'* in the Introduction.

Identifying and essentializing categories of people as tribal and categorizing them in lists of Scheduled Tribes by state is a legal act confirmed and updated by Parliament and rooted in the Fifth and Sixth Schedules of the Indian constitution. There the following criteria are formulated in Article 342 (25): primitive traits, distinct culture, geographical isolation, shyness of contact with the community at large, and (economic) backwardness. Based on these dubious criteria, Scheduled Tribes (ST) are distinguished from Scheduled Castes (SC) and Other Backward Classes (OBC), thus ignoring the specific quality of the linkages within the tribal society of the Plateau which was outlined in the introduction. An example of the conceptual arbitrariness of this process of categorization in the research area is revealed in the "Voters' List as Issued by the Election Committee in the Year 2006" (Jamda Block *panchayat* 2006), which classifies the community of the weavers as members of the OBC category in one ward, while in another ward weavers are listed as members of the SC category. Of course, this arbitrariness is not a regional specificity but a pan-Indian feature. Ho people displaced by the Kalinganagar Industrial Complex in the Sukinda subdivision of Jajpur District in Odisha, for example, complain that government functionaries and revenue officials have identified and recorded them in their registration papers as members of the Munda tribe. They claim that they are Ho, that Kolhan is their centre of orientation, and that they have migrated from Mayurbhanj, "part of Ho *disum* (country) before state reorganization" (Moharana 2012: 105).

In the ethnically, culturally, and linguistically heterogeneous terrain of the Chota Nagpur Plateau tribal people speak languages that have been classified as members of the (North) Munda branch of the Austro-Asiatic language family and the Dravidian language family of Southern India, alongside the Indo-Aryan languages Hindi and Odiya. According to Anderson (2008) the Munda languages Ho, Munda, Mundari, Santali, Kharia, Juang, and others whose distribution is given in map 2 are spoken by ten million people in that region of central and eastern India. Of these, according to Pucilowski (2013: 2), Santali, Mundari, and Ho are the most widespread with respect to the number of speakers. The language status of Ho is described as developing, and their language use as "vigorous. Positive attitudes" (*Ethnologue* 2017). A distinction is made between Chaibasa[24] Ho and the Mayurbhanj variety. On the Plateau, especially around the Ranchi area, Kurukh, a Dravidian language, is spoken by Oraon people. Many tribal people are bilingual. More than a few use three or more languages in

---

24 Chaibasa is the district headquarters of West Singhbhum. In fact, it has been the district headquarters ever since the creation of the district of (undivided) Singhbhum following the establishment of the Kolhan Government Estate in 1837.

speaking and writing. In contrast, in the course of my fieldwork I did not even once hear an official speak or attempt to speak one of the indigenous languages. Moreover, officials never seemed too surprised that those "backward primitives" whom they despise so much were capable of conversing with them in Odiya or Hindi.

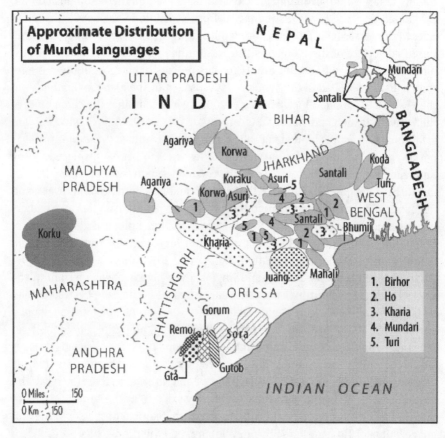

Map 2: Approximate distribution of the Munda languages
Kurukh (or Kurux), spoken by the Oraon, is a Dravidian language and as such not included here.
(Source: Anderson 2008: 2).

Kolhan, Ho country (*Ho disum*), and the Ho

Map 3: Kolhan/*Ho disum*
The research area, indicated by the red square, crosses the contemporary administrative border between West Singhbhum District in Jharkhand (left) and Mayurbhanj District in Odisha (right). Source: suedasien.info (retrieved November 2013).
In 1912 the areas of Bihar, Chotanagpur, and Odisha, then called Orissa, became a state named Bihar and Orissa. Orissa and Bihar became separate states in 1936, and Jharkhand was separated from Bihar in 2000.

It is in the two adjacent districts of Mayurbhanj and West Singhbhum in the states of Odisha and Jharkhand that a majority of the Ho live, in quite a compact area (Deeney 2008; Das Gupta 2011; Areeparampil 2002) approximately the size of Northumberland in Great Britain. Here Ho is the dominant language. It is also spoken as a lingua franca by approximately fifty thousand non-Ho (Deeney 2002: ix). In this area village elders (*munda*) and ritual guides (*diuri*) are mainly Ho, village meetings are held in Ho, and Ho is the language that prevails at the village markets (Deeney 2008: 67). Almost 150 years ago Dalton became quite lyrical about this part of the Plateau when he referred to "a series of fair and fertile plains broken, divided, and surrounded by hills" (Dalton 1868: 11). This is the area that Ho people refer to as Ho country (*Ho disum*), translated in much of the literature as Kolhan (Dalton 1868; Tuckey 1920; Majumdar 1950; Areeparampil 2002; Das Gupta 2011; Yorke 1976; Verardo 2003b). Majumdar (1950: 1) gives 1,919 square miles as the extent of the territory of Kolhan. This equals 4,970 square kilometres and is an accurate estimate. According to *Ethnologue* (2017), Pucilowski (2013), and the Census Atlas (1988), Ho is also spoken in the Dhalbhum area, in Keonjhar District, and in the state of West Bengal.

It was in the mountainous southwest of Kolhan in the Saranda Forest Division where Yorke did fieldwork among the Ho, in an area where Ho are recruited as labourers for the mining industry exploiting the local iron-ore mines, whose deposits are considered among the richest in the world (Yorke 1976: 13). In this densely forested part of Kolhan open mines coexist with shifting cultivation in the hill regions and settled agriculture in the valleys. Fifteen years earlier Dhan (1961; 1962), herself a Ho, conducted an ethnographic study of the Ho of the same region focussing on their socioreligious lives. Bouez stationed himself in two villages near Champua in the very south of Kolhan, right on the border with Keonjhar. He published the results of his research on kinship and alliance among Ho and Santal in 1985.[25] Verardo, on the other hand, did fieldwork among Ho, Munda, and Mundari people in Porahat, which is an area within today's West Singhbhum, but which in terms of the definition given above would be to the north of and outside Kolhan. According to Ho oral 'histories' in that region, some of Verardo's Ho informants claimed to have migrated to Porahat from the south, from Kolhan, and others from the ex-princely states of Kharsawan and Seraikela to the east of Porahat. This is interesting for two reasons:

First, some of my most elderly informants in the research area proudly recollected relations with the Raja of Seraikela. A senior member of the dominant Bage clan even claimed to have been regularly invited to the Raja's court, as he was a famous *chhau* dancer in his younger days, and Seraikela was the centre that staged and promoted the art of this sophisticated dance, whose origin, he claimed, was tribal. Second, Verardo's suggestion of Ho people migrating north into Porahat is important because according to the information I was given Ho have migrated southwards from the north and northwest. As their point of departure in the northwest one informant mentioned Rewa, which is a town in today's state of Madhya Pradesh. In any case, migratory movements by the Ho appear less speculative in the Ho's oral 'histories' and seem quite probably to have taken place between today's towns of Bandgaon and Chakradharpur, linking Porahat and Kolhan by the Ranchi road. Here, the names of forty-three villages are identical with the names of the same number of Ho clans. This correspondence will be explored in chapter 3 when I analyse the names of Ho clans and subclans.

To my knowledge Deeney is the only scholar to have drawn attention to this phenomenon of overlapping. He for this reason suggests that Ho may have migrated into Singhbhum from this area (2002: 146; 2008: 96). This would indicate that Ho people are not and have not been limited to the terrain of Kolhan in an

---

25 R. Parkin (1992) in his book on "The Munda of Central India" extensively draws from Bouez's publication when he analyses and compares Ho and Santal social organization, relationship terminology and marriage patterns. Parkin's monograph is not based on his own participatory fieldwork, but "relies completely on the previously published work of others" (1992: 13).

exclusive sense and that it indeed makes sense to speak of Ho country (*Ho disum*) instead. In fact, Deeney himself only occasionally uses the term Kolhan but rather focusses on the Ho of West Singhbhum and Odisha. In this context it should be kept in mind that Odisha came into being as an independent state only in 1936, when it was known as Orissa (see map 3). Bihar and Orissa formed one state until then, which means that before 1936 no administrative boundary separated Ho country.

Lupungutu: a Christianized region of Ho country

Identifying *Ho disum* as a territorially rather coherent region does not mean that it is a culturally uniform or undifferentiated area. On the contrary, there are significant cultural distinctions, not only between tribal communities, but also between and within Ho communities.

It was in Lupungutu near Chaibasa where I entered Ho country for the first time in 2005. Lupungutu is a Jesuit stronghold and has a significant Christianized Ho community. The Jesuits whom I have met there are highly committed people working as priests, teachers, project managers, social workers, legal advisors, drivers, gardeners, doctors, and lawyers.

Future priests are given language courses in the Ho language by Ho scholars, as communication with local Ho is to take place in Ho and church sermons are to be given in Ho for Ho people. In parish services Jesus is addressed as Sinbonga, the Ho's creator God. This was a major issue that required negotiation with Rome and was a request that was not easily granted (J. Deeney, personal communication). As trainees Jesuits have to acquire fluency and precision in the Ho language before they do social work 'in the interior', assist with the cultivation work there, and initiate diverse agricultural development projects and irrigation schemes. As priests Jesuits live, often for decades, in the tribal villages, where almost every one of them catches malaria but continues to work.

Parental demand is great to run Hindi and English medium schools and colleges, which Jesuits do as headmasters and qualified teachers, but there are also hostels and schools built for tribal girls and boys, where they are given decent food and taught in their Ho mother tongue. Here boys and girls wear school uniforms in the English style, and girls have their thick black hair tamed into neat braids. A night school system right in the forested tribal areas was also about to be set up, though eventually given up.

Hospitals and a medical ambulance are managed by Jesuits and run in the Ho language to serve the local Ho people. Ho women are trained as nurses and encouraged to qualify as part of the staff.

As lawyers, Jesuits assist Ho women and men if they happen to be taken to court and defend them free of charge. Jesuit lawyers are consulted regularly by Ho in cases of impending land dispossession, which is a constant threat in this mineral-rich area. By 2005 more than one hundred thousand acres of tribal land had been sold for the opening of mines (Das Gupta 2006) despite legislation to the contrary. Since the institutionalized *manki* and *munda*, employees of the (Jharkhand) state, are often held to be corrupt and collaborating with the mining boards, Ho turn to Jesuit lawyers instead. From the top floor of the Tribal Research and Training Centre, I could see and smell the furnaces and hear the trains transporting iron ore day in and day out, continuing all through the night, just beyond the walls of the gated community.

The regional Tribal Research and Training Centre (TRTC) of Lupungutu, established in 1984 by the Jesuit Mathew Areeparampil and run by him until his death in 2002, is a busy place. It offers classes, workshops, and seminars for those interested in tribal issues and informal educational programmes for adult and young tribal people from the surrounding villages, especially for *adivasi* girls. For those attending such courses the TRTC provides access to a library, computers, sewing machines, basketball facilities, a football ground, and spacious gardens.

Lupungutu is a well-kept and well-organized place. Jesuits are hard-working people, disciplined, and efficient. Jesuits whom I met criticized the Indian government policy of "advancing the tribals into the Indian mainstream" as a strategy of assimilation contributing eventually to the loss of tribal identity, as outlined above. This strategy, they say, they attempt to counteract in their day-to-day interactions. In their own ways they try to advance the Ho's lot by improving their material and spiritual well-being according to their general humanitarian approach. But, having said all this, it is, of course, a Jesuit approach. At Easter 2006 I was present when a huge screen was set up in the middle of a field and an emotionally charged American documentary on the life of Jesus drew crowds of Ho people from the vicinity to watch the film, which lasted more than three hours. It had been dubbed into the Ho language.

What conversion does to Ho people, their worldview, their sociocosmic ideas, and their Ho-ness could be a highly fascinating project for anthropological research to be done from the Ho's perspective, since the Jesuits at Lupungutu with whom I have been in touch for years are nontribal, non-Ho people, many from Tamil Nadu or Kerala and all fluent in the Ho language, who collaborate with local Ho people with an attitude of respect. Focussing on the Jesuits and studying their interaction with the Ho tribals would also be a resourceful research topic, and Lupungutu a suitable region in which to study this. However, neither conversion nor the issues related to it nor the 'Jesuit project' was my research focus. My focus was on locally defined Ho priorities and local Ho perspectives. I was interested in observing how Ho communities and Ho people are faring without the assistance of the Catholic Church, social activists, Chaibasa academia, disciplined formal education, and nongovernmental organizations. My site for doing fieldwork was further south, where members of tribal and nontribal categories live side by side in an area less than forty kilometres away from Chaibasa, not at all remote in terms of distance, but significantly remote ideologically from Hindu and Christian perspectives – despite the existence of (government) schools, often boarding schools located on the outskirts of the villages, proselytizing activities of sorts, close relations living in nearby towns, and knowledge about the world outside transmitted by people doing migrant wage labour in different parts of India, mostly Northern India, Gujarat, Assam, and Bhutan.

Deeney and the Ho

John Deeney is a scholar of the Ho who had lived and worked in Lupungutu for more than sixty years when he died in 2010. Born an American of Irish origin, he died as an Indian citizen. Before he left for India, his early training as a Jesuit involved deep immersion into the grammar of English, Latin, Greek, French, and Gaelic. Once in India, he studied Hindi. As soon as he entered Ho country in the 1950s, he began to systematically learn that language. He became fluent in Ho, in both conversation and writing: "pure Ho," as my Ho informants used to acknowledge with great respect. By the end of the 1970s Deeney, in collaboration with a Ho graduate, Dhanur Singh Purty, had developed a modified Devanagari script for Ho, a spoken language, and published his first Ho-English dictionary. At the time of my main fieldwork in 2009 – 10 he was in his late eighties and still busy trying to grasp the complexity of the Ho's sociocosmic world. It was he who introduced me into the very practical first steps and the poetics of the Ho language in 2005, as well as into the intricacies of the Ho's tribal universe and kinship matters.

Deeney published widely on the Ho, and I was also given access to his unpublished material. Not only the analysis of Ho relationship terminology in chapter 6 draws heavily on our discussions and his publications, but also my overall understanding and representation of the Ho's spirit world in chapter 4.

Deeney collaborated with anthropologists to make sense of his observations and offer reliable ethnographic material. He discussed his findings with Ho people in order to check their correctness before going to press. He made it a point to present his material from the Ho's point of view – also in his dictionary, which offers cultural background knowledge and insights into Ho perspectives that turn it into a Ho encyclopaedia rather than a body of lexical entries and an isolated collection of denotations.

Having spent the majority of his adult life among Ho people, Deeney conveyed a spirit of being unaffected by any kind of cultural pessimism and free from any inclinations to despondency. He portrayed Ho culture as vigorous, subtle, and very much alive. However, his books have been published only regionally, by Xavier Ho Publications in Lupungutu, Chaibasa, and Ranchi. Unfortunately, they may be known and accessible only to a limited number of academics, and this scholar and his in-depth knowledge may easily be overlooked. For this reason, appendix 1, "Scholarly Commitment: John Deeney and the Ho of Kolhan," seeks to fill this academic gap by giving an introduction to this philologist, his immersion into Ho matters, and his written work. It also includes information gained in personal encounters and talks with him over many years, as well as some additional fieldwork background.

The field

Getting there

Accessing Ho country via Odisha, from Mayurbhanj through the southeastern Kolhan plateaux, may be logistically difficult and at times quite time-consuming, although not impossible, as there is an existing transport infrastructure – one that becomes more and more challenging, however, the closer one gets towards the Jharkhand border. But there are trains and buses to supply the periphery of the plains, and there are four-wheel-drive vehicles when nothing else works. Trains from Howrah Station in Kolkata, West Bengal, regularly reach Tatanagar Station in the modern industrial centre and steel city of Jamshedpur, Jharkhand, with its over six hundred thousand inhabitants in about three to eight hours, severe pollution advertising the blessings of modern, advanced, and economically developed India long before the train eventually comes to a halt at the station. Tatanagar is some eighty kilometres or roughly fifty miles from Manbir, a village in the research region with a large Ho population (map 4), and the Ho's kin and friendship ties include relationships across this distance from Tatanagar. From Tatanagar public buses run southwest to Rairanpur in Odisha, sometimes along newly paved roads that have been cut through tribal settlements. Thus, tribal people and their shaded mud houses have become prone to exhaust pollution, traffic noise, sun, and rain, as trees offering shelter and intimacy have been cut down. In 2012 it took the bus three hours to reach Rairanpur, whereas three years before it took more than six hours along roads that were bumpy and at times full of potholes. Potholes are regularly the result of heavy monsoon rains turning roads into muddy tracks by undercutting the tarred road surface. But then, the bus drivers are competent experts and know where and when to leave the road altogether in order to cross some fields instead. They also know how to repair the engine and change the tyres.

Rairanpur is a bustling town of more than thirty-four thousand inhabitants (Census 2011). It has electricity and a controlled twice-daily power cut of one hour each time. There are roads, schools, colleges, doctors, hospitals and pharmacies, many shops, tea stalls and stalls selling cooked food, a regular permanent market, fairly reliable internet access, a large bus terminal, and a considerable number of job opportunities in the iron and iron-ore mines in the vicinity. Its two or three small hotels are often fully booked by groups of engineers and mining experts exploring ways of exploiting the mineral wealth of the area and driving around in shiny, expensive jeeps. While in ten years I never saw a white person in the villages where I did research, in Rairanpur occasionally, though not very often, some European, American, or Australian project assistants might turn up. They enjoy the safety and comfort of a hotel there while some doing short-term research in the tribal vicinity. Others are assigned to some project, such as the National Geographic Genographic Project or the same organization's mitochondrial DNA project. Their 'fieldwork' consisted of finding tribal people who were prepared to donate their saliva for genome analysis and racing from one tribal village to the next for this purpose. They did not really understand why I refused to collaborate.

In Rairanpur, Odiya is the official and dominant language that people speak along with Hindi. English is hardly used and only rarely understood. Tribals who have found a job here (*nala:*, to work for wages) prefer to speak Odiya in this nontribal environment rather than their respective mother tongues.

From Rairanpur, a few jeeps used as buses occasionally spend an hour or so struggling their way west along mud roads towards Jamda, a spread-out market town of perhaps two thousand inhabitants (Census 2011) quite close to the research area. Up to fifteen people, sometimes more, squeeze into such a four-wheel-drive vehicle which constitutes the local shuttle service between these two places. Some people will have to stand at the back (men only), while the top is reserved for poultry, baskets, luggage, household, and construction items.

Map 4: The region of research
The region of research, indicated by the orange ellipse, can be accessed from Rairanpur to the east. The twice-weekly market is in Jamda. Manbir to the west is right on the border between Odisha and Jharkhand and at the foot of a mountain (*buru*) considered sacred and inaccessible by the local Ho. It is an extension of the forested mountain ranges conventionally said to divide North and South Kolhan. (Source: India and Pakistan AMS Topographic Maps, Perry-Castaneda Map Collection, Austin, University of Texas Library Online, sheet NF 45–6. Series U502. Retrieved October 26, 2014; orange ellipse added.)

On the way, the latest news is exchanged, and the anthropologist's plans are discussed, in Ho or Odiya, first among the women, usually at the back of the jeep, and then passed on to the front rows. Having spent quite some time with women on trains all over India enjoying their passionate discussions on all different walks of life, I am still stunned by the undaunted straightforwardness and self-confidence of the tribal women as reflected in their interactions with men on the jeep and elsewhere. As soon as the jeep leaves the main road and turns inland towards Jamda, the tribal hinterland becomes immediately and visibly present: instead of urban brick houses or houses made of concrete and painted in bright, sometimes gaudy colours, the mud houses of the Ho people appear, easily recognizable from outside and easily distinguishable from the mud houses of the Santal. Tribal houses are usually clustered in groups and tucked away in the shade of tamarind, neem, and mango trees, and they are usually spotlessly clean. Before reaching Jamda the jeep will cross a bridge across a tributary of the Kharkai River. It will pass the police station, a recently erected, quite massive *diku* building safely positioned towards the outskirts of Jamda, in garish colours and an alien architectural style, and occupied by Odiya-speaking staff from the plains; the General Post Office, which is more often closed than open; and the fenced-in *panchayat* buildings of Jamda Block, guarded by policemen with rifles over their shoulders.

Jamda is the jeep's final destination. *Jamda* is a Ho word which denotes an "arbour or shelter of branches and leaves, especially that used on the occasion of a marriage feast" (Deeney 2005: 172) and, in a different context, on the occasion of secondary burials, when such shelters of branches and leaves (*jamda*) are erected for a deceased person's affines who are invited to participate in the celebrations or funerary rituals and stay overnight in these shelters for this purpose (see also plate 10). In the town of Jamda, in administrative terms Jamda Block, which is a district subdivision, the twice-weekly market on Wednesdays and Saturdays is an event of some social significance in the region. Members of various indigenous categories come together from distances of up to two hours on foot to see and be seen, to exchange news and views, and to initiate new relationships, possibly including love or marital relationships.[26] Ho women sell homemade rice-beer and rice-liquor (*diyan, rasi*) and produce collected in the jungle, such as red ants, a delicacy to be eaten with lemon juice and chili, twigs of the sacred sal tree (*sarjom daru*) to be used as toothbrushes (*karkad*), leaves of the sal tree, from which plates and cups are made to be used in ritual contexts, and fresh fruit. Ho men sell fresh vegetables from their gardens and, at times, black beans (*ramba*), a pulse needed for ritual purposes, and unhusked rice (*baba*, paddy) if some extra money is urgently needed. Muslim tailors offer different kinds of ready-made clothes for men and women that they have either sewn themselves or bought elsewhere in the cities, where tribal people do not like to go. Potters (*kunkal*) sell earthen pots (*mandi chatu*) in which family meals are prepared and that regularly need to be replaced when a relative has died. Still other vendors, located some distance away and partly outside the covered market site, sell poultry, fish, and meat.

According to the 2011 census, Jamda Block includes no towns but sixty-seven villages. The total population of Jamda is given as 2,356 with an ST population of 1466 and an SC population of 32. This reveals that even if the census figures may not be very reliable, more than 63 percent of the population have been scheduled, of whom 62 percent are registered as tribal. On the way from Rairanpur to the research area Jamda is the last place to house a Hindu temple, if quite a small one. Only since 2012 has Jamda been connected to Bhubaneswar by a bus making the trip regularly twice a week. When I took this bus once, it was packed with parents on their way to visit their children who attended either KISS or KIIT in Bhubaneswar.[27]

Heading west from Jamda towards the border between Odisha and Jharkhand, the quality of the roads or paths becomes poorer. Local people usually walk or go by bicycle. From Jamda the villages of Manbir and Tarana can be reached on foot in another hour or so (see map 4). The 2011 census gives a

---

26 see in chapter 3: "How to establish a relationship".

27 Both institutions were founded by A. Samanta in 1992–3 for tribal pupils and students. KISS is the Kalinga Institute of Social Sciences providing free accommodation and education for 27000 children from kindergarten to post-graduation including vocational training. KIIT, a private university, is the Kalinga Institute of Industrial Technology also primarily addressed to tribal students.

total population of 2,006 for Manbir, with 1,315 (65 percent) registered as ST and 84 (4 percent) as SC. In the course of my fieldwork I was never able to figure out what had happened to those who had been omitted or forgotten by the scheduling system, since all of my informants had been administratively compartmentalized within the nationwide system one way or the other. If one is prepared to trust official figures at all, it might be interesting to know that of the 1,725 inhabitants included on the Manbir voter rolls, a total of 1,061 are entitled to participate in the local *panchayat* as well as in the national elections. In Tarana 1,318 people are registered as ST (65 percent) and 63 as SC (3.1 percent), out of a total of 2,012 inhabitants. These are the officially fixed administrative facts and figures. To most Ho people they reflect a *diku* mindset that separates and continuously subdivides indigenous categories and territoriality irrespective of local understandings of coexistence. Tarana with its numerous hamlets is one of the regions of research. Officially, it is subdivided into four administrative wards given numerical labels, "13," "14," "15," and "16." To local Ho and Santal people this bureaucratic way of anonymizing and tearing apart their sacred landscape and the population cultivating it is foreign talk (*diku kaji*). They instead refer to a multitude of hamlets (*sai*), some of which became meaningful to me during fieldwork, such as Gara Sai, Santal Sai, Kharia Sai, Pathan Sai, Boja Sai, and Rasika Sai.

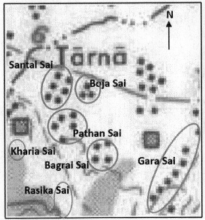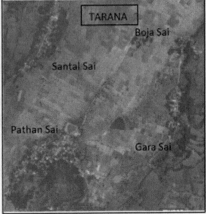

Map 5: The village of Tarana and a few of its hamlets
Left: Source: As given above for map 4. Right: Source: Google Earth, retrieved July 31, 2015. Names of hamlets added by author. Tarana is also pronounced or spelt Taran or Tarna.

The first name on this list refers to a *sai* through which a rivulet (*gara*) runs, hence Gara Sai. S. Kondangkel,[28] Gara Sai's secular head (*munda*), does not know the exact number of its inhabitants, but he is precisely aware of the number of its households, as in preparation for the annual village festivals (*porobko*) it is his duty to collect a share (*baga*) from each household. So he can report that in Gara Sai there are forty-seven Ho and six Santal households. It is one of the hamlets inhabited by tribal people only, in this case Ho and Santal. According to S. Kondangkel, neither Scheduled Caste people nor Gau people live in Gara Sai; the latter are the Ho's cowherders, who have been classified in the region as members of the OBC category. Despite being administratively separated from Ho and Santal people, the local ritual guide of the Gau people is regularly involved in Ho rituals at the village level, just as the Ho's ritual guide is involved in the Gau's festivals.

Santal Sai is a hamlet populated predominantly by Santal people, hence Santal Sai, along with a few of the Santal's clients. The blacksmith (*lohar*) lives right in the centre, almost next door to the Santal *naeke*, the hamlet's ritual guide, and the local secular head (*majhi*) with his two wives. A single weaver (*dom*) used to live at the southernmost end of Santal Sai, where he made a living by selling fish in the markets until he died. In 2009 I stayed in Santal Sai for more than two months, before I moved to Boja Sai.

Boja Sai is a pure Ho settlement, perhaps a twenty-minute walk along the embankments from Santal Sai. Boja Sai is a cluster of houses with roughly a dozen households, most of whom are members of the Kondangkel clan. *Boja* has the denotation 'a load; a bundle of wood, leaves tied together', but some informants claimed that Boja was the name of Boja Sai's founder-ancestor.

I do not know what the history may be of Kharia people giving their name to Kharia Sai, a hamlet close to the jungle. I was involved in marriage negotiations in Kharia Sai, but the people I met who lived in Kharia Sai spoke Ho and identified themselves as Ho of the Sinku clan. To assist the bride's side during the marriage negotiations, the secular head and ritual guide of Pathan Sai had been invited to participate.

Pathan Sai is a larger hamlet probably so called by the local Ho people because of its considerable Muslim community, who live in the immediate vicinity of the Ho. Ch. Purty, who shortly after my entering the field established a ritual friendship (*saki*) with my husband and me, is the secular head (*munda*) of the Ho

---

28 S. Kondangkel has proved a most reliable informant over the years. He became my younger brother. As *munda* he was a person much respected by the villagers. His portrait is given in chapter 7.

here.[29] The Muslim people of Pathan Sai identify themselves as members of the category Sheik and refer to their separate section as 'Muslim Sai'. They have their own secular head (*sadar*) and ritual guide. According to Deeney, *patã* "originally meaning a Pathan, is used for Mohammedans in general" (2005: 284) among Ho people. Officially, Muslims were not registered in this area at all in the 2001 and 2011 censuses of Jamda Block as Muslims, but they are administered – for revenue reasons – as members of "ward no. 13," along with households of the cowherd (*Gau*) category.

Rasika carries the meaning "happy, to rejoice," but I am not aware of a narration or myth to explain the name. Where there are people who are socially linked within a *miyad mandi chaturenko*[30] and who have land in both Pathan Sai and Rasika Sai, there is economic collaboration. All of these hamlets are separated by rice fields, rocky outcrops, or small rivers, but they are within walking distance of one another.

The book shows that these hamlets are not isolated from each other. They are connected by kin and marriage relations, by economic cooperation, and by ritual interaction. In ritual affairs the two *munda* will cooperate, as they did when a new ritual guide (*diuri*) was selected, since the former one had decided to step down. At the same time, in their secular lives Ho people from Boja Sai and Gara Sai will turn to S. Kondangkel from Gara Sai, whom they recognize as their *munda* in the same way that when his father was still alive, their fathers recognized him as their *munda*, from whom the duty to be *munda* was passed down to his son. Ho people from Pathan Sai, which is perhaps some two kilometres from Gara Sai, will turn to Ch. Purty as their *munda*, while Santal people from Santal Sai have their *majhi* and Muslims their *sadar*. Ho perform as *munda* strictly within their immediate vicinity, otherwise cultivating their fields and without any privileges or executive powers vested in them. This reflects the fact that people's perspectives are locally centred on their own hamlet and those hamlets related to them by kinship or marriage links rather than on the all-embracing, yet more remote administrative unit of the village (*hatu*) as such.

---

29 Ch. Purty will be referred to throughout this book. Many of my observations in the field have been discussed with him, and he himself proved a reliable source of relevant information. The *saki*-relation with him is discussed in chapter 6 as a form of ritual friendship.

30 This is a relevant social unit of Ho people analysed in chapter 3.

Being there

In terms of accessibility or distance this site is not really remote, a factor which in quite a few monographs on tribal issues constitutes one of the decisive markers to qualify for solid fieldwork. On the contrary, the chosen site for research is comparatively close to the more urban centres of Rairanpur to the east (one hour on foot plus one hour by jeep), Chaibasa to the north (three to four hours and thirty-eight kilometres by Chaibasa *gari*), Jamshedpur to the northeast (one hour on foot plus one hour by jeep plus three hours by bus from Rairanpur), and, since 2012, Bhubaneswar to the southeast (eight to twelve hours by bus from Jamda). The point I want to make is that logistically and pragmatically one can get from Kolhan to the world outside and vice versa fairly easily – travelling within Kolhan is much more strenuous – and the means of transport connecting the peripheries and the centres are always packed. Ho country is not isolated and probably never has been, and people are not ignorant of what is going on outside their tribal terrain, as their kin and friendship system includes relations in Rourkela, Jamshedpur, Simlipal, Chaibasa, Rairanpur, Cuttack, and Bhubaneswar. I argue that in the absence of the caste system, temples, and Brahmanical priests, the tribal society of Kolhan as outlined in the introductory chapter constitutes a world that is essentially different from Indian mainstream society in terms of its value-ideas, norms, and practices. This is so not because of its geographical remoteness from Brahmanical values as enacted in the coastal plains of Odisha, only some hundred kilometres or so away, but despite its relative closeness. To me this made the choice of the research area especially fascinating and rewarding, as the book will attempt to contribute to questioning the powerful discourse according to which globalization's impact on indigeneity is always and everywhere unilateral. The book will question the evolutionist bias hidden in the assumptions about the modernization of indigeneity that Sahlins has criticized as "sentimental pessimism" (Sahlins 2000: 507). According to this set of assumptions, indigenous people live the way they do because and only as long as they do not have access to the modern, globalized world. Because of an alleged universal rationality, that access will initiate processes of transformation with objective necessity, with the effect that once the bridge into modernity has been built, tribal people will instantly cross it, wanting to get rid of their backwardness and start modernizing their cosmos and their behaviours. In the course of my fieldwork, however, I experienced the opposite. I could observe that my Ho and Santal neighbours keep crossing these bridges and usually return as fast as they can. My Ho mother never minded me leaving for Chaibasa, as this is pure Ho country, but she minded my staying overnight in Rairanpur, which, though fairly close, she considered *diku* terrain. It just so happens that as symbols of progress and Brahminic civilization, urban centres do not seem to hold attractions for tribal people as such. When they leave their villages, they do so because a social obligation so demands or for a particular purpose. My Ho informants went to Rairanpur when they had decided to see a bio-doctor there or when they had saved enough money to buy a pressure cooker, to Jamshedpur to visit their kin, and to Chaibasa when they had been asked, sometimes by a written invitation, to attend a secondary burial. Whenever they went, they did so accompanied by a group of relatives and often only after a thorough consultation with the *mamu* (mother's brother) of a member of the travelling party. Tribal solidarity reaches far, but tribal purity is at stake outside tribal terrain.

Conversely, apart from policemen, government employees, teachers, and representatives of the mining industries, nontribal townspeople and nontribal plains people do not enter tribal regions as a matter of principle. For them, tribal terrain is not geographically remote, but it is notionally remote and culturally quite distinct. That this has turned into an embodied attitude became empirically obvious to me when I once missed the last bus that leaves Rairanpur for Jamda in daylight in the late afternoon. I found nobody prepared to take me home, as that would have implied returning through the tribal zone after dark. This is telling indeed, as I was usually treated with utmost respect and offered help generously at all times. To nontribal people, however, in Rairanpur and elsewhere, tribal territory and its specific multi-ethnic pattern of coexistence is a no-go area.

The fieldwork situation

The decision to do long-term fieldwork and do it among Ho people developed only gradually, in phases over many years, and really took time to take concrete shape. As this decision-making process has impacted my understanding and representation of how to go about doing fieldwork and how to decide on the focus of this book, I will next briefly discuss how my biography and my reading social and cultural anthropology led me to prepare for fieldwork and to continue it over a decade. These prerequisites are necessarily subjective and selective. I mention them because the person of the fieldworker, that is, myself, is considered an inseparable and constitutive part and aspect of fieldwork itself. The world of the Ho that I will be representing is my perception of it. Whatever I have experienced, listened to, and observed in participatory research has been processed and perceived through the filter of the cultural narratives that I have grown into and that have become mine. Boas remarked in this context that "the seeing eye is an organ of tradition" (quoted in Sahlins 1994: 99) and that in order "to understand human behaviour we must know as much about the eye that sees as about the object seen" (quoted in Pöhl and Tilg 2011: 14).

Biographical prerequisites

After having finished my professional career and before deciding to enrol in the Institute of Ethnology at the Free University of Berlin as a regular student in her first term at the age of almost sixty, I spent almost a year in Southeast Asia and India. This was meant as a kind of separator before entering a new and unknown phase of my life. The culture shock came, rather unexpectedly to me, after my return home, when I tried to get re-integrated into the routines of the Western individualized way of life. The decision to start from scratch and read social and cultural anthropology was to a large degree informed by what I had experienced and observed in Asia that year but did not understand, by what I found fascinating and awe-inspiring but could not make sense of. I will give just one example which became a major focus in my anthropological commitment later.

One of the things that had impressed and at the same time startled me was a grand death ritual that I happened to be invited to participate in and that I was allowed to observe for a full day near Rantepao, Sulawesi, Indonesia, among Toraja people. What startled me was that despite all the knowledge and wisdom that I thought I had acquired in a long life as a mother, a married woman, and a professional person, I was utterly unable to grasp the meaning or rationality of what I was observing, while at the same time it was clear that the people involved were collectively following a meaningful routine, their performances reflecting a local culture that seemed very much alive and not on the brink of dying out. During this ritual, some fifty or more buffaloes were to be sacrificed in the midst of terraced rice fields located in the island's steep mountain ranges. People of different ages and sexes were assembled, all uniformly dressed in black and red. The most elderly men were repeatedly talking and shouting into their mobile phones with a note of urgency, obviously passing on orders of some significance. These elders were ceremoniously dressed all in black, in contrast to the other participants, and, exuding authority, they were choreographing the whole ceremony in standardized ways according to a well-known schedule. Taking turns, groups of men and women serenely sang in repetitive rhythms and tunes, quite monotonous as they sounded to me at the time, and danced in circles around several buffaloes before they were expertly sacrificed. The procedure of ever-new groups singing and dancing and buffaloes being sacrificed was repeated for the major part of the day. The animals were eventually divided up such that certain young men carried home a buffalo's head, others half a head, still others a hind leg or two feet, the tail, a shoulder, or other parts. I was amazed, because I could not imagine that anybody would eat an animal's head or feet. Men and boys right next to the sacrificial site would carry a coffin on their shoulders and run along a path with it, zig-zagging with it, dashing backwards and rushing forward in circles while simultaneously shouting and screaming. The whole situation looked chaotic and ordered at the same time, bizarre and full of contradictions – or what I thought were contradictions. I could not connect the slaughtering of buffaloes and the issue of death. I could not relate the matter-of-fact use of posh modern icons such as cell phones to the whole nonmodern ceremonial set-up. And my Western rationalities and explanatory models were no help in deciphering the ritual. It seemed obvious, though, that I had been witnessing a culturally alive, significant, and ordered routine uniting several hundred people and centring around death in collective, nonprivate, public ways. This was clearly not a thing of the past performed by people who had not yet been in touch with modernity. I was able speak to some participants in the ritual in English and learnt that they had come all the way from the United States of America and Canada to participate in these rituals on behalf of their dead, some of whom had died several months before. They had arrived in big jeeps, and the road was packed with new cars. A lot of money was clearly involved, but from my utilitarian perspective, the sacrifice did not make economic sense to me. Yet people behaved in a way that indicated that they were doing what needed to be done. In no way did they convey to me any notion of depression, shyness, or the awkwardness that may creep in once people have learned or are taught to despise their culture. Also, this was no foray into exoticism, folklore out of context performed to attract ethno-tourists, although a small handful of tourists were there. They looked utterly out of place to me, but they were welcome, I was told, since their presence would contribute to confusing and scaring off the spirits of the dead.

Reading social and cultural anthropology

Anthropology is the subject offering theoretical expertise on how to study human societies other than our own. So, digging down to the roots and studying cultures in depth offered itself as a logical and constructive project for my future. Theory, future fieldwork, participant observation, a second socialization, language learning – this was exactly what I was looking for. I enrolled at university and became a regular student. Peter Berger had just published his first book on the Toraja of Sulawesi and the ritual treatment of their dead. Good start.

In hindsight, the project of becoming immersed in tribal issues and the Ho universe introduced itself while I was still reading social and cultural anthropology. Promising young scholars, members of the Orissa Research Project headed by Professor Pfeffer, were either returning from fieldwork among diverse tribal communities of Middle India, teaching about their research and writing up their theses, or on their way back to the field. It was an exciting and stimulating teaching and learning environment. Work in progress. Theoretical issues became empirically grounded.

Still, I soon realized that I had more questions than I dared to ask during the seminars and that the answers that I was given often did not explain what I needed to know and understand. I wanted to connect, to visualize, to grasp whom and what I was studying. I did not doubt, for example, that kinship in less complex societies is a decisive cultural factor patterning intimate structures of relatedness, but to me such statements remained a type of algebra rather than a lived experience. Joking relationships? Asymmetric alliances? Shamans? Hereditary affines? Descent groups and categories? Time and again, it was the anthropology of death that fascinated me most, since I could better connect issues and theories with what I had already encountered elsewhere, though not understood. Essays by R. Hertz on death and secondary burials (1907), by M. Bloch on the meaning of death (1988), by Bloch and J. Parry on the relationship between death and life (1982), by Marcel Mauss on the category of the person (1938), and by Vitebsky on the continued agency of the dead after their physical death, as elaborated in his monograph *Dialogues with the Dead* (1993), opened up a new world as the authors explored and traced historically, sociologically, anthropologically, and linguistically alternative, nonindividualistic ways of constructing *Anthropos*, social relationships, and meaningful active relations between the living and the dead. This and other anthropological literature suggested to me the idea of investigating death from an anthropological perspective as a sociocultural topic embedding the biological phenomenon in a wider culture-specific context. I wondered how ideas and concepts alive elsewhere and people living according to them could be studied.

Time for fieldwork in the field, now that I had learned about the first steps into fieldwork. I wanted to see with my own eyes and find out for myself. I talked to Professor Pfeffer, who was then my university teacher and who became the supervisor of my doctoral thesis. Why don't you go and find out about the Ho? he said. He mentioned J. Deeney, a former American missionary, who he knew had written on several aspects of Ho culture. I was given the name and email address of M. T. Raj, a Jesuit, then in charge of the library at the Tribal Research and Training Centre (TRTC) at Lupungutu near Chaibasa, Jharkhand, India. He did not forget to point out that the terrain was malaria infested and that people die from cerebral malaria. So I should be careful.

Until then I had never heard of this tribal community in Middle India. Of course, before going to Ho country, I read whatever I could get hold of about the Ho. Awkwardly enough, it was not the literature by D. N. Majumdar (1950), C. P. Singh (1978), R. Parkin (1992), or S. C. Roy (1912) that inspired me to get going. K. S. Singh (1966) made a difference, though, because in several parts of his book he comes close to representing local history from the Ho's and Munda's perspective and conveys the spirit of Ho politics and poetry. Google at that time, early 2005, came up with only two fairly morbid bits of information: one concerned the now-abandoned Koel-Karo dam project causing Ho people to become dispossessed, and the other was about nuclear waste being dumped on tribal, specifically Ho, land in Dhalbhum, resulting in children born with physical deformities, severe pollution of the soil, and poisoning of the agricultural produce.

Preparing for fieldwork

In March 2005 I entered Ho country for the first time. Before arriving, I had tried to get in touch with a few people in the area via email, received no answer, bought a ticket to Kolkata, and eventually arrived in Chaibasa with nobody really expecting my arrival. Everyone in the Jesuit community working with or on behalf of Ho people was busy, as sketched above, or hosting some international delegation. Deeney, who at the time was about to finalize the drafts of his Ho-English dictionary to be published that summer, made it very clear that he would not have a single spare minute to spend with me. M. T. Raj was busy supervising the construction of a new three-storey building sponsored by the German charitable organization Miserior which would later house the TRTC's enlarged library, a kitchen, dormitories for groups and individuals, study and computer rooms, and facilities for students to qualify as future car mechanics, as well as providing the space for a huge irrigated vegetable garden. At the TRTC I browsed through the literature they had on the Ho, including Major Tickell (1840), Bouez (1985), Yorke (1976), the six volumes then published of *Tribal Studies* edited by Behera and Pfeffer, the complete Census of India series up to 1991, an *Introduction to the Ho Language* (1991) and a *Ho Grammar and Vocabulary* (2002 [1975]) both written by Deeney, the sixteen volumes of the *Encyclopaedia Mundarica* by J. Hoffman and A. van Emelen, and impressively more. Books, brochures, and papers were neatly catalogued and carefully kept behind glass in a place on the outskirts of the Chota Nagpur Plateau to support research on tribal issues in a tribal environment. The library looked somewhat unused, however, and during the years that I kept coming back, not one single person ever made use of it while I was there taking notes. All in all, it was a splendid place for me to get a first feel for my unfolding project. I had a safe place to stay with regular meals and a room to myself, electricity, running water, and secure means of transport into the 'interior', as tribal settlements inside the jungle were referred to, with any of the Fathers, if they went there to supervise, for example, the night-school system.

A young Ho student who attended a secondary school run by local Jesuits knew a little English and was willing to take me on my first excursions into the Ho vicinity. He introduced me to his family. I remember how surprised I was when he addressed his biological brothers and sisters (younger than he) and his father's brother's sons and daughters (younger than he) by the identical kinship term of younger brother or younger sister (*undi*). Reciprocally, he was ad-dressed by all of them as elder brother (*bau*). His father's household members and his father's elder brother's household lived in houses sharing the same courtyard. What I had found difficult to grasp or even to visualize in a seminar on kinship back home in Germany, that in Ho country and elsewhere brothers live and work together for a lifetime as a norm, immediately began to feel real. I was also invited by my young Ho assistant to participate in a secondary burial in his village. Because of his presence, people approached me without hesitation. I was immediately invited by Ho women to learn how to make leaf cups and leaf plates and to drink rice-beer. They were incessantly talking, drink-ing, and laughing, and, of course, I did not understand a word. Eventually I was invited by a few Ho to attend their flower festival (*ba porob*) in their village in the hills. I could not go, however, as the Fathers thought it might be too insecure for me to be in a hilly forested area without their protection. I realized that for field-work purposes later I would need to learn the language fast, become independ-ent to set my own agenda, and find a site in a Ho-dominated area that was not governed by Christian values and norms, efficiency, and discipline. But in sum, this had been a safe first stay and a sensitive introduction into Ho society.

At the end of the same year, when I went again, I was fortunate enough to find Manbir (map 4), a Ho village in Mayurbhanj. A young man and a young woman, both Santals who had graduated in anthropology, volunteered to assist me in the field as long as I was struggling with the language. When I decided on the young woman, for the reason that she might better help me gain access to the female Ho domain, she was no longer available all of a sudden, or so I was told. That was a hard lesson, as I was refused a reason. Sauna Majhi, the male assistant, was a wonderful cook and highly motivated. While I wanted Sauna to assist me in getting in touch with the local people, in translating our conversations, and in finding my way into the village, he had a clear but quite different understanding of his role as assistant. He had been trained as a physical anthropologist and was interested in data collecting. He left after the first month.

After the village elders, so I was told, had decided to have me among them, I was offered an abandoned former government house with an open roof right in the middle of the village, where I spent four months in 2006. The house was ideally situated, as one of the two village wells was right in front of it and hence it was a busy site, especially in the early mornings and evenings. Of course, this was no Ho house, and the kitchen inside was not equivalent to the sacred space within a Ho house, the *adin*. The building was easily recognizable as a *diku* building, as it was made from bricks and had windows in the kitchen also, through which Ho women and girls fetching water kept watching out for the female *diku* inside and offering a sort of free crash course in the Ho language for me. Of course, Deeney's language books helped me survive among people who were for the most part fluent in Ho, Santali, Hindi, and Odiya but not in English.

My focus from 2005 until 2007 was on death, death-related rituals, and the relations between the living and the dead in tribal Middle India, especially in Ho country. I worked up my fieldwork-based research data related to that topic into a book published in 2009 by Manohar in New Delhi.

That was only the beginning. So in 2008 it was suggested to me to continue and intensify my research among the Ho, which meant doing long-term field-work. This, however, was postponed for a year due to an organized outbreak of considerable unrest in Odisha and pogroms against the Christian community following the murder of Swami Laksmanada Saraswati in the district of Kondhmal in August 2008. Though a group of Naxalites claimed responsibility, the murder was blamed on 'the Christians' (Mallebrein 2008).

Before my main fieldwork began in October 2009, necessary arrangements had been made in previous and consecutive visits to the research area concerning the choice of hamlet or village, purpose and length of my stay, accommodation, food, and language assistance. Ever since Sauna had left Manbir in 2006, G. Hansda from Santal Sai (map 5) had become my assistant. Since 2009 he has also become my host and my son. I have kept going back to the research area for shorter and longer periods of between two weeks and two months to deepen the relationships that began to develop in the field and to continue fieldwork concerning certain aspects that required further research and that I became aware of only in the process of writing up the book. The fieldwork situation was ideal: I had a lot of support and was welcomed to participate in all different walks of people's profane and ritual lives. I felt safe at all times. Lupungutu was a day's journey away from the research area but close enough to serve as a retreat once in a while when I needed some rest to think and a table to write on or to clarify some language issues with Deeney and interview others.

3 Living in a world of relations: of Ho social categories

"How do you marry in your society without having clans (kili)? How can we marry our daughters in your country if we do not know who are our affinal relations (bala-saka)?" This is what I was asked by my saki *(namesake) when the* saki *ceremony had been performed and we began to talk about mutual support and the overall potentialities implied in this ritual relation.*

Ho people are comprehensively and collectively born into and embedded in a web of social relations within which they order and organize their lives. This chapter is about Ho understandings of what accounts for their specific ways of constituting and regenerating social cohesion within and beyond their society. It is an ethnographic account of what it means to Ho people to belong to relevant social categories such as tribe, clan, subclan, house, brotherhood, village, and *miyad mandi chaturenko* ('people of one rice pot'), a specific Ho category. These categories are relevant because Ho people's interaction, their sociocultural lives, their meaning and decision-making are firmly and dynamically rooted in these social categories over the generations. Ho people live them and live in them, and in everyday and ritual practices these social categories keep being reproduced and recreated. They offer orientation to how things may be done, should be done, or must not be done. They impact whom (not) to eat and drink with, how to marry, where to live, what kind of work to do and whom with (and whom not), and where (not) to be buried. They are no outside imposition by the anthropologist, and they are not outdated.

Based on my data, I will concentrate here on those social categories that I could identify as relevant in the region of research and that Ho and Santal informants pointed out as meaningful. They often referred to those of their social institutions that are functionally and semantically overlapping by making use of Ho nomenclature. An example of this is the Ho category *miyad mandi chaturenko*, which is known to Santal people there: when they explain their Santal institution, they use the Ho designation synonymously with the Santali terms *alehor*, literally 'our people', and *gusti*.

This implies that categories that others who have published on tribal Middle India and the Ho have suggested as essential in their regions are not always considered in this book. Dhan, for example, describes an indigenous distinction be-

https://doi.org/10.1515/9783110666199-007

tween agnatic (*owa: goe:*)[31] and affinal ancestral spirits (*hortenko*)[32] for the Ho of the Saranda region of Kolhan. Given the dichotomous division of the Ho's social universe into a person's agnatic and affinal relations, this distinction indeed makes cultural sense, but as I have never come across the term *hortenko* during fieldwork, I will not enlarge on it here. I was also unable to trace in the region of research the social categories that Verardo elaborates for the Ho and Munda of Porahat, such as *kupulko*, *khunt*, and *bonso* (Verardo 2003b: 32, 33).

I will not discuss Ho social categories here as analytical or static isolates, since I have not observed them as such during fieldwork. In fact, the following section on how to establish a relationship is a case in point to illustrate the inseparability of how on the one hand relations are always latent, dynamic, and in the making, involving an empirical Ho's likes and dislikes, aspirations and determination, and how on the other hand a person's subjective whims and desires may find orientation and guidance within an acknowledged formal frame and within normative patterns of ordering or classifying relations.

How to establish a relationship

When asked to define relevant sources of their identity as Ho persons, Ho people invariably and immediately begin by referring primarily to the names of their village (*hatu*) and their clan (*kili*). In the course of fieldwork, it soon turns out, however, that village and clan are further distinguished into smaller units and that in fact these smaller units at grassroots level figure more prominently in Ho people's lives than the more remote and encompassing categories of village and clan. Still, these two constitute relevant points of reference which will also determine the nature of an emerging relationship between Ho young men and young women who are strangers to each other and who may want to establish a personal relationship. As a piece of evidence, I was given a nonindividualizing kind of model conversation suggesting a fixed order of questions as the most 'natural' way of becoming acquainted, by exchanging information in the following six standardized steps:

---

31 Literally these are "the dead of the house". For Ho ancestry see also below "*Mmc:* the structural significance of Ho ancestors".
32 Dhan defines this term as the ancestors of the "mother's clan, wife's clan, brother's wife's clan, and sister's husband's clan" (Dhan 1962: 20).

- Step one: "Where are you from?" (*Okon hatuetebena?*)[33]
- Step two: "Which clan (*kili*) is yours?" (*Abendo chikan kili?*) As possible answers I was given for person A *kili Hasda:*[34] and for person B *kili Bage.*[35]
- Step three: "Did you happen at some time or other to see my X, Y, or Z?" (*En kukudom nela:iya chi?*)[36] Possible answers could be "Oh yes, that relative is my mother's brother" or "That relative is my mother's brother's wife" (*Eya, en kukudo mamun/hatomin*).[37]
- Step four: The questioning technique will have been successful if the relationship can be pinned down by both agreeing on positive relationship terms. "Then you must be my ..." (*Ente amdo...*).
- Step five: If no relationship can be traced within the immediate vicinity, other villages will be checked to come up with a positive result. "This can take between fifteen and forty-five minutes," I was told, sometimes even more, and it is absolutely necessary, as it will decide the type of relationship to build.
- Step six: If still no relationship can be discovered, the young man and young woman may try to establish a *sango*[38] relationship. If they are on their way to the market, I was told with a fine sense of humour, they may then slow down their pace considerably and begin to joke with each other.

---

33 Literally: Which village (*hatu*) are you from? -ben- in 'hatuetebena' is a 2nd person dual pronoun used when addressing someone and showing respect; 'hatuetemeya' would be the more informal address in the 2nd person singular.

34 *Hasda: kili*, sometimes also referred to as *Hasada* or *Hansda kili*, is the name of a Ho as well as a Santal clan.

35 The *Bage kili* is the dominant clan in Manbir.

36 *Kuku* is the vocative of *gungu* which is an important Ho relationship term including and uniting relatives of the uneven generation of *ego*'s great-grandparents and that of *ego*'s great-grandchildren, relatives of *ego*'s parents' generation and relatives of *ego*'s generation younger than him-/herself. As an inclusive term it is used here generically to denote a person's relatives as such.

37 There is one term, *hatom*, for a female and a male *ego*'s mother's brother's wife (MBW) and father's sister (FZ). Deeney gives *kuma* for MB as reference term; people in the research area, both Santal and Ho, preferred *mamu* instead as address and reference term.

38 *Sango* is a self-reciprocal address and reference term used irrespective of a person's relative age and gender. In a broader sense it is also used as a generic term within *ego*'s generation to relate to the position of a joking relation. *Sango* constitutes one of the categories of a potential spouse. See chapter six for "*Sango*: the semantics of an enigmatic term".

Plate 6: Multilingual Middle India
Hape se sangat would be *sango, hapanme* in pure Ho ("shut up / be quiet, *sango!*") *Sango* in Ho is *sangat* in Santali and Odiya, *se* is taken from Hindi, and *hape* is adopted from Ho. *Hapanme*, or the shortened form *hapa!*, is very colloquial and often heard in Ho country, usually to rebuke a young child or – among adults – to address a joking relation in a colloquial and joking way.

This may seem a mechanical, almost trivial enumeration, but, in fact, it reveals how a developing, emotionally charged, and intense situation is navigated by and embedded within a standardized, down-to-earth, and dispassionate system of relationship terminology, with the compass needle firmly pointing towards the reciprocal relationship term *sango*. It also reveals a few important social categories framing Ho people's constructions of belonging and relatedness: village, clan, and kinship. All three of these domains or units hint at interrelated and structured collectivities which will remain collectivities even if disentangled into their smaller components: a Ho village (*hatu*) is subdivided into a number of hamlets (*sai*) and notionally opposed to the realm of forest (*buru*) and jungle (*bir*); many but not all Ho clans (*kili*) are subdivided into totemic subbranches and further into local groupings, and all clans are notionally differentiated from other non-Ho tribal categories and conceptually opposed to nontribal categories; Ho kinship distinguishes between a Ho's agnatic relatives (*haga*), living and dead, and a Ho's affinal relatives (*bala*), both of which are to be differentiated from a Ho's ritual friendship ties (*saki*). Social cohesion is defined by this web of social categories choreographing existing and future relations between two empirical Ho individuals, as the example given above illustrates.

A Ho identifies herself or himself and is identified by others in relation to someone else or to a collectivity of others bearing importantly on people's behaviour and patterns of social interaction. None of my informants, not even the most politicised, emphasized their being individual, independent, autonomous, and equal citizens of a modern Indian nation-state.

When my husband came for a visit to the field in 2009, my Ho mother was not only looking forward to meeting my husband, an individual stranger unrelated to her, but by virtue of me being her daughter (*mai*), to meeting her son-in-law (*ara*), to whom she was *hanar*, an affinal relation. The village headman of a neighbouring hamlet, to whom she was also mother (*kaki*),[39] had constructed me into his elder sister. He looked forward to meeting my husband because he would meet his *teya*, his elder sister's husband, which is a joking relationship. He would encounter not only an unknown individual but also an already known relation implied in the relationship term *teya* (WyB-eZH). So, while people in the research region were unknown to my husband, a web of kinship relations already existed before his arrival there. The system of disregarding individualizing personal first names in public and instead making use of relationship terms in address and reference emphasizes relatedness, collectivity, and inclusion rather than separation, individualization, and exclusion.

The language of relatedness

Ho social categories are specific in that they are indigenously not expressed as linguistically abstract nouns. The social category *owa:*, in anthropological convention 'the house', is referred to by Ho people as *owa:renko*, 'people of the house'. Ho people speak of 'people of one rice pot' (*miyad mandi chaturenko*) when they refer to a local and translocal entity that unites people in ritual interaction and that is a corporate unit at the local level. What anthropologists conventionally define as 'brotherhood' or an agnatic category is linguistically ren-

---

39 As a reference term *kaki* is terminologically father's younger brother's wife (FyBW) or mother's younger sister (MyZ). As address terms I often heard *kaki, kaki-ma*, or just *ma* used synonymously by both, Ho and Santal.

dered in Ho as 'brothers' (*hagako*), in Santali as *alerenko*, which again is identical with the Ho compound, literally meaning 'our people'.[40]

There is no Ho term given in Deeney's dictionary to denote affinity or collective marriageability. However, Ho do make a distinction between those whom they have "*prospective* relations through marriage with" (Deeney 2005: 25; my emphasis), *bala-saka*, the term used in the introductory lines of this chapter and the one that probably comes closest to denoting an individual Ho's affines, that is, the marriageable as a category, and *bala-bundu* (ibid.), a collective term denoting a Ho person's in-laws, that is, those with whom empirical affinal relations have already been established. In practice, however, Ho people tend to cut both expressions short and simply use *bala* or, in the plural (for three or more people), *balako*. This may create some confusion for those who expect unambiguous denotations as I initially did, since *bala* used as an isolated lexical term refers to one's son-in-law's or daughter-in-law's parent, in the vocative *balatadi*, and since *balako* are also those who go to a young woman's or young man's house to arrange a marriage. Some terms are multivalent, their meanings and connotations varying according to the specific context.

Bala in its abbreviated form or complemented by various suffixes is a term that I heard frequently in the field and quite from the beginning. For example, during secondary burials people come together for a few days and stay overnight. However, *bala* and *haga* stay in separate places, and the rules of commensality differ depending on who is considered *bala* or *haga*. Having said this, however, the boundaries around these opposing categories are not necessarily rigid. Depending on the context, they may reveal a processual nature rather than a static character.

Complications: linguistic, colonial, and anthropological

This section is intended to briefly illustrate the necessity of defining indigenous terms and institutions on the basis of fieldwork data.

The linguistic and conceptual confusion that exists about these terms and institutions was initially caused by British colonialists equating languages with the speakers of those languages and reifying formerly flexible and unde-

---

40 The compound consists of three parts: *ale+ren+ko*. *Ale* denotes 'we' (1st person plural, an exclusive pronoun), *-ren* is a postposition to closely link two words translatable as 'of', *-ko* is the plural marker put at the end of animate nouns and the bound form of the 3rd person plural personal pronoun. Often, as in the examples above, *-renko* can be translated as 'people of'.

fined social compositions as Munda, Ho, Ho-Munda, or Mundari.[41] It has been continued by some anthropologists, as when Parkin identifies "Munda as the whole group of languages and tribes" (1992: 23), "Mundari when this [Munda] tribe alone is mentioned" (ibid.), and consequently Ho as an "offshoot of the Mundari" (ibid.: 25). Others have separated populations such as Halbi and Gondi speakers into members of castes and tribes on linguistic grounds, whereas Gregory points out the identical semantic value of their respective kinship systems despite differences in lexicon (Gregory 2009: 68). Drawing a linguistic divide unrelated to the specific context does not make sense in an area where people are regularly fluent in two or more languages.

It is worth making a few remarks on the linguistic pitfalls and the complexity that comes along with the cultural diversity of the region and giving a few examples from fieldwork to account for the language of social cohesion. Verardo (2003b: 32), who did fieldwork in the Porahat region north of Kolhan, but still within the district of West Singhbhum, opposes the affinal category *kupul(ko)* (guest) to *haga*, the agnatic category of 'brothers'.[42] When I explicitly enquired

---

41 'Mundari' has conventionally been classed as the name of a language (Deeney 2002: vii; *Ethnologue* 2009: 392; Anderson 2008: 195). According to Verardo Mundari was introduced as a "category among the 'forest people'" (2003b: 13) in the fourth settlement report of Porahat only in 1966. It seems that the practice of confusing ethnicity and language against which Anderson warns (2008: 195), has been continued in India after independence.

42 Consider the entry *kutum-kupulko* consisting of *kupulko* (guests) and *kutum* (relationship and relation by marriage) (Deeney 2005: 218, 219). Maybe this compound relates to the totality of a Ho's social universe by uniting the conceptual contrasts of agnatic and affinal relations. In anthropological perspective Deeney's definition of this term may seem too vague. But then he is a philologist and not an expert in alliance theory. Bouez (1985: 54, 55) opposes the terms *kutum(ko)* and *bala-bondhu* as inclusive categories to relate to a Ho's consanguines *(kutum)* as terminologically opposed to a Ho's affines *(bala-bondhu)*. *Kupulko*, according to him, is synonymous with *bala-bondhu*, the first used among the Munda, the latter among the Ho both terms including all those who are not *'hagako'* ('brothers') and hence not marriageable. Berger (2007: 83) did fieldwork in Odisha among the Gadaba the senior section of whom speak Gutob which is an Austro-Asiatic language such as Ho and Santali. Berger refers to *kutum* as local patrilineal descent group and in an extended sense also as family. Parkin, on the other hand, in his book on the Munda categories of Central India opposes for the Munda as categories *kutum*, "potential affines", and *kupul* defined as "those persons with whom an affinal relation has been established" (Parkin 1992: 148) which would be the in-laws. According to him Ho would use *kutumko* and *hagako* as synonyms (Parkin 1992: 145) which is a statement that I cannot confirm for the Ho of Mayurbhanj, just as Munda people would use *kutumko* and *hagako* as conceptual opposites (ibid.). Parkin draws from Bouez who has not listed *kutum* for Keonjhar, and there "allies in general are *balasaka*" (in Parkin 1992: 149), a term that is also used by Santal (ibid.: 145; Bouez 1985: 98). Again, in my research area I cannot confirm this, since Santal people there would use *pera* or *perako* (with plural marker) for their affines instead.

about *kupulko* in the Chaibasa area, I was told that this is a term to refer to one's daughter or sister after their respective marriages or to one's mother's brothers (*mamu*). In other words, it was used for empirical in-laws. As usual in such cases, Ho never offered a generalizing answer to my general question but rather a number of precise examples taken from their life experience.[43] Of course, beyond the realm of relationship terminology, *kupulko* in a broad sense denotes all those with whom one is on visiting terms.

Hagako in the Porahat area seem to correspond to the category of *hagako* in my research area; *kupulko* there seem to be the Ho's *bala-saka* here; and the Munda's category *kutum* seems to be opposed in meaning to the same category among the Ho. In the Mayurbhanj area of research I have not heard Ho people resort to compounds such as *kutum-kupulko* at all or to single kin terms such as *kupul* and *kutum*. While Ho in the research area usually refer to a couple's marriage as *bapala* – the -*p(a)*- infix added to *bala* indicating an aspect of mutuality and reciprocity, hence two categories becoming affinally related in marriage, S. C. Roy translates 'betrothal' as *bala* for the Munda of the Ranchi area (1970: 251).

However, linguistic complications will also be met beyond the domain of Ho kinship terms. Roy gives *sarna* as the Munda's sacred village grove (ibid.: 227), but this term was used in the research area only by Santal, whereas Ho insisted on *jayer* or *desauli*. In socioreligious discourse, however, *sarna* also functions as a political concept addressed to the tribal populations of the area. In academic circles in the Chaibasa area the implementation of *sarna dharam* as a unifying indigenous "religious belief system" (P. Sen, forthcoming: 10 f.) is meant to support, unite, and represent *adivasi* people. This idea was rejected by my Ho informants as clearly beyond the pale.

The data and examples given above and in the footnotes reveal that identical terms are used by different ethnic categories in different regions of Middle India. These terms may then carry identical or different or even opposite meanings. It also holds true that in different regions the same ethnic categories, in this case Ho and Santal, seem to use different terms to refer to the same social category. It thus becomes obvious that the meaning of specific (relationship) terms depends on context and region as well as on the anthropologist's perspective (for example, whether a distinction is made between a person's affines and his in-laws in the first place or not). The semantics of an expression cannot be inferred linguis-

---

43 Concerning the term *kupulko* Bouez makes the following interesting remark: "Si on demande à un Ho d'énumérer ses *kupulko*, il se trouve très embarrassé, car la catégorie est si souple qu'il semble impossible de pouvoir la cerner indépendamment des situations concrètes où le terme est utilisé." (Bouez 1985: 55).

tically, terms need to be defined in context, and if unrelated to the region where they are used, they often do not offer reliable orientation. There is no universally unambiguous lexicon of Munda kin nomenclature, not even one that is universally agreed upon by all Ho all over Kolhan and beyond. When discussing Ho ways of constituting social categories and cohesion I will for this reason rely first and foremost on my own data and the terms I learned in fieldwork in my specific research area, as Ho people themselves are highly sensitive about the ways in which they and their culture are spoken about.

The category 'tribe'[44]

Whereas clan (*kili*) was among the first Ho words that I was taught, I hardly ever came across the rather abstract category 'tribe' (*jati*). Still, Ho people would rather twist their tongues and try to somehow pronounce the word 'tribe'[45] than use *jati* (tribe, caste, race). As a word borrowed from Hindi, *jati* perhaps rings even more foreign (*diku*) to Ho ears than the English term 'tribe'. Second, the Ho tribe as such, like every other tribe, is not a functionally united political unit or decision-making body and hence is locally of little importance, as Sahlins (1968: 16) and Leach (1977 [1954]: xv, 49) argued long ago. In terms of social organization it is a distant and weak category when compared to the social cohesion and the relations that matter at the local level where "social interaction is greatest and co-operation most intense" (Sahlins 1968: 16). It is at the local level and in membership in localized groups where an individual Ho's life and aspirations are collectively embedded. This is not to say that tribal membership or the category of tribe are altogether irrelevant. Ideologically and quite generally, to be Ho – rather than to be a member of the Ho tribe – was pointed out to me as a matter of pride. My fieldwork, in fact, intensified and people were prepared to interact with me only after I was in the process of becoming a Ho myself – at

---

44 There has been a hot debate in anthropology surrounding the issue of 'tribe' in India which has recently been resumed, discussed and analysed in its consequences for the 'tribal' situation in Middle India by Skoda (2005: 49 – 60), Hardenberg (2005: 52 – 70), Berger (2007: 55–58), Pfeffer (1997: 3, 2002: 9–31), Verardo (2003b: 8 – 26), Shah (2010: 9 – 28), Das Gupta 2011. In my book (Reichel 2009) I have outlined essentials of the ongoing controversy within the context of a globalizing interest in indigeneity as well as the 'family resemblances' concerning tribal value-ideas in all of tribal Middle India. This discussion will not be resumed here. I will focus in this chapter on the fieldwork-based ethnography of 'the tribe' as a Ho social category.

45 In the Ho language there are no words beginning or ending with consonant clusters. In the case of loan words that contain such clusters the pronunciation then is often re-adjusted.

least to a certain degree. Likewise, before the village headman's wife offered to establish a ritual *saki* relationship with me, she inquired whether I was a Ho, not whether I was a member of the Ho tribe.

It is especially on the occasion of local festivals (*porobko*) to ritually accompany the annual crop cycle at the village level that the Ho, the Santal, and the nontribal communities of the service castes perform their distinct festivities in grand public style. When Ho address their Ho deities during their specific Ho feasts, prominence is given to the distinctiveness of Ho cosmology and the Ho's spirit world; here Ho celebrate and recreate their Ho-ness. Despite the existence of kinship relations and pronounced ritual interaction[46] between the tribal and nontribal communities at the village level and beyond, it is here where cultural distinctions are visibly – and sometimes audibly – emphasized and celebrated at the same time. I argue that in ritual contexts, in practice, the otherwise abstract, anonymous, and distant notion of tribe comes alive as it attains, expresses, and conveys an overall relevance by constructing (Ho) identity on the basis of "considerations of sameness," as Sahlins puts it (1968: 19), of belonging to "the same kind" (ibid.), in the Ho language *mid* (to be one, oneness). This surely is a phenomenon transcending the category of clan and constitutive of the larger framework of (the Ho) tribe. It is a phenomenon that pays respect to the cultural significance of the tribe as notion and concept – not to the sociological entity or administrative unit as a bounded substance – and irrespective of its organizational weakness. Linguistically the tribe's distinctiveness is captured in the designation 'Ho' denoting 'man'. Of course, Ho people do acknowledge that there are fellow hill-tribe 'men' who also refer to their respective tribes in their mother tongues as 'man', as mentioned above. From this it does not follow that Ho would "ignore the other families of the human race," as S. C. Roy puts it in his book on the Munda (1970: 207), implying that they equate their tribe with humanity as such, a collectivity referred to by the Ho, if at all, as *manwa*, a term not unsurprisingly of Sanskrit origin. I simply argue that their focus is different. "Une tribu ne se représente qu'elle même," as Bouez says (1985: 30). I often found that Ho people have a detailed knowledge of how non-Ho communities perform their distinct rituals in the vicinity. But when it comes to performing Ho rituals, it is Ho values that are celebrated the way they have always been (correctly) celebrated – as seen from the Ho's perspective.

---

46 See below chapter 5 which deals with the ritual interaction between the Gau (cowherder) community and Ho people on behalf of several Gau *festivals*. Plate 17 shows *shivratri* which is choreographed jointly by both the local Gau's and the Ho's ritual guides (*diuri*).

To belong to the category 'Ho' is not a moral value judgement but a cultural classification, including some people within the category of 'sameness' while excluding others who as non-Ho are then conceived of as belonging to a different kind. This indigenous sociocentric logic of 'othering', however, is not done in uniform ways, since these 'others' are further differentiated and ranked, as has been shown above for the category of *diku* (outsider). *Diku* are notionally excluded from and opposed to the Ho's social universe and do not belong. The Ho's clients as another category of 'others' are conceptually distinguished but included in the Ho's sociocultural world. They belong (see chapter 5).

Of course, this self-identification by Ho people as belonging to one (*mid*) named category with blurred boundaries is ignored by the modern state and its bureaucracy, as already mentioned in the case of census reports and elections. Consequently, on their identity cards a Ho's collective identity is unequivocally pinned down to a combination of letters and up to twelve numbers. My Ho father (*kaka*) has his identity rendered as OR/01/003/244523 [BVV4652442] on his identity card. OR perhaps is short for Orissa. To him this is a *diku* codification that he was reluctant to waste time on and explain. A Ho's residence and house are similarly identified by a code of fixed numbers, and the names which Ho people never use to address each other, and the names of their clan are administratively identified as their first names and surnames, more often than not bizarrely misspelt.

Village, clan, kinship

A Ho village is the centre of a network of relations (Berger 2007: 65) connecting tribal persons, alive *and* dead, their nontribal neighbours, who are often members of several distinct service castes, and their spirit world, including Sinbonga, their creator God. In this respect a Ho village can be defined as a territorial site, a social category, a sacred space, and the materialization in ritual at the micro-level of a sociocosmic whole.

A Ho village is a territorial unit, because it is here where the jungle was cleared by Ho ancestors and where those ancestors' living offspring are ploughing and cultivating their ancestral lands. Ho people live in houses which many claim their ancestors built and which they have kept rebuilding and repairing ever since. According to the late Jado Bage, the oldest member of the dominant Bage clan in Manbir, this village was founded five generations ago by Domke Bage, his FFFFF. This might be some time around 1780. Jado Bage, his SSSSS, could orally pass on the pedigree of a total of nine generations. Ho villages in the research area are usually multiclan villages. They are divided into several hamlets where members assigned to the same clan (*kili*) live next to each other, and some of them are classified and cooperate as *miyad mandi chaturenko*.

A Ho village becomes a social category because Ho people acquire membership and identity by social, that is, ritually accompanied birth into their village, into their clan and its localized group, and, of course, into their agnatic kin group as constitutive parts of it. The making of a Ho person and his or her eventual transformation into a Ho ancestor is accomplished in a village. Ho villages are social units in that they "appear in charge of the entire social life" (Sahlins 1968: vii). Villages, however, are not social isolates, and they may be linked affinally with other villages over the generations. Chapter 6 will show how diachronic affinity creates a social web that is rooted locally in hamlet and village and that constitutes a gift of relatedness waiting for every Ho from birth.

A Ho village is an overall sacred space segmented into a multitude of sacred subspaces. It contains, sometimes on its outskirts, the sacred village groves that Ho in the research area call *desauli* or *jayer*. While *desauli* is homonymous with the main male protecting spirit of a village, his wife *jayer buri* is considered an ancient female spirit and the primordial mother of the Ho. It is during annual festivals when sacrificial offerings are made to the spirit world, including *desauli* and *jayer buri*, that the village is symbolically united. In rituals performed inside the sacred grove and outside it in the fields, the populated sociocosmic whole is re-enacted and celebrated. The process of linking the living of the present and their spirits of some mythical past across time and space is linguistically reflected in the vocative forms of *desauli hon* and *jayer buri* or *jayer buri hon*. *Hon* denotes 'child' and *buri* 'old woman, wife'. Used after the name of a spirit it is a way of showing respect "and no connotation of smallness" (Deeney 2005: 155). At the same time, by attributing human characteristics to otherwise immaterial and remote spirit beings, it humanizes these beings and thus links them to the world of the living.[47]

Although the spirit world is conceived of as highly differentiated into distinct realms of responsibilities, I was often unjokingly told that the Ho's true deities are their ancestors. Ho houses as such are permanently linked to notions of the sacred by the ancestors who dwell in the sacred space within every Ho house, the *adin*, and by the continuous interaction between the living and the dead there. This is equally true of the threshing floor (*kolam*) adjoining Ho houses and the rice fields surrounding Ho hamlets. Rice fields are manifestations of *baba enga* ('paddy mother'), "the primordial paddy seed" (Deeney 2005: 177) that

---

47 For a discussion of the spirit world, its structure and accounts of how the living and their spirit world are interrelated see chapter 4.

is annually paid respect after the harvest in a paddy ritual (*ked bonga*). Ho conceive of rice, the land on which it grows, and their ancestors as integrally linked to each other and a sacred unity. They acknowledge this sacred quality by taking off their flip-flops – and by making sure I did not forget to do the same – before entering the sacred grove, the threshing floor, the house, or the *adin*. They especially forbid entry into the *adin* to those who are not entitled to trespass there, that is, those who are not 'brothers' (*haga*) or 'people of one rice pot' (*miyad mandi chaturenko*).

A process similar to the one outlined above, according to which spirits are constructed as variously distant or, depending on context, close and almost human, seems to also apply to Ho ancestors. When Ho people refer to their ancestors quite generally and as a distant and anonymous body, they will refer to them as *tata-gunguko*. When they have in mind those beings transformed into almost human fellow inhabitants of their houses, they will call them *ham hoko–dum hoko*.[48]

The category 'clan' (*kili*)

In otherwise relevant anthropological literature on the Ho, the structure and semantics of the category 'clan' has sometimes been represented in a way that my fieldwork data do not agree with. For this reason, I will begin by making three critical comments concerning the representation of the dimension and character of Ho clans, the relation between clan, local subclan, and totemic designations, and lastly, the analytical language used to describe Ho social organization and its semantic implications.

Ho clans (*kili*) have been defined as "corporate descent-based groups" (Verardo 2003b: 31) that "share putative ancestors" (ibid.) or "common ancestors" (S. C. Roy 1970: 228). The emphasis on corporateness and common descent may be true of the local segments or groups representing a clan at village level, which I will call 'local subclans'[49] henceforth, but not of the transregional

---

48 This notional and denotational ambiguity is again highlighted in the following section on *Mmc*. For better readability I will usually continue in this book to refer to ancestors as such but will specify if the context demands to distinguish between *tata-gunguko* and *ham ho – dum hoko*. As *ham ho – dum hoko* are co-terminous with a male Ho's immediate and remembered lineal and collateral forefathers of the previous four and more generations, 'ancestors', 'forefathers' and 'the dead of the house' will occasionally be used synonymously.

49 Dhan refers to the localized segments of a clan as "sub-clan" (1961: 61f), too, as does Bouez (1985: 47f); Deeney speaks of the sub – branches of a clan or of "sub-*kili*" (2002: 135); Verardo

unit of a Ho clan. Majumdar has already been criticized by Yorke for also assuming a corporate character for the entire clan and a capacity to take "collective political action" (Yorke 1976: 62) which would be manifested in a "clan/*kili* council" (Majumdar 1950: 103) equal to the village council (*panchayat*). A similar notion of "clan assemblies" is taken up by Parkin (1992: 75) in the case of breaches of marriage regulations. Such breaches and other problems of a similar dimension were discussed in my research area many times when the purity of the local subclan, including that of the ancestors attached to it, was at stake. But it was always the concern of the male members of the local segments of the subclans, who met at the dancing ground (*akara*), sometimes two or three times a week, in order 'to pass a judgment' (*bichar*). The possibility of incest (of which I will give an example below in the section on "Clans, brother clans, and marriage"), the question of how to deal with a 'sudden' (*tataka*) or 'violent' death in order to safeguard the villagers, of what to do in the case of a theft or the felling of a sacred tree – in the research area these were considered matters of some urgency which needed to be seen to at the village level. Men would meet immediately, flexibly, and repeatedly to consensually come up with a good decision (*bichar*). Neither a 'clan council' nor a 'clan assembly'– given the overall extension of Kolhan – would allow for an immediate response to such violations. In other words, I simply doubt the existence and practicability of a pan-tribal, supravillage 'clan body'.

My second comment concerns the notion of 'totemism' and exogamy in the context of Ho clans and subclans. Majumdar speaks of "totemic exogamy" (1950: 12), S. C. Roy of a clan as "totemistic sept" (1970: 230), Parkin of the tendency of all tribes "to identify the higher-order descent groups with totems" (1992: 72), and Pfeffer of "a finite number of exogamous totemic patrilateral clans" of Ho and Munda, Oraon and Kisan (2014: 273). I will argue below, however, like Bouez (1985: 47), that while Ho clans are exogamous and patrilateral, the clear majority of them are not totemic. In contrast, the majority of the countless local subclans represented in villages or hamlets carry totemic names that are prefixed to the name of the clan. The presence of a totemic attribute, however, neither suggests nor implies exogamy,[50] since exogamy remains a quality of the overall clan irrespective of whether a clan is segmented into totemic subclans or not.

---

does not mention 'subclans' at all, and Yorke identifies subclans as "local lineage" (1976: 53) at village level.

50 "Avec le sous-clan, qui n'est pas exogame, [...]" (ibid.: 47), and: "Dans l'ensemble les noms de clans de type totémique sont rares, [...]" (ibid.).

In my research area I was able to make a closer examination of the pedigrees of some people who were members of the Bage and Kondangkel clans. These two clans are two of the Ho clans that are not further divided into subclans. So for a very long time during my fieldwork I was completely unaware of the existence of subclans: I did not ask, I was not told. To illustrate: it will conform to Ho marriage patterns for a boy of the Soso Pingua subclan to marry a girl of the Soso Purty subclan, since the girl will marry outside her clan (Purty) and hence clan exogamy will have been observed. In arranging a proper Ho marriage (*bare-misi bapala*) it does not matter whether the names of the respective – totemic – subclans are identical, as in this example (*soso [daru]*, the marking-nut tree), since no common ancestry is assumed among the members of totemic subclans affiliated with different nontotemic clans. Hence as far as the Ho are concerned there is no link between totemic designations and exogamy. A source of this confusion may be that in practice Ho people refer locally to their named, that is, totemic subclans exclusively by giving the names of the encompassing, nontotemic, umbrella clan designations (Verardo 2003b: 31) – as if there was a restriction on giving away a public secret by communicating about it. The *munda* (village headman) of Pathan Sai belongs to the Purty clan, but only when I took down the members of his *miyad mandi chaturenko* (people of one rice pot) did I learn that he is a member of the Holon (rice flour) Purty subclan. How subclans are good to think with will be explained in the course of this chapter.

It seems that there are kin 'household names' that are publicly given without hesitation and shyness, such as *haga* (brothers), *bala(saka)* (affinal relations), *owa:renko* (people of the house), *kili* (clan), and *ham hoko–dum hoko* (forefathers). But there are other kin-related designations for which a sort of veiled language is resorted to. This applies to the named social category of the local subclan that transforms into the Ho category *miyad mandi chaturenko* when focussing on aspects of commensality, corporateness, joint landed property, and descent. It also applies to Sinbonga, the Ho's highest deity, who is regularly and directly addressed by the *diuri* (ritual guide) of a village during the yearly village festivals (*porobko*) but not by ordinary villagers. Whenever people refer to him in their daily lives in nonritual contexts, they never pronounce his name directly and aloud but rather point a thumb skywards.[51]

---

51 To give an example: when it is raining people will say *gamatanae:*, which literally means that 'he is making it rain' using 'rain' as a transitive verb and suffixing –*e:*, a subject marker. There is no Ho equivalent to express English 'it'. When I enquired: *okoe:* (who?), the response was non-verbal, but the thumbs-up signal towards the sky was given instead.

My last critical comment relates to the language of descent theory in which much of Ho social organization has been elaborated so far in anthropological literature. It seems that some anthropologists' own genealogical perspective has been projected onto the social structure of the Ho and imposed on other tribal societies of Middle India as well.

The analytical model of the 'African' clan as "a system of lineages and a lineage [as] a genealogical segment of a clan" (Evans-Pritchard 1969 [1940]: 192) represents the Nuer clan as "a genealogical system" (ibid.) and "a highly segmented genealogical structure" (ibid.: 192–93). According to this theory, the focus is "not on residence" (ibid.: 6) but on genealogical depth and descent, a clan's known and common ancestry, knowledge of genealogical links between a clan's dispersed segments, and traceable and known linkages between a clan's members, who are genealogically rooted in maximal, major, minor, and minimal lineages (ibid.).

Just as Barnes had already pointed out that "*poly*segmentary stateless systems of the Highland [...] societies fit awkwardly into African moulds" (Barnes 2007: 97; my emphasis) Parkin has convincingly criticized the applicability of descent theory originally worked out for Africa to communities outside of Africa (Parkin 1992: 53). Although, according to Parkin, the theory's overall relevance has now also been dismissed "for Africa itself" (ibid.), Parkin continues to make use of its perspective and vocabulary, thus documenting its powerful and long-lasting impact in anthropology on those interested in analysing tribal social organization at all. By defining "sub-clans as lineage" (Parkin 1992: 71) and clans as "maximal descent groups" (ibid.: 71) and by referring to "maximal agnatic units" (ibid.: 74), "lineage unity" (ibid.), a "founding lineage" (ibid.: 77), and "lineage settlers" (ibid.), Parkin is a case in point of how despite professed statements to the contrary, lineage theory may linguistically sneak in through the backdoor.

The case is different and similar with Yorke, Dhan, and Verardo, who otherwise have relevant fieldwork-based things to say about the Ho. All of them (Bouez being the exception) make use of lineage-theory vocabulary and lineage-theory classification as if obliged to a code of conduct imposed by British social anthropology's internationally recognized dominant narrative of descent orientation. Unfortunately, they impose the *diku* system of maximal, major, minor, and minimal lineages on Ho society, and, I argue, they do so to little avail: whereas Verardo defines the social category *owa:* (house, household, family) along genealogical lines of up to six generations as a maximal lineage (Verardo 2003b: 33), Dhan defines subclans "occupying a single village or a group of villages" (Dhan 1961: 61) as maximal lineages, and Yorke splits the indigenous category of *miyad mandi chaturenko* into maximal lineages and major or local lineages (Yorke 1976: 86). What in Verardo's case is identified as the maximal lineage (the house), becomes the Ho's minimal lineage for Yorke and is missing in Dhan altogether.

In contrast, I will argue below that Ho perspectives are not concerned with notions of a clan's or subclan's common ancestry, which is not even hypothetically postulated. Instead, locality and corporateness are what matter in terms of the localized segments of Ho subclans. The collective or joint pedigrees of the localized subclans do matter as agnatic relations, but they do so not as a constituent branch within a genealogical system but morphologically within the Ho's social construct of *miyad mandi chaturenko*. Ho people's agnatic kinship relations reveal a comparatively shallow genealogical depth. They are complemented by affinal relations, thus emphasizing a synchronic and horizontal rather than an overall vertical and lineal perspective. Since conceptual understandings of the nature of the 'African' clan with its genealogical pyramid are encapsulated in the vocabulary of lineage and descent theory, I will try in this book to avoid misleading connotations as much as I can and to refrain from using terms evoking lineal perspectives charged with the burden of their anthropological past. I will stick instead to the social constructs as they unfolded in the field and as they were indigenously passed on to me.

The following systematic discussion of the Ho's social categories of tribe, clan, subclan, and *mmc* is primarily concerned with the social relevance they are assigned in organizing the Ho's contemporary sociocosmic lives.

Tribe and clan

It has been argued above that the Ho tribe is a distant and structurally weak category. The same is true of Ho clans, though to a lesser degree. Never do members of the whole tribe meet or know each other; neither do members of one of the 133 different Ho clans.[52] The tribe as such and clans per se – apart from providing membership in an exogamous category – are never units of political relevance at the village level. Of course, the names of clans are present and known in the form of the named local subclans, which in fact are inclusive segments of a clan that are locally known and referred to by the name of the whole clan. In addition, every Ho's surname is administratively identified as the name of the clan into which that Ho individual is born. Mere membership in the same

---

52 This is the number that Deeney (2008: 96) and D. S. Purty have been able to trace.

clan, however, does not suggest a bond of intense solidarity or sense of belonging among its members as opposed to members of other clans.

The same Ho clans are scattered all over Ho country and beyond. The village headman of Pathan Sai, a hamlet in eastern Kolhan, is a member of the Purty clan, as mentioned above, and so is Deeney's anthropological Ho collaborator from Karlajuri near Chaibasa in northern Kolhan. Bouez mentions the Purty clan for Champia in southern Kolhan, and Yorke mentions it for Saranda in southwestern Kolhan. My neighbour in the village of Manbir in Odisha was a member of the Sawaiya clan, and so was a Ho scholar from Tantnagar in Jharkhand whom I met in the linguistic department of Ranchi University, quite outside Kolhan territory. My *iril* (HyZ) in Manbir, with whom I maintain a joking relationship as her *hili* (eBW), is from the Deogam clan, which is mentioned as the dominant clan in Dhan's research region in Saranda – across the mountains dividing North and South Kolhan.

So Ho clans are dispersed indeed. They may differ significantly in size. Ho clans are never corporate units with an organizing potential or organized structure (Dhan 1961: 61). Ho clans are exogamous categories, not descent-based groups. They are patriclans that reckon membership through males only. Infants, both male and female, are born into their father's clan and acquire social membership after the naming ceremony that takes place an odd number of days after their birth. Wives are ritually introduced to their husbands' ancestors after marriage and gradually acquire their husbands' clan membership. However, despite an awareness of being related within one's clan as *haga* ('brothers'), there is no construct of a common (clan) forefather, as already argued above. Genealogical links to trace and prove a common patrilineal descent line of the entire clan are neither known nor seem to be of any interest. Not even Ho elders who were pointed out to me by others as the most knowledgeable would be bothered with genealogical depth in terms of the wider clan – but they would certainly know about the pedigrees revealing their local subclan's agnatic linkages.

Clans, brother clans, and marriage

Whereas the tribe is of conceptual significance, Ho clans – as exogamous categories – are important status providers in organizing marriages. It is mainly in this regard that clans are relevant Ho social categories.[53] Marriages within the

---

53 According to Verardo (2003b: 35) Ho and Munda people in Porahat talk about exogamy in terms of brotherhood and brother clans rather than in terms of clans.

same *kili* are disallowed and punished by outcasting (*jatite bar*), since all members of a clan – despite the lack of or disinterest in genealogical linkages – consider each other agnatically related and siblings within *ego*'s generation. In terms of Ho society, however, this is a cultural and structural rather than a biological classification, since most people united within a clan will remain unknown to each other throughout their lives. Also, the quality of agnatic clan linkages includes what Ho people refer to as 'brother clans' (*haga kiliko*). Knowledge of a clan's one or more brother clans is passed down from the elders, but it is not unambiguous. Clans that are considered brother clans in one region may be considered affinal categories in another. So, while the semantic value of individual clans as either marriageable or nonmarriageable may differ regionally, intermarriages between affinally and permanently related categories are perpetuated over the generations.

I was given the names of brother clans without reservation by both Santal and Ho informants. Purty in Pathan Sai will not intermarry with the Bari and Alda clans, since both are constructed as the Purty's brother clans, in this case as their younger brothers, a classification that at the same time is a statement about the Purty clan's superior status as the elder brother. In the same area Kisku and Sinku are conceived of as brother clans, indicating that the concept of brother clans crosses tribal boundaries, since Kisku is the name of a Santal clan (*paris*) and Sinku that of a Ho clan (*kili*). In such cases people of the respective brother clans are referred to as 'people of one clan' (*miyad kilirenko*).

Clan exogamy is a norm that is known and respected by both Santal and Ho. That people of neighbouring tribes are not considered notional others (*diku*), however, will be illustrated in an ethnographic example from the Holon Purty clan of a *saki* bond of ritual friendship that transcends tribal boundaries (see in chapter 6: "Relatedness across tribal boundaries").

In fact, towards the beginning of my fieldwork, when I inquired into marriage patterns and behaviour, this was the positive rule that I heard many times: you can marry anybody, but outside your own clan. During fieldwork I only once came across a situation in which a young couple from the same *kili* was said to be intent on getting married. It was the talk of the area for days, and people were really upset, insisting that the couple give up their plans immediately. Obviously, the two waited a few days for the situation to calm down, but when it did not, they eventually left the area for good.[54]

---

54 Shah documents a few examples of young Munda people who run away to the kilns to make an independent living far away from the social restrictions imposed on them in their natal villages (2010: 130 f.)

Of course, I soon learnt that there is a lot more to consider, but at least it was a prominent and convincing starting point in that it revealed that Ho conceptualize clans as sociocentric affinal categories between which marriages are arranged rather than as egocentric descent categories. This assessment is also reflected in the Ho language. As noted above, a Ho's marriageable category is *bala*, and a properly arranged marriage between two parties is called *ba-pa-la*, the *-p(a)-* infix expressing reciprocity. So two individuals about to marry will be members of two distinct and encompassing – sociocentric – social units that are defined reciprocally as affinal categories to each other.

The next section contains a descriptive stocktaking of Ho clans and subclans, followed by an ethnographic account of the Holon Purty origin myth to illustrate how the social categories of clan and subclan contribute to bringing about social cohesion in Ho people's lives.

Ho clans: stocktaking I

Numbers and names

Risley (1891) is quoted in Majumdar (1950: 91) as giving the names of forty-six Ho septs. Majumdar writes about fifty to sixty clans in his time (ibid.). Parkin (1992), following Bouez (1985: 47), assumes more than a hundred. Eventually Deeney (2008) published a list of 133 Ho clans plus their respective brother clans (*haga kili*) with whom intermarriage is proscribed and the names of the villages in which his Ho informants of the listed clans were living. Earlier, in 2002, he had published a list of 132 clans, 48 of which had more than 190 'sub-*kilis*' between them (2002: 136–45), while the remaining 84 Ho clans had no subclans whatsoever. Deeney also provides a nonexhaustive list of nineteen *kili* names shared by Ho and Munda. It includes clans such as Champia, Hembrom (Munda: Hemrom), Purty (Purti), Soy (Soe), and Bodra[55] that are found throughout Ho country and that have the largest numbers of subclans (see below). To my knowledge there is no compilation of Ho clan, brother clan, and subclan names that is more complete and linguistically reliable than this one.[56]

---

55 Neither Hoffman and Van Emelen 1990 nor Deeney 2002 provide meanings of any of the above clan names but for Hembrom/ Hemrom which is a small tree.

56 Deeney has also published on regional differences within the Ho language, on differences between Ho and Munda, on Ho compared to the Hasada and Naguri dialects of Munda, on the influence of Sadri on Munda and of Odiya on Ho. In a scenario of non-written languages, the expert knowledge of the language situation may constitute a degree of reliability when it comes to spelling indigenous terms and offering profoundly researched denotations.

Hoffman in the *Encyclopaedia Mundarica* has done a comparable exercise for 106 Munda clans. While Hoffman's list *in*cludes the subclans that he could trace as "34 groups of seemingly connected clans" (Hoffman and Van Emelen 1990: 2407), Deeney's list *ex*cludes the 190 Ho subclans he counted. Summarizing his effort, Hoffman claims that only sixty Munda clan names have a "known" denotation, thirteen a "doubtful meaning," and thirty-three "not even a fancied meaning" (Hoffman and Van Emelen 1990: 2411). Hoffman's article on *kili* is an intense argument against S. C. Roy and his characterization of Munda clans as totemic. According to Hoffman, none of his Munda informants with a reference to a plant or animal in their clan names knew of food restrictions or taboos concerning their clan totem, nor did they claim identification with or "descent from a totem" (Hoffman and Van Emelen 1990: 2407). For this reason, Hoffman says, even if more Munda clans carried totemic names, there would still be "no reason to call them totemic clans" (ibid.).

The point of the argument is not to deny the fact of totemic naming of Ho and Munda clans as such but to criticize its interpretation as impacting and determining people's religious convictions. The speculative assumption of a link between totem and religion was comprehensively analysed and rejected by Lévi-Strauss in 1962. Totemism since then has been dismissed as an illusion, as an arbitrary construct in the minds of anthropologists. Whereas totems continue to be generally acknowledged as a means of social classification, totemism is no longer acknowledged as a religious system or as constitutive of a religious system.

While it is assumed that clan names common to Ho and Munda, as mentioned above, reflect a common past in agreement with Ho oral 'history', there are many Ho clans which with some certainty are not found among the Munda. This will be explored next.

I will argue here that by looking at the meaning of Ho clan and subclan names more closely, some light may be thrown on the process of continuous segmentation, which may account for the large number of Ho clans. Bouez refers to this process as the "fission" (1985: 48) of originally homogeneous clans.[57] The Ho situation contrasts strikingly with other Middle Indian tribal communities in the Ho's neighbourhood, with Kharia and Oraon in the Chaibasa area and further

---

57 I will not discuss Bouez' hypothesis concerning the segmentation of Ho clans because my data neither confirm nor contradict his findings. But I have strong doubts. According to him Ho clans are segmented into named "non-exogamous sub-clans" (1985:48). He defines a sub-clan as "unité provisoire" (ibid.: 48) that transforms in the course of two or three generations "en une unité parfaitement exogame" (ibid.) thus continuously generating more clans out of previous subclans. (see the following section).

north, and especially with the Ho's immediate neighbours in the research area, the Santal, who organize their social lives within their twelve clans *(paris)*.

Clan names

To my knowledge no systematic research concerning Ho clan names has been done so far, and no such study is attempted here. While it is true that it is often not possible to assign an unambiguous meaning[58] to Ho clan names, I have been able to do so for at least half of the known Ho clan names and for a majority of the subclan names.

Of the 133 clan names, 15 may with some certainty be identified as totemic.[59] This equals approximately 11 percent. Of these, five refer to animals: an uncastrated male pig, a jungle bison, a white heron, a cock, and a potter's wasp. Six refer to plants, such as different kinds of trees, grass, and a herb. Four refer to material objects (frying pan, arrowhead) or environmental features (grinding stone, flat rock). So classification by totems is not entirely absent, but at the level of the clan it does not seem to be a prominent feature.

There are three clans that have the names of other ethnic communities: Mutukan (a term for a member of the Bhumij community), Munda,[60] and Bhumij. The names of two clans refer to the human species: Honhaga (child of one's own agnatic category) and Kora, which is Mundari (a man).

A prominent feature of some consequence, though, may be the correspondence between forty-three Ho clan names, almost a third of the total, and the names of villages in what is considered to primarily be Munda country, North Singhbhum and parts of Ranchi District. In their oral 'history', Ho claim that they lived in this area together with Munda people before their migration south (see "The Ho's oral 'history'" in chapter 1). All of these forty-three villages can be identified along both sides of the Ranchi-Chaibasa Road, today's National

---

58 Example: *Tiu.* According to Verardo *Tiu* (rice that is boiled before husking) – as opposed to *Adwa* (unboiled rice) – refers to a ritual distinction within each clan (2003b: 32). According to Bouez *tiu* is a root denoting 'to fall', 'to let fall' and its meaning accounts for the inferior status of the local sub – clan *Tiu* Bodra within the Bodra's myth of origin (1985: 82). According to Deeney *Tiu/Tiyu* is a Ho clan name (meaning unknown; it is a name that Ho and Munda share); 'to fall from a height' in Ho is not *tiu*, but *iyu:* (2005: 168). See above "Complications: linguistic".
59 The semantic value of the clan names has been verified with Deeney's Ho – English Dictionary (2005).
60 The name of this clan is co-terminous with the Ho's village headman and the Ho's brother tribe.

Highway No. 75.[61] Heading north from Chakradharpur the villages – not too close to the road[62] – are scattered in the terrain of the Tebo Ghat, where the road climbs towards the town of Bandgaon and beyond towards Ranchi. Of the forty-three Munda village names that have become Ho clan names, thirty-nine are not found among Munda people as Munda clan names. Whereas the identity of village and clan name is known among other Middle Indian tribal communities as well, though to a lesser extent, the correspondence between this large number of Ho clan names and Munda village names restricted to a comparatively limited area seems exceptional. It has led Deeney to come up with an informed speculation about a possible interrelation between the exceptionally large number of Ho clans, Ho clans' village names, the likely process of Ho clan segmentation, and the Ho's oral 'history' of migration.

I will next briefly sum up Deeney's hypothesis, for the following reasons. There is a sociocultural dimension reflected in Ho understandings that structure their past as the history of their migration. Migrating to Ho people means inviting their ancestors to come along, too. However, as Ho ancestors are understood as humans, including humans' erratic nature, migrating may involve leaving behind and hence neglecting one's ancestors, who then cannot be ritually taken care of in their living descendants' new destinations. How this situation is ritually dealt with was told to me by my *saki* from Pathan Sai. His narration of the Holon Purty origin myth will be given in the next chapter.

Back to Deeney's hypothesis (2002, 2008). While most data on clans, subclans and brother clans were directly passed on to him by people of the given *kili*, conclusions concerning the Munda village–Ho clan identity are entirely his. To him it seems likely that Ho over a period of centuries may have migrated into South Singhbhum along the Tebo Ghat, as mentioned above. When they eventually settled in Kolhan, Deeney suggests, Ho people may have prefixed the name of the village where they had settled last to the name of their *kili*, perhaps in order to distinguish themselves from other groups of the same *kili* in the new settlements. Thus members of the Bodra *kili* from the village of Ban(d)ra may have called themselves Bandra Bodra, whereas members of the Bodra *kili* from the village Icha:gutu would refer to themselves as Icha:gutu Bodra. Today the Icha:gutu, Ban(d)ra, and Bodra clans exist as independent clans. An explanation for this could be that in the course of time, the clan names Icha:gutu Bodra and Ban(d)ra Bodra were transformed into simply Icha:gutu

---

61 Google Earth shows the region below the entry "Bandgaon map".
62 According to Ho elders Ho people show a tendency of moving towards the 'interior', away from the roads if these are trespassing through their countryside.

and Ban(d)ra. While the original clan name Bodra was dropped in the process, the knowledge that these clans were agnatically related as *haga* was maintained by Ho elders and passed on by them. To this day the Icha:gutu, Bodra, and Banra clans are conceived of as *haga kili* and as such do not intermarry – as a rule. Empirically, though, marriages by elopement (*kepeya andi*) are widespread among the Ho, and elders reluctantly condone elopements that happen among members of such *haga kili*, when young people are not much concerned about past links either to original villages in North Singhbhum and Porahat or to original clans. This example of how two village names developed into two *kili* names may be a likely model of the extraordinary formation of distinct Ho *kili* that carry the name of a Munda village and are at the same time not found among the Munda.

My fieldwork data confirm some of these assumptions, and I will give two examples. "How do we know whom they are talking with and what they are talking about?" I sometimes heard Ho parents who themselves had married by eloping complain about young people who were using a mobile phone and who were not prepared to pass on any information. "They might be talking to just anybody! In the old days it was our responsibility to arrange marriages properly! These days young people do just as they please without consulting us first. And there is nothing we can do about it." The message implied here is that a marriage between members of putative or original brother clans is considered next to incest by the elders, though not by all younger Ho. Marriages by elopement are inferior in terms of status when compared to properly arranged marriages, but marriages between brother clans constitute a completely different class altogether. Marriages by elopement are conceived of as a behavioural slip in the code of conduct that can be expected under certain conditions and that can be readjusted. Marriage between members of brother clans is seen as a serious offence, a violation of tribal values. However, as the example shows, tribal values are also subject to change, and it is perhaps for this reason that Deeney calls elders' knowledge of separate clans that in former times were considered one historic rather than social.

The second example relates to the Deogam and Kondangkel clans. These two clan names are village names in the terrain of the Tebo Ghat, as discussed above, and large localized groups of the two clans are present in the research area of Mayurbhanj, with a village headman (*munda*) from the Kondangkel clan acknowledged by the villagers as belonging to the group of the founding clan of Gara Sai (map 5). In terms of his pedigree, which includes three ascending generations, the village headman knows about his local clan group's roots pointing north, but he is not aware of his clan name's identity with a village in Jharkhand, and this identity does not seem to matter in any way. What matters more and was given to me in his pedigree are his kinship links pointing to Jharkhand. His father's two elder sisters (FeZ, *hatom*) married two brothers from Alda *kili* in Godsereng, Jharkhand. They are buried in their husbands' burial sites. Relations with his father's sisters' husbands and their children have remained close, since these are his *mamu* (FZH) and *sango*, as father's sister's children (*hatom honko*) or mother's brother's children (*mamu honko*) are frequently and generically called in the area in address and reference. At the same time, S. Kondangkel has become *mamu* to his *boronja* or *gekowa*, literally his elder sister's son, more precisely his FeZSS. These affinally based relations are known, they matter and remain diachronically alive, and people are on visiting terms. They are social relations, lived relations, as opposed to the historical ones that existed when Munda village names were transformed into Ho clan names, probably centuries ago. Similarly, my *iril* (HZy) from the Deogam clan in Manbir whom I mentioned above is unaware of a link with an original village of the same name in Jharkhand.

Just as the large number of identical Munda village and Ho clan names and the overall nontotemic naming of Ho clans came as a surprise to me at the level of the clan, so did the nonpatterned and irregular assignment to Ho clans of named subclans and the naming of those subclans.

Ho subclans: stocktaking II

Numbers and names

It was mentioned above that of 133 Ho clans, 85 are not assigned any subclans, but 48 do have subclans. The overall number of subclans is probably beyond counting. According to Deeney's list of 190 subclan names, there are 16 clans with 1 subclan, 9 with 2 subclans, 4 with 3 subclans, 3 with 4 subclans, and 4 with 5 subclans. The Sinku, Sawaiyan, and Ban(d)ra clans have 6 subclans each; the Tiria, Purty, and Pingua clans have 8 subclans each; the Soy clan has 9 subclans; the Boepai clan has 10 subclans; the Bodra, Hembrom, and Sundi clans have 12 subclans each; and the Champia clan is alone in having 17 subclans.

As explained above, a subclan is specified by prefixing one or two, very rarely three, words[63] to the name of the clan: if the encompassing clan is Purty, Sukuri Lutur Purty is one of its eight subclans (*sukuri* – pig; *lutur* – ear). The numbers of subclans assigned to Ho clans and the known subclan designations

---

63 *Boda Kaira Susi Hembrom* is the only one in Deeney's list (*boda* – uncastrated male goat; *susi* – shoot [of a plant]; the meaning of *Kaira* is unknown).

reveal no regularities whatsoever. Most of the designations are unique, with only a very few occurring in different clans.

Siń (सिञ – tree) is perhaps the root of the name of the district today often spelt Singhbhum, a name whose two aspirations are foreign to the Ho way of spelling or pronouncing words. *Siń* is attached as a subclan designation to the Ho Angaria, Digi, Hembrom, Laguri, and Sinku clans. *Chauli chapi* (to wash husked uncooked rice) is the name of a subclan of the Kora clan, along with three other subclan markers assigned to the Kora clan, and of subclans belonging to the Angaria, Bankira, Bari, and Champia clans. Generally speaking, however, Ho subclan designations are unique, allowing for specifications such as Murmu Kinbo (the subclan name *Murmu* here is the name of one of the Santal clans), Bobonga Sinku (*Bobonga* is the name of another Ho clan), Bir Sawaiya (*bir* – jungle), Sadom de: Champia (*sadom* – horse; *de:* – to ride), Lo Benta Buriuli (*lo* – to burn; *benta*, turban, something wrapped around the head). The diversity of the designations makes sense in expressing distinctions and status differentiations between the subclans within a clan (Bouez 1985: 48), as the story of my *saki* will reveal, rather than between clans. To repeat: there are no two clans with identical subclan designations in identical order.

Subclan names can be roughly classified as follows: more than a hundred may be characterized as totemic. There is a strong focus of sixty names referring to plants, mainly different kinds of trees, grass, rice in different forms, and vegetables. More than thirty refer to animals, mostly terrestrial ones: bullock, tiger, rabbit, bear, field rat, mouse, dog, buffalo, horse, goat, monkey, and more. There are a few aerial ones – crow, owl, egret, grey pelican, and others – but definitely fewer than the terrestrial ones, and not a single aquatic one, save perhaps for the white heron. Almost thirty have miscellaneous denotations, referring to human activities such as to pour liquor, to set aside, to entwine, to go backwards, to leave (something that will make sense in the origin myths of the respective subclans), to people, to the spirit world, to titles and environmental features such as Raja, Brahman, Bhuiya, and Murmu, to spirits of the mountains, forests, low-lying fields, rivers, and more. More than fifty subclan prefixes are clan names affixed to another clan name. Of these, more than twenty are identical with village names in Munda country, as discussed above. The combination of two clan names can be exemplified by the segmentation of the Kinbo clan into the Bage Kinbo subclan and of the Bodra clan into the Bansin Bodra subclan.

Subclans, brother clans, and marriage

The above classification of Ho subclans reveals the following if seen in the context of known brother clans and marriage patterns. I have argued above that exogamy is a characteristic of the clan. It includes a clan's brother clans over the generations. I have given above an example of two people belonging to different clans (Pingua, Purty) to which subclan segments with identical names (Soso – a tree) are assigned. They may marry, since both belong to different clans and since no exogamous character is attached to or implied in the subclan designations, as argued above. Although this statement is true, it needs to be qualified given the different classes of Ho subclans.

My data show that if the name of a subclan is totemic, there will be no marriage restrictions – at the normative level.[64] However, if the name of a subclan is the name of another clan, irrespective of whether the clan's name is identical with a village name as explained above or not, the property of exogamy usually attached exclusively to the clan is extended to the subclan. Three examples are given to illustrate this.

1. People from the Siń Sinku, Siń Digi, and Siń Angaria subclans may intermarry, as Siń is a totemic subclan designation and Sinku, Digi, and Angaria are distinct clans. Hence the rule of exogamy will be observed.

2. In line with the cultural logic unfolded above, two people from Jerai Balmuchu and Jerai Sinku may not intermarry, since *Jerai* is the name of a Ho clan and, prefixed to another clan name as a subclan designation, it carries with it the notion of brotherhood. Hence in cases like this one, the property of exogamy is extended to and implied in the subclan's designation. In other words, a clan's property of exogamy remains when the clan's name becomes the specifying designation or determining prefix of a subclan.

3. People from the Tiria clan cannot marry into the Bage or Samad clans, since of the eight subclans that the Tiria clan is segmented into, two have names that are those of these two clans: Bage Tiria and Samad Tiria. Now, for *all* members of Tiria's eight subclans the Bage clan and the Samad clan are con-

---

64 This statement is valid in the context of clarifying distinctions within the category of subclans. Otherwise it is too general. Just as in the case of marriages by elopement groom and bride do not just run *any*where – in other words there are fixed rules how and where to 'run away' (*nir*) – it does not follow from the norm of exogamy that people will marry into *any* clan other than their own even if they may claim to be able to do so. As will be shown in chapter 6 the concept of diachronic affinity expresses a sense of continuity by confirming established marital relations over the generations between affinal villages, allowing at the same time for flexibility and interest in establishing 'new roads' (*hora*).

sidered brother clans, and intermarriage is proscribed. In other words, a young woman from the Ko:kuia Tiria subclan (*ko:kuia* – egret) may not marry a young man from the Bage or Samad clans, even though the *ko: kuia* subclan designation is totemic. This is at least what the elders know and pass on to the younger generations, irrespective of whether the latter are interested in listening or in following the social restrictions between *haga kili*.

When I wanted to check the correctness of a few pedigrees that I was readily given by Ho informants, people initially considered the accompanying paper-work part of it quite a nuisance, a culturally alien activity. On the other hand, on second thought, some said to me, "You know, we elders know about (*adata-nale*) these things. We do not need to write them down. But once we are dead, perhaps it will help the young ones in case they forget."

I have argued above that tribe and clan are distant and weak categories, yet meaningful ones, if in different degrees and ways, that clans are dispersed, and that most members of a tribe or clan will remain unknown to each other through-out their lives. The same is true of subclans in general, including those homon-ymous subclans – Bouez speaks of "homonymie patronymique" (1985: 48) – that are scattered throughout Ho country, that do not form corporate groups, and whose members do not share a common pedigree[65] or mutual obligations. As I am not aware that this phenomenon has been dealt with in anthropological lit-erature, two examples from my research area involving the Holon Purty subclan and the Kondangkel clan will illustrate the point.

1. I mentioned above that my *saki*, the village headman (*munda*) of Pathan Sai, belongs to the Purty clan and the Holon Purty subclan and resides in the re-search area in Mayurbhanj. I gave his pedigree in Reichel (2009: 108). He is in charge at the household level of performing rituals addressed to the an-cestors of the local segment of the Holon Purty subclan and remembers the names of dead subclan members across up to four generations, residing as far as away as Chaibasa, Cuttack, and Bhubaneswar. D. S. Purty, Deeney's collaborator and the author of several booklets on the Ho, is a resident of Karlajuri in the Chaibasa area. He is also a member of the Holon Purty sub-clan. Although both are knowledgeable persons in terms of Ho norms and values, neither knows of linkages between the Holon Purty subclans in ei-

---

65 Though in a different line of argument, Dhan (1961: 62) for her research area mentions differ-ent subclans that are affiliated to Deogam clan and that are "not geneologically related" (ibid.) Bouez in yet a different context writes that "on peut trouver des individus portant le même nom de clan et n'ayant aucune ascendance commune" (1985: 48).

ther area or elsewhere, and what may be more significant, neither is at all eager to find out.

This confirms that it seems to be socially irrelevant that homonymous subclans affiliated to identical clans continue to regionally exist in different places. The fact of homonymity does not transform unrelated subclans into translocal homogeneous units, as there is no economic or ritual interaction between them. What ultimately matters is a Ho's social rootedness in the localized segment of the (sub-) clan in the Ho's hamlet or village, the perspective being a strictly localized one. It is here where burial rites are performed, where cooperation is lived, and where marriages are autonomously arranged. Elders of the Holon Purty subclan in the research area will not consult elders of the Holon Purty subclan living near Chaibasa or wherever else segments of the Holon Purty subclan may be found.

2. Boja Sai, another research site where I did fieldwork, is a hamlet inhabited almost exclusively by members of the Kondangkel clan, but for the members of two affinally related households belonging to Hembrom clan. The eleven households of Boja Sai include between one and seven members each, for a total of forty people. In such a comparatively small hamlet with nine coresident households sharing common Kondangkel clan membership I had expected to find one social and ritual unit with well-known and clear-cut boundaries and common ancestry. I was wrong. Boja Sai is mentioned here for the reason that although all of its Kondangkel inhabitants consider each other agnatically related as a matter of cultural logic and classification, they do not constitute a corporate unit, they do not share a common pedigree and ancestry, and they do not constitute a homogeneous group. This underlines the fact that being members of the same clan or subclan does not make Ho people feel *one* as being "people of *one* rice pot" does. As outlined above, neither Boja Sai nor Gara Sai nor Pathan Sai are localities registered in the official census documents. They are indigenous inventions, relevant relative points of local reference, but this does not turn their inhabitants into equal members of an exclusive unstructured social unit even if they are all members of one clan. Hamlet and village are centres of a network of relations whose boundaries are nonetheless open and differently defined in different contexts. It will be seen in the following section on the *miyad mandi chaturenko* that the territorial boundaries around hamlets and villages are comparatively irrelevant in terms of defining the boundaries around a Ho person's *mmc*. The *mmc* of my classificatory (Kondangkel) parents' household in Boja Sai included two other (Kondangkel) households in Boja Sai but also extended into Gara Sai, a neighbouring hamlet in the immediate vicinity. In times of ritual interaction and necessary consultations

they would turn to and cooperate with members of their *mmc* in Gara Sai and not their (Kondangkel) neighbours next door in Boja Sai. In fact, there had been some serious trouble in the past, resulting in members of the Kondangkel clan passing by other members of the Kondangkel clan without greeting one another. But even without lingering conflicts I have not observed economic cooperation outside people's *mmc*.

To make things more confusing, the Kondangkel clan is one of the eighty-five Ho clans that are not subdivided into known and named subclans. How then do Ho people organize their daily corporate and ritual lives without the structure of named subclans? The answer is similar to that given in the first example, as follows: Every Ho, who after the naming ceremony is socially and notionally admitted into his or her father's clan as an encompassing category, grows up in a localized corporate group that is only nominally related to the clan. This group is smaller than the clan or subclan and larger than the unit of the 'people of the house' (*owa:renko*) into which a Ho is born. These localized segments may be either the named localized segments of a given clan or subclan or, as in the case of the Kondangkel clan, an unnamed localized segment of the clan. People know who belongs.

Irrespective of these formal distinctions between named or unnamed groups, in indigenous terms the localized social units are indiscriminately referred to as *miyad mandi chaturenko*. I argue that this social unit is the most significant source of Ho identity construction in that it constitutes the frame and field of action of Ho people's secular and ritual lives by accommodating the living and the dead within its structure. It is here where social cohesion is lived out and most intense.

The people of one rice pot (*miyad mandi chaturenko*)

To my knowledge *miyad mandi chaturenko*, henceforth called *mmc*, has not been addressed so far by Ho ethnographers as a social unit in its own right, although some scholars have singled out some of its relevant aspects (see Pfeffer 2002: 223). Verardo confirms the term for the Ho and Munda of her research area in the district of Porahat in the state of Jharkhand (personal communication) but chose not to enlarge on it in her 2003 thesis. Dhan opposes the noncorporate, nonorganized category of the clan to "agnatic descent-based groups, corporate localized segments of a clan within and beyond the village boundaries" (1961: 61) but does not mention the term *mmc*. However, if we leave aside the previously mentioned problems with this terminology's association with 'Africanist' de-

scent theory, she makes an important contribution when she sees a causal relation between the existence of groups of "lineal and collateral descendants [...] of
territorially contiguous lineages" (ibid.: 65) and their feelings of *oneness* (my emphasis) and solidarity with their "common ancestry" (ibid.),[66] which is demonstrated in the course of Ho death rituals. The names "of the ancestral spirits
[...] of the paternal clan" (Dhan 1962: 20) are called out, goats are sacrificed,
and their blood is sprinkled over the sepulchral stones. This '*oneness*' in Ho is
expressed by *miyad*, the first word in the term *mmc*. Semantically, it extends beyond the mere indefinite article, as I will show in this section. Bouez refers in the
case of the death of a Ho villager to members of a "même groupe local de sous-
clan, [qui] sont tenus de casser et de jeter tous leurs pots en terre" (1985: 53)
without introducing the term *mmc*. But the passage quoted mentions a decisive
moment of re-enacting the *mmc* when its members throw out their rice pots in
the event that one of them dies. Yorke is the only ethnographer to mention the
term *mmc*,[67] which he defines in his chapter on lineage structure as the indigenous term to describe the "maximal lineage" (1976: 86) and symbolize the "unity
of the local lineage" (ibid.). According to him, it is a "corporate group of people
in that all the members know each other [...], co-operate in their daily lives [...]
and often hold joint rights in the communal land of their lineage." (ibid.) Apart
from Yorke's structural-functionalist perspective and the bias of lineage theory
that has been criticized above, this is true as concerns the localized segments
of a Ho person's *mmc* at the level of the hamlet and village, sometimes also extending into the immediate vicinity. Deeney in his dictionary entry focusses on

---

66 The term for ancestors in general, for example not distinguishing between agnatic and affinal ancestors or opposing ancestors as an undifferentiated category to the living as a unit, is
tata-gunguko. This term breathes an air of temporal remoteness and spatial distance as outlined
above.
   There is another term for a Ho's ancestors who are in fact those dead forefathers of the immediate and previous generations whose souls have been called into the *adin* in a particular ritual called *keya ader*. These ancestors are known by name and ritually remembered. Ho (and Santal) people feel close to them. They feed them and communicate with them. They construct them
in analogy to human people with human traits. They are co-members of the 'house' and as such
are referred to and addressed in ritual as *ham hoko-dum hoko* (old men, sleeping men). Contrasting *owa:renko* (the people of the house) encompassing the living and the dead Dhan (1962:20)
calls them *owa: goe:* (the dead of the house).
67 In the course of his fieldwork Yorke got in touch with Deeney who became interested in
Yorke's data concerning *mmc* and discussed them with Dhanur Singh Purty, who became Deeney's collaborator at that time (personal communication with Yorke and Deeney). Deeney eventually published entries concerning *mmc* and related aspects in his dictionary (Deeney 2005:
242). *Mmc* is not mentioned in S. C. Roy 1970, in Majumdar 1935/ 1950, in Parkin 1992, or in
Das Gupta 2011.

mmc members' "common ancestor" (2005: 242), their right "to enter one another's kitchen (*adin*)" (ibid.), and the obligation "to remove from service the rice pot then in use" (ibid.) upon the death of any one of them.

The aspects listed are relevant characteristics of a Ho's *mmc*: territorial contiguity, a specific ancestry, face-to-face relationships, corporate group(s), communal land, death rituals, and a sense of oneness. But how do these isolated aspects interrelate and contribute to constituting an integrated whole, an exclusive social unit? How is membership in an *mmc* acquired? And how does the *mmc* differ from or overlap with Ho people's *hagako*, their 'brothers'?

In his essay on the Halbi kinship system in Bastar District, Chhattisgarh, Gregory glosses the distinction of tribal people's social universe into "us" and "them" as "brotherhood" and "otherhood" (2009: 68). In this sense *mmc* and *haga* both belong to the category of brotherhood, but they are not identical. I will discuss the differences in the section "*Mmc* and *hagako* (brothers, brotherhood)" later in this chapter.

Mmc: a metaphor of commensality

Miyad mandi chaturenko is a culture-specific Ho kin construct that expresses the unity and oneness (*miyad*) of its living and dead members (*-renko*) in a metaphor of commensality (*mandi chatu*, the earthen pot in which rice and rice-beer are prepared). *Miyad* carries the meanings 'to be one with; to become one with; to be united with; to have sexual intercourse' (Deeney 2005: 250). This concept of *oneness* keeps being regenerated at different levels. Ho people, it was explained to me, feel one with their dead, especially with their forefathers who are remembered in ritual and who cleared in the process of settling the land that their living offspring own and cultivate today. By daily feeding the collectivity of the dead of the house before starting to eat themselves, Ho people, young[68] and old, reciprocate and re-enact this oneness in intimate communion. Commensality of the living and the dead is "us-centric," because eating together underpins that people are one or become one in a process of continuous transformation, as the maturing status of in-marrying wives will show. Commensality causes social cohesion and creates relatedness.

---

68 My assistant's six-year old son one day put a comparatively larger portion of cooked rice (*mandi*) on the floor intended to especially feed his grandmother (*jiya*) who he remembered as a particularly frail person. This shows that children grow into a concept of ancestry that is constructed in analogy to the living and material rather than anonymous or esoteric.

For ritual purposes and on the occasion of the grand Ho feasts, meals of which rice (*mandi*) usually is the major part are prepared inside the kitchen (*adin*). The *adin* has already been defined as the sacred part of every Ho house, since the earthen pot in which rice is cooked and rice-beer prepared is considered the abode of the collectivity of the dead of the house (*owa: goe:*). It is by preparing and eating rice from the pot inside the *adin* that a pregnant Ho woman expects her foetus to become ensouled by her husband's ancestors.[69] This earthen pot is treated with special respect to keep it pure and unpolluted from any defiling eyes of 'others', of those who are not part of this specific one-ness. For this reason it is kept inside the *adin*, which only 'the people of the house' (*owa:renko*) and generally members of the respective *mmc* from elsewhere are allowed to enter. The right of access to other people's *adin* is not vested in membership in the same clan or subclan but in affiliation with a shared *mmc*. So, finding out who is entitled to enter the *adin* may in fact be the ultimate test and a most reliable way of finding out who is definitively reckoned a member of a specific *mmc*.[70] The living coresident and locally dispersed *mmc* mem-

---

69 see *Gift exchanges between the living and the dead* in the appendix. In this text the focus is on the process of ensouling a foetus in a process called *jom-sutam* and a rite called *rowa sarub bonga*.

70 According to Dhan a male *ego*'s daughter after marriage on the one hand loses the right to enter her natal *adin*, but on the other hand she speaks of visiting obligations of sons and brothers towards their sister also after marriage (1961: 59). Unfortunately, I have never been able to witness this myself because the relational constellations within which I was living would not allow this. However, in the course of my fieldwork I could observe continued obligations of daughters towards their parents also after marriage. The married daughter of my classificatory Ho mother, for example, kept coming back to help with the work especially on the eve of the grand festivals when considerable extra chores were waiting to be done. She cooked inside the *adin* and served the meals from there. On certain feasts she cleaned the *adin* and whitewash-ed it. Her entering the *adin* seemed in no way restricted. Her husband, however, who helped with the work on the threshing floor, never entered the *adin* once.

On the other hand, whenever my Santal assistant's wife, my *kimin* (son's wife) had run back to her parents after severe quarrels with her husband, it was usually her father who kept drop-ping by, had a chat with his son-in-law and evaluated the situation until eventually his daughter was prepared to return. When another time my *kimin* ran away to a town nearby, her husband immediately informed his wife's parents. Her father came the next day to inquire about the sit-uation. When I informed him that his daughter had returned the previous day in the late after-noon before dusk, he seemed satisfied and returned home without having met and talked to his daughter or his son-in-law. – Of course, neither he nor his wife ever entered the *adin* of their son-in-law's house.

These are just two instances that reveal social cohesion between adjacent generations. They express the continued interest of a father/ of parents in and their obligation to take care of their daughter also after marriage (the Santal example) and also of a daughter to take care of her pa-

bers are interrelated through their dead forefathers of the previous generations, who also as ancestral spirits are constructed as mobile in analogy to the living. Hence they are assumed not to be restricted to the single *adin* into which they have been called at their death. The earthen pot thus becomes the ubiquitous symbol of the unity of an *mmc*, transcending the unit of 'the people of a house' (*owa:renko*) by constructing a unit of interrelated living and dead beings assigned to it. It is polysemous, as it encompasses a putative or known first 'one' rice pot and as rice, land, forefathers, their living offspring and, on the figurative level, fecundity, growth, continuity, protection, unity, and solidarity are identified and symbolized in this key metaphor.

The re-creation of the oneness of a Ho's *mmc* in commensality is regularly expressed in a sacrificial meal whose preparation and consumption I have never been able to observe and participate in myself. It takes place inside the *adin* that I was never and nowhere allowed to enter, clearly revealing the ambiguous nature of my adoption into Ho clan membership as *haga*. Bh. Sawaiyan, a Ho graduate from Ranchi University, informed me about the preparation of the sacrificial meal as follows:

> In an *mmc* the wife of the family head prepares the sacrificial meal in the evening time of festivals such as *mage, ba, jomnama porob*. The sacrificial meal is prepared in the form of gruel. It is made up of *adowa chauli* (rice husked without previous boiling) and pulse. In some cases, rice and pulse are prepared separately. *Chipa* (fermented rice-beer brew pressed between palms) is one of the essential offerings to Sinbonga and the ancestors sheltered in the *adin*. After the offerings gruel is served and shared strictly among members of *mmc*. (personal communication, email, April 16, 2014)

Only when I was given this piece of information was I able to begin to make sense of two scenes that it brought back to mind and that I had witnessed in Manbir in February 2006 outside the *diuri*'s house where I was staying at the time.

After the harvest was completed and shortly before the celebration of *mage porob*, two of the *diuri*'s men (*diuritekin*) were sitting – facing east – in the courtyard of the *diuri*'s spacious house while it was quickly getting dark. Each man had a few large earthen pots (*mandi chatu*) in front of him. The pots were full of fermented liquid cooked rice (*maya*) which the men now ladled out in por-

---

rents after marriage (the Ho example). My assistant, who had become my son, used to complain to me that with tribal people a daughter's parents would always take her side in a run-away situation and that it was an awfully hard job to get one's wife back.

tions with their hands (*goe:*). They squeezed out (*chipa*) the substance with the palms of their hands (*ti*) and obtained as a result *rasi* (juice; the pure watery liquid resulting from the fermentation on top of the rice-beer). Usually, in secular situations, this is done with the help of a strainer (*chala*) and by women. Here it seemed an utterly male affair, and consequently I was made to feel that my presence was not welcome. I wondered at the time whether the rice-beer or rice liquor was made from *adowa chauli*, as the colour of the rice was whitish and the substance of the brew rather soft. *Adowa chauli* is used especially in ritual situations and carries a "connotation of 'sacred'" (Deeney 2005: 4). I was not able to observe what happened to the *ti chipa rasi* when its preparation was finished, as it was dark by then and the men had disappeared into the *diuri*'s house.

Plate 7: Preparing ritual rice-beer (*ti chipa rasi*)
Preparing ritual rice-beer manually, the *diuri* and one of his men squeeze (*chipa*) fermented rice between the palms of their hands (*ti*). This is done in the *diuri*'s courtyard when dusk begins to fall. The semifluid substance, which is more liquid than rice-beer (*diyan*) and less liquid than rice liquor (*rasi*) will be offered on the eve of the grand Ho festivals first to Sinbonga. After the offering it will be shared among the members of the local segment of a *miyad mandi chaturenko*. While *ti chipa rasi* is reserved for ritual situations, *diyan* and *rasi* are drunk and shared on mundane occasions without any restrictions.

Simultaneously in the days before *mage porob* the women of the house assembled in the courtyard. For hours on end they sat there gossiping and giggling while gently opening the dried pods of *ramba* and mindfully beating the seeds onto the ground. *Ramba*, a coarse, almost black pulse, is considered sacred in the research region and routinely used in ritual situations. If it is not available to a household, it is bought in the market or acquired in exchange for a day's cultivation work in the fields.

I now suspect that *mage porob* and other Ho festivals, as hinted at by my Ho informant, is preluded at the household level by the ritual handmade *ti chipa rasi* prepared by the *diuri*'s men and offered by the representatives of the respective *mmc* to Sinbonga, the Ho's male God, and to the collectivity of the *mmc*'s ancestors (*ham ho–dum hoko*) whose male members of perhaps four generations are called out by name, while their wives are remembered generically and not by name. After that, the sacrificial meal prepared by the *diuri*'s wife and consisting probably of cooked *adowa chauli* and *ramba* is consumed. Men and women of an *mmc*, contributing to the sacrificial meal in separate ways, become united in ritual with their creator God and their ancestors in the act of commensality. This conclusion, however, is speculative, as I have never observed or participated in the ritual during fieldwork myself.

A conceptual counterpart revealing female agency by women interacting publicly with the world of the divine may be assumed during *ote ili*, a ritual in the course of which it is women who feed Mother Earth (*ote enga*) by pouring rice-beer onto the earth (plate 15). This ritual is highlighted in chapter 4.

Mmc and membership

An *mmc* is an exclusive, specified, and defined unit within a subclan or clan. It is an empirical, egocentric, transgenerational unit into which "no one can be included if s/he does not belong" (John Mundu, D. S. Purty, personal communication 2012). Membership is reckoned patrilaterally, including a male *ego*'s unmarried sisters and daughters and – beyond agnatic linkages – his wife or wives. Membership is acquired through the performance of the birth rites,[71] in the course of which baby girls and boys are introduced to their father's forefathers

---

71 These are basically purification ceremonies (the first held three days after birth: *niyar era:*, the final rite about 30 days after birth: *tiki era:*) to remove the social impurity in which a newborn baby and the baby's parents find themselves after birth. A preliminary link (*sutam* – thread) is implemented before birth by the dead of the house (*ham hoko*) ensouling the foetus as mentioned above. See also Deeney (2008: 70 – 1).

and given one of their names as a gift. In this process the infant is transformed from a (biological) being into a (social) person with membership in *mmc* and clan and the right to complete funerary rites at death.

Plate 8: Burial site in the case of a bad death
The child buried here died before the birth ritual was accomplished. Thus the child was not eligible for complete funerary rites. The secondary burial was missing altogether, and the first burial also differed in relevant aspects. The body was buried outside the village boundary. The burial site was marked by a stone which was not taken there from the jungle for that particular purpose and which got lost after some time. In a case of such a so-called bad death a child will not be transformed into a beneficial ancestor, as its soul is not invited into the ancestral abode, the *adin*, by a ritual necessary to bring this about (*rowa agu*, to bring the soul back).

For male Ho, membership in their father's *mmc* is permanent. Membership is not discontinued when brothers migrate or split up for other reasons. In such cases, not only do the names of the living and dead members keep being remembered in ritual, but also the different localities where segments of the *mmc* have settled and cleared the jungle. In the case of migration, the recollected common last place of origin before migration – as a kind of unifying focus – will receive special attention (Reichel 2009: 109). By uniting the remembered forefathers of usually up to four generations plus another three generations of their living offspring, an *mmc* may be comprised of an impressive number of members.

Out-marrying women are excluded from their father's *mmc* as a rule. In-marrying wives during the liminal phase of transition will acquire membership in their husbands' *mmc* only after being introduced to their husbands' *ham hoko* in the *jom-isin* (eat-cook) ceremony. Before a wife may enter the *adin*, the sacred part of the house, touch the *mandi chatu* (rice pot), and cook the meal in it, a sacrifice of a *suka kaluti* (young hen of yellowish-brown colour that has not yet hatched eggs) is made and offered to the dead of the house dwelling in the *adin*. They are asked to accept the new daughter-in-law (*bala-saka kimin era*) as a new member of the household, clan, and tribe. By preparing the meal in the 'one' rice pot of the collectivity of 'the people of the house' (*owa: renko*), by eating together, by sharing the rice meal (*mandi*) with her husband, by adopting her husband's ancestors and eventually 'forgetting' her natal ancestors, a wife is in a permanent process of becoming one with and a member of her husband's *mmc*. The rice pot is instrumental to and at the core of this process. A wife's transition into her new status as a member of her husband's *mmc* is symbolically documented by the former cooking pot being withdrawn from service to be replaced by a new one. Whereas an unmarried daughter belongs to her father's *mmc* and *hagako* (and clan), a wife will become a member of her husband's *mmc* (and clan) only, but never of her husband's *hagako* (D. S. Purty, personal communication 2012).

Mmc: the structural significance of Ho ancestors

Unlike the case of the sociocentric categories of tribe, clan, and subclan that I have discussed so far, genealogical relations among the living and the dead members of an *mmc* should be known by the heads of the *mmc*'s households, as they are substantiated in individual pedigrees and commemorated in ritual at the household level. An individual male Ho's knowledge of his membership in a specific *mmc* is accounted for egocentrically, implying that the generational depth of his known forefathers moves along with its members. In other words, as every *mmc* contains members of several generations, there will be some considerable overlapping concerning individual members' pedigrees. While the males of the same generation within the same *mmc* may share identical pedigrees, there is nothing like *one* identical pedigree or ancestry that is common to all members of different generations of a given *mmc*.

The same logic seems to apply in the case of Santal people in the research area. They also make use of the Ho term *mmc* and refer to it synonymously as *gusti* in their language, Santali. My Santal assistant began the pedigree of his *mmc*, represented in figure 18, with his FF and FFB, that is, going two generations back, and so did his FFBS, the consequence being that I was given two different pedigrees with one generation missing in my assistant's pedigree. This shows that pedigrees are individual, relative, and not absolute and that the *mmc* of people of different generations is not identical, even though they are agnatically related as brothers (*haga*). In both cases the assumption of originating from a specific ancestor and of sharing a body of traceable forefathers (*ham hoko–dum hoko*) with their living fellow members is passed on to their offspring.[72]

In this respect a Ho's specific ancestry (*ham hoko–dum hoko*) and the ties resulting from it are the powerful structural glue that holds an *mmc* together – so much so that all *owa:renko* (people of the house) united within a specific *mmc* 'mutually get rid of' (*epera:*) their current rice pots upon the death of any of the *mmc*'s members. This ritual visibly demonstrates and re-creates the structural oneness of locally dispersed segments of an *mmc*, as it is observed by all its members irrespective of whether they can attend the funerary ceremonies or not. The ritual – according to indigenous knowledge – for the time being[73] transforms the 'people of one rice pot' (*miyad mandi chaturenko*) into 'those who reciprocally throw out their rice pots' (*mandi chatu epera:ko*). Once again, the living (-*ko*) and those ancestors assigned to them (*mandi chatu* as physical rice pot and as personification[74] of the collectivity of the dead) are linguistically united in this key metaphor of commensality.

It would be biased, however, to assume that an *mmc* is predominantly and exclusively ancestor-focussed, connoting a perspective oriented towards the past. This is wrong for several reasons.

– In a society with an overall cyclical worldview, the integration and ritual treatment of ancestors as a matter of cultural logic is as much oriented towards the future as it is towards the past.

---

72 For *gusti* and/or *mmc* from a Santal perspective see also chapter 7, 2nd portrait and figure 18.
73 'the time being' in this case relates to a rite of passage when the living – due to death pollution- are separated from the sociality of the community and undergo a transition in the preliminal and liminal phases. The pots should be broken, before the living are reintegrated socially and the soul of the dead becomes integrated into the community of the ancestors inside the *adin*.
74 The trope of the rice pot works in different secular and ritual contexts and is quite common in Ho country. There is nothing exceptional about it. Two examples: *kuma chatu ka huju:wakana* – the maternal uncle's (*kuma* – MB) people have not yet come. This is literally: the earthen pots in which they will bring rice-beer (*diyan*) has not yet come. Example two: *nama chatu*, literally new earthen pot, in a figurative sense defines a freshly laid egg offered in divining to *nage era*, a female spirit residing in low-lying fields, ravines, and pools.

- In the present Ho ancestors have quite practical duties towards the living (and vice versa), and they are considered to remain active members of their *mmc* (Reichel 2017: 116).
- Ancestors are rescued from oblivion and notionally kept alive by their names being called out for up to four generations in ritual, and they are kept alive physically in the present and the future by passing on their names in an infant's naming ceremony.
- In Ho country there is no rigid and absolute line isolating and separating the dead from the living. Dead forefathers turn into protective ancestors and are sheltered by the same roof. Ancestors within a Ho's *mmc* are not a generic or anonymous category (*tata-gunguko*) and as such opposed to the living. Communication and commensality with them continue (*ham hoko*).

I argue that instead of limiting Ho people's perspective to a focus on times past, the structural significance of Ho ancestors consists in reproducing relatedness among the dead, among the living, and among the living and the dead. Thus, although the structural bond within a Ho's *mmc* is the overlapping known ancestry of the ancestors' living offspring, its perspective and outlook lie very much with the living and their present and future lives.

- To illustrate, in the cases when I was given the pedigrees of my informants' *mmc*, the living members in all cases far outnumbered the dead. My *saki*'s *mmc* as far as I documented it (Reichel 2009: 109) consists of approximately[75] 101 members. Including his deceased only son, 27 of these are his remembered forefathers from three different localities (Chaibasa, Cuttack, and Pathan Sai in Jamda) over five generations. Perhaps 74 are the living members of the *mmc* over four generations. Of these 74 living members of my *saki*'s generation (0) plus two descending generations (-1, -2), about 26 people are the living members of the local segment of his *mmc*, which is identical with the local segment of the Holon Purty subclan that I have referred to above.

The decisive conceptual difference between the Holon Purty subclan and a Holon Purty *mmc* is that the Holon Purty subclan is a category implying that despite bearing an identical subclan's name, members of segments of the Holon Purty subclan elsewhere are unrelated and hence unknown to each other, whereas a Holon Purty *mmc* constitutes a group of widespread known linkages among

---

75 'Mistakes' happen. For that reason, separate offerings in ritual are generically addressed to all those who accidentally have been forgotten, I was told.

its members. A subclan cannot claim a primordial ancestor to be the source of knowledge of the category as such, other than of a mythical nature, and hence a subclan's members cannot assemble beneath a joint roof. Empirical members of an empirical *mmc*, however, share an empirical ancestral peak, a forefather who is often identified as the empirical founder of the particular locality whenever oral 'history' in the area suggests doing so. As pointed out above, however, both are units within the boundaries of the Purty clan – given the assumption that wives become permanently included in their husbands' clan.

Mmc: a local and translocal group

An *mmc* is a unit that takes material form locally and regionally. It often ignores boundaries drawn around hamlets and villages for administrative purposes. Locally, it has its own boundaries that become visible only in particular situations. I was able to catch a glimpse of that when in the case of a severe illness suffered by the son of my younger 'brother', medicines were buried in the ground around the land and houses of members of the local segment of his *mmc* extending from Gara Sai to Boja Sai (see map 5 above).

At the local level, an *mmc* constitutes a corporate, ritual, and commensal group; at the regional level, it remains a social and ritual unit and group. Although an *mmc* may lose its quality of organizing economic collaboration at the translocal level, it does not turn into a distant and weak category due to its considerable size, even if its segments may be dispersed throughout Kolhan and even if its members will never meet in person in the course of their lives. An *mmc* even then retains the quality of a group with exceptional unity in ritual (inter-)action and mutual support.

To sum up: an *mmc* lives out and re-enacts a dispersed group's unity, which is symbolized in the metaphor of 'one rice pot' and which includes those who have migrated or moved on. The awareness of oneness is demonstrated by its members throwing out their rice pots on the occasion of a death, being allowed to enter each other's *adin*, remembering common though locally dispersed forefathers in ritual, and knowing the names of and the relations among their living comembers, together with reference to known places of origin and active solidarity (*denga em* – to give help) among the living members.

Mmc and *hagako* (brothers, brotherhood)

Whereas membership in an *mmc* is definitive and exclusive, as I have argued above, Ho brotherhood (*hagako,* short form *haga* – brothers) is an inclusive social category with fluid boundaries that are culturally defined. *Hagako* in Ho may be coterminous with *mid mayom hapatinko* (those who share the same blood / one blood) or *ale miyad hitaren honko* (we are children of one seed),[76] suggesting people of a common substance, of a common kind, of some primordial essence. This again suggests agnatic relations, as which *haga* relations are indeed conceived. *Haga* relations, however, are not solely biologically defined as blood relations or with genealogical regard to a common original ancestor as the decisive determinant. Who is considered *haga* may vary in extent and meaning in varying contexts, as has been shown above for the classification of certain clans as brother clans in one region and others in other regions. *Haga* is not an absolute but a relative categorization and classification. The agnatic link opposing "us" and "them" – whoever the 'others' are – is a putative one. "Us" unites people without shared pedigrees and without known linkages within an "us-centric" category such as clan or brother clan *as if* they were related to each other in known ways. In broad and general terms *haga* is an idiom of social discrimination, of cultural classification. It is not a biological concept, although people make use of the idiom of blood or blood-based relationships. The "us" / *haga* / *mayom* category works at different levels, house, subclan, clan, caste, hamlet, or village implying different layers of relatedness and opposition. I will give some examples.

At the level of clan membership *haga* ("we") are distinguished from *bala* ("they," marriageable), thus identifying a category of people as related by blood, hence the rule of exogamy. The notional opposition between *haga* ("we") and *bala* ("they") becomes physically visible in the course of secondary burial rites. While *haga* attending the ceremony will spend the night near or inside the deceased person's residence, *bala* will spend the night separate from them, outside in a field; while *haga* will stay in a 'proper' house, *bala* will stay in temporary huts; while *haga* will fast (drinking rice liquor and rice-beer and smoking are allowed and not considered contradictory to the concept of fasting), *bala* will exchange food with each other, cook (separately from each other and from their *haga*) and eat (separated in their respective huts from members of

---

76 "*hita* – a seed (for propagation); a progenitor or ancestor" (Deeney 2005: 153). Deeney translates *ale miyad hitaren honko* as "we are children of a common ancestor" (ibid.). In a more encompassing sense the collectivity of all Ho conceive of themselves as the seeds of Sinbonga.

other *bala* categories). Eventually *bala* women will sing and dance, and *bala* men will drum all through the night. *Haga* women and men will do the same but among themselves and separate from their *bala*, in the yard of the deceased person's house. In terms of residence, food exchanges, commensality, dancing, singing, and drumming, the opposition between *haga* and *bala* is publicly manifested, the boundary between the two categories upheld, but also bridged by food transactions. An example from fieldwork is given to illustrate the situation, especially the empirical impact of the fluidity of the cultural classification as *haga* and the relativity of the *haga / bala* distinction as an idiom of social discrimination.

I was invited as *haga* to a secondary burial in Pathan Sai in February 2006. I was not given any reason why I was classed as *haga*. While still in the process of becoming a (Ho) person after a little more than five weeks in the field, I interpret(ed) the situation as the result of partial identification[77] with the *munda*'s wife, who was also invited and present as *haga* and with whom I entertain(ed) a *saki* relation.[78] I realized to my amazement mixed with a note of disappointment[79] that I was grouped along with *bala* on 'bala terrain' outside

---

77 About degrees of identification in ritual relations see "Ritual friendship" and "Distinctions in identification" in chapter 6.

78 A detailed analysis of the *saki* relation is given in chapter 6. – Concerning the possible link between *haga* and *saki* relations in the case of the secondary burial here my argument runs as follows: before her marriage the *munda's* wife, my *saki*, was a member of *Sinku kili* as was the deceased male. Although in marrying my *saki* had adopted her husband's *kili* Purty her presence at the burial may be seen as the continuation of her social obligations towards her natal *kili* and the relativity of the "radical severance" (Gregory 2009: 71) of a daughter from her father's *kili* at marriage. My (female) *saki*'s relation to the deceased was defined as a *haga* relationship which was demonstrated as she (and her husband) stayed in the deceased person's residence in the course of the three days of the secondary burial – as opposed to where the *bala* stayed. The *saki* relation as link to my being defined as *haga* in *this* context, I argue, reveals the *saki* relation as bringing about a certain degree of agnatization and identification. This classification, however, is not absolute as my being placed among *bala* clearly expresses. It may be seen as running parallel with the permanently ambiguous position of women and their status as beings "in-between" (Strathern 1972).

79 I was obviously walking around in ethnocentric shoes of which I was, however, not aware at the time, but which may account for my emotional state: as yet unable to make sense of the whole set up of an extremely intense situation in which people kept talking to me while I was still quite averbal, I fell victim to my home made common sense and projections of ranking *haga* relations superior and *bala* relations inferior. While trying hard to adjust and behave adequately, 'correctly ' in order to become one of "us" which at that time was synonymous for me to become integrated as *haga* I realize in hindsight that by being put on ,bala terrain' I felt de-graded, as if I had failed, as if I hadn't performed well enough. The message of the card-

the main house in a temporary hut, although my *haga*-ship and status had been previously announced to me and was documented, as can be seen in plate 9.

Plate 9: Ambiguities of the *haga* relationship
The piece of cardboard fixed to the top branch of the temporary hut assigned to me on '*bala* terrain' reads in Devanagari script, "Borlin (Garmany) HAGA."

Each of the other thirteen temporary huts was marked with a piece of cardboard indicating in Odiya script the village and the relation of the specific *bala* party to the deceased person, such as *mamu* (MB) from Tarana, *saragi* (WZH) from Tendra, *hon era* (HeBD) from Jamda etc. My status was obviously ambiguous and processual, relative and not absolute: I was advertised as *haga*, "us," but I stayed with "them."

The widow of the deceased, accompanied by my *saki*, eventually came to the hut assigned to me and shared the meal that I had prepared in a ritual that Ho call *mid jom*[80] (to become one by exchanging cooked food from each other's plates and feeding each other; see also plate 22). The meal itself was the result of as many raw food exchanges as there were temporary *bala* parties in *bala* sheds. As there were thirteen of them, I had previously exchanged, that is, given and received, thirteen small portions of raw meat, uncooked rice, pulses, onions, garlic, and spices. By combining the uncooked ingredients given by thirteen *bala* parties into one meal and by eating and incorporating it, the category of the different *bala* sections became represented as one unit. This *bala* unit was opposed to the *haga* who were locally separated in the main house. This separation, however, was not absolute, as beforehand I had been given a portion of meat by a member of the Sinku *kili*. The widow herself eventually performed

---

board inscription read to me: good effort but do keep trying. You are on the way, terminologically you may have already become one of us, but *de facto* you have not.
80 *Mid* – one; short for *miyad*; *jom* – to eat. The meaning is: to become one in the act of commensality.

the procedure of *mid jom* with each of the thirteen other *bala* units in their respective huts. Other Sinku *haga* ate cooked food in their affines' huts as well. I argue that in this act of commensality with the widow my status as *haga* in relation to the deceased was confirmed, and that in the act of positioning me on *bala* terrain the relativity of this status was documented.

Plate 10: The placing of in-laws (*bala*) at a secondary burial
Temporary huts erected for the in-laws (*bala*) on the occasion of a secondary burial in Pathan Sai. My hut is to the left (see plate 9 for the inscription); the hut to the right is assigned to *hon era* (eBD, ms; HeBD).[81]

To continue illustrating the spectrum of Ho understandings of the concept of *hagako*, at the level of brother clans that are proscribed for marriage, the example of the Holon Purty subclan discussed in chapter 4 will show that according to my *saki* a clan may be classified as a brother clan and social junior if the same god is worshipped, as is the case for the Purty and Alda clans. This clearly is beyond any biological reasoning.

There is another component of classificatory Ho brotherhood within *ego*'s generation. It is considered a *haga*-like relation, although it crosses clan boundaries and hence again in a strict biological sense does not match the criterion

---

81 *Hon era* – eBD(ms); HeBD; eZD(ws); WeZD; D (Deeney 2005: 156).

of people united by sharing the same blood (*mid mayom*). It is embedded in the terminological system of Ho kinship relations and verbally explicit in Ho relationship terminology. I refer to the category of a Ho person's spouse's siblings' spouses (spsibsp) in generation 0. For this category as such there is no linguistic equivalent in Ho. Pfeffer calls this category "quasi-consanguines" (2004: 393). In terms of relationship terminology those who fall into the category of *ego*'s spsibsp are terminologically reckoned nonaffinal relations. They are addressed like *ego*'s brothers and sisters (elder and younger). In this sense, members of the spsibsp category terminologically and structurally assume the quality of a Ho's "quasi" *hagako* (in *ego*'s generation). To illustrate, a male Ho addresses his WyBW by the same term for 'sister' (*misi-kui, misi-era*) that he uses to address his 'own' younger sister; a Ho woman addresses her husband's elder brother's wife as 'elder sister' (*aji*) just as she and her husband are used to addressing their 'own' elder sisters.[82]

At the level of the hamlet and village, agnatic *haga* kin relationships in the sense of *mid mayom* (one blood) are the most obvious ties, relating as 'brothers' through individual pedigrees the coresident males of usually up to three generations (FF, F, S), including the brothers and sons of a male *ego*'s FF and F and their unmarried daughters. It has already been emphasized above that women after marriage will not become classified as their husbands' *hagako*.

The following remarks hint at the relation and differences between *mmc* and *haga*. A man's *haga* in certain contexts is coterminous with *mid ote hapatinko* (those who share one land; Deeney 2008: 41) which is a term that clearly reveals a male bias, as it excludes a man's (unmarried and married) sisters and wife (or wives) as a matter of principle. Ho women do not own land, they cannot inherit it, and they cannot pass it on to their sons, but they are entitled to continue cultivating it should their husbands die. This may create problems in the event that there is no son or no (husband's) brothers who can inherit the land. *Haga* in terms of land (*mid ote hapatinko*) refers exclusively to those 'brothers' among whom the land will be divided if one of them is to die. Here 'brothers' are those who communally own and cultivate (ancestral) land, while their 'sisters' and daughters are excluded *in this context* from the category *haga* or *mid ote hapatinko*. Where land is concerned, instead of private property, the notion of communal or mutual ownership of ancestral land by 'brothers' prevails. Indeed, it is inscribed in the language as such: *hatin* denotes 'to share', and *hapatin* by infixing *-p(a)-* expresses reciprocity.

---

82 The sociocultural intricacies implied in this terminological category will be analysed in chapter 6: *Relationship terminology I and II*.

4 Ho accounts of social cohesion in history, myth, and the present

Hierarchy, history, and myth

The data discussed in the previous chapter have shown that the diversity of sub-clan names contributes to expressing status distinctions and hierarchical relations between the subclans within a clan and that clans as such are important status providers in arranging marriages. The present chapter will illustrate in several fieldwork-based ethnographic accounts aspects of status and hierarchy embedded in Ho constructions of history and myth.

Given a multitude of Ho clans and subclans, hierarchy in its etymological sense provides and accounts for a ranking and ordering of Ho social categories in relation to the Ho's sociocosmic whole, independent of and separate from political and economic power inequalities and social stratification (Dumont 1970: 66). Hierarchical relations are given substance in myths about the first settlers (*munu hoko*), in various subclans' myths of origin, and in their 'histories' of migration and settlement (*disum amin–disum nam*), which are kept alive by being transmitted orally and which impact people's interrelations and interaction in the present. Myths convey a perfected, abstracted, or meta model, an order that Lévi-Strauss contrasted as a "thought-of" order (Lévi-Strauss 1953: 548) to "lived-in" social orders, of which kinship is one, and human statistical or empirical praxis. Of course, these two realms are linked, as Leach points out, since all myths constitute "a charter for a community's beliefs or actions in the present" (Leach 1990: 229). According to Leach, a myth is timeless and constantly re-enacted in ritual performance[83] – as opposed to (written) history that is time-bound, that cannot be repeated, that is oriented towards and anchored in the past, and that remains there. A myth, however, is a story about the past "pegged to an identifiable relic and a place on the map [...] its chronology at best ambiguous" (ibid.) and its orientation directed towards the present. I argue that Ho subclan myths of origin are about hierarchical relations choreographed by totemic and other designations as 'identifiable relics', while in this respect localities as discrete 'places on the map' do not matter.[84] On the other hand, in Ho

---

83 Assmann (2007: 57) similarly stresses that myths (orally) stored in human memory and constitutive of a people's cultural memory construct 'reality' and keep the world going.

84 1. See above the subchapter on (sub)*clan names* that are identical with village names in today's Jharkhand. 2. In the origin myth of (the Santal) clan *Murmu* an allusion to Champa is made

https://doi.org/10.1515/9783110666199-008

narrations of their history of migration which "purport to be history" (ibid.) and which contribute to constituting status in yet another context, 'places on the map' do matter and are remembered in ritual. In the relevant myths concerning which members of which clan had settled in the research area, first precedence is given to the Kondangkel clan. The 'identifiable relic' is an outwardly inconspicuous small broken stone, and the 'place on the map' is its location in the middle of a remote field outside Gara Sai where annually the members of the local segment of the Kondangkel clan meet to celebrate, sacrifice, and pass on the story of their clearing the jungle in this region. In other words, the myth is being publicly and constantly re-enacted in ritual performance. It legitimizes S. Kondangkel as *munda*, and the community in and near his hamlet of residence insists on his performing as *munda* in a region where and at a time when the *panchayat* (village council) has long replaced and officially abolished the *manki-munda* system.

It is obvious that Ho myths of origin and Ho myths of migration are at quite opposite ends of a fictive linear timeline, the first related to myths about the origin of the universe, Sinbonga, and the creation of man (*hic*, Ho), the second to a rather recent past. However, in the Ho's awareness both narratives are often thought together and easily interwoven, as the example of the Holon Purty myth of origin in this chapter will show. Majumdar also mixes elements of mythological origin with discrete references to Ho migration to and their settling in Kolhan in his brief outlines of the myths of origin of several Ho clans (Majumdar 1950: 97 f).

Myths matter locally. They are passed on with authority by those entitled to do so, often the most aged men available. When I once wanted to find out about the local version of the Ho's creation myth, I was directed to a roughly eighty-year-old man.[85] However, when I addressed him, he asked me to consult an even older Ho because – due to his age – he considered him even more knowledgeable. Another time a Ho teacher was pointed out to me. A few people even hired a car and took me to a distant village because they had heard that this man was widely acclaimed for his knowledge. He had a thick book with drawings and handwritten notes on diverse cultural topics which none of the group that invit-

---

(Bouez 1985: 88). This, however, confirms the above argument insofar as Champa as I was told many times by people of Hansda and Murmu clan is a mythical site and as such an information on superior status rather than a geographical place.

85 Ho people are usually neither aware of nor interested in their exact biological age. In situations like this when seniority becomes an issue they make an informed guess by linking their biography to events of some prominence. This old man mentioned that as a young man he had served in the army before Independence and fought during World War II.

ed me had seen as yet. It then turned out, however, that in the man's account elements of Ho and Santal mythology got mixed up, that he identified the Ho's creator God as Thakur and replaced Sinbonga by Luku-ham and Luku-buri.[86] After our return home, people informed me that they were quite unhappy with the man's presentation and asked me not to make use of it in my book. To me, this showed that mythical knowledge is a highly valued good and that 'educated' people who command such knowledge are highly respected – relatively speaking. I gained the impression that people themselves are keenly interested in refreshing their knowledge concerning their mythical past, but not to the extent of uncritically giving up what has been orally passed on to them by their elders so far.

Plate 11: Stones as a medium of commemoration "A myth is a story about the past pegged to an identifiable relic and a place on the map" (Leach 1990: 229). G. Hansda joins the broken parts of the Kondangkel commemoration stone (*bid-diri*, an upright memorial stone) testifying to their claim of precedence in the area.

As already outlined, homonymous subclans – unrelated to each other – reside throughout Kolhan. So do segments of the Holon Purty (sub-)clan, and it seems likely that, unrelated as they are, they have different myths of origin that are equally unrelated to each other. This may at least be an explanation

---

86 He turned Luku – ham and Luku – buri who in some Ho creation myths figure as the first man and woman, sometimes also called Lutukum haram and Lutukum buri into the creators of the world thus replacing Sinbonga.

for why the origin myth that Majumdar gives for the Purty clan (1950: 99) differs in content and in the number of subclans from the one that I was told. Roy's information on subclan names assigned to the Purty clan also deviates from local knowledge in the research area (S. C. Roy 1970: 235).

The Holon Purty myth of origin

Introduction

The Holon Purty myth of origin as given here was narrated by Ch. Purty, *munda* of Tarana, Mayurbhanj, Odisha, on March 10, 2006, at his house in Pathan Sai, a hamlet within (Tara or Taran or) Tarana. It was announced as the story of the Purty clan (*kili*) and its altogether five Purty sub-*kili*. I have not added to the account any information that I gained in later discussions. Contextualizing annotations are given in the footnotes instead, and an interpretation and comments at the end. I will render the myth by sticking with the original in terms of content and order as much as I can. I did not interrupt the narrator by asking questions – although at times the temptation was great – in order to leave the lead and the storyline fully with him.

The myth

By being married to Manai Purty, a woman became the first wife of a Purty and a member of the Purty clan herself. She became pregnant and gave birth to quintuplets, to five sons. At the time of delivery her husband was absent.[87] She gave birth to her sons in a bush of reeds called *hatu* or *asul mail* in Ho, the hollow stems of which are used for the shafts of arrows. Nearby was the hut of a man from the Bari *kili*. He offered his help and took four of the sons to provide them with suitable places to live. He left the eldest son in the reeds and set off with the other four infants, carrying them in two baskets tied to a carrying pole on his shoulder (*go:*).[88] Along the way, he passed a rat hole. What a good home

---

[87] Perhaps this piece of information hints at some social drama. It is especially noteworthy in a Ho context, as Ho are the only tribal community that I know of among whom a wife's husband performs as 'midwife'.

[88] Transporting heavy loads on the shoulder like this is a common practice of Ho men when they carry home bundles of harvested paddy from the fields which women transport on their heads, or when they carry trunks from the jungle to build houses or to make firewood (*san*).

for a son, he said to himself, and he left one of the children there. All those descending from (*adu*)[89] this son belong to the *Huni* (field rat) Purty subclan. He went on and realized after a while that one of the infants had fallen through a hole in the basket at his back. The man thought to himself that, well, this might as well be a suitable place to grow up and establish a home. The son who was left there established the *Puchu:* (to pass or fall through a hole) Purty subclan. Another son was left lying under a *soso daru* (marking-nut tree). His descendants are called Soso Purty. Now the man had only one more child left to find a good home for. While walking on, he stepped on the excrement left on the path by a dog (*seta*). This is not good, he thought, but he left the child there. His descendants belong to the Seta Purty subclan.

The son who was left in the tall grass (*mail*) at the very beginning was the eldest son. He was vested with special powers by the god called *maran bonga* (great spirit/god)[90] and became *disum maran bonga*[91] (great spirit/god of the country). With the help of *maran bonga* and due to his special powers, the eldest son was able to build a large house. The material that he used for this was *holon* (rice flour). His descendants (*hon-ocho:ko*)[92] are called Holon Purty. The Holon

---

However, in ritual contexts, the person to accompany the ritual guide (*diuri*) to the sacrificial site of the village (*desauli*) carrying in earthen pots the water (*da: go:*) needed to perform a sacrifice needs to be nominated by the community and selected and confirmed by the gods in a special ritual (*mad pata:*).

89 This is a graphic way of illustrating otherwise biologically based genealogical reckoning of descent: *adu* always implies a downward movement. It literally means "to lower" and, in a reflexive sense, *adun*, "to get down, descend; to put down as an offering an egg or eggshell or turmeric to propitiate some spirit [...]; of chickens to enter into a field (usually over an embankment, and hence down)." (Deeney 2005: 4)

90 *Maran* may be translated as 'great, big' or 'previous, former' or, in this context, the *bonga* of something big e.g. a hill or mountain. Deeney calls *maran bonga* "one of the more prominent spirits" (2005: 243), Dhan the "clan deity of the Hos" (1962: 22). As a tutelary male spirit, he is called upon to protect the work on the threshing floor, to protect those going to the jungle, to protect cattle and silkworm cultivation. Within an ideology of reciprocity regular sacrifices may be offered to him for his continued protection by the head of the household. As *maran bonga* is considered a *clan* spirit, regular sacrifices by the village *diuri* are not offered to him in the main feasts on the village level.

This seems to be a spirit that my male *saki* is used to addressing himself, since when telling this part of the myth he referred to *maran bonga* as *maran tadi bonga*, '*tadi*' being the regular way of informally forming the vocative. In any case, I was often told that spirits (*bonga*) usually bear more on Ho secular lives than the more distant creator god Sinbonga does.

91 According to Dhan (1962: 22) each kili gives their own name to *maran bonga*, and it would be the members of the Purty *kili* to refer to him as *disum maran bonga*.

92 *Hon* – child; "*ocho:* – to detach with the hand grains from a cob of maize or the husk from a grain e.g. of paddy" (Deeney 2005: 270). In analogy to the human capacity of reproducing more

Purty are recognized as the elder brothers of all other Purty sub-*kili*, there being altogether five.

Members of the Bari *kili*[93] are considered the Purty clan's younger 'brothers' and as such not marriageable. People of the Alda *kili* who worship the same god *maran bonga* as people of the Purty clan are likewise classified as the Purty clan's younger 'brothers' and as *haga kili*[94] and hence proscribed for marriage.

In the event of trouble,[95] the shaman (*dewa*) will investigate by divination what it is that has annoyed the great spirit of the country (*disum maran bonga*), using *sinduri* (vermillion) and *chauli* (husked uncooked rice). The *dewa* will suggest what is to be sacrificed (*bonga*) in order to appease the spirit.

In the course of *hero: porob* (sowing feast)[96] members of the Holon Purty clan prepare a special festival bread (*lad*)[97] made from *holon* (rice flour). *Holon lad* is prepared by being cooked in boiling water only. Then it is offered to

---

of their kind a multitude of descendants is identified with the multitude of the grains from the cob of maize in the metaphor of *ocho:*.

93 It was a member of *Bari kili* who had helped distribute the four sons. To tribal people quite generally work *for others* is considered an activity of low status. In other words: for tribal people to work on their own fields reflects superior status. This is a relevant observation as the distinction 'work for your own group' as opposed to 'work for others' structurally qualifies the distinction between the tribal patrons and their nontribal artisan categories (see chapter on "The Ho and their clients").

Mutual help (*denga em* – to give/ offer non-paid help), however, is a respected and expected concept of tribal solidarity.

The help offered by the member of the Bari clan in the origin myth and its classification as the Purty's social junior thus expresses the hierarchical ranking in terms of seniority as a means of (social) discrimination, but not of discrimination against another person, group, or category.

94 By classifying Bari and Alda *kili* as social juniors *and* simultaneously as 'brothers' reveals once again that hierarchy is *not* synonymous with power relations, inequality or stratification, but an idiom of social order.

95 As *maran bonga* oversees fields and crop, trouble in this context may relate to periods of little or no rain. Spirits and gods communicate with the living in this way pointing out their dissatisfaction at something that needs to be discerned and that needs to be made good. This is the shaman's responsibility.

96 *Hero: porob* refers to the sacrifice and feast held after all the sowing has been completed (*her* – to sow; *o:* is a marker to indicate passive voice and attached at the end of a word) about the month of July.

97 Ritual food made on the occasion of special festivals such as this bread is usually prepared without spices, oil and salt. The flour used to form flat shapes of this particular bread is made from *adowa chauli* (rice husked without previous boiling), which is rice used in ritual, i.e. high-status situations. Pucilowski has the transcription of a narrative of the complete process of preparing *hero: porobreya: holon lad* (2013: 229 – 236) which after the offering is eaten up. Pucilowski unfortunately does not mention among whom this sacrificial bread is shared.

maran bonga. In the month of *hero:* no member of the Holon Purty is allowed to touch *holon* until this sacrifice has been offered.

Members of the Holon Purty clan migrated to Tarana from Katigutu, Ch. Purty added. The first to have settled here were Manai Sinku[98] and Gardi Kondangkel.[99] Only after these had settled here did Kirsai and his men of the Holon Purty clan arrive. Pathan Sai in the village of Tarana is the second site where Holon Purty people settled, after Katigutu.[100]

Interpretation and comment

Quite of his own accord, Ch. Purty eventually jumped from narrating the process of the Purty clan splitting up into various subclans in some mythical past containing no hints whatsoever at places, locations, or territoriality to the more recent process of Holon Purty people, known by name, migrating from a concrete, named place and settling in another concrete, named place at a period of time perhaps less than two hundred years or four generations ago. The two narrations were inspired and intertwined by two male protagonists with an identical name, Manai. One of them is identified as the mythical/remote progenitor of all Purty subclans (*munu* – origin; original; first beginning). The other is Ch. Purty's and his brothers' known and more immediate forefather *(ham ho–dum hoko)*, their FFFF, a member of their *mmc* remembered by name (Manai Purty) and place (Katigutu) in rituals at the household level. To this day the name Manai recurs every other generation[101] in their pedigree, connecting a total of seven generations of kin.[102]

---

98 My female *saki's* natal clan is Sinku. Both the Santal clan Kisku and the Ho clan Sinku that are related across the tribal boundary as brother clans convey connotations of royalty.

99 For the Kondangkel commemoration stone see plate 11.

100 The repetition of certain parts by word pairs and poetic parallels in oral accounts is a typical feature not only of Ho narratives. Fuhrmann (2013: IX) and Vitebsky (2008: 244; 2017: 3) mention a similar feature for the Karow and the Sora.

101 Vitebsky speaks of a process of "recycling ancestors' names into new babies" (2012: 184).

102 Manai is also the name of my male *saki's* only male grandchild whose mother's father (MF: *tata*) he is. His only son died very young. His only daughter gave birth to five daughters, before eventually Manai was born who, however, as a member of my *saki's* son-in-law's *kili* Birua may have adopted his name from his paternal forefathers. By belonging to a different clan and patriline Manai will not be entitled to inherit land from his (maternal) grandfather's side one day. – In 2016 news was broken that my *saki* was about to adopt one of his younger brothers' sons.

The process of settling (*disum amin–disum nam*)

Introduction

The process of settling in a particular area is a specific moment in a (sub-)clan's collective memory. The precedence of the original settlers and the chronology of those arriving later is publicly acknowledged and not contested. In the research area precedence as first settlers is attributed to the Bage clan for the villages of Manbir and Jamda (see map 4) and to the Kondangkel and Sinku clans for Tarana (see maps 4 and 5).

The Holon Purty subclan's account of *disum amin–disum nam* is part of their migration construction. It is about the process of how, due to an increase in population in the Chaibasa area in Singhbhum, they selected land (*disum* – country; to establish one's country somewhere) about forty kilometres to the southeast, how they decided it was suitable for cultivation and settling, how they cleared the land of trees, shrubs, and grass (*amin*), how they by clearing the jungle acquired the right to settle there (*amin-nam*),[103] and why they called the site Tarana.

The myth was recollected as follows by my (male) *saki* in collaboration with his three younger brothers and a few fellow villagers who had joined us for the public lesson, at dawn on January 3, 2006, my fifth day in the area. In his role as *munda* my *saki* had been summoned as a witness in order to negotiate and sign a document concerning a mortgage of 1500 Rs given to a villager on half an acre of land for two years. When the deal was done, people stayed on, and my *saki* chose to point out the relevance of land for Ho people by narrating the story of their settling in the area. Characteristically, sitting with the others on a bed (*karkom*) in the courtyard of his house, my *saki* did most of the talking and did so with authority. The others complemented his report occasionally, while some of my *saki*'s brothers' children, *gungu* (HyBCh) to me, squatted down listening attentively. The myth was translated by G. Hansda, my assistant.

---

103 With much the same meaning as *amin-nam* such a process of acquiring the right to settle in a new area is also referred to as *ma:-nam pu-nam*; *ma:* – to cut, to slash e. g. a tree or shrub with an axe; *pu* – to uproot by hitting the stump of a shrub.

The myth

About four generations ago there were two marketplaces, Dongol Hat and Garh Hat, as Chaibasa and Rairanpur were called in the 'olden days'. Kirsai Purty, my *saki*'s great-grandfather and Manai's son, and a few of his men were walking all the way (*hora* – road; path; passage) to Garh Hat on foot, while watching out for a suitable site. When they thought they had found a good one, before making the final decision they had to ritually put the area to the test according to criteria that they had learned from their forefathers and have passed on to their own sons, as follows:

A tall tree in the prospective area was cut halfway through its roots by the *diuri*, the ritual guide, from Katigutu, who accompanied Kirsai and his men. A red cock (*ara: sandi*)[104] was tied to the tree by a rope. Rice, husked and uncooked (*chauli*), was put on a large plain stone which served as a dish or plate (*patra*) within the cock's reach. A hollowed-out bottle gourd (*suku tumbu*) was filled with water and left at the foot of the tree. Before the cock was left at the scene for seven days, a prayer was addressed to Sinbonga and the men's forefathers back in Katigutu asking for protection and support. The site was considered suitable for settlement if the tree did not fall down in these seven days, if the cock stayed alive, and if a little water and rice was left over. This will make for enough water and rain in future and for fertile soil. All of this worked out for Kirsai Purty and his men. They called the site Tarana (*tara* – half) to commemorate that (the root of) the tree had been cut halfway through in the ritual. Ever since, Kirsai and his descendants have lived in Tarana, just as Randor and Sorgod, Kirsai's two brothers, settled in Cuttack and Rasika Sai after having successfully performed the respective rituals there (*bonga manatin* – to obey a ritual). As outlined above, in the event of migration Ho ancestors are invited to accompany their living descendants, but Ho people are never sure whether all of them really come – for example, due to potential physical disabilities. So, in order to ensure all of their ancestors' continued protection, a male red-brown cock (*ara: sandi sim*) and a black hen (*hende sim*)[105] need to be sacrificed at the *new* site in memory of the ancestors at the *former* place of residence. This is regularly done on the occasion of *mage porob,* the big village festival after the completion of the harvest.

---

104 *Ara:* – red-brown, *sandi* – male; a cock of this colour is regularly offered to *desauli,* the spirit of the sacred grove, on the main village festivals.

105 In the village festivals a black hen is offered to *nage erako,* tutelary female spirits associated with places where water gathers or may gather and assumed to dwell in low-lying fields, in springs, pools, or ravines.

Interpretation

The narrative of the Purty clan's process of settlement as presented here can be seen as a continuation of the Holon Purty myth of origin, which towards its end was rounded off by referring to those named forefathers who had chosen and ritually approved the site. By clearing jungle territory in the area, Purty people have acquired the right to land and thus notionally come close to but are not identical with those who are acknowledged as the first settlers. Both accounts make sense on their terms. However, some questions remain open when confronted with other ethnographic data from the region.

While Santal, Gau, and Muslim residents confirm that Ho are the first settlers (*munu hoko*), in Tarana without differentiating between individual Ho clans in this context, Ho people, including those of the Holon Purty subclan in the area, specify this by attributing precedence to the Kondangkel and Sinku clans. So, there is no question which clan is that of the first settlers. Also, I have several times been assured that the obligation to perform as ritual guide (*diuri*) and secular head (*munda*) ideally lies with members of the clan of the first settlers and hence is hereditary. Exceptions will be tolerated only in exceptional situations, if, for example, a *diuri* or *munda* dies early or has no son, if his son is too young, or if someone leaves the area for an extended period in order to make a living elsewhere.

In this respect and due to this logic, S. Kondangkel as a representative of the clan of the first settlers is the legitimate *munda*, and the same is true in the case of the former *diuri*, G. Kondangkel from Pathan Sai. But what about the legitimacy of Ch. Purty as *munda*? Initially, it was quite confusing to me that while in ritual respects Gara Sai and Pathan Sai are indigenously considered *one* unit of Tarana (see map 5) sharing *one* sacred grove (*desauli*) and *one* diuri, there are *two* munda, sometimes cooperating, sometimes not, sometimes conveying a mild air of hostility. Ch. Purty of Pathan Sai, considerably older than S. Kondangkel, commands a high reputation as *munda* whose duties he has seen to for the past twenty years. He emphasizes himself that it was due to his initiative that a new tank was built and a new burial site established. I suggest that it is a case of ascribed status for S. Kondangkel, as he inherited the prestigious responsibility of being *munda* from his father, and it is one of achieved status for Ch. Purty. I eventually learnt that the (male) Ho community had asked the latter to take on the responsibility of being *munda* two decades or so ago when S. Kondangkel's father died quite unexpectedly, followed only a little while later by his eldest son. At that time S. Kondangkel, unaware of what was going on back home, was working in Bhutan (*nalatani:* – someone who works for wages) for an extended and indeterminate period of time. He was too young then, he says, and did not feel sufficiently trained to fulfil a *munda's* duties anyway, since he had not expected it would be his turn so soon.[106] The necessity of an extended training period to meet the demands of performing as *munda* is indeed a serious and acknowledged argument. It also holds true for the duties of the *diuri*. G. Kondangkel, *diuri* of Tarana, confirmed that he acquired all of his knowledge from his father, that he started to accompany him to the sacred grove (*desauli*) regularly when he was a very young boy, and that it took a process of more than fifteen years of learning before he began his duties as the main *diuri* by being in charge of an offering in the course of a ritual aimed at bringing about rain (*da: gama*) at the time when S. Kondangkel's father was *munda*.

The lack of training of a future *munda* or *diuri* may constitute the mentioned exceptional case that calls for intervention and action for the community's benefit. I suspect that in the situation outlined above, the Holon Purty myth of origin, as well as the myth of their settling in Taran(a), came into play and gained importance in Ch. Purty's having been invited to fill the gap, as follows:

- The Holon Purty myth of origin reveals that the Holon Purty segment is the most senior of all the segments into which the Purty clan is divided and thus accounts for its most senior status. This is a prerequisite for eligibility as *munda* or *diuri*.
- The myth of settlement (*disum amin–disum nam*) reveals that people of the Holon Purty subclan cleared parts of the jungle in the region, thus linking them to the spirits of the locality and to Mother Earth, as emphasized above. This is a status-elevating quality that they share with the first settlers (*munurenko*).

---

106 In the neighbouring village of Manbir there was a similar situation relating to the *diuri* there: Ks. Bage of the dominant Bage clan was too young when M. Bage, his father and *diuri* of Manbir died. He was succeeded by Lokon Bage, his FFFFBSS and *kaka*, who was supposed to wait for Ks. Bage to grow up and become *diuri* himself. When I enquired into who was the *diuri* of Manbir at the beginning of my fieldwork, Lokon was pointed out to me by my immediate neighbours, but whenever I approached him he absolutely refused to collaborate. He claimed that he was utterly ignorant and that the true *diuri* was Ks. Bage. I should go and ask him. There was ritual interaction between the two, though, and both lived in the immediate vicinity, though in two distinct hamlets. As can be seen in plate 7, for example, it is Ks. Bage (right) who is in charge of preparing ritual rice-beer (*ti chipa rasi*) to be offered first to *Sinbonga* at *mage* and *ba porob* and afterwards shared among the members of the local segment of the *mmc* to which both, L. Bage and Ks. Bage, belong. But the commensal act is being done inside Lokon Bage's enormous compound.

I presume that such situations lead to there eventually being two men negotiating and performing the respective duties as either secular heads or ritual guides – cooperatively or separately.

- According to their myth, it was they who imposed the name Tara(na) on the (whole) village and not the Kondangkel clan.
- After S. Kondangkel's return, his settling in Gara Sai, his getting married, and his becoming father to a son, local people eventually resumed their former habit of seeking out and addressing him as *munda*, while Ch. Purty, once elected and re-elected, has continued to this day to the best of his ability and also keeps being consulted as *munda*.

Both myths contribute in different ways to rooting the local segments of the Purty and Kondangkel (sub-)clans in history, understood as a meaningful and structured past providing status in and directed towards the present. The duties of the living and their representatives are authorized by and embedded in matters of mythology, land, and ancestry.

The Ho and their spirit world: of social cohesion in the present

In difficult times, we turn to Sinbonga, to our ancestors and to the protective bonga, *but not to the malicious ones. We turn to them for help and protection in difficult times. We address our ancestors like this: "Ham-hoko, dum-hoko, horo jangilepe!" To Sinbonga we say, "Horolem!" We do not say, "Horoleben!" We address a protective* bonga *by name first, before we ask for help.*[107]

(D. S. Purty, personal communication 2014, Chaibasa, Jharkhand).

---

107 1. *Ham hoko-dum hoko* collectively refers to the dead of the house (also *owa: goe:*) dwelling in the sacred part *(adin)* of the house alongside the living; when asked for help they are usually not individualized by specific names. For the distinction with *tata-gunguko* see above.

2. *Horo, jangi* are poetic parallels meaning "to protect, to guard". As this formula is used whenever tutelary spirits are addressed in much of the literature these are also referred to as *guardian* spirits.

3. *Horole-m* (protect us!): -m indicates 2nd person sg to be distinguished from the more formal and distanced forms *horole-ben* (2nd person dual) and *horole-pe* (2nd person plural) which may be used e.g. to address the *munda* of a village or the *manki* of the region. *Horole-m* is respectful, but also the closest, most intimate way of addressing someone, free of formalities.

Introduction

In chapter 3 social cohesion was outlined primarily as a structured phenomenon and the result of the Ho's system of social organization ordering interaction and relations among Ho people and coexistence among the tribal societies in this area of the Chota Nagpur Plateau. The focus was on the living, although Ho ancestors were structurally included in the *mmc*.

I will argue in this section that social cohesion in Ho country is not confined to the material and visible world of the living. In a holistic society such as that of the Ho, the unity of society and the cosmos surrounding it includes the Ho's spirit world, which as the sphere of the divine is assigned superior value and addressed with politeness and respect. The cosmic-societal whole is understood as being governed by principles and values and subjected to one universal order (*niyam*) that is assumed to be operative in the world of the living as well as in that of the spirit world.

The overall approach so far has been systematic and analytical. The focus here is different. The Ho's spirit world and the relations between diverse categories of spirits and the living is a huge and complex topic that would make for yet another comprehensive analysis and book.[108] Of course, this cannot be done here. However, in order not to utterly neglect a dimension of considerable relevance that cannot be isolated from Ho people's everyday lives, their empirical interaction with the spirit world will be highlighted here by my giving accounts of a few incidents I observed in the field. This is done without aiming in any way at a complete survey. The basic introductory remarks that follow are thus meant to selectively outline the setting necessary to understand the context within which the ethnographic verbal and visual illustrations gain meaning and make sense.

---

108 Deeney had a sense of the extensiveness of the domain and did continuous ethnographic and linguistic research into the topic. This shows by relevant differences including the etymology of the name Sinbonga between a first draft of "The Spirit World of the Ho Tribals" and its publication in 2008. Only reluctantly did he go to press in that year (personal communication) as he felt he was getting weaker and there was a danger of his findings not being published at all. But in honour of the Ho's attitude towards their spirit world he felt obliged to publish what he had researched in collaboration with D. S. Purty. Himself a Ho he had made interviews on the topic with many elders in several Ho villages in Jharkhand which were taped first and then systematically transcribed.

The structure of the spirit world

Living in a world of plenty: this holds particularly true for the Ho's perception of the diversity of their spirit world and their reciprocal exchange relations with that world, which are regularly re-created in ritual at the household and the village level.

The Ho's spirit world as such is structured in such a way as to imply the idea of a "triple world" (P. Sen 2006: 314) – one within which, however, the boundaries are blurred. Sinbonga, male and unmarried, is recognized as supreme spirit and creator of the universe. The spirit world then falls into two distinct but related spheres: *bonga* and the dead of the house *(owa: goe:)*, who are not thought of or referred to as *bonga*, although both are categories of spirit beings. Disembodied and invisible to the living, *owa: goe:* or rather their souls *(rowa)* are classified as protective and helpful or, depending on their kind of death, harmful spirits. Once constructed as protective spirits, *owa: goe:* are assumed to dwell inside the sacred part of the house and remain close to the living. They are classed as *ham ho–dum hoko*. Harmful *owa: goe:* are made to stay outside the house, as various accounts below will show. They are not classed as *ham ho–dum hoko*. Conceptualized as individuals, they are treated individually in ritual.

Owa: goe: are to be distinguished in status and sphere of activity from those *named* spirit beings that are conceived of and referred to as *bonga*. *Bonga* are also said to be the spirits of dead people. By involving themselves in the lives of the living, *bonga-ko* cause themselves to be perceived as living spirit beings. They are basically identified as those spirits that revealed themselves and their protecting role when the original settlers in a village cleared the jungle. These spirits are specified as *ma:-nam chalu:-nam bongako*.[109] They subsist on the sacrifices offered to them by the living in exchange for protecting people, their harvests, their cattle, and their possessions. As place spirits, they are closely linked to a specific terrain, transforming hills and mountains, pools, tanks, and trees into a sacred landscape.[110] In analogy to the dead of the house

---

109 see *The Ho's oral 'history'* in chapter 1. *ma:* (to cut, to slash) and *chalu:* (to hoe) are used as poetic parallels in *ma:- nam chalu:- nam* (to find by hoeing). The symbol of a hoe relating those 'ancient' spirits and the first settlers (*munu: hoko*) in the present is commemorated in death rituals. When the purified *rowa* (soul) is guided from the tank back to the house it is fastened to a hoe carried on the left shoulder of the widow of a deceased husband (*see* jacket illustration of Reichel 2009).

110 According to the Asur myth female Asur *bongako* are the spirits of dead women who also belong in this category of *bonga*. Deeney introduces them as a relevant section of the Ho's spirit world (2008: 15) referring to D. S. Purty (1978, vol.7, 13), to Bodding's Santali Dictionary (A/142; B/

(*owa: goe:*), who may be tutelary or harmful, *bonga-ko* are spirit beings that may be supportive or malign[111] in their attitude towards the living.

Ho people's notional entwinement with and dependence on their spirit world is constantly present in their lives and a constitutive aspect of it. Ho tend to personalize and humanize these spirits. This shows in the way the living address them when asking for their protection and assistance. Spirits are constructed in analogy to the living. In fact, they are perceived as "living beings" (Dhan 1962: 18, quoting Hoffman and Van Emelen 1990 [1950]: 612) and assumed to retain their intellects and wills and a capacity for caring about the affairs of human beings. As the living feel free to make demands on their spirits, the spirits are reciprocally said to be able to make demands on the living – and to punish them if they are not treated with respect. In every aspect, this is an active interrelation.

The dead of the house (*owa: goe:*) within the Ho's spirit world

The dead of the house as a social category in their own right, distinct from though not unrelated to the world of the living, have been referred to above when discussing the spatial and social aspects of a Ho village.[112] Communication and commensality continue within an *mmc* after the death of one of its members.[113] Their overall significance and active involvement in every Ho's life in the region of research has also been the focus in Reichel 2009. Arguments and fieldwork data discussed there will not be repeated here. Instead, I will give accounts from fieldwork of the consequences when the spirit of a dead person is classified as potentially harmful, such that the soul is not invited into the *adin*. To enable understanding of the problem and the context, I first provide some basic information.

Immediately after death the *rowa* (soul, shadow) of a deceased Ho is perceived as erratic. In a painstaking process, it is socially transformed through a series of rituals and ceremoniously 'called back' (*keya*) from the grave to the de-

---

324) and Hoffman and Van Emelen's *Encyclopaedia Mundarica* (H/164 ff). I will not enlarge on them here as they were not mentioned to me during fieldwork. For the purpose of this book Bodding is listed in the References as Bodding (1932–1936), Hoffman and Van Emelen's *E.M.* as 1990 [1950]. A brief outline of the Asur legend is given in Glossary I.

111 I will not discuss the class of the Ho's malign *bonga* here. See below "The spirit world of the Gau" in chapter 6 for malign *juguni* and *baram buri* spirits.

112 See above *Village, clan, and kinship* in chapter 3.

113 *See* above *miyad mandi chaturenko* in chapter 3.

ceased's former residence. This is done by members of the *miyad mandi chatur-enko* and the in-laws, all of whom assemble for that reason on the occasion of a death. The soul (*rowa*) is invited to take up permanent residence in the sacred part of the house, the *adin*, in the company of its newly acquired fellow coresident dead. Standardized though variable patterns of how to ritually treat and purify (*sabsi*) their dead are assumed to have been passed on to the living by their forefathers (*sida: kaji* – narratives of 'olden days') and need to be observed (*man-atin* – to obey) precisely in order for the whole village to come to grips with the notional disaster that any death socially presents. Invisible and bodiless, the dead who will eventually dwell inside the houses along with the living are transformed into benevolent protective spirits. They have entered the Ho's spirit world and as such have access to Sinbonga, the supreme being and the epitome of purity. Much concerned with their own and their family's social purity, which is prone to becoming polluted if, for example, clan codes or norms are violated, they mediate between the world of the living, the spirit world, and their creator God.

Linguistically, the dead of the house or *ham hoko–dum hoko* are not gendered, since Ho, as explained above, has no separate masculine and feminine forms: "old men, sleeping men" refers to the dead of either sex. In this formulation their human character is emphasized, while they are simultaneously identified as spirits. The responsibilities they acquire at death include and range from duties towards newborn babies, to whom they provide a name and status; towards recently married wives who need to be ritually introduced (*jati ader*) into the local segment of the *mmc* before they may touch the rice pot (*mandi chatu*); and quite generally towards protecting and keeping watch over the people of the house (*owa:renko*), their lands, cattle, and crops, and their in-laws.

Social cohesion between the living and their dead in this respect is not so much a given state as the result produced by continuous bilateral interaction. This aspect of social cohesion extends beyond the world of the living in the present. It links and relates the living and the collectivity of the dead by rooting them in the social web of the village, as an individual death affects the whole village and representatives of each household are involved in the choreography of the death rituals, and it adds a dimension of historicity by including the dead of many generations.

Accounts from the field: on the soul-spirits of persons who have suffered a bad death[114]

The ritual treatment of a dead person's *rowa* (soul) in the case of what is considered a deviant kind of death is something that can be empirically witnessed in participant observation. Ho people have no generic term to denote a class of 'bad' death. They speak instead of different *ways* of dying, of various deviating *kinds* of death, in quite concrete and descriptive terms, for example, a death due to being bitten by a snake or tiger (*hab-gonoe:*), to be distinguished from death caused by being bitten by any other animal (*huwa:-gonoe:*), by being burnt or having fallen into fire (*urub-gonoe:*), or by committing suicide (*goe:en / gojen*). In a case recounted below, when it was not clear whether a woman had been murdered or committed suicide, the death was characterized as *tataka gonoe:* ("stupefaction; amazement; to be stupefied, amazed," Deeney 2005: 371) and *roka gonoe:* (sudden death). The following accounts cover four deviating kinds of death and dying requiring distinct ways of dealing with the respective *rowa* spirits.

Suicide (*goe:en*)
A Ho boy, approximately fourteen years of age, hung himself in R., where he was attending secondary school. By committing suicide (*goe:en*), he was considered to have made himself an outcast (*jatite bar*),[115] and his soul (*rowa*) was judged (*bichar*) ineligible to be invited inside the *adin* and become an ancestor. The *keya ader* (to call back inside) ceremony in the course of which a purified Ho soul is invited to participate in the sociality of the dead of the house (*owa: goe:*) was not arranged. He was buried outside the village boundaries, so that his soul's defilement or social uncleanness (*bisi:*) could not adversely affect the purity of the village and the villagers (*bisi: tala* – to include in defilement; pass., to share defilement). Ho people assume that a wandering soul may turn vengeful if left unattended, as it is unsheltered and without the company of its fellow souls. It may harm the living and needs to be propitiated. In this case, a large, flat stone (*sasan diri*) did not cover the grave, but an inconspicuous upright stone (*bid-diri*) about forty centimetres tall was set in the ground. It was

---

114 Parry (1994: 159) and Bloch and Parry (1982: 15) give an in-depth discussion of the concept of a 'good' death occurring in the right place, at the right time, voluntarily and controlled versus a 'bad' death which is considered flawed as it comes "untimely, sudden, abrupt [...] uncontrolled and involuntarily" (Parry 1994: 162).

· 115 *Jati* – "race; tribe; caste; type, kind"; *bar* – "outside; to put outside" (Deeney 2005: 31, 177)

erected in memory of the deceased on top of an embankment next to a field. "He was a member of our community, which now is incomplete without him. Placing the stone is a way of making our community complete again," I was told. "His soul will linger around the stone. When it is hot (jete), it may sit in its shade. It should not feel inclined to roaming about."

In this example, the boy's soul-spirit (rowa) was permanently excluded from the community of the living locally and socially but remained notionally and visibly included by being provided a memorial stone. His story as I have narrated it here was told to me by an elderly Ho. He was cultivating his field when I was wandering around (honor) in the vicinity and happened to see the stone.

To die and leave behind (goe: bage)

A woman from a neighbouring hamlet, Baru Sai, married and the mother of two sons, left for Kolkata in 2006. She did not return for many years. Eventually she was considered dead, and her social death was referred to as goe: bage (to die and leave behind), a term that is conventionally resorted to in order to refer to a widow and her children in the event that her husband dies first. A stone similar in size and shape to that mentioned in the preceding case was erected, and the reasons given for doing so were similar. When I was in the area in 2013, however, the woman unexpectedly returned, old, ill, and on the verge of dying. She wanted to stay with her husband and sons and die where she had married virilocally. Her request was first bluntly refused, then grudgingly granted. Her husband and sons, however, made it very clear that none of them was prepared to bury her or to have her buried in their ancestral burial site behind their house. As it remained unclear what exactly she had been doing in Kolkata, the situation was widely and hotly debated. I learned about it in a shed in the marketplace where it was discussed over a bowl of rice-beer. It became a matter of bichar (judgment, to judge, to pass judgment on), a Ho institution also mentioned above in the boy's case.

In my experience, bichar was always called for when a death was about to be classified as bad, a category that includes different kinds of deaths, as mentioned above, and hence requires different ways of dealing with it and the spirit of the deceased. It is exclusively men who meet for bichar to debate whatever may possibly affect the purity of the village. Although men do talk important matters over with their wives, I observed, however, that more often than not women first discuss matters with other women in the vicinity, often when meeting at the well at dawn, before they turn to their husbands. Men freely admitted that it was wise not to ignore their wives' advice.

The judgment concerning the woman's situation was that the purity of the ancestors in the burial site and in the *adin* was at stake and needed to be preserved by all means. The *bichar* ruled out *jate bonga*, a ritual (*bonga*) to purify something or someone after some defilement (*jate*) which might have been an option in such a situation.[116] It was debated but not agreed upon. The quarrel continued and sharpened; the situation remained unresolved. The woman was still living, but the erection of the memorial stone years before meant that the burial rites were conceived of as having already been finalized. The *diuri* of the hamlet, concerned with the well-being of the whole village community, was consulted and asked to take care of the matter. After all, a *diuri*'s main role is to solicit the protection of *desauli*, the village's main guardian spirit. The *diuri* accepted the responsibility and started to discuss the matter with his two assistants (*jomsimkin*). When I left the field to return to Germany, they had not yet decided what needed to be done to comply with the code of conduct towards the ancestral and the village spirits. This involves quite practical steps, which as such are, of course, embedded in the Ho's encompassing value system and their concept of hierarchy and order (*niyam*). This is also revealed in the following situation.

A sudden death (tataka gonoe:)

There was a disturbing event that happened in January 2010. It never became clear whether it was a case of murder, attempted murder, complicity in murder, suicide, or death due to a fit of epilepsy.

A woman, Site K., was said to have succumbed to severe burns after having been pushed or having fallen into an open fire.[117] Site K. was the mother of a married son who had died in 2006 in Gara Sai and who had gone through the complete funerary rites.[118] His *rowa* spirit (soul) was inside the *adin*, his body beneath a *sasan diri* (flat burial stone) next to his house, where his wife lived to-

---

116 There are diverse reasons for people to undergo the *jate bonga*, and it is not only done in a case of death. S. Kondangkel had asked the *dewa* (shaman) to perform it on him after he had consulted two physicians in Rairanpur, a larger town near-by, to help his dying son, because he felt that too much contact with *diku*-people outside the village boundaries might have annoyed or defiled his ancestors. He did the same when he came back from Gujarat where he had been for some time to earn money (*nala* – to work for wages). In such situations, the *jate bonga* is meant to propitiate the ancestors and re-purify the living.

117 *udur-gur* – to push (*udur*) so as to make someone fall from a standing position (*gur*); *gur* (to fall), although an intransitive verb in Ho, is considered passive and takes the passive form. Where we would say 'someone falls', Ho language implies that 'someone is made to fall'.

118 They are given in detail in Reichel 2009.

gether with their four young children. Site K. was the third wife of her husband, who had died two years earlier. His first wife had one married daughter only; his second wife had no children. So, Site K.'s body was taken to her dead son's house to be buried there.

The burial procedures were supposed to be guided by the two *dakuwa* (the village headman's helpers), but only one of them turned up. The other one was on his way to a cockfight. Afraid that his cock's fighting spirit might be undermined by being surrounded by death pollution, he refused to appear. Site K.'s husband's three brothers were present and took part in the *bichar*, which diagnosed a 'sudden' death (*tutuku gonoe:*). They opted for the performance of a *jate bonga* (purification ritual) and asked the dead woman's son-in-law (*ara*) to see to it that it was done properly. This man was the husband of the only daughter of Site K.'s husband's first wife. He belonged to his father's *mmc*, with which Site K. was also associated by marriage. He had come from outside for the occasion. I was not allowed to participate in the all-male affair of the *bichar*, so my assistant recorded the negotiations on a voice recorder. The males who were present (*hagako, balako, haturenko* – people of the village) discussed whether the body was to be purified or rather the members of the house or all members of the *mmc* or the whole village and how. The question was raised of whether the body should be burnt instead of buried to preclude a possible postmortem investigation by the police. It was decided and announced after the *bichar* to bury the body but not to oil it, not to wash it, and not to apply turmeric. There would be no *keya ader* ceremony (calling the *rowa* into the *adin*). Each household of the village was involved by contributing five rupees. The *diuri* gave ten. It was discreetly argued whether one chicken or twenty chickens should be sacrificed to pacify the supreme clan spirit, *maran bonga*. The *dewa* (shaman) who was consulted suggested sacrificing a red-brown cock (*ara: sandi sim*) to *desauli*, the village's main guardian spirit, in order to purify the whole village. The members of the *mmc*, however, considered the situation to be so sensitive that it was decided to also sacrifice a *pundi kaluti* (a white hen that has not yet laid eggs). A sacrifice of that colour is offered exclusively to Sinbonga. The fellow villagers stayed away during the proceedings but watched intensely from a distance. They were curious; the *owa:renko* and their *balako* were nervous. The body had to be disposed of the same day; the soul-spirit (*rowa*) had to be kept in check. A grave was dug in front of a thorn bush (*ram*) at the furthest possible edge of the compound, but within its fenced-in boundaries. The Ho *diuri* from Pathan Sai was among those who dug the grave. He belonged to Site K.'s *mmc*. While usually on the occasion of a burial people are quite talkative, this time the atmosphere was tense, and there was little socializing. Having done their duties, people left as soon as possible.

While the men were busy preparing the grave and away from the house, where the body was kept inside on a rope-bed (*karkom*), the women investigated the body thoroughly and in silence. The body had been stabbed several times. As Site K. had previously been taken to a hospital in R., where her death was confirmed, this must have been an open secret, and the women were obviously determined not to reveal it. Contrary to what the men had decided, the body was washed, lavishly oiled, and covered with plenty of turmeric, and *chauli* (husked rice) was put into her right hand. Site K.'s mother carefully looked for lice in her hair, caressed her dead daughter's face, and oiled it repeatedly. Many new saris eventually covered the body, and worn and torn ones were removed. All of this ceremonious treatment was concealed from the men. Carried on her bed to the grave by male *haga* and *bala*, the body was lowered into the grave only at dusk. It was covered not only with rupee coins, as usual, but with banknotes, something that I have seen nowhere else. Site K.'s mother examined each note carefully to make sure there were no fake notes. All the money was left with the dead, whereas otherwise towards the end of a burial those who have helped dig the grave are given a certain number of the coins in reciprocity. A branch of the thorn bush was placed on top of the grave. The thorns were supposed to make sure that the soul-spirit could not escape. The thorny branch of a plum tree (*bakara daru*) is sometimes used for this purpose.

Death due to a snakebite *(hab-gonoe:)*
My last account is about a girl who was bitten by a snake (*hab-goe:*) and died at the age of sixteen. Sunai Kondangkel was the daughter of my *kaki-ma* of Boja Sai, whose classificatory daughter I had become and in whose house I lived for several months. Sunai was buried inside the fence surrounding the hamlet and separating it from the adjacent rice fields but outside the fence surrounding the houses, yards, threshing floors (*kolom*), and burial sites. Separated from her younger brother, who had died from disease and who had been given a flat burial stone (*sasan diri*) next to and in line with his forefathers, Sunai was buried at the far end of and within the compound, but as far away from the house and as close to the fence as possible.

Sunai had died before I entered the field. An excerpt from an essay (Reichel 2017) on how her soul-spirit (*rowa*) continues to be ritually treated many years after her death is given in the appendix, "Sunai Kondangkel: ethnography of a bad death."

The outcome of a bad death can never be a protective benevolent spirit or ancestor. This is a matter of cultural classification and distinction, not a moral statement. Even if Ho people assume different degrees of harmfulness of such an untransformed spirit, communication and ritual treatment, although not commensality, may continue and contribute to appeased relationships, as in Sunai's case. Social cohesion thus includes not only the living and the dead of the house in the *adin*, but also those who have suffered a bad death. Territorially excluded, they are not forgotten. They belong.

Plate 12: The grave of Sunai Kondangkel
Sunai Kondangkel's grave is at the far end of the compound behind the threshing floor, within the fenced-in area. Her soul may not enter the house. Her brother is buried beneath one of the large slabs of stone in front. His *rowa* is sheltered in the *adin*.

Bongako (spirits)

A Ho's *ham hoko–dum hoko* are considered the 'house spirits' within the relational frame of a Ho's *mmc*. They remain spatially close to their offspring. They are neither thought of nor linguistically referred to as *bonga* (a spirit, to sacrifice, a ritual). Transgressing the social and local boundaries of the local agnatic group, *mmc*, hamlet and village, *bonga-ko* are known but more distant spirits who involve themselves in the lives of Ho people. They usually do this only when they have been called and invited to do so. Their scope of responsibility is socially more comprehensive and not restricted by kinship ties. There are tutelary and malign *bonga* spirits, female and male. Many are associated with places where they are assumed to dwell permanently. There is a long list of the spirits of various mountains, high hills, swamps, rivers, ponds, lakes, and tanks.

The boundary between the spirits of the dead of the house (*owa: goe:*, *ham hoko*) and those spirits defined as *bonga* is at times blurred, something that can be illustrated as follows: the two main tutelary spirits of any Ho village are the place spirits of its two (separate) sacred groves, the *desauli* grove and the *jayer* grove. The male spirit of the *desauli* grove is referred to as *desauli bonga*, the female spirit of the *jayer* grove as *jayer buri*. *Jayer buri* is considered to be *desauli's* wife. Of the two, *desauli* is addressed as *bonga*, which clearly anchors him notionally within the spirit world. *Jayer buri*, however, celebrated during the *ba* feast as a source of human life and in the obscene language of the *mage* feast as the primordial generative force of the community, is referred to as 'old woman' (*buri*). *Buri* is the identical term with which young children address any old woman (like me). Attaching this characterization to the female village guardian spirit lexically highlights the human qualities assigned to her and the link connecting her to the human world.

The Ho's tendency to humanize their spirit beings, as elaborated above, is further expressed by the fact that both *desauli* and *jayer buri* are indigenously thought of and ritually treated as and like ancestors (Deeney 2008: 20). Again, *jayer buri* especially is addressed in ritual by formulas identical with those used when addressing Ho forefathers and ancestors. During Ho village festivals such as *mage* and *ba*, the same type of offering that is made to the ancestors, a *suka kaluti* (a hen which has not yet laid eggs and which is of a yellowish colour spotted with brown), is made to *jayer buri*, thus classifying her in this context in one category with the dead of the house (*owa: goe:*) and assigning her the role of an original mother. *Desauli* and *jayer buri*, humanized though they may be, are in charge of a village's well-being in their role as main village guardian spirits. They are not to be confused with the mythical first two human beings who became the first parents of the Ho creation myths, Lutukum Haram and Lutukum Buria. The latter are not commemorated or offered sacrifices in Ho village festivals alongside *jayer buri*.[119]

Bonga spirits are considered relevant social actors in the Ho's secular lives, actors who are notionally ever-present and who are regularly communicated with in ritual at the individual, household, and village levels. Tutelary *bonga* spirits are those living beings with whom Ho people live in a reciprocal relationship: sacrifices are offered to them to honour and nourish or sustain them so as to reciprocally receive their continued protection. This relates to their protecting peo-

---

119 According to Deeney (2008: 19, citing the *Encyclopaedia Mundarica*/B: 387) the names of the first parents are specified in the *Munda* rite for the *ba* feast right after *jayer buri* is addressed, but not so in the Ho rites.

ple, their crops and harvests, their cattle, and all their possessions. The principal yearly celebrations such as *mage* and *ba*, at which the *diuri* presides in the name of the village community, are held in honour of the tutelary spirits. On these occasions, offerings in the villages' sacred groves are not directed to Sinbonga, who is invited as a witness to the scene, but instead to the pantheon of the Ho's protective spirits, each of whom is referred to by name and recognizable by the colour of the sacrificed animal and a separate compartment (*okowa*) it is given next to other *bonga* spirits at the site of the sacrifice.

Plate 13: *Okowa*
During the principal yearly celebrations, Ho tutelary spirits (*bonga*) are invited to assemble and eat in separate compartments (*okowa*) made for them by the *diuri* and his men (*diuritekin*) at the

foot of a sal tree (*sarjom daru*) inside the sacred grove (*desauli, jayer*). There are as many *okowa* as there are *bonga* asked to participate in the ritual. The *diuri* dabs spots of *sinduri* on the stones, with a fixed number of spots assigned to each *bonga* he is calling. The *bonga* are offered turmeric, *sinduri*, crushed *adowa chauli*, water, *rasi*, and the blood of the sacrificed animals. The heaps of rice are referred to as *punji* (wealth).

The relationship between Ho people and their spirits is an active, working relationship. It is conceptually distinct from a passive or one-way relationship of worship, adoration, fear, subordination, or submissiveness shown by the living towards the spirit world. As the living Ho are attributed agency, so are their *bonga* spirits. Ho people, often their ritual specialists such as the shaman (*dewa*) or ritual guide *(diuri)*, pose requests, expect them to be granted, and make promises (*agom, mansik*) to lure the spirits into fulfilling their demands.

Accounts from the field: how *bongako* (spirits) are involved in Ho lives

In a difficult situation, specific and specialized *bonga* spirits will be addressed individually by name to intervene in support of those who call on them, as if specialization and a division of labour among the *bonga* spirits was a matter of course. My first account is about an individual request addressed to a local mountain spirit in a rite called *bonga-nam* (by a shaman, to find out). It concerns a theft and includes a promise (*mansik*) made to the spirit.

Bonga-nam and mansik

T. K., a neighbour in Boja Sai, had left his house to pay a visit to his daughter and grandchildren. When he returned after three days, he realized that *chauli* (husked rice) was missing from the room where he had stored it inside his house. It was a sack of government rice that he was entitled to each month as someone of the category BPL (Below Poverty Line). He assumed it had been stolen. Determined to get it back, catch the thief, and have him punished, he turned to the local shaman (*dewa*). Inside the room where the rice had been stored, the *dewa*, assisted by T. K., squatted down in front of the wall facing west[120] and performed a *bonga*. The *bonga* was addressed to Manbir Pat. A *pat* is a spirit dwell-

---

120 While the village guardian spirits, the place spirits (*buru bonga*) and Sinbonga are addressed by those who call them facing east, Manbir *pat* contrastingly is addressed towards the opposite direction. This is also done during the rituals on behalf of the whole village community (*gram bonga*).

ing in a mountain. In this case the *pat* spirit was associated with Parwa Buru, a sacred mountain in Manbir and the highest in the immediate vicinity. A *pat* is usually called upon for help by a shaman in an act of divination (*bonga-nam*) to discern who is causing the trouble – in this case, who stole the rice and where to find the thief and the stolen rice. The scene was prepared by the *dewa* sprinkling water on the floor. The demand made by Manbir *pat* and mediated through the shaman was *ara: sim mansik*, a promise (*mansik*) to be made by the householder to sacrifice a red-brown (*ara:*) chicken (*sim*). While in an *agom*, which is also a promise, an earthen pot (*mandi chatu*) is put on top of the roof, in a *mansik* the pledge to sacrifice is documented by dabbing *sinduri* on the floor and the wall, as was done here. Although T. K. was convinced he had done the right thing, he was not too hopeful. "The *bonga* will only be successful if the rice has not yet been sold outside or eaten up. Then nothing can be done. Also," he added, "the *bonga* (ritual) will only be effective within the limits of the sphere of influence of Manbir *pat*. Beyond that he has no power. Irrespective of the outcome of the *bonga*, giving a *mansik* means that the sacrifice of the chicken has to be made in any case."

Plate 14: *Bonga-nam* and *mansik*
The *dewa* (shaman, right), T. K. (householder, centre), and a male witness (left) requesting the support of a mountain spirit in a case of theft.

The *bonga* lasted less than fifteen minutes. It was a simple, individual, unspectacular,[121] and down-to-earth affair at the household level, performed in a mood of severity and requiring a *dewa*'s competence, a local witness (here a member of the householder's *mmc*), water (plain: no basil, no leaves from the mango tree), *sinduri*, and T. K.'s willingness to reciprocate for Manbir Pat's services by keeping his promise. The *dewa* received a bowl of rice-beer for the occasion. I chose to recount this episode because it illustrates how as a matter of course and almost naturally Ho turn to their spirits for support in their everyday lives and recognize them as a resource – unquestioned, uncontested.

Mad pata:

This account is about a critical, sensitive situation of collective relevance at the village level in which the collectivity of the regionally known *bonga* spirits was called upon. This was about neither a favour to be asked nor a request addressed to the *bongako*, but a matter of reaching a decision about the election of a new *diuri*, a process which culminated in the spirits revealing their final say in a ritual called *mad pata:*. In this ritual of about thirty-five minutes, the spirits publicly disclosed their decision.

The context

Gulam Kondangkel was the *diuri* in the area in 2006. He was about to step down and had trained two successors to take over, which one of them did. When I returned to the field in 2008, however, the newly elected *diuri* had resigned, and in 2010, his successor was intent on also backing out in view of the requirements that he could not meet, saying that his house was too small to keep the ritual items safe from defiling gazes from outside. During all these years, whenever I returned to the field, Gulam K. kept performing as main *diuri* or assisted the main *diuri* by prompting him or feeding him the sacrificial formulas. "Only I know all our *bonga* spirits, only I know how to correctly perform the *bonga-buru* (generic term for sacrifices addressed to the spirits) in the *desauli* (sacred grove). That is why I keep being asked so often."

---

121 Dhan characterizes such "private rituals [...] concerned with the problems of the individuals rather than the community [...] business-like [...] and devoid of elaborate proceedings" (Dhan 1962: 32). They are performed any time in a situation when someone or one of his animals suffer from a particular disease, when a child is born, before building a house, or before the tiles are attached to a roof.

At the end of January (*mokor chandu:*) 2010, before fixing a date for *mage porob*, the great village festival after the harvest has been completed, the new *diuri* had to be (s)elected, and this time I was able to participate in the necessary proceedings and observe the ritual called *mad pata:*. Again, G. Kondangkel oversaw the ritual. Immediately afterwards, he, the newly elected *diuri*, and the two *munda* (secular headmen), who were also present, settled the days for the village festivals: *gau o:l, ote ili, mage porob,* and *ba porob.* All of them were to take place within four weeks or so (*mage chandu:*, January-February; *pagun chandu:*, late February-early March).

For the ritual about sixty to seventy male villagers assembled on the *akara* (meeting place, dancing ground), sitting on the ground in a circle. Each household of the village was represented that way. Among them and in a prominent position were Ch. Purty, the *munda* of Pathan Sai, and S. Kondangkel, the *munda* of Gara Sai. S. Kondangkel opened the meeting. Only a few minutes before, he had confirmed in a discussion we had on the way to the *desauli*, as he had done previously, that in Odisha the positions of *diuri* and *munda* were legally inexistent and hence irrelevant.

The ritual

First, the resigning *diuri* was asked to sit inside the circle and confirm his decision to step down, which he did briefly. No pressure was exerted; no questions were asked. Then, several men were suggested by the villagers. and those who agreed stood as candidates. Having expected to become involved in communication with the sphere of the divine, they confirmed that they had been fasting beforehand. Two boys, perhaps eight or nine years old and, due to their age, constructed as ritually pure, were the intermediaries with the divine sphere in this ritual. They stood opposite each other, holding under their armpits two split bamboo (*mad*)[122] halves in a horizontal parallel position. Throughout the ritual, the boys did not move at all. The *diuri* sat on the ground looking east and watching the bamboo halves. He had purified the space in front of him with cow dung and by sprinkling water over it. The water had been consecrated by leaves from a mango tree (*uli daru*) and some *tulsi* (basil) placed inside the vessel, the bamboo halves by *sinduri* marks applied by the *diuri*, and the boys by the *diuri* placing a

---

122 The bamboo had to be cut in the jungle immediately before the beginning of the ritual. Ho make a distinction between village bamboo (*hatu mad*) and bamboo growing in the jungle (*buru mad*). Deeney's entry describes *buru mad* as follows: "[...] not too thick, but with a very thick hole and quite strong; prob. Dendrocalamus strictus, Nees, Gramineae, B.139/15, H.139/2/1" (Deeney 2005: 56). See plate 30.

little *sinduri* and *adowa or bonga chauli* into their palms before they picked up the bamboo. The *diuri* began by addressing a long list of tutelary *buru bongako* (the local spirits of high hills near a village) by name.

Their range of influence, he said after the ritual, reaches from the Nilgiri Mountains in the southwest to Simlipal in the southeast and Manbir in the north, and they are valued as protectors (*bakai*, to fence off) against epidemics, poor harvests, and the failure of the monsoon. They are closely tied to *desauli* and considered his helping spirits. When participating in a *bonga*, the *diuri* continued, all spirits will stay until the end. They leave only when water is again sprinkled to make them leave.

Now, the *diuri* made the spirits enter the scene, one by one, by dabbing dots of *sinduri* on the ground. He dabbed five dots of *sinduri* for the prominent spirit *maran bonga*, four for his wife *pangura bonga*, five for *jayer bura*, and four for *jayera* (these being intimate ways of addressing *desauli* and his wife *jayer buri*). Fewer dots of *sinduri* were put on the ground for the spirits of the mountains, the hills, the jungle, the pools, and the tanks, in accordance with their relatively lower rank in terms of the hierarchical relations that are projected to exist among different categories of spirits. Sinbonga was also invited by name and as a witness, but he is never indicated by *sinduri*. The spirits once present were assumed to be prepared to actively announce their consent or dissent in the following manner: whenever the *diuri* called out the name of one of the candidates, it was interpreted as a sign of divine consent when the bamboo halves, though not moved by the boys, as I could clearly observe, began to entwine (*pata:*). This happened several times. If they did not interlace after the name of a candidate was uttered, it was understood as an expression of dissent. This also happened. In this way, not only the next *diuri* was elected, but also the two men (*oron sakowa*) to blow the jungle bison horns on the occasion of all village feasts, those who carry the water needed for the sacrifices to be performed at the village grove (*da: go:*), and those (*ramba rid*) entitled to grind black lentils, the coarse or *bonga* pulses whose relevance has been shown above, for the same purpose.

I was utterly stunned and speechless when I saw the bamboo halves twist and entwine several times. While I was still absorbed in my thoughts, wondering how to make sense of this,[123] the *diuri* approached me and said, "They are so powerful, our *bonga-ko*. Now you have seen with your own eyes."

---

123 I was wondering how to pass on this piece of information to my scientifically-minded husband, a physicist and mathematician and how to respond to his questions that I would not be able to answer.

In this ritual at the village level, representatives of each household symbolized the village's unity. Representatives of the spirit world and Sinbonga were present, documenting the unity of the people and their spirit world in ritual, with the two young boys mediating between the two worlds. As mentioned above, Ho people do not perform a *bonga* but rather they 'obey', 'observe', or 'respect' it (*bonga manatin*) and its inherently given rules. In other words, the *bonga-ko* obey or respect the living by attending the ritual and doing their duty, and the living obey or respect their *bonga-ko* by following the ritual accurately and by living according to Ho values and rules (*niyam*). The living and their spirits actively live out a reciprocal relationship, interrelated and sustained by their reciprocal duties.[124]

The first ethnographic account above was about a specific spirit's involvement in a Ho person's secular life. It was a request to find something that had been lost. The second account was about involving the collectivity of the locally known spirit world, including Sinbonga, in a ritualized decision-making process. By having the final say in selecting the next ritual guide and his associates (*diur-iteko*), the *bonga-ko* were assigned a prominent role in restoring order and in keeping the village's sacral life going.

The following account is about a ritual in honour of, as I will argue, Mother Earth. The ritual is one at the village level but not performed inside the village's sacred grove. It is performed by a female at around noon, in the courtyard of the *munda*'s house, and separately, at the onset of darkness, by the *diuri* at his house, both on the same day.

Ote ili

Within the cycle of the major Ho village feasts (*porobko*),[125] *ote ili* is the only one in which lexical reference is expressly made to the earth (*ote*). In the research area people construct *ote*, literally 'land' and 'field', as Mother Earth (*ote*

---

124 I have highlighted the role of the two boys in the ritual to elect the *diuri* in a lecture held at Bhubaneswar, India that became published in 2014 as an essay in *The Oriental Anthropologist*, vol. 14 (2). An extract and a photo are given in the appendix under the heading: "Concepts of Children and Childhood in Anthropology [...]".

125 For a concise and comprehensive survey see Dhan (1961:33). For an analysis of key notions coming to the fore in the course of the major village feasts see Deeney (2008: 18ff). For a description of folklore data ignoring the concept of Mother Earth see Majumdar (1950: 210). For the names and a brief characterization of the major feasts as celebrated in the research area see the entry *porob* in glossary 2.

enga), and special offerings are made to her during all village feasts (Dhan 1961: 25; Munda 2014: 11, 14). In fact, when looking into the sky at night in a contemplative mood and philosophizing about kinship relations among the planets, people confirm that they associate the earth with a mother, the sun with a father, and the moon with a mother's brother (*mamu*).

I will argue here that *ote ili* is directed exclusively to Mother Earth, honouring her after the paddy has been harvested, threshed, boiled, dried, husked, and stored. Simultaneously, ideals of abundance, reciprocity, and continuity are celebrated. I have been able to observe *ote ili* at the household and the village level five times. This account is based on the data collected in the area.

Context

Following *gau o:l* (cowshed or cattle feast), at which the cattle mother (*gau mata*) is honoured and rice-beer is fed to the cowherds performing as and transforming into cows,[126] *ote ili* is celebrated by ceremoniously feeding rice-beer to Mother Earth. The message and obligation implied in the rite of rice-beer overflowing is 'We had *diyan* abundantly this year, give us abundantly in the year to come! Give us as much rain and fertility as we give *ili* (rice-beer) to you!' *Ote ili* precedes the *mage* feast, which in *mage kaji* (obscene language spoken during the *mage* feast) linguistically emphasizes ideas of fecundity and fertility while separately stressing both the female and the male elements.

Ote enga (Mother Earth) is neither considered the spirit of a dead person nor assigned the status of a *bonga*[127] affiliated with the Ho's spirit world. Ho people say that the spirits (*rowa*) of the dead, the *bonga* spirits, and Sinbonga, though basically considered beneficial and protective, may punish the living if they are not treated with respect. Ho people, however, will not relate this capacity to punish to Mother Earth, and no shaman will discern that Mother Earth is inflicting any calamity on anyone. Thus, the reason to classify her here is her being considered to have been created by Sinbonga and given to the Ho as a gift, as the creation myth has it – in analogy to the rice mother (*baba enga*),[128] the millet

---

126 for *gau o:l* see "The spirit world of the Gau" in chapter 5 and plate 19.
127 Dhan relates to Mother Earth as "earth deity", "earth *bonga*", "mother earth", and "Mother Earth" (Dhan 1962: 25; 1961: 85). Dhan is the only one to confirm a relation between *ote ili* and Mother Earth. Deeney who has so much to say about the *concept* of rice mother, millet mother, cattle mother, does not at all mention Earth Mother. Unrelated to *ote ili* which is not his focus, Munda underpins the notional relevance of Mother Earth alongside Sinbonga (Munda 2014: 14).
128 The concept of Mother as a way of gendered personification has been referred above. As concerns the Rice-Mother, it will be further elaborated in chapter 7 in the ritual called *ked bonga*.

Plate 15: *Ote ili*
A "sacrificial action held two days before the *mage* feast. Rice-beer (*ili*) is poured into vessels so as to overflow into the earth (*ote*)" (Deeney 2005: 276).

mother (*kode enga*), the silkworm mother (*lungam enga*), and the cattle mother (from Hindi, *Gau mata*). The concept of 'mother' – symbol of fecundity and fertility – implies the idea of the living propagating more of their kind, of generations to come. It is the personification as mother of the generative power communicated by Sinbonga. In exchange for sustaining the living, the Ho's deities receive reciprocal attitudes and acts of respect. *Ote ili* is such a ritual to pay homage to Mother Earth. Beyond being a nutritious drink, *ili* (here: rice-beer; usually: *diyan*), of course, in a sociocosmic context hints at the initializing role it is assigned in the Ho's creation myth in originating mankind (*manwa*) as such.

The ritual performance of *ote ili* at the *diuri*'s house is recounted next.

The ritual

The setting for the ritual at the *diuri's* house which will be described here is prepared by the female head of the house (*owa:rini:*) purifying the courtyard (*racha:*) and the veranda (*pindigi*) with cow dung mixed with water (*guri:*) and collecting fresh leaves of the sal tree (*sarjom daru*) from the jungle and making ritual cups (*pu:*) out of them, and by the *diuri* and about fifteen men taking a ritual bath.[129] While at the *munda*'s house the ritual takes place in daylight at around noon, at the *diuri*'s house the ritual is performed only after dusk.

When it is completely dark, the *diuri* and his men assemble on the *pindigi*. Facing east, they squat down behind twenty-five leaf cups filled with oil. Invoking as many village *bonga-ko* as they have leaf cups, the men simultaneously, clearly, and loudly pronounce their sacrificial formulas.[130] The women of the house and their children watch. The core element of *ote ili* which gives the ritual its name is a matter of no more than fifteen minutes:

Gandu (low stools) are arranged in two rows in the courtyard, waiting for the men to sit down after having first addressed the spirits of the village. Separate from the men and at a ninety-degree angle, a ceremonial mat (*jaṭi*)[131] is put

---

129 The ritual character becomes visible as all the men assemble inside the house first and leave it in a queue with the *diuri* at the top. On their way to the tank and on their return, they will neither talk nor will they look back in between. If someone addresses them in the process, they are supposed not to respond.

130 This is not a natural given, but reflects an acquired qualification that the men in charge of the ritual take pride in. The *diuri* of a neighbouring hamlet was repeatedly mocked at because of his slurring the words and formulas during ritual and people were sure he was trying to hide his incompetence of recollecting things properly.

131 In the area, a *jaṭi* is made from leaves of *buru kita*, a stemless dwarf palm growing in the mountains (*buru*). A *jaṭi* is used exclusively in ritual situations. Rolled up it is kept inside the house fastened to a wall and not exposed to defiling gazes from outside. It had been one of the reasons of the former *diuri*, as elaborated above, to resign as *diuri* as this purity could not be guaranteed within his small house (see example of *mad pata:* given above). A *jaṭi* is made by women, and in the situation above used by the women only, while the men were sitting on stools.

on the floor, and the women of the house sit down on it in rows facing south. First, he *diuri* serves everybody repeatedly, men and women, by pouring rice-beer into the leaf cups, from which it overflows onto the earth. The final step is performed by the oldest woman present. She pours plenty of oil (*neem sunum*) on the heads of everybody participating in the ritual.

This ritual unites the living and the dead by the living symbolically drinking the rice-beer that is made from the rice that grows in the fields that the ancestors once cleared and that they and their forefathers have cultivated ever since. The rice-beer lavishly overflowing onto the ground is symbolically offered by the living to Mother Earth and the spirits that have revealed themselves in the process of clearing the jungle, thus uniting the living and their spirit world, which during *ote ili* takes material form in Mother Earth. These elements, especially the role of rice-beer in the origin of mankind, are conceptually linked in Ho versions, different though they may be, of their creation myths. Through oil overflowing on people's heads, hair, and faces and through *ili* overflowing onto the earth, the relations established by these linkages adopt the character of marriage relations, conjuring up ideas of abundance and the continuity of a permanently ongoing chain or circle. In this, the process and metaphor of matter overflowing resembles the rite of *baba* and other substances overflowing from the right hand of a dead person into the palms of the living related to that person within the *mmc* (see plate 20).

Sinbonga

Sinbonga has been referred to many times in this book, which, of course, makes sense, since despite great variations in Ho creation myths, he is unequivocally believed to be the creator of the universe, of all things animate and inanimate. Out of water Sinbonga is said to have created firm land, trees, plants and animals, and in the end mankind, all of whom are constructed as his seed (*hita*

Kita is a symbolically charged material. During *gonon* (bridewealth) negotiations representatives of the groom's and the bride's side will sit on two separate *jati* (*bala jati* and *haga jati*) made from *kita*.

Also, in the liminal phase of guiding the *rowa* (soul) of a deceased from the grave to the house, the female relative in charge of this duty will put the *kita* to which the *rowa* is assumed to cling to after the burial of the body, between the toes of her right foot. For this duty and purpose no other 'grass' is allowed to replace *kita*.

For *kita* as part of the substances pouring from a deceased person's right hand into the palms of members of their *mmc* see plate 20.

– a seed for propagation; a progenitor or ancestor; *jan* – a bone; the pit of a fruit; a grain, e.g., of paddy, a seed) and his possession. The "life-giving force" (Dhan 1962: 19) or "generative power" (Deeney 2008: 52) that causes seeds to grow, increase, and multiply is related to and identified and personified as Sinbonga. In Ho awareness the power to generate more of their kind has been conveyed by Sinbonga to rice and other plants, to cattle and other animals, and to human beings. Thus, Ho conceptualize Sinbonga as the *continued*, beneficial, ever-active and ever-*present* source of their sustenance. In personifying, as outlined above, *jayer buri*, the village's female guardian spirit (*bonga*), as the Ho's proto-mother and ancestress, rice as rice mother, millet as millet mother, cattle as cattle mother, and silkworms as silkworm mother, Ho people honour these gifts as aspects of Sinbonga as their origin and ultimate source, from which they have been propagated. So, even in rituals and sacrifices at the household and village level that are not primarily addressed to Sinbonga, he is always implied notionally and sometimes visibly, which can be seen if the colour of a sacrificed animal is white. After all, Ho people live on the earth and in the jungles that he created and gave to them as a gift.

Though beneficial towards the living and invisible and bodiless like the spirits of the dead of the house and the domain of the *bonga-ko*, Sinbonga's role as supreme being, creator of the universe, and generative power personified singles him out from the spirit world in which he is otherwise included.[132] When calling on Sinbonga in a *bonga* at the household level, the male head of the household in his ritual role will refer to himself as Sinbonga's subject (*ama: porja hon, ama: paiki hon* – your subject-child) and address Sinbonga in the second-person singular, which is a colloquial as well as intimate way of talking to someone, as mentioned above. This lexical closeness to Sinbonga is embedded in and respects the idiom of seniority by defining the householder as a junior (*hon* – child) in a serving attitude (*seba-sara* – to serve). Before then asking a favour of Sinbonga, the householder will make a reference to his defining characteristics, such as "*baikenam, sirjonkenam* (you have made, you have created)" (D. S. Purty, personal communication 2012). To describe these characteristics of Sinbonga, the Ho language has a number of synonyms that are used interchangeably: *upan* (to bring into being), *japan* (to create), *upan-japan* (to create, here: poetic parallels), *undub* (to give birth to).

Ho visualize Sinbonga as a grandfather. They call him *tatan* (my grandfather). The relation between a grandparent and a grandchild is a close relation-

---

132 Deeney considered replacing the denotation of Sinbonga in his dictionary (2005) from God to Creator in the next edition (personal communication).

ship among the living, in terms of kinship relations a joking relationship. Ho people see Sinbonga as someone who talks to them in their dreams. Sinbonga is not constructed as a distant God who in a kind of one-way relationship demands to be worshipped (and feared) by men, which would run counter to the all-pervading principle of reciprocity. He is assumed to expect to be commemorated and honoured in ritual. Offering the proper sacrificial formulas and a sacrifice of a white animal, thus metaphorically feeding him with the blood of a white victim (*pundi dae*), is considered such a respectful action.

Sinbonga is involved in people's secular and ritual[133] lives in a constructive way, if less so than the tutelary spirits of the village to whom the *diuri* addresses his sacrifices (*bonga-buru*) in the name of the whole village when he presides during the principal yearly celebrations such as *mage* and *ba*. But people turn to him in desperate individual as well as collective situations as a last resort, as the example of a sudden death (*tataka*) above revealed. The *bichar* (judgement) might also have resulted in offering a sacrifice to the ancestors, to *jayer buri* or *maran bonga*, in which case a *suka kaluti* (a chicken of a yellowish-brown colour that has not yet laid eggs) would always have been decided on, to *desauli*, in which case a cock of a red-brown colour would have been sacrificed, or to *nage era*, the female *bonga* spirit of the rivers, in which case a black hen would have been chosen. As in my perception those assembled were so exceptionally nervous and the situation, not excluding murder, so extremely sensitive, I assume the decision in favour of a white *kaluti* (chicken that has not yet laid eggs) addressed to Sinbonga instead of a white cock was resorted to in order to make sure that the purest possible, most respectful, and most effective sacrifice was offered. Similarly, maybe it was for the same reason, to propitiate Sinbonga most successfully, that two sexually immature, unpolluted youngsters were the appropriate choice in the example of *mad pata:* given above.

Sinbonga's generative or creative power is not limited to bringing human beings, animals, plants, and trees into being, but also, as mentioned above, natural phenomena such as rain, hail, wind, and clouds. Linguistically, Sinbonga becomes or is the force – in terms of grammar the subject or *agens* – that makes it rain, hail, etc. In Ho there is no word for "it," so sentences such as 'it rained', 'it stormed', can literally not be expressed or even thought. In addition, there are cases where what in English is expressed by intransitive verbs such as 'to be

---

133 *see* the ritual of *mad pata:* above that Sinbonga was invited to attend as witness. Without his presence the new *diuri* could not have been elected. When I plucked up courage and asked when Sinbonga was expected to arrive, the response was (perhaps triggered off by so much ignorance on my part): "Stupid (*dondo* - stupid, foolish)! He is here already!"

born' or verbs such as 'grow', 'increase' in their intransitive sense, in Ho takes the form of transitive verbs requiring a personal subject in a sentence in the active voice. In Ho, children, plants, and animals do not intransitively grow or increase, but instead someone causes them to grow or increase. In these semantic fields, Sinbonga is the personal subject. His name may be replaced by an animate personal pronoun as subject marker, but it is still Sinbonga who is notionally implied, since he is the only one who is accorded the capacity to infuse life. Considering Wittgenstein's propositions in his *Tractatus Logico-Philosophicus*[134] on the correlation between language and thought and the impossibility of thinking and perceiving the world beyond the boundaries established by language, this may be seen as a powerful statement about Sinbonga as lexically and semantically involved and ever-present in Ho people's daily lives.

Hence, Ho understand Sinbonga's creation of man and his role in giving life (*jonomkenam*, you have given life, you have caused birth) not as an abstract piece of information or a myth unrelated to their present lives. Instead, they believe that his life-giving force and capacity to make things grow is lived out in every human being's conception, growth inside a mother's womb, and birth. Ho people say that a foetus talks to Sinbonga in the womb. Moreover, it is Sinbonga to whom a baby is said to return if it should die before the naming ceremony. This is usually held between the ninth and the twenty-first day after birth and constitutes the period in which the baby is introduced to its forefathers, thus acquiring the status of a (social) person. While Sinbonga is literally conceived of as the ultimate cause for a foetus to grow inside its mother, it is the dead of the house who are assumed to en-soul the foetus during pregnancy in the course of a rite called *rowa sarub bonga* (the soul taking possession of someone), as mentioned above. In this rite Sinbonga, the spirits of the dead of the house, and the living become actively and materially interrelated in reciprocal gift exchanges during a woman's pregnancy.

Deeney phonemically distinguishes *siṅ* [ङ्] as in Siṅbonga (सिङ्‌बोंगा) from *sin* [न्] as in *singi* (सिंगि – the sun; daylight) and *siń* [ञ] (सिञ – a tree; a stalk) as in Singhbhum (सिञभुम). From a lexical perspective, these distinctions run counter to the assumptions made by Tickell (1840: 797) and Majumdar (1924: 194) in equating Sinbonga with the sun or defining him as a sun god.[135] "To refer to Sin-

---

134 "The limits of my language mean the limits of my world", Wittgenstein 2003 [1921]: 5.6.
135 This assumption indirectly holds true for Dhan, too, by her defining *chandu: homol* (moon) as a *bonga* and Sinbonga's wife. Otherwise, however, she presents Sinbonga as "omniscient, omnipotent [...] creator and master of all things animate and inanimate [...] pure, eternal, the only *bonga* who is regarded as true god" (Dhan 1962: 19,21).

bonga as a sun-god, i.e. in any way equated to the sun or considered as dwelling in the sun, is to misunderstand the Ho's attitude towards Sinbonga" (Deeney 2008: 14). In the research area, as mentioned above, people do associate the sun with a father, but they do not associate the sun with Sinbonga other than that he has created the sun, as he has created the moon and the earth. Apart from potentially being everywhere, Sinbonga is believed to live in the sky (*sirma* – sky; heaven; year) but not in the sun (*singi*).

Conclusion

The Ho's spirit world is constructed as a tripartite body of living beings that are accorded distinct competences, rights, obligations, and agency within a holistic ideational frame. Spirits are less deified or worshipped than sustained and honoured in ritual at the household and village level. They are commemorated and communicated with. They are publicly acknowledged as resources, active on demand, in Ho people's secular lives. In return for their continued protection, Sinbonga and the spirits are offered animal sacrifices. The reciprocal nature of the interrelations between the Ho and their spirit world is, of course, also true of the relationship between Ho people and Sinbonga.

Social cohesion among the living was outlined in chapter 3 with regard to the Ho's social organization. It also interrelates the living and their overall spirit world, as this chapter has illustrated. In yet another perspective, it is consolidated by ties reaching beyond the Ho's tribal horizon to their nontribal clients, as the following chapter will show.

Only once did I come across a *dewa* who in the course of a *bonga* buried some substances in the ground and exclaimed "Sinbonga" several times while pointing expressly at the sun. This *dewa*, however, came from outside the village and was not a Ho.

5 Relatedness across tribal boundaries: the Ho and their clients

Tailors and traders

"We never talk to them, because they don't talk to us," my kaki-ma *explained.*

Introduction

Sheik Imran and Sheik Abdul, the present secular head (*sadar*) of the Muslim community of Pathan Sai (plate 16, on the right) and his predecessor (left), agreed to meet for a talk, which was followed by another one two weeks later. As usual on such occasions among the Ho, a larger crowd, perhaps fifteen to twenty-five people, immediately gathered, in the Muslim case all male, listening intently, participating actively, negotiating meaning, staying on, or leaving. Others joined, young and old, children sometimes kept at a distance or hushed by their elders – trained into the principle of seniority the Muslim way.

Plate 16: The secular headmen of the Muslim community (Pathan Sai, December 2012)

https://doi.org/10.1515/9783110666199-009

This chapter is based mainly on information gained in these two basically un-structured interviews in December 2012. Consequently, the data collected are few and not acquired through participant observation. The situation was rather one of veranda ethnography, although it was a veranda in front of the village store, which was run by Sheik Abdul, and not that of the anthropologist. The eth-nographic description is necessarily thin, which shows especially in the para-graph on marriage, even if interesting enough to have been included here. The reasons why I had not initiated direct communication with the Muslim commu-nity until then and why this communication was established at a time when my main fieldwork was assumed to have been completed reflect aspects of the par-ticular kind of distanced coexistence that exists between Ho, Santal, and the Muslim category of their clients.

One of the reasons is the lack of communication and ritual interaction be-tween the tribal categories and their Muslim clients, which is significantly differ-ent from interactional patterns between Ho and Gau people, for example, the Ho's herders. Three examples are given to illustrate the point of conceptual dis-tinction.

Muslim tailors live opposite my *saki's* house in Pathan Sai, at a distance from their front door of maybe less than five metres, on the other side of the mud road dividing the Ho and the Muslim community spatially and ritually. Any-one who opened the front door could not avoid perceiving the 'other' or being perceived by 'them'. Whenever I was visiting my *saki*, I used to step over to the Muslim tailors, all of them males, who were busy working at their Singer sew-ing machines in the courtyards outside their houses. We would converse in Ho, and they did not mind my coming over to them and asking questions. However, I never observed my *saki* paying them a visit or talking to them informally. When too many Muslim children were curiously watching the scene through the open entrance door of my *saki*'s house, this door would often be closed in their faces. My *saki*, who was generally keenly interested in introducing me into the Ho uni-verse, obviously did not consider social interaction with the Muslim community part of this. She did not object to my going there, but she never commented on it. It was as if both sides kept a carefully balanced distance between each other – physically, socially, and conceptually. As the wife of the *munda* of Pathan Sai, she was surely aware of the invisible boundaries that were to be respected in this multiethnic convivium within which the Ho and their various client catego-ries cooperated in interdependent, interrelated, yet clearly separate ways. In a process of identifying with Ho views and attitudes and without my being aware of this process up to 2012, I, too, had begun to exclude them from my per-ception and focus of research.

As regards the absence of verbal interaction, I had made a similar observation with my *kaki* from Boja Sai. Whenever people met, saw, or passed by each other, the latest news and other bits of meaningful information would usually be exchanged, often without people ever halting or turning back. There is no gender differentiation in that Ho women address and respond to others as readily as men do. If, however, it happened that someone passed by someone else in silence, an unresolved conflict or social punishment was often the reason behind it.[136] The silence in passing by was always meaningful. The case with the Muslims, however, was different in that the pattern of intentional nonperception between spatially close neighbours was extended indiscriminately to the category as such. "We never talk to them, because they don't talk to us." This was all my *kaki* was prepared to explain, and she could otherwise be a very long-winded person indeed.

My Santal assistant, who had lived in the area for more than forty years, claimed to have never been on social terms with any Muslim of Pathan Sai in his life and to have never entered a Muslim house, although he knew that I knew that he went to Pathan Sai regularly to order and buy beef. Was this classified as a purely economic transaction and as such accepted behaviour – though not for his wife, who never went? When he once received a written invitation to a Muslim wedding, it was clear to him that he would not consider going: "They invite us, because they know we don't come. We don't go, because they kill cows and eat beef, and they wouldn't come to us, because they know we eat pork." He was quite averse to the project of getting in touch with the Muslims for fieldwork purposes. "Oh no, that is not possible," he said. "You cannot do that." Only when I threatened to go without him was he prepared to accompany me and even took pride in initiating the talks by getting in touch with the Muslim *sadar* of Pathan Sai. The atmosphere of the meetings was rather pleasant, and an unexpected invitation to lunch at the *sadar's* house two days later was extended and verbally accepted. The invitation was even handed around as a kind of symbolic capital, but he did not go: "We can't. They don't really mean it." So, a socially competent person's behaviour reflected and expressed the strength of the principled conceptual distance and distinction between the category of (Ho/Santal) patron and the category of client.

---

136 From an epistemological point of view this is important to know, because useful information was to be gained not only by listening to what was being said and not only by observing what was being done, but by becoming aware of what was not being said and not being done. At the same time it became obvious that these public non-reactions were socioculturally controlled and not the result of some spontaneous intrapersonal emotion such as anger or resentment, of indifference or mere coincidence.

History and the Sheik category of Muslim Sai

The Muslim community of Pathan Sai does not live in a separate hamlet, as the *kunkal* (potter) community does in the neighbouring village of Manbir. Their houses have been built close to each other in a compact area of Pathan Sai and, though spatially separate from the Ho, are visibly a constituent part of it, with a mosque in its centre. They have separate wells, their own *banda* (tank, pond), and a separate school attached to the mosque.

My informants claim to have been in the area for a long time, at least five generations. They arrived, they said without my prompting them, because the Ho needed them. They recognize the Ho as the first settlers in the area and mention the Sinku and Kondangkel *kili* in this context, which matches the information passed on to me by Ch. Purty, as narrated above and illustrated by plate 11. To the best of their knowledge, the Ho first invited the Gau (members of the Gaur or Gope caste, cowherds; see below). Before the Muslims were invited as tailors, they say, Pano had settled in the area as weavers. They characterize Pano as Hindu people who carry the title Patro and with whom Muslims have never been 'one people'. There is no professional specialization within the Muslim community, as all are tailors and traders. As traders they speak and understand Ho, Odiya, Hindi, and Santali. They speak a local form of Bengali as their mother tongue. Today, they add, they have also learned cultivation from the Ho, and some have bought land. Others refer to a First Settlement of 1906, when land "was given to us by the British and even before the British came." Now history is the topic, and many get really excited.[137] Sheik Abdul begins to lecture: "In the old days we were also Hindu. Actually, we have not migrated here; we have always been here! We are related to a dynasty in Ajmer."

These remarks are revealing for several different reasons. The information given does not make sense in the academic understanding of history: there was no settlement in 1906, and if they had the Chota Nagpur Tenancy Act of 1908 in mind, this act says that nontribals cannot acquire tribal land, and Muslims were surely not considered tribal. Moreover, my Santal assistant's comment to enlighten the ignorant anthropologist was "We call this settlement from 1906 the Permanent Settlement." Even though the Permanent Settlement of 1793 (see glossary 1) settled the conditions of revenue collection rather than the conditions of tribal land acquisition, all my informants' references to history underpinned

---

137 Whenever a lively discussion like this comes up, I am happy to have decided against a rigid questionnaire beforehand that might force me to interrupt my informants and ask them to please "stick to the point".

their appreciative assessment of things ancient and past as adding some ultimate flavour of superior authority to a statement. In other words, history is
not conceived as a scientific collection of past facts and figures structured chro-
nologically in time and space but rather as the embodiment of the principle of
seniority. As such, it offers guidance and meaning to the present.

No *Patā* in Pathan Sai!

What Ho and Santal people refer to as Pathan Sai[138] its inhabitants call Muslim
Sai. All Muslims in Pathan Sai have been Sheik all along, my informants tell me;
there is not a single Pathan around! Of their own accord and without my intervention, they characterize the Pathan as one of four Muslim *kili*. As far as status
differences are concerned, they rank the four categories Sayed, Sheik, Mongol,
and Pathan in this order. Sayed are acknowledged to have superior status, because they are the direct descendants of the Prophet. Sheik come second, followed by the Mongol, who are said to have migrated from Mongolia. Pathan of
the title Khan claim a history linking them to Rajasthan and Afghanistan. The
four categories are referred to simultaneously as *kili*, *jati*, *kandan* in Urdu, and
bongso.

Marriage and ancestors

Sheik marry Sheik; they do not marry outside their category. They are very clear
and concise about this and explain that there are two ways of finding a spouse
for a son. When two brothers have children, these can marry, or when a brother
and a sister have children, these can marry, too. The former model was preferred
in former times; nowadays, the latter is preferred. They confirm that both MBD
and FZD marriage are possible. Then Sheik Abdul, the former *sadar*, smiles
and adds, "We call a father's sister's daughter *fufu* or *hatom hon*.[139] Well, I am
married to my *fufu*." And "Our mother's sister is our *monsi*, or in Urdu, our
khala. We would never marry our *monsi's* daughter." If a Ho woman and a Muslim intend to marry, the young woman has to convert to Islam first in order to be
fully recognized. If a Muslim young woman marries a Ho, she will become an
outcast. Marriages are arranged. Runaway marriages? No! So, are these the an-

---

138 As relates to the Ho usage Deeney denotes *patā* as "a Mohammedan – (This word, originally meaning a Pathan, is used for Mohammedans in general)" (2005: 284) – which really is cor-
rect- from the Ho point of view.
139 Sheik Abdul used the Ho term *hatom hon* for FZCh to explain *fufu*.

swers that one receives on the normative plane when one interviews people instead of doing participant observation? At least in the case of the Ho, there is more to marrying than meets the normative eye.

Inside the Sheik's houses there is no *adin*. What about their ancestors' souls? They are believed to remain attached to their graves and their bodies, which are buried and not cremated. Once every year, there are readings from the Koran and prayers all through the night inside the mosque, also in commemoration of the ancestors. This special night is identified as *shab-e-barat*, and then the informants become very precise. It is the night preceding the fifteenth day of the eighth month of the Islamic lunar calendar, Sha'ban, which is the month preceding Ramadan. Following that night, all males will go to the burial ground. The ceremonies on behalf of the ancestors inside and outside the mosque are never attended by women.

The village: secular and sacred

Like their Ho and Santal neighbours, brothers in Muslim Sai live together for a lifetime – unless there is trouble. Quarrels of a secular nature are solved by a village council meeting that is referred to as *panchayat* and includes the *sadar* (secular head) and male representatives of Muslim Sai. The meeting site, equivalent to the Ho's *akara*, which is a term they know but do not use, is the *idgah*.[140] The discussion is a court-like procedure, with the quarrelling parties each accompanied by a witness and each lodging their complaints. The case is settled when the guilty party apologizes (*mafi*),[141] which will be expected and accepted. The two parties hug and embrace each other, lifting each other briefly into the air.[142] In the case of a conflict between Muslims and Ho, two of the ward members from the village council (*panchayat*) will be called in. Can they think of a situation or remember one when they decided to call the police? The adults look at each other and shake their heads: no, never ever would they do that. In their rig-

---

140 *Idgah* is an Urdu word. As far as I could ascertain back home it denotes an open-air place for public (mass) prayers used twice a year and usually situated at the outskirts of a town, settlement etc. In the case of Pathan Sai I am not aware which site was referred to as *idgah*; in any case, no religious overtones seem to have been implied.

141 Most of the discussion was done in Odiya with some Urdu, Ho or Hindi terms some of which loanwords of Persian origin sprinkled in such as *namaz* (praying five times a day); *mafi* is Hindi.

142 This lifting each other into the air could be observed in the course of Ho marriage negotiations, too, after the *gonon* (bridewealth) had successfully been agreed upon.

orous attitude towards the police the Sheik of Muslim Sai seemed quite Ho to me. They point out the democratic character of their public conflict management, stressing the equality of the structure. Similarly, they say, if a *sadar* dies, the *nahib sadar*, his assistant, will perform the former's duties only until a new *sadar* has been elected, which is by no means a hereditary affair, never! The important qualities of a man eligible to stand as a candidate? He must be married, be educated in the Koran, have a beard, and be prepared not to get involved in and interfere with spiritual matters.

Those are the responsibilities of a hierarchy of males with a *mufti* at the top and a *maulana* under him. Their activities are focussed on and restricted to the mosque. As a matter of principle, there is no cooperation between the *sadar* and the spiritual 'officials'. It is the *maulana*'s duty to regularly lead readings on Koranic topics inside the mosque and to pray as prescribed five times a day (*namaz*). The call over the mosque's powerful loudspeakers makes the existence of a Muslim community an auditory reality for every non-Muslim in the vicinity. The *maulana* of Muslim Sai, S. K. Banaullah, who participated in the discussion, was a man in his early thirties. He had completed his secondary education. There followed five years of training and qualification at a religious institution in Uttar Pradesh, which he left as a graduate. After that, he was allowed to fulfil duties in the mosque. Festivals such as *id* are celebrated by the males in the mosque, from which Ho, Santal, and members of any other community are excluded. Muslims generally do not mix with other categories socially. In that respect, they remarked that our talking together had been very interesting for them, too, as previously they had known people like me only from television. I should feel free to make use of all their information, write my book, and finish it soon!

Conclusion

As a related and constituent part of the tribal universe, the Sheik of Pathan Sai are a category of tailor and trader clients who have lived permanently in the area ever since they were invited by the Ho, whom they recognize as their tribal patrons. They trade their products at the various local markets; in the villages they offer stitching or repair services with the sewing machines fixed on the back of their bicycles. Obviously, there is no social taboo against the Sheik of Pathan Sai meeting with outsiders and discussing aspects of their secular and ritual lives. Their rootedness in history, their social organization, and their active religious life centring on the mosque contribute to maintaining strong, if distant, in any case reliable relations between clients and patrons. Some essential Ho vocabulary has been incorporated into their Bengali vernacular. There are restrictions on intermarriage between Muslims and Ho. The practice of shifting from parallel-cousin marriage to cross-cousin marriage within an overall endogamous marriage pattern is assessed as a given and accepted fact.

Weavers

"There are no relations between Ho and Pano, because there is no more weaving," a Ho said.

"Our relations to the Ho? You better ask the Ho," a Pano said.

À la recherche d'une catégorie perdue

In Santal Sai, in the very last, poorest, and southernmost house of the hamlet, a widowed Pano who is a trader in fish lives alone. In Pathan Sai, there live Ho, Sheik, and Gau but no Pano at all. In Gara Sai, there are Ho and Santal but no Pano and no SC (Scheduled Caste) people. In Boja Sai, there live only Ho, no Santal, no Pano. In Manbir, Ho and Gau live intermingled, and potters live in a separate hamlet, but there are no Pano. In Deokundi, there are Santal and three Pano households right at the end of the village. The only Pano there who had until recently been weaving cloth that Ho and Santal need for marriages had died. As he had not taught his only son, no weaving is done in the village any more. In Tendra, there are Ho and a number of Pano households, in which no one is weaving. A Pano from Patro Sai, the name by which he referred to his village, cycled from hamlet to hamlet selling textiles and blankets to the tribal villagers. He knew of no Pano who were weaving nowadays. His fellow Pano made a living as casual labourers. The Sheik elders of Pathan Sai refer to Pano as a Hindu weaving caste of former times. Nowadays, they say, they are not in touch with the Pano, as they buy the necessary material for tailoring in the larger towns.

These examples immediately reveal some basic differences between the client categories of tailors and weavers and the difficulty of doing research into the Pano category in this particular area. Can they be called clients at all under the given circumstances?

Some say that Pano more often live in Santal-dominated villages than in Ho-dominated ones. As a category, weavers are known and present in the collective consciousness, but as weavers who have stopped weaving. Ho prefer to call Pano *peyae*.[143] Knowledge about Pano was generally vague. Many knew of some village where they had heard Pano lived or where an occasional Pano was still weaving, but this information in all cases proved to be incorrect. In the Chaibasa and Lupungutu area of Jharkhand, as well, highly knowledgeable Jesuits who are engaged in long-term work among the Ho in the interior are unaware of the fate of the Pano, except for their name, given as *tanti*. As empirical beings, Pano continue to live individually in tribal villages.

In order to hear from Pano how they see their present status and their future perspectives, two villages were chosen, Deokundi and Tendra. Unfortunately, this again is a kind of veranda ethnography, though revealingly different from that concerning the Sheik.[144]

Pano on Pano: an emic account

In both villages, Pano houses are spatially integrated into the village, although at the very end of the village, where they are found on both sides of the road; from the outside they look no different from Ho houses. In both villages, a *karkom* (bed) and chairs were offered, not within the courtyards but outside on the road. People converse in Odiya but claim to have their own Pano language, too. They refer to their category by speaking synonymously of *tanti*, Pano, or Patro. Contrasting themselves to Brahmans, they clearly categorize themselves as "Sudro, Hindu, and SC." They are certain that they have lived in the region for a very long time, actually since the creation of the earth. As they are no longer able to make a living from weaving nowadays, they do work like digging ditches, working in quarries, chipping stones for road construction, serving in hotels elsewhere, helping in the fields with the harvest, and threshing other people's rice paddy (*baba*) as wage labourers (*nalatani:*). Pano houses are built with a west–east orientation and have an *adin* inside, but unlike in Ho houses, the wall separating the *adin* from the rest of the house is relatively low. The *adin* is a sacred site where the ancestors are supposed to dwell and Hindu gods and goddesses are worshipped. Whereas ancestors are primarily conceived as protective, they may turn out to be harmful if not treated correctly. Adequate ancestor worship is demanded once a year inside the house in the *adin*, to which

---

143 *peyae* – "member of a weaving caste; to become socially defiled, e.g. by child birth" (Deeney 2005: 288).

144 The results are really poor, since participant observation was not possible, since Pano households were neither known to me nor visible in the course of fieldwork, and since the few Pano informants were comparatively less talkative and less prepared to pass on information.

they refer as *shraddho*,[145] and 'outside' – this was not further specified – in a cattle ritual.[146] While in one Pano house I was allowed to enter the *adin* and take a photograph,[147] *kutum balako*, those representing the affinal side, are not entitled to do so, as I was expressly informed. In another Pano household, I was invited to enter the house but not the *adin*.

As their highest gods and goddesses, they point to a pantheon embracing Brahma, Vishnu, Shiva, Lakshmi, and Maheshwar.[148] In terms of their social organization, they have so many *kili*, they say, that it is impossible to mention them all. In any case, Dhosboyo, Boruda, Mohua, Borudi, Kheserari, and Benkura[149] are some of these. Quite of their own accord, they refer to these categories as *kili*. "We marry outside our *kili*," a Pano informant says. "I am a Dhosboyo, my marriage is an arranged one, and my wife's *kili* is Kitchinga. In our marriage ceremonies *sinduri* (vermillion) is given." Runaway marriages may happen. However, a couple is expected to elope within their caste. Both *mamu hon* (MBCh) and *hatom hon* (FZCh) marriages are accepted forms.

Death, ancestry, and affines

After death Pano's bodies will be buried in their separate burial sites, which they call *pitr-grh* (cremation ground)[150] irrespective of whether a corpse is buried or cremated. Cremations are considered the more expensive version and as such occur only rarely, but they do happen. The graves are dug into a field in such

---

145 I have spelt this term as I understood and noted it down in the field. This Odiya term, if it is Odiya, is possibly related to Hindi *sraddh* which McGregor (2011: 958) defines as "a ceremony in honour and for the benefit of deceased relatives, observed at fixed periods and on occasions of rejoicing as well as of mourning (libations and offerings of *pindas* are made to the spirits of the deceased [...])."

146 In the Santal context *uri: bonga* is a ritual at village level in the course of which the raw meat of two cattle is redistributed to the Santal households in equal shares.

147 Entering the *adin* is something quite unheard of for people from outside their *mmc* as outlined above.

148 "[...] having to do with Siva (*Mahesvara*): the name of a Saiva sect" (McGregor 2011: 801). As my Pano informant explicitly claimed Hindu identity, this reference as quoted in McGregor may make sense.

149 The spelling is derived from the pronunciation and may slightly differ, as informants sometimes found it quite irksome if they were asked to repeat certain words time and again until the anthropologist was satisfied.

150 The Odiya term is *masani*, but when asked about their *masani* our Pano informants who had claimed to speak Odiya and their Pano vernacular only, understood but then used the Hindi word *pitr-grh* in their answer.

a way that the body will lie along a north-south axis with the head to the north and the face turned towards the east, and a visible but rather inconspicuous stone is placed on top of the grave, above the head. The burial sites are outside the village boundaries and contain the corpses, while the ancestors' souls are believed to be inside the *adin*. This information contains so many – for me, unexpected – parallels to the Ho way of visualizing their ancestors, whom they conceive of as basically old and sleeping beings, that I ask about the Pano term for ancestors. A long silence and long thinking follow. Eventually, I am given the terms *mora pitor* (*mora* in Ho denotes a corpse, *pitar* or *pitr* in Hindi an ancestor) and *adhmara*, which in Hindi is defined as "half dead, or close to death" (McGregor 2011: 25). This certainly deserves more exploration in future fieldwork.

Ten days after the burial of the body, the soul will be invited into the *adin*. A well-informed elderly woman joins in the discussion and begins to explain the ritual labour to be performed by the affines. Everybody listens intently, as she proves to be such an eloquent, knowledgeable, and fluent speaker. A group consisting of male affines, *bala bundu* or *somodi*, and agnates, *haga*, goes from the deceased's house to the grave. They carry a *topa:* ("very small four-cornered basket," Deeney 2005: 388) and a slightly larger basket with *tulsi* leaves, *elaichi*, and a water pot. The grave site is purified by sprinkling water. The soul is then invited by a *bala*, maybe the deceased's son-in-law, to enter the small basket. In order to keep the soul purified, the *topa:* is put into the larger basket and covered with a *lija* (cloth). This is the *bala*'s responsibility, and this is where and when the *bala*'s responsibility ends. I am quite sure that I am privileged to witness a moment of Pano elders' indigenous knowledge being orally passed down to the younger generation. *Haga* or agnates are then handed the *topa:* with the soul in its purified state and carry it to the *adin* of the deceased's house. On their way back from the grave, the party sings, drums, and shouts *Haribol!* There is another purification procedure in front of the house, where each member of the party washes his hands and feet with turmeric water, and one of the *haga* asks the soul to enter the *adin*. Alas, I was unable to observe this being done with my own eyes; consequently, I depended on the ritual being recollected verbally. As if summing up the activities for me, the Pano woman ended by calling this ritual *keya ader bonga*. This is exactly the term that Ho people use when inviting the soul of their ancestors into their *adin*.

Conclusion

Pano or *peyae* are remembered in the area as a former category of weavers. Just like the potters, basket makers, blacksmiths, and tailors, the weavers had also contributed to a societal whole of which they were a constitutive part. They were socially embedded in a multiethnic universe in which members of tribes and castes, patrons and clients, interact in interdependent yet separate ways well beyond the economic plane. They had their identity, their distinct professional qualifications, and their duties. They mattered; they belonged. The similarities in the ritual treatment of the ancestors of both Pano and Ho are striking.

Nowadays, many make a living as unskilled wage labourers pursuing their own individual lives. They continue to live in the tribal villages, at least those who have decided to stay on. However, I argue that although they may be close neighbours spatially, they have become isolated, a category apart conceptually. In fact, whenever I enquired about Pano or *peyae*, I never encountered a patronizingly derogatory air of contempt, disdain, or scorn towards members of a low caste and their ascribed low status. I rather had the impression that as Pano have stopped performing as clients[151] in this area, they have turned into modern individuals. As such, they have begun to conceptually fall out of this multidimensional society, and people have lost interest in them; they are simply beginning to forget (about) them.

Cowherds

"There are ancient relationships between the Gau and the Ho; they are the Ho's purifiers, as they provide the necessary water in the course of a Ho wedding ceremony," the Ho munda of Pathan Sai once remarked.[152]

"You know, in ancient times Gau people were related to Brahmans like this:[153] *Brahmans were allowed to receive cooked rice (mandi) from Gau; however, Gau were not prepared to receive cooked rice from Brahmans. Will you accept cooked rice from us Gau people?" This was one of the first questions that the Gau diuri of Pathan Sai asked me.*

---

151 Due to the specific situation that I found the Pano in in that part of Mayurbhanj I am unaware of possible other duties of Pano as described in Berger (2002; 2007:127 – 132) and Niggemeyer (1964), such as performing as musicians in marriage and death rituals, as traders, as messengers, as suppliers of animals for their patrons' sacrifices.

152 Berger also relates to the Goudo's duty of fetching water, however "for the king [...] at the Dosra festival" in former times (2002: 68).

153 The conceptual link between Gau and Brahman is supported by denotations given in Gatzlaff – Hälsig and in McGregor below the entry Gaur: "1. *hist.* a particular grouping of brahman communities; 2. a particular brahman sub-community" (McGregor 2011: 280) and "sub-caste of the Brahmans; a member of such a caste" (Gatzlaff-Hälsig 2002:401; my translation).

Introduction

Gau are a vigorous and omnipresent category interrelated in many ways with the Ho in whose villages they live. Gau[154] is a term to denote a "member of the Gaur or Gope caste" (Deeney 2005: 120), who prefer to refer to themselves as Mahakud, in Jharkhand also as Mahato. There is intense social and ritual interaction between Ho and Gau. As each Gau household regularly contributes its share for joint sacrificial activities, S. Kondangkel, the Ho village head of Gara Sai, knows with certainty that there are twelve Gau households in Pathan Sai. Like the weavers and tailors, Gau also confirm that they came as they were invited by the Ho. They claim to have migrated from Gopapur in Uttar Pradesh.

Tailors (*patã*) and potters (*kunkal*) primarily become visible outside their residential areas when carrying their products to the weekly markets. Potters will push bicycles; most tailors will ride on motorbikes. But both, potters and tailors, are always on the move, in a hurry, heading towards their goals. I have never seen *kunkal* stop along the way, in the villages, in order to sell their pots right there or just for an occasional (brief) conversation. On the contrary, I was strictly advised by Ho to go all the way to the market rather than buy a pot from a *kunkal* on his way there. In that respect members of these communities are socially more distant from the Ho than the Gau. In contrast, the herders are always there, audible and visible in many ways: they move around on foot, either on their way through the village in order to collect the cattle in the morning or on their way back from the grazing ground outside the village towards evening. They are also ritually present by performing several distinct Gau festivals that contribute to constituting the Gau community as a distinct category, though not an isolated one, since there is ritual collaboration between the Gau and the Ho *diuri*.

Shivratri (Shiva's night)[155] is such an instance. During this festival, loud Hindi film music is played in honour of Shiva all through the day and the following night. Four loudspeakers installed outside the Gau *diuri*'s house, as the ritual centre of the Gau community, blare ear-piercingly loud music over the surrounding non-Gau hamlets. Although this festival is distinctly Gau and Hindu in char-

---

154 According to McGregor *gau* or *go* are "words recorded in early Hindi (Brajbhasa) literature" (2011: XII, 276, 280).

155 Ho pronounce it as *sibrateri*. It is the "name of a festival in honour of Shiva (kept, with a fast during the day and night and sometimes with observations extending over a longer period, on the 14th of the dark half of the month Phalgun)" (McGregor 2011: 951). In the Gau community of Pathan Sai this festival in 2010 lasted two days and took place on February 12th and 13th. I was invited to observe all of the ritual and enter the Gau *diuri*'s courtyard.

acter, as it is addressed to Shiva and as a procession departs from and returns to the Gau *diuri*'s house, Ho women participate in it, dancing in trance along with Gau women through the village towards the large water tank and back again. Also, the Ho's ritual guide is actively involved in choreographing the ritual process alongside the Gau *diuri*.

Plate 17: Ritual collaboration of Gau and Ho *diuri* during *shivratri*
The choreography of *shivratri* lies in the hands of the local Ho and Gau ritual guides of Pathan Sai. Here the two negotiate details of an offering made on the way to the Gau community's tank. (The Ho *diuri* is at centre left, the Gau *diuri* at centre right, and both are squatting.) February 12, 2010.

On the other hand, there are the grand yearly Ho village festivals (*porobko*), in which not only do the Gau's ritual guide (*diuri*) and (male) members of the Gau community participate, but Ho-Gau transgenerational interrelatedness is the very focus of the rituals. The information in this chapter on the Gau and their secular and ritual life was obtained by participant observation[156] and in in-

---

156 At the beginning of my fieldwork among the Ho in Manbir/ Mayurbhanj/ Odisha in 2005 my immediate neighbours were Mahakud and referred to themselves also as General (see *Prologue* in Reichel 2009). Like a number of other Mahakud households they lived right in the centre of the village on both sides of the road surrounded by Ho. It took me quite some time to become

terviews in 2010 and 2012 with the ritual guide of the Gau, Krstang Mahakud, who conversed in Odiya and Ho. According to him, however, Gau also have a language of their own. Their mother tongue is called Gop(a)ra in Odisha or Mogda[157] in Jharkhand and Bihar and is unwritten in both cases. When I talked to the Gau *diuri*, I sat on a bed, *karkom*, in the *diuri*'s courtyard. His younger brother and his wife were also present, and so was his son, to whom the responsibility of being a Gau *diuri* will be passed on one day. As in my interview with the Sheik of Pathan Sai, many other Gau people joined in, listening actively and discussing or rather negotiating issues until everybody agreed. As usual for me by now, children were curious enough to follow what was said.

Gau on Gau: an emic account

The Gau's administrative category, they told me, is OBC (Other Backward Classes). Jokingly, they added that there was an advocate who told them what to do in order to transform into members of a Scheduled Caste (SC), as there would be government money for them then. The way they are willing to manipulate these administrative terms clearly indicates that they do not identify with these alien labels. Their blacksmith, the advocate advised them, should identify himself as *lohar* instead of *bindhari*,[158] and they should call themselves *gopari* instead of *gope*. Many Gau have become landowners, *gusiya*, in the course of time, as they have been able to acquire some land which they cultivate. They primarily make their living, however, by herding the Ho's cattle, for which they are paid in kind.[159]

Where their social organization is concerned, Krstang Mahakud, the Gau's ritual guide, pointed to a number of Gau clans or *kili* such as Muteri, Tela, Bahag, Pur, and Purwa. The Gop(a)ra term for *kili* was given as *gusti*. These Gau *gusti* are related to and correspond to the following specific Ho clans: Kalundia, Kondangkel, Bage, Birua, and Purty. As so often in similar situations when

---

aware of their status as members of the Gau community and the particular kind of relationship with the Ho.

157 Berger (2002: 68) mentions the category of Mogda Goudo for Koraput in Odisha, Yorke (1976: 58) the Magadha Gowalla for Singhbhum in Jharkhand.

158 The spelling might also be *bhindani* according to how I understood people's pronunciation.

159 The Gau *diuri*'s wife showed a *dabba*, a tin holding 250 grams of *chauli*, husked rice ready to be cooked. She is entitled to this handful of rice daily and will receive it when returning the cattle in the evening. Additionally, she will be rewarded by each household whose cattle she is herding by being given 20 *poyla* of *baba*, unhusked paddy, once a year. This exchange in Ho is called *usul* ("to pay up; to pay back; Hindi 'wasul')" (Deeney 2005: 404).

talking about marriage and descent, people became really interested and eager to come up with examples from their own experience. Here it was the Gau *diuri* who explained that he is from *kili* Purwa, whereas his wife was a Pur or Birua before marriage – the identification of Pur, which is a Gau clan, with Birua, which is a Ho clan, is the *diuri*'s own formulation. Marriageable categories are MBCh (*mamu hon*) or FZCh (*hatom hon*), as well as *sango*, explained as the Gau's term for a sibling's spouse's sibling. Krstang emphasized that Gau and Ho have many things in common despite Gau feeling themselves to be Hindu rather than *adivasi*, although this might be changing gradually. Sure, Gau and Ho are not supposed to intermarry, but both marry according to the same pattern – outside their *kili/gusti* – and both assess the same categories as marriageable. Also, the Gau deities marry according to the same pattern and rules.

These marriage norms are presented and elaborated in such a matter-of-fact way that the anthropologist keeps being surprised when realizing that at the empirical level things can and will be quite different at times. To give two examples:

One day in 2010, my Ho *kaki* (mother) from Boja Sai, a member of the Kondangkel *kili*, took me along to a secondary burial at Pathan Sai in which she was involved and to which she had been invited as one of the agnates, as *haga*. As usual in Ho secondary burials, the *haga* stayed in their agnates' main house and the attached courtyard, including overnight, while temporary huts were built for the *balako/kupulko*, in anthropological terms affines, as discussed above. It is usual that *haga* take a walk around in the course of this ceremony and also walk to and interact with their in-laws outside. While following my *kaki* to the site of the temporary huts, I was introduced by her to a Ho woman who is married to a Gau. She gave her natal *kili* as Kunkal, which is in fact the name of a Ho *kili*, and she explained that she has become a member of her husband's Kondangkel *kili* after marriage, which in Gau terminology would be membership in her husband's Tela *gusti*. Their daughter was also present. She proudly claimed to be bilingual, as she can converse in Ho as well as in a mixture of Odiya and Bengali which may perhaps be identified as Gop(a)ra. On leaving the scene my *kaki* summarized, "These are our Gau *bala*."

Another time, on the occasion of *shivratri*, the major Gau festival, which took place in the courtyard of the Gau *diuri* in February 2010 two days after Ho people celebrated *mage*, one of the possessed Gau women was pointed out to me by my (Ho) *kaki* as her *iril* (HyZ) and my *hatom* (FyZ). Her daughter was introduced to me as my *sango*, my father's younger sister's daughter (FyZD),[160] and *ge-kui*

---

160 *See Sango: the semantics of an enigmatic term* in chapter 6.

(HyZD) to my *kaki*, and moreover, yet another Gau woman was addressed by my *kaki* as her *saki* or namesake.

As if to prove the point of conceptual contiguity, Ho and Gau kinship terms were also used interchangeably in the interview at the Gau *diuri*'s house. The Gau *diuri* observed that Gau had the same number and kind of kinship terms as the Ho, a powerful statement that could, however, not be verified further. Even if the statement should prove to be empirically and statistically incorrect or only partly correct (I just don't know), it does reflect metaphorically how close Gau people like to feel to their patrons in terms of worldview – the more so since this contiguity, almost identity, was formulated publicly and by the community's most senior authority, the Gau *diuri*. He and those present later came up with more examples to confirm this interrelatedness: on the occasion of a number of rituals Ho and Gau will reciprocally contribute to their respective festivals by collecting and exchanging *chauli*, preboiled and husked rice, and chicken.

Gau ancestors, women, and ritual purity

Like the Ho, the Gau bury their dead, quite amazingly for a community insisting on its specific Hindu character. Apart from the absence of cremation, on the other hand, there are significant differences between the Ho and Gau ways of burying their dead. There is a separate Gau burial site outside the village boundary, the Gau's *mosani*.[161] Inside the grave, a deceased person's head will point north and their feet south, their face will be turned to the east, and their hands will be in the *jowar* position. A dead person's bed will be broken and placed inside the grave, just like the person's valuables and food. In Kharia Sai in 2012, there were two fresh graves, protected by the shade of larger shrubs and sal trees. Two legs of the broken beds stuck out; cloth lay around. On top of the two graves were two small, empty, orange plastic containers with an image of Parvati holding a trident and inscriptions in Hindi reading *ganga jal* (water from the river Ganges) and *satyam, shivam, sundaram*.[162] In the ground at the northern end of the graves, above the deceased persons' heads, was a commemoration stone, perhaps as big as two fists. This looks like the Santal burying their dead, quite unlike the Ho treating their dead to huge flat burial stones, the famous *sasan diri*.

---

161 The Gau's complex burial ritual including the secondary burial is described in Reichel (2009).

162 Truthfulness, goodness, and beauty.

Gau ritually address their ancestors, whom they call *agur budha* in their mother tongue, in their *adin*, their *goptir*. This part of the house is separated by a wall which, however, is not as tall as that in Ho houses, but taller than in Pano houses. To the anthropologist's amazement, the Gau seem not to sense the Ho's urge to protect this sacred compartment from any defiling outsider's gaze. I was instantly invited to have a look inside the *diuri*'s house and even to take photos in the *adin* beyond the separating wall. In what they refer to as *korun* in their Gau language, I could detect the Ho's *keya ader* ceremony, a ceremony in the course of which a deceased person's soul is lured into the *adin*. There the Gau's ancestors are offered sacrificial food of sweet bread (*lad*) made from unboiled husked rice (*adowa chauli*) and rice-beer (*diyan*). I was told that only *hagako*, members of the agnatic category, are allowed to enter the *adin*, whereas *balako* or members of the affinal category are not. What about in-marrying women? Are they considered *haga* or *bala*? Well, if the marriage has been an arranged one, a wife will be considered *haga* and may enter the *adin*; in the case of a runaway marriage, she may not.[163]

Gonon or bridewealth is given to the bridal side, but no cattle as the Ho would do! The Gau give 25 rupees (the symbolic amount given in a Ho wedding is 101 rupees) and a number of *dhotis* and *sarees*, as agreed upon between the negotiating parties. A bride may bring along a bicycle, a ring, and bowls for water; however, these gifts would not be considered part of the obligatory bridewealth.

The spirit world of the Gau

Gau people believe that their origin goes back to primordial times. They refer to the *Mahabharata*. In fact, they claim divine descent and a direct relationship with Krishna. They refer to him as the protector of herdsmen. They argue that on one particular day, he became a cowherd himself. *Go, Gau, Gaur,* and *Gop:* the very denominations reflect the cowherds' linguistic and ideological embedd-

---

163 This piece of information may require further research: in the Ho case, at least, also a wife won in the course of a run-away marriage will eventually be introduced to her husband's ancestors. These are demanded to accept the new bride as the legitimate wife and invite her to enter the *adin*, allow her to touch the rice-pot and prepare the family meal inside the *adin*. A married Ho woman, however, even if 'properly' married, will not be classified as one of her husband's *haga*, as discussed above.

edness in both the profane and the sacred spheres.[164] These mythologically constructed links to Hindu gods and goddesses are re-established and re-enacted in
the Gau's distinct yearly festivals. In *shivratri*, Shiva and his associates are the
focus; in *gau o:l*, directed to both cows and cowherds, Krishna, avatar of Vishnu,
is conceptually implied. The presence of these gods, which to Ho people are *diku*
gods, may contribute to accounting for the Gau's high status, which they ascribe
to themselves and which is attributed to them by the Ho.

This on the one hand conceptually important, though perhaps on the other
hand somewhat distant, pantheon of Hindu divinities is complemented by a
number of named spirits (*bonga*) that are conceived of as residing in the fields,
hills, and mountains, in forests (*buru*), in the jungle (*bir*), and in watering holes,
ponds, rivers, and lakes in the vicinity. *Bonga* constitute the joint sacred landscape of Ho and Gau, and they are ritually addressed by both. These spirits, protective as well as malevolent, matter in the Gau's and the Ho's everyday lives –
maybe more than the distant top-level sacred beings, as they are held responsible for inflicting epidemics and diseases and also for warding off all kinds of
danger from the village, both the people and, most importantly for the Gau,
their patrons' cattle. The Gau presented their divine idiom to me as an overarch-
ing bovine idiom: just as their profane lives revolve around the cattle's well-
being, so does their divine sphere.

Some Gau informants say that Gau and Ho share a major part of their spirit
world, while others claim that it is identical. In this respect, then, it does not
come as a surprise that the Gau *diuri* performs sacrifices addressed to their
(joint) spirits at the Ho's sacrificial sites and not only at those of the Gau. Gau
do have a sacred grove (*jahera*) of their own, close to the Ho's *desauli*. Both
are right in the middle of the rice fields and serve as sacrificial sites (plate 18).

A few examples will be given to illustrate the Gau's integration into the Ho's
spirit world and their ritual interaction with their patrons' ceremonial life. There
is a ritual called *boro-bunji* (Deeney 2005: 50) which is performed about twice a
year in the Gau's *jahera* and which is addressed to *baram buri*.[165] This is a sacrifice in which the whole village is involved, including Ho and Santal. It is meant
to drive beyond the village boundary the *baram* and *juguni* spirits assumed to
live in fields, hills, and the jungle. These are malign, dwarf-like spirits who are

---

164 Whereas *go* or *gau* denote a cow, a bull, or ox (McGregor 2011: 276), *gop* translates as a cowherd, a leader of a group of cowherds, a community of cowherds; the compound *gopendra* relates to "the lord of the herdsmen [...] and a title of Krishna" (ibid.).

165 *baram* – "a dwarf (usually referring to a spirit)", (Deeney 2005: 31); *buri* – an old woman.

believed to cause epidemics and serious sickness.[166] At the core of the ritual is the well-being of cattle and villagers, and it is the Gau *diuri* who is in charge of appeasing these spirit-beings. In Hubert and Mauss's terminology, Ho and Santal constitute the sacrifiers, whereas the Gau *diuri* is the sacrificer (Hubert and Mauss 1981: 20, 22). All Ho households[167] contribute to the ritual like this: Ho boys from each Ho household, perhaps six to ten years old, take one hen that has not yet laid eggs, a *kaluti*, to the Gau's sacred grove. The head meat of the sacrificed *kaluti* will then be prepared and eaten by the Gau *diuri* and his helpers inside the *jahera*, while the body meat will be redistributed to Ho and Gau households and eaten there, thus uniting and distinguishing Ho and Gau in ritual commensality. In order to appease *baram buri* more comprehensively, once every five years a goat which is sponsored by Ho households is sacrificed in the Gau's sacred grove by the Gau *diuri*.[168]

Some Gau argued that *baram bura* (*bura* – old man) is the Gau's main male deity, residing in the Gau's sacred grove, and his wife, *baram buri*, is the main female deity, residing in the jungle. *Baram buri*, it is said, is his *mamu hon*, as *baram bura* has married his mother's brother's daughter.

Gowa bonga is a tutelary female spirit who protects the cattle and the cattle shed (*gowa* – cattle shed). Gau people conceptualize this spirit as *gau mata* or cattle mother in her role of caring for cattle and in analogy to the Ho's concept of rice mother and millet mother. To get her protection for the cattle, a sacrifice of a black hen is made inside the cattle shed on the occasion of the cattle feast ("in many parts of the Kolhan held on the *ote ili* feast preceding the *mage* feast"; Deeney 2005: 131).

During my time in the field, *gau porob* in Pathan Sai was called *ponai porob*, as it was held on January 31, 2010, at full moon (*ponai*). It was an affair of one night and one day. In my bed in Boja Sai, a few kilometres away, I could hear the deafening music, interrupted by equally loud dialogue from two different Hindi films, all through the night. *Gau porob* takes place before Ho people celebrate *mage porob* and members of the Gau community – in collaboration with Ho – perform *gau o:l*.

---

166 Revealingly, the principle of seniority in Ho country is not only operative among human beings, but also rules the spirit world: "*baram bongako* [...] are considered to be servant spirits to the *juguni* spirits." (Deeney 2005: 31).

167 I do not know about the contributions of the other communities.

168 Interestingly, for the same purpose Santal perform a cow-ritual, *uri: bonga*, once every five years, in the course of which a cow and a bullock are sacrificed. The ritual guide of the Santal (*naeke*) is in charge of the process; the Santal secular head, *majhi*, and one male from each Santal household are present.

Plate 18: Sacred groves
A Santal *jaher* (top) near Jamda, a Gau *jahera* (centre) near Tarana, and the Ho *desauli/jayer* of Pathan Sai (bottom).

Plate 19: *Gau o:l*
Cowherd boys transform into cows rollicking on all fours. As such, they drink the *diyan* which they are offered towards the end of the rite straight from the bowls, without using their hands. The heaps of *baba* (paddy rice), the lump of earth (hidden in the photo), and the twigs broken from trees growing in the jungle represent ancestors (*munurenko*), the spirits of the hills and mountains (*buru bongako*), and the spirits of the jungle (*bir bongako*) that are addressed by the Gau *diuri* in the ritual.

Gau o:l[169] is a major annual Gau feast. It is the Gau *diuri*'s duty to perform the *bonga* at the Ho *munda*'s and the Ho *diuri*'s sacrificial sites. It is the Gau *diuri* who determines the exact day for this feast, and it is the Gau patrons' obligation to prepare the necessary *diyan*. This is done by Ho women. To symbolically further confirm the ritual interrelatedness between the two categories of patron and client, all cowherds are invited and assemble in the Ho *munda*'s and the Ho *diuri*'s courtyards. The ritual begins by invoking the village spirits (*hatu bonga*). In the course of this ritual, a few cowherd boys transform into cows rollicking on all fours. As they charge other cowherds watching the scene, they are whipped, scolded, educated; it is serious and funny at the same time, and there is lots of laughter throughout this part of the ritual. All the male Gau are anointed with oil, adults and children – as cows, as cowherds. They are offered and

---

169 Deeney calls this feast *gau mara* ("a feast […] at which rice-beer is given to cow-herders", 2005:120). He defines *mara* as a Ho term to refer to a cowherd in a ritual context. Yorke describes it under this name in Yorke (1976: 56). Purty (1978) has a chapter on *gau mara*. In my area of fieldwork, I have not heard this expression. Judging from Yorke's photos there is no doubt that *gau mara* and *gau o:l* are identical.

drink plenty of *diyan* that they are served by Ho women. It is during *gau o:l* that the herders are compensated for their services and contracts renewed. *Gau o:l* is structurally important for the village as such – beyond the Gau segment – as only now may roofs and houses be repaired and fences renewed, and some say that only now may fruit from the jungle be picked.

Between January 31 and February 28, 2010, I could observe how Gau people performed six different major rituals within a period of only four weeks, some in collaboration with Ho: *gau porob, gau o:l, gowa bonga, ote ili, shivratri,* and *gram bonga*.[170]

Conclusion

Gau cowherds do not herd all the cattle of the village, as there are Ho and Santal households that either cooperate in herding each other's cattle or have sufficient children to herd their own cattle. Still, because of the ritual interaction between Ho and Gau and their time-consuming herding services, Gau people are a physically omnipresent category in and of the tribal universe. Whereas in Manbir they lived scattered among the Ho households, in differently coloured and hence externally identifiable houses, in Pathan Sai the Gau community lived in a separate ward, next to the tailors, yet closely attached to the main village.

Economic and ritual interaction between the Gau community and their tribal patrons is intense and systematic. Gau and Ho people share central values in that they share their spirit world and their understanding of the role of the spirit world in the lives of the living – despite their supreme deities being distinct and honoured in distinct ways.

---

170 *Gram bonga* has not been elaborated here. It is a Ho ritual addressed to the spirits relevant for the village (Hindi: *gram*). Male Gau people participate in the sacrifice which takes place at the Ho *munda*'s sacrificial site of Gara Sai.

6 The *saki* relation as ritual friendship

Ritual friendship and the *saki* relation will be elaborated for the region of research as yet another way of bringing about – across tribal boundaries – reliable, long-lasting relations independent of economic needs and kinship obligations. The focus is first on the academic controversy concerning the concept of ritual friendship, after which fieldwork-based anthropological studies of different types of ritual friendship in the wider region of Middle India will be addressed. This is followed in the second part of the chapter by an ethnographic report of the process of a *saki* relation coming into being, its gender implications, and its kinship and affinal linkages.

Ritual friendship

Ritual friendship has been variously referred to as ceremonial, bond, institutionalized, arranged, or formal friendship, as 'friendship', as a ritual relation, and as ritual brotherhood (Berger 2007, 2015; Desai 2010; Hardenberg 2005, 2018; Mohanty 1973–74; Pfeffer 1982, 2001, 2016; Skoda 2004, 2005). It is an analytical umbrella term to conventionally circumscribe a distinctive type of social relationship cutting across the boundaries of the categories and units discussed in this book so far. The question will be raised whether the term 'ritual friendship' for a *type* of social relationship is a suitable one if people refer indigenously to specific *kinds* of ritual friends or simply to ritual friends by specific terms instead. I will stick here with 'ritual friendship' as a working formula for the time being and will replace it later by the indigenous term when elaborating on the Ho's *saki* relation.

The concept

The study of friendship as a key social relationship, which claims Firth (1967 [1936]: 108–15) as one of its ancestors (Desai and Killick 2010: 15), has led to an anthropology of friendship (Bell and Coleman 1999; Beer 2001)[171] collecting and comparing concepts and practices of friendship, ritual friendship, and kinship in a worldwide context. A controversy has developed concerning the usefulness and value of including and indiscriminately merging social relations in a

---

171 Firth (1999) wrote the preface to Bell and Coleman's book of the same title.

https://doi.org/10.1515/9783110666199-010

diffuse category of relatedness (Carsten 2000: 3) encompassing conceptually distinct forms of friendship and kinship relations. This approach has been criticized for masking indigenously relevant boundaries and ignoring indigenously relevant distinctions and practices (Killick and Desai 2010: 5). Other criticism concerns the appropriateness of imposing the ethnocentric dichotomy of spontaneous voluntary (Western) concepts of friendship versus constrained and arranged friendship understandings upon the academic debate about this subject, as well as the question of whether to study ritual friendship within the domain of kinship and according to criteria informed by the study of kinship or as a category in its own right. The latter is the position that I will argue in favour of here.

The decision to treat ritual friendship here as a separate, though not unrelated, intra- and interethnic social category in its own right, contributing to social cohesion among the Ho and also between Ho and their various neighbouring communities, was inspired by my fieldwork, in the course of which I myself became involved in the intricacies of a ritual friendship.

Without implying that friendship and affinal and agnatic kinship represent mutually exclusive concepts and domains, I will argue in this section that ritual friendship is to be distinguished from both nonformalized friendship (*juri* – friend) and kinship ties (*haga* – 'brothers'; *bala* – affines), while borrowing elements from both. Translocal social networks created by ritual friendship relations are a well-known feature of the tribal societies[172] of Middle India. In Odisha, according to Mohanty, bond friendship "is one of the most important forms of social relationship and found amongst all categories of people" (1973–74: 130). Likewise, my Odiya-speaking informants, when asked about ritual friendship, immediately pointed out alternative terms supposed to be known in all of Odisha. They mentioned Odiya designations such as *phulo*, *dadhi*, *mito*,[173] and *sangato*. However, as I have not been able to experience and explore

---

172 The concept of 'Tribal Society' as prevailing in Middle India has been outlined above in the *Introduction*.

173 Desai (2010: 130) refers to Jay (1973) and Parry (1986) who mention *mitan* for Chhattisgarh as does Froerer (2010: 133). Jay translates this term as 'friend'. McGregor does not only give 'friend, sweetheart' for this term, but as a second denotation '*female* namesake' (2011: 815; my emphasis). This would again correlate with the gender bias of Ho *saki* and Hindi *sakhi* as outlined above.

Mita seems to relate to more than someone's 'friend' (McGregor 2011: 815). For the Aghria Skoda defines the *mita* friendship of namesakes as a "relationship between equals comparable to brothers" (2004: 171) and refers to the case of the Birhor and the Kharia among whom the *mita* friendship (of namesakes) is known, too (ibid.). S. C. Roy (1970: 262) and Parkin (1992: 206) refer to *mita* and *saki* synonymously as namesake for the Munda, the person after whom a baby is

the specificity of any of these particular relationships in the field myself, I will leave them and their underlying divergent or overlapping meanings out of consideration here.[174] I will also not consider Froerer's fieldwork-based study of children in Chhattisgarh, because her article is exclusively concerned with what she terms "ordinary friendship," which she defines as a domain of voluntary, achieved rather than ascribed, unconstrained, companionable nonkin relationships. These relationships are explicitly contrasted to "kinship and caste relations" as "the least institutionalized of all social relationships" (Froerer 2010: 134).

As a category in its own right, ritual friendship has in its various facets been explored from an anthropological perspective for Middle India and contextualized for the Gadaba of the Koraput district (Mohanty 1973–74: 130–55; Pfeffer 2001: 99–125; Berger 2007: 173–78), for the Dongria Kond of the Niamgiri Hills (Hardenberg 2005: 82–87, 199–202), for the Aghria of the Sambalpur district (Skoda 2004: 167–77; 2005: 147–64), and for the eastern region[175] of Maharashtra (Desai 2010: 114–32).

According to these scholars, different types of ritual friendship have different names and distinct, at times overlapping, qualities depending on the region. These differences concern the individual or collective nature and the sacred or profane character of ritual friendship, notions of equality and hierarchy implied in this relationship, the degree of identification between those so related, senti-

---

named. For the Ho Majumdar mentions the term *saki* in the context of the name-giving ceremony. Otherwise "the saki is a living relation, a villager or a mere friend" (1950: 187).

174 The category *sango* has been contextualized above in "How to establish a relationship". Among the Ho *sango* is known as a relationship term to refer to an individual ego's classificatory sibling's spouse's sibling representing a joking relation and indicating a category of collective marriageability or prospective spouses. Hence in the Ho's case it would be misleading to assume a semantic and denotational identity due to the linguistic resemblance of *sango* and *sangato* since a ritual friend – usually of the same sex – is a friend and by definition of ritual friendship not a potential marriage partner. Mohanty has the "bisexual" exception of *babu* for the Gadaba (1973 – 4: 148) which may lead to marriage. Otherwise, Mohanty defines a same-sex *sangat* relationship (ZHZ/ BWZy: ws) as "kin-based ritual friendship" (ibid.).

175 Desai did fieldwork in a "multi-*caste* village located in a 'tribal area'" (Desai 2010: 132; my emphasis). However, apart from this reference to a 'tribal area' Desai has chosen not to give the name(s) of the communities among whom he worked, and there is no information whether these are tribal, mixed or otherwise and whether the ethnic composition of the population matters at all in discussing ritual friendship in that region of Middle India which is the border zone between Maharashtra and Chhattisgarh. According to Skoda (2004, 2005) this matters. Skoda who did fieldwork in a mixed tribal and caste society of north-west Odisha among the Aghria reports that ritual friendship is widespread, but strictly at an inter-community level only and prohibited for Aghria at an intra-community level altogether.

ments such as love and affection implied and expressed, and the distinction between ritual friendship and fictive kinship.

Not only is ritual friendship quite generally a neglected topic in anthropology, but to my knowledge, concepts and practices of ritual friendship among the Ho in particular have so far not been explored at all. For this reason, I will first look in some detail at the various communities of Middle India in order to better understand and assess the Ho category *saki* and its classification as ritual friendship.

Ritual friendship in Middle India: collective and individual

Ritual friendship may create lasting bonds over several generations between collectives, as has been shown for the Gadaba (Pfeffer 1982, 2001; Berger 2007; Mohanty 1973–74), or between two individuals. In both of its forms it creates, at least at the normative level, an arena in which personal ties are unhampered by status distinctions, authority, and kinship entanglements. Internally, among the parties included, it is hence supposed to be safe from disputes and quarrels. Within a wider social context, though, the relationship as such may be prone to disapproval and criticism exactly because of its levelling potential, its "caste blindness and the emphasis placed on commensal dining," as Desai reports from his field (2010: 131, note 17). Ties evolving in the course of and reflected in ritual friendship may be accorded a sacred character, albeit to varying degrees, as there are different types of ritual friendship[176] and as the notions of friendship implied are highly variable. Despite this variability, it has been argued that the very concept of ritual friendship as practised in the tribal societies of Middle India, which are otherwise ordered by hierarchical considerations, promotes notions of similarity, equality, and even sameness. Moreover, the bond of ritual friendship presupposes, just as it brings about, mutual respect if not deference, solidarity, sharing, and gift-giving among those so related.

In its *collective* form, Pfeffer argues for the Gadaba that it "ties together villages as collectives" (Pfeffer 1982: 48). Mohanty confirms the collective form of Gadaba bond friendship as complementary to friendship established between two individuals (Berger 2007: 179; Mohanty 1973–74: 131, 141), to which he refers as *maitar* or *sangat*. According to him, collective *mahaprasad* bond relations are

---

176 Covering all of Odisha Skoda (2004: 167–177) gives a compact survey and comparison of relevant forms of ritual friendship such as *mahaprasad, makra, bensagar, sahi, karamdal, sahay and baula, mita, phul, ganga jal.*

a widespread feature and the most durable "group friendship," an "elaborate inter-village bond friendship at the subclan level" (Mohanty 1973 – 74: 145). The collective nature of this type of ritual friendship turns Gadaba villages so related into *mahaprasad* villages in reference and the villagers into *mahaprasad* or *moitr* in address.

Mahaprasad moitr friendship is classified as the most sacred of all forms (Mohanty 1973 – 74: 141; Skoda 2004: 168; Berger 2007: 174), unbreakable and divine, as it is sanctioned by divine witnesses in ritual (Desai 2010: 119) and, as Skoda holds for the Aghria, sealed in commensality by sharing *prasad* (leftovers from the gods, a divine gift), preferably from the Jagannath temple in Puri, with each other. Collective forms of friendship are also the focus in Berger's book. Although he refers to Mohanty's term "bond-friendship," he nowhere uses the expression of ritual friendship himself, and he renders *moitr* as "ritual relation" in his glossary (Berger 2007: 528). By focussing on the relation's key features instead of glossing it as one of friendship, he avoids ethnocentric connotations that may be evoked by the term 'friendship'.[177] He distinguishes three kinds of *moitr* relations connecting and cutting across different "segments" from within "the same (or from different) descent categories" (ibid.: 173, 175). For the Dongria, Hardenberg, who writes about "friends, 'friends' and friendship" (2005: 82, 199, 201) with and without inverted commas, that way avoiding the term 'ritual friendship' altogether, reports the collective nature of friendship relations (*tone* for males, *ade* for females) between "whole groups [though] not total clans" (ibid.: 202) and "villages and families" (ibid.: 82), though not between brothers or, as Desai adds, "other close relatives" (Desai 2010: 117). In his book, Hardenberg primarily elaborates the bonds created by individual friendship ties across the generations (Hardenberg 2005: 82 – 87), and the same is true of Desai, who does not mention the phenomenon of collective *moitr* at all.

I have not come across any collective type of ritual friendship among the Ho, which, of course, does not mean to say that it does not exist. As I was unaware of the theory of the phenomenon in its collective form at the outset of my fieldwork, it may well have escaped my perception. Moreover, I was emotionally quite overwhelmed by being offered a *saki* relation 'out of the blue' – after all, I was fresh in the field and fully ignorant of the Ho language then – and obsessed with finding out what this specific relation implied. Was it a ritual friendship? A kind of ritual or fictive kinship? A mixture of both or different from both? And how were

---

177 Similarly, I will criticize in this chapter below misleading connotations of brotherhood when characterizing the relation between ritual friends as one 'like brothers'.

we supposed or expected to behave? What follows centres around the individual form of ritual friendship.

In its *individual* form ritual friendship is forged between two hitherto unrelated same-sex individuals (two females or two males), simultaneously binding their families and thus contributing to enduring relationships between them (Skoda 2004: 168; Hardenberg 2005: 82; Desai 2010: 117). Desai speaks of a rather "chaotic system" crossing "the clean-untouchable divide" in that ritual friendships may be established between any two persons independent of otherwise socially relevant status distinctions due to their particular tribe, clan, or caste affiliations and irrespective of their specific age or economic situation at the moment of becoming ritual friends – as long as the two friends are "at a similar stage in their lives" (ibid.: 120).[178] One might as well see it the other way round: that it is the very core of the system of ritual friendship that as a complementary social resource it can afford to ignore otherwise relevant social boundaries. According to the mentioned authors, utilitarian motives, economic considerations, material concerns, or obligations of mutual assistance may not be absent, and such motives have been documented by Berger (2007: 173), Hardenberg (2005: 84), and Desai (2010: 128). However, the same authors claim that these motives do not seem to be the driving force for two people or the parents of newly born babies to initiate or formalize a relationship as ritual friends. Support, especially offered as a pure, ideal gift, may well be one of the results, since ritual friends are expected to give without any expectation of a return gift.

Though formalized, ritual friendship is not nonemotional. Desai and Pfeffer, who discuss the *moitr* "bond-brother" relation in the context of the Gadaba's secondary mortuary rites, are the most explicit about this. Both agree that the idea of love is the foundation of ritual friendship and its key characteristic, differentiating it from the bonds and constraints of kinship and affinity. Desai calls the *mahaprasad* relation a "matter of affection" (2010: 114) and its motivating force "sentiment and love, only love (*sirf prem*)" (ibid.: 126). Moreover, ritual friends' love (*prem*) for one another is assumed to increase over the course of time. *Moitr* relations, according to Pfeffer (2001: 113), are likewise noninstrumental in character and based on "mutual devotion" and "unconditional love" (ibid.: 114). Mohanty echoes this by summing up this relation as involving "noble feelings, mutual love and self-sacrifice" (Mohanty 1973–74: 148).

This emotional component of love, devotion, and esteem is complemented by *moitr* friends' dignified (speech) behaviour towards each other. When greeting each other, according to Pfeffer and Mohanty, Gadaba ritual friends bow deeply.

---

178 This may relate to the two friends' marital state or the size of their respective families.

Desai adds that in contrast to ordinary friendship, ritual friendship is distant, formal, and strictly nonjoking (Desai 2010: 128). This last component is further developed in Berger's (2007: 177) analysis of *mahaprasad* among the Gadaba into almost an avoidance relation: a high standard of hospitality is expected but can only with some difficulty be offered to visiting ritual friends at any time, he argues, so the best ritual friends would be those who live in villages far away. Hardenberg, in contrast, claims that joking (and demanding at any time) is the very essence of Dongria ritual friends' relationships and that it is joking that brings about the egalitarian bonds. Such fieldwork-based observations reveal that at the conceptual level, overlapping ideas about affection and equality in ritual friendship allow for variations at the empirical level.

Although it makes sense for analytical reasons to distinguish individual and collective forms of ritual friendship, relations subsumed within the individual category betray notions of embeddedness and collectivity reaching out beyond the two individuals. The Ho's *saki* relation may illustrate the point. It represents an individual form of ritual friendship for the reason that in my case it began by being initiated between two (female) individuals. It then immediately into a wider network by including familiar, that is, already existing social relations and eventually included our respective families. Only later did I find out that my *saki* relation with the *munda*'s wife was itself embedded within an already existing transtribal network of *saki* relations, all of which I inherited by initially becoming the *munda*'s wife's *saki*. So characterizing the *saki* relation as an individual type of ritual friendship does not mean that it is socially disinterested and isolated from the social networks within which the individuals involved lead their profane and ritual lives. In *this* respect the individual aspect is a relative rather than an absolute feature. It signifies a point of departure into a diachronic process of establishing a wider union of relations.

Desai gives a fine example of this dichotomy between the individual and the collective forms of ritual friendship in his account of how in eastern Maharashtra friendship between two men from two different *adivasi* villages led to their eldest sons becoming ritual friends (*mahaprasad*) about eighty years ago. Although the ritual friendship as such was not passed on to the two ritual friends' sons (which otherwise is a common and acknowledged practice), the closeness of the *mahaprasad* relation still favourably affected those related to the ritual friends as their respective kin or in-laws. Along the way and in the process, this relationship terminologically included the ritual friends' parents as *phul baba* and *phul dai,* and one of the ritual friends became elder brother to his ritual friend's sister. The relationship eventually included an adopted son and inseparably integrated the original two ritual friends' agnatic and affinal kin of both sexes across altogether four generations. The quality of the ritual relationship found expression in (work) cooperation, commensality, mutual support, and invitations, including sleeping at each other's houses rather than at their in-laws' places in the same village (Desai 2010: 120).

Equality, hierarchy, and identification

Ritual friends in Middle India address each other reciprocally by specific and identical terms, contributing to the symbolic manifestation of a relationship of and between equals (Skoda 2004; Berger 2007; Desai 2010; Hardenberg 2005). The taboo on the use of any other forms of address and individual names "superimposes equality in status relations" (Hardenberg 2005: 86). Whereas kinship relations are often associated with "hierarchical distinctions based on relative age, generation or status as an affine or consanguine" (Desai 2010: 12), ritual friendship aims at "total identification" (Pfeffer 2001: 113) between the ritual friends as a key characteristic of the relation. Apart from the identical address, identification and sameness[179] are emphasized by the assumption that *mahaprasad* friends' *jiban* (heart, spirit, life energy) has virtually merged in the process of transforming into ritual friends.

Relationship terms (including affinal relationship terms), which reflect an idiom of seniority, express hierarchical relations, while friendship terms do not. Moreover, the language of ritual friendship is equally and reciprocally honorific: depending on context, Ho people may address others informally by the colloquial second-person-singular personal pronoun 'you' (*am*), whereas ritual friends will address each other even in informal situations as, literally, 'you two' (*aben*), the dual honorific form of the pronoun expressing respect. At least, this was one of the first instructions I was given after the *saki* ceremony. There are no inferior or superior, no senior or junior ritual friends. When this friendship is sealed in a ritual, status distinctions and hierarchical ordering that will continue to exist outside the ritual relation become quite practically and materially annihilated in an act of commensality by exchanging food and rice-beer, by eating from the same plate, and by using identical address terms.

---

179 Desai (2010: 12) quotes Paine (1969) who following and reversing Leach's remarks on "opposed pairs" (Leach 1968:57) such as father-son or husband-wife characterizes ritual friends as persons "paired in the *same* role "(Paine 1969: 507; my emphasis) thus highlighting notions of identification and equality.

Ritual friendship and kinship

Ritual friendship has been characterized as creating a relation *like* brothers and even closer than brothers. However, it is not imagined as one *of* brothers or creating a relation *as* brothers. The distinction is important in that the lexical distinctions (like/as) hint at underlying, semantically opposed concepts of ritual friendship and kinship or brotherhood. Although ritual friendship may be interpreted as modelled on kinship patterns by including ritual friends' respective kin relations and leading to the use of kin terms to address them, it is not a kinship relation itself (nor identical with fictive kinship). Indeed, my use of affinal relationship terms for my male *saki*'s agnatic kin (in the total absence of my female *saki*'s kin) initially confused me a lot – so much so that for some time I was convinced that the *saki* relation was first and foremost some kind of a kinship rather than a ritual relation.

Ritual friendship may mean a relation *like* brothers mainly in terms of the durability and intensity or closeness of the relationship between brothers, which means it is a comparison of limited value. Also, it has been reported as a common practice for Middle India (Hardenberg 2005: 83, 84; Desai 2010: 117) that children of ritual friends can themselves become ritual friends over several generations. *If* the relation between two ritual friends were accorded an agnatic quality, the relation between their children, about to become ritual friends themselves, would be considered agnatic, too. It would be a relation between two brothers or two sisters, and, as noted above, establishing a ritual friendship relation between brothers or sisters is ruled out as a logical possibility. The example underlines the fact that ritual friendship as such at best brings about a relation *like* brothers and prohibits one *as* brothers.

Things are different at the level of ritual friends' children, though. Among the Ho, the children of ritual friends are considered brothers and sisters and are thus not eligible for marriage. A process of agnatization that is conceptually denied between ritual friends is obviously initiated and triggered among their children. While ritual friends do not fall into the category of brotherhood and kinship, their children do. For these reasons, I find the connotations of kinship and brotherhood conjured up in the context of ritual friendship misleading rather than enlightening and not really helpful.

Ritual friendship among young children is often sealed on their parents' initiative (Majumdar 1950: 187–88; Hardenberg 2005; Desai 2010). In the case of Ho and Santal this may happen soon after birth, or more precisely, after the naming ceremony, but also at a(ny) later stage. My Santal assistant, whom I frequently accompanied when his wife, my *kimin* (daughter-in-law), sent him on some errand, was constantly in search of a suitable *saki* for his roughly six-year-old son.

This was how I learnt that Santal people in that area value that social resource, too, make use of it themselves, refer to it by the identical Ho term, and conceive of it in similar ways. When eventually my assistant thought he had perhaps found a suitable boy who was roughly the same age, he actually became increasingly agitated whenever they met, which was usually on the way to the market in the next market town. Didn't I think that he behaved quite similarly to his own son, who was a very curious, creative, and funny young boy, agile, active, outgoing, communicative, and self-confident? And didn't that other boy even look a little similar? Such aspects of similarity seemed to matter a lot. In fact, he never mentioned the importance of the boy's clan, caste, or tribal affiliation in the process of deciding whether and when to get in touch with the boy's parents about his plan to initiate a *saki* relation between the two.

Clans and brother clans are effectively constructed as one and the same category, and their members are considered agnatically related *as* kin, in *ego*'s generation *as* brothers (or siblings). As marriage within a clan is prohibited, so is intermarriage with someone of a brother clan.[180] Brothers, classificatory and actual, are kin to each other. *As* brothers, *as* kin, they are subject to kinship demands and restrictions. Brothers are fully rooted in the profane domain of household management and quite generally in the economics and politics of their respective localized groups (see above). Although bonds between brothers may be among the closest of all kin relations, they are also "recognized as the most difficult to maintain successfully" (Desai 2010: 123). Their relation by necessity and definition is "interested" (ibid.), while the relation between ritual friends ideologically is not. Whereas before marriage brothers ideally work together for the good of the common undivided household, after marriage or at their father's death there is a risk of jealousy, disputes, and quarrels over issues of land and inheritance. The potentially conflictual experience of brotherhood contrasts sharply with the vision of ritual friendship as nonconflictual and free from any such concerns.

Ritual friends are unmolested and unconcerned by kinship responsibilities. Where cooperation among brothers is a kinship demand and obligation, it is ideally a matter of solidarity and commitment among ritual friends. Gifts among ritual friends should be given without expectation of return, as outlined above. Account-keeping, on the other hand, is characteristic of exchanges among close kin, which are subject to the cultural logic of reciprocal and long-term give-and-take in the classical Maussian sense.

---

180 See above the subsection "Clans, brother clans, and marriage".

It has been argued in this chapter on ritual friendship so far that ritual friends, individual as well as collective, are structurally attributed the status of equals, in a relation that sometimes has sacred connotations, as in the case of *mahaprasad* or *moitr*, and that is situated outside, independent of, and across clan, caste, and kinship boundaries. It constitutes an alternative mode of social interaction, a resource for people so related that runs complementary to relations of kinship and affinity. Ritual friendship in its distinct ways contributes to social cohesion.

Ritual friendship and fictive kinship

I will briefly discuss here the concept of fictive kinship in order to show that ritual friendship should be conceptually conflated neither with kinship nor with fictive kinship.

According to Desai (2010) and Mohanty (1973–74), fictive kinship has been considered synonymous with ritual friendship in various ways in literature on ritual friendship. This is a position I do not share. I rather follow Barnard and Good (1984: 150), who contrast fictive and figurative kinship. According to these authors, fictive or adoptive kinship tends to be "*jurally* recognized as such, in certain *legal* contexts" (my emphasis), while figurative or ritual kinship creates relationships such as godparenthood that are "complementary to kinship rather than an essential part of it" (ibid.), but expressed in the idiom of kinship. An example of fictive kinship in this understanding is Skoda's elaboration of "*Dharma* Kinship" (2004: 172). As a type of intergroup relation among the Aghria and their neighbouring communities and as a category apart from ritual friendship, it is the adoption of daughters and sisters into families with sons only. By creating sibling relationships between (*dharma*) brothers and (*dharma*) sisters *as* brothers and sisters, it creates fictive or adoptive kinship relations among persons of *different* sex, who by definition are excluded from becoming ritual friends. For this reason, at least at the level of analysis, it does not make sense to confuse or conflate ritual friendship and fictive kinship. Unlike kinship relations and like ritual friendship, though, *dharma* relations are accorded a sacred character. Despite being reckoned as siblings, however, *dharma* sisters do not live with the family into which they have been adopted, nor are they eligible to inherit.

To conclude: ritual friendship in fact deserves to be treated as a category in its own right, as postulated in the introduction to this chapter. Independent of persons' clan, caste, or kinship affiliations, ethnic background, gender, or age, different types of bond friendship link different units of the segmentary societies of Middle India in individual or collective ways, thus contributing to creating a landscape of nonhierarchical relatedness. This landscape is inhabited by ritual friends constructed as equal individuals or by whole groups and villages linked by long-term relations based on mutual respect, affection, and commitment. The honorific character of the relation is reflected in the use of honorific language, as shown above. Social cohesion comes structurally alive at contrasting yet complementary layers: the same people who experience and live out the value of similarity or sameness as implied in the ideology of ritual friendship experience and live out the idea and value of hierarchical distinctions as expressed in the idiom of seniority and implied in the ideology of kinship relations.

The *saki* relation

When the news was broken to me that my elder brother had died in Germany on February 7, 2016, while I was in the field in Tarana, Mayurbhanj, Odisha, I decided to tell S. Purty the next day. We had agreed to inform each other about important family matters ten years before. She reacted in a way that according to my European perception or understanding was a mixture of sadness, reflectiveness, empathy, respect, awe, distance, and at the same time nonphysical closeness. No touching, no embracing. No anger, no wailing, no tears. She referred to my elder brother as her elder brother (bauṅ – my elder brother). She sat down contemplating the course of the world (duku – suffering, any kind of grief, whether physical or emotional) and sharing memories of her ten brothers and sisters, none of whom was still alive. "I wish I was a butterfly, or maybe better a bird," she said. "Then I could fly to your country. I could join you in diri dulsunum (secondary funerary rites) and meet our relatives (hagako) and in-laws (balako) there." I promised to cover my brother's body back home with the white linen that she would buy and give me the following day. She insisted on supplying me with plenty of chauli (husked rice) that had been harvested from her family's own fields. She requested that I share it at home with my family (owa:renko, people of the house). She also told me to let the deceased have his share the Ho way: his head bedded on rice, his hands filled with it, and his body spread all over with it. In Ho country this is a reciprocal gesture towards the dead, to feed them on their awesome journey. Before that, rice flows from the dead person's right hand down into the palms of several haga relatives, beginning with the spouse and including those related to the deceased as grandchildren.

S. Purty responded to the news as friends in Ho country do. S. Purty is my *saki*.

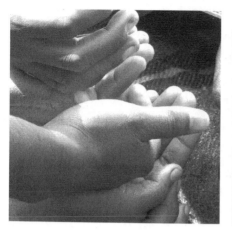

Plate 20: Gift exchanges between the dead and the living
Sustaining the dead and sustaining the living in a continuous circle of give-and-take, thus blurring the onlookers' and the participants' perception of who is feeding whom, grains of paddy, goat droppings, black lentils, and grass are made to continuously overflow from the dead person's right hand into the palms of *haga* below and back again. The rite (*baba tela-ura*) begins with the surviving spouse opening his or her hand and includes those related to the dead as grandchildren (*jaitadi*).
In marriage negotiations goat droppings (*merom ii:*) represent cattle; black, coarse lentils (*ramba*) represent buffaloes; *kita* is the grass-like material from the jungle from which ritual mats (*jaṭi*) are made to accommodate agnates and affines; and paddy (*baba*) is an indigenous currency representing wealth, abundance, plenty, and ancestral links.

Saki: the lexical field

Saki literally means "witness; namesake; to name after another" (Deeney 2005: 324). As outlined above, Ho people use *saki* to refer to a particular single person in address and reference, usually a living individual. They do not use it as an abstract noun or a generic term or to refer to the relationship as such. If the possibility of a semantic correspondence between *saki* (Ho) and *sakhi* (Hindi) is allowed, the gendered specificity of the relationship as I experienced it in the field is relevant, since in Hindi *sakhi* is defined as "*female* friend, companion" (Gatzlaff-Hälsig 2002: 1304; my emphasis) and as "a woman's or girl's *female* friend" (McGregor 2011: 972; my emphasis). An element of the sacred and an "attitude of religious devotion" are emphasized in compounds that have *sakhi* as one of their elements (ibid.), and I have referred above to the connotations of the sacred implied in the *mahaprasad* relation.

None of my informants has ever mentioned a linguistic link between Hindi and Ho in that respect. Instead, they treated the *saki* relation as an indigenous, non-*diku* (i. e., non-Hindu), tribal concept. They used the expression as if it was a term of Ho origin.

Fieldwork and the *saki* relation[181]

In the preceding section on "Ritual friendship," in which I addressed ritual relations that have been documented for Odisha, some conceptual parallels and distinctions have already been outlined.

This section is about the *saki* relation as I experienced it in the field, relating Ho, Santal, and members of nontribal communities in the region of research and beyond. In fact, it was to a considerable extent the *saki* relation or rather two *saki* persons who initiated my husband and I[182] into the field, who by formalizing our relation as *saki* authorized and paved the way for our being "there," who contributed to our becoming social beings, and who proved constant and reliable sources of valuable information and authentication.

Alongside other sincere and serious informants, Ch. Purty, as village headman (*munda*), was centrally involved in the rituals at village level[183] and in all kinds of village affairs. As *munda* he kept being asked by fellow villagers to act as witness and mediator.[184] As our *saki* he committed himself to taking us along and introducing us into Ho culture. He really took his time to make us understand. While others understandably grew impatient, became confused, or got lost, as I did myself,[185] when working through the genealogical relations of their

---

181 The *saki* relation has already been referred to in this book many times touching upon the following aspects: the relation as one between two females, potentially parallel meanings of the terms *saki* (Ho) and *sakhi* (Hindi), areas of similarity between two *saki* persons, honorific speech behaviour among *saki*, intentional search and parental initiative to provide a *saki* for their children, *saki* relations between Ho, Santal, and Gau, denotational and connotational aspects of a *saki* relation, *saki* versus kinship/ *haga* relations, *saki* and *mita* as synonyms (see Skoda 2004: 171– 172).
182 My husband stayed with me for four months in 2006 when the *saki* relation was established.
183 Plate 3 shows him (far right) lying on the ground honouring Mother Earth during *mage porob* along with the ritual guide (*diuri*) of Pathan Sai (far left).
184 An example of this has been given above in *disum amin – disum nam*.
185 The relations within our *saki's mandi chaturenko* have been published in Reichel 2009. It took me several times to take notes, sort them out, make sense of them and get them confirmed. While working through the generations along the grid as Barnard/ Good suggest (29 – 32) I got

individual pedigrees and generations of remembered forebears and living off-spring, he kept going on. As the villagers trusted him, so did we. More than that, apart from being ignorant of the rights and duties implied in a *saki* relation, we, of course, felt privileged for having been offered a ritual relation and so soon. After all, we were given the chance to experience and simultaneously ob-serve the relation from the inside. It became more than an abstract matter of theory. We became part *of* it. We greatly profited from it in practical ways that came as a one-sided gift-giving that was "not predicated upon calculation of a return" (Desai 2010: 115). When towards the end of our first stay in the region some villagers made clear demands for the few things that we had acquired in the course of doing fieldwork and began to publicly divide them up among each other, our *saki* helped us out of this situation before it could become awk-ward, as we did not want to cause discord among the villagers by giving to some and leaving others empty-handed. The day before we left, he came with an ox-cart, loaded it with everything, including us and our bicycles, walked the two oxen and their load on foot all the way back to his home a few kilometres away, invited us to sleep at his house, promised to keep our property until our return the following year, and without our being aware of it, ordered a jeep for the next day to take us smoothly to where we would catch a bus.

Establishing the *saki* relation

In hindsight, things developed really fast and kept taking us by surprise. To make it easier to understand the context within which the *saki* relation was es-tablished, I will first outline the setting.

For the purpose of doing fieldwork, my husband and I had been offered an empty house in Manbir[186] by the villagers there. It was a proper *diku* site for *diku* people like us: a former single-room government *pakka* (made of bricks) building that had fallen into disuse, an alien architectural object. We were informed that

---

really lost one day. I kept to the two questions: how do you address her/him (*chikaiyaben*)? How does she/he address you (*chikabenae:*)? Although my *saki* was clearly interested in all kinship related matters and willing to cooperate I observed how tiring this procedure was for him (and how confusing for me). So, when again I asked my *saki* the first question, I received an answer and almost mechanically made a note of it. But when I asked the second question, my *saki* looked puzzled and eventually said: "Don't be silly, he can't even talk!" Without realizing the generational depth, I had enquired about my *saki*'s FFBSSSS, a grandchild of the (-2) generation that had been born just a few months before.
186 For Manbir and all other sites referred to here, see map 4.

the villagers had met and discussed the matter first, before they finally agreed to have us stay among them and in this house. This took a few days. We remained outside the decision-making process, and I have no knowledge of who was included. But news may have spread announcing our arrival, since on the second day after our moving in, to our bewilderment, G. Hansda from Santal Sai, a hamlet of the village of Tarana and itself adjacent to the village of Manbir, banged on the door, introduced himself, and advertised himself as our assistant. He turned out to be fluent in Santali, Ho, Hindi, Odiya, and English (and he has knowledge of Pali and Sanskrit as well). As at that time we were utterly averbal in the Ho language, we welcomed the possibility of collaborating with someone who was rooted locally, married, and the father of two sons. He agreed to accompany us in and introduce us to the area and the people. *Disum amin–disum nam*, the story of the Holon Purty clan choosing the site of Tarana and settling there given in chapter 4, is a result of the three of us walking through the rice fields and meeting Ch. Purty in the courtyard of a Ho house. As *munda*, Ch. Purty had been asked to negotiate a mortgage of some consequence for a fellow villager. When this job was done, everyone stayed on while he narrated the Ho's history of their settlement in the area. Like everyone else, we were sitting on string cots (*karkom*) and listening, and G. Hansda was translating. This happened on our fifth day in the field, at seven o'clock in the morning. It was our first encounter with Ch. Purty. Of course, we had not met him just by chance, as G. Hansda knew of his appointment in the morning and had arranged for us to meet him there, just as it was no coincidence that he suggested a few days later that we walk along the embankments between the harvested rice fields from Santal Sai to the *munda*'s house in Pathan Sai. I thoroughly enjoyed these early morning walks as a protected and safe way of learning about the field and gaining vital orientation. When we had almost reached the *munda*'s house, approaching it from the back, a woman was there cleaning the yard. She was the *munda*'s wife, perhaps in her sixties, as was I. Not at all taken aback at seeing us and obviously on familiar terms with G. Hansda, but without any form of greeting, to my surprise, though she was not at all unfriendly, she looked at me closely, pointed first at her grey hair and then at my even greyer hair, inquired whether I was a Ho, and suggested that she and I become *saki* to each other. This was all. She turned around and continued her work. Her husband was not at home. We left.

The entire encounter had been a matter of a few minutes. In my field diary it occupied one or two lines. The meaning and content of the *saki* relation would unfold to me only gradually, by living it out in the course of fieldwork. However, the very practical and immediate next things to be *done* were announced in a first talk (*jagar*) with the *munda* and his wife soon afterwards.

We were invited to their house as soon as my *saki* had prepared a pot of rice-beer (*diyan*), which during the cold season usually takes four days. This time we were greeted the Ho way.[187] While my *saki* kept ladling out the rice-beer into steel glasses for all of us, my male *saki* did most of the talking, with an air of dignified serenity, as follows:

My (female) *saki* and I would address each other from now on as *saki*, and as *saki* only. Because of that, her husband and my husband had instantaneously become related as *saki*. From this it followed that the *munda* and I became related as *saki*, just as the *munda*'s wife and my husband became *saki* to each other. All four of us would reciprocally address each other from now on as *saki*, as all of us would be equally and reciprocally *saki* to each other.[188] There would be two ceremonies to seal the *saki* relation. He invited us to the first ceremony to be held at his house, following which it would be our turn to host the second ceremony at our place. We were informed, and in great earnest, that on the occasion of the first ceremony it was our duty to bring along *saki lija:* (*li*ja: – cloth), meaning a new *saree*[189] and a (white) *dhoti* for our *saki*. We should also bring along two necklaces that we were asked to make from the blossoms of flowers of our choice. They would provide the rest – whatever the rest was.[190] He would an-

---

187 The proper Ho way of greeting (*jowar*) is always preceded by being offered with both hands a jar filled with water (*muta*). On receiving it one lifts the jar with both hands a little upwards while simultaneously slightly bowing one 's head. Outside every Ho house there is a fixed site for the purpose of washing one 's hands and feet (*abun*) by pouring water from the jar. One then takes a sip of water into the palm of the right hand (*jom ti*), gurgles with it and spits out the water. With a similar gesture as before the jar is handed back. The hostess, usually the female head of the house (*owa:rini:*) will then empty the jar completely, refill it and hand it over to the next guest. Only after everybody has completed this procedure, one will either be asked to sit down in more informal situations. In more formal situations the greeting ceremony (*jowar*) is done with always two people greeting each other individually. In this, a guest will stand opposite the host both holding their hands in front of their chest, palms and fingers put together with the fingertips pointing downwards. Guest and host will then approach each other until their fingertips touch, after which the balls of the thumb are lifted upwards and the heads are bent downwards.

188 I have above mentioned the linguistic phenomenon 'poetic parallel' which is the Ho way of doubling the meaning when expressing parallel content in parallel phrases and in parallel syntax. As the example above shows, this speech behaviour is not restricted to ritual situations.

189 When I showed my neighbours, members of the category General in Manbir the saree that I had bought without mentioning the *saki* ceremony they immediately sensed the context and responded: 'so this is a Sambalpuri saree as *saki lija:*?' This shows that not only the *saki* relation as such is known among other non-Ho communities in the area, but that they as non-Ho refer to certain elements of the relation by identical Ho terms.

190 At that time, I was not yet able to ask questions in the Ho language myself, our male *saki* did not tell us and our assistant refused to translate as he considered himself competent to announce the exact day of the first ceremony to us in due time. G. Hansda was requested to come along, too, and act as witness to the scene.[191] We were told that from now on, their door was open to us anytime. We were asked to learn the Ho language fast.

This get-together was the first of its kind for the four persons who would constitute the core of the *saki* relation. The encounter was formal in character, instructional, and strictly nonexplanatory in terms of content. As for the *sango* relation, which has been described above as coming into being through an almost fixed chronology of known steps within an acknowledged frame, we were given here a script, a matrix of the technicalities to be followed, of what was to be *done* in a known order. Almost as an aside, we were made to understand that the *saki* relationship was not meant as an addition of two distinct relationships, as a case of my *saki* and me on the one hand as separate from, opposed to, or complementary to my husband and his *saki* on the other. Elegantly and almost inconspicuously, the *saki* relation as one between same-sex individuals included another pair of *saki* of the opposite gender, affiliated, as we concluded, by similar age, marital status, and the existence of children and grandchildren.[192]

The *saki* relation within the web of kinship

After that and before the *saki* relationship was sealed in the upcoming ceremonies, we met frequently, usually at the *munda* and his wife's house, usually at dawn or in the later evening, after the cultivation work was done.

Our two *saki* lived by themselves in a modest house. Their only son had died young, and their only daughter was married in Kuleibira, a village at a distance of less than two hours' walk on foot. She visited frequently with her children. Our male *saki*'s three younger brothers lived with their families in houses adjacent to our *saki*'s, sharing the same courtyard, as is usual in Ho country and has been pointed out already. While we sat with our *saki*, their nephews and nieces,

---

swer the questions himself. In this initial situation a structurally problematic aspect of assistanceship during fieldwork became visible that would continue to cause irritations and has been well documented elsewhere (Berger et al. 2009).

191 This does not seem to have been a pragmatic decision only in order to provide us with a competent translator as I had initially thought. Only some time later did I find out that my *(female) saki* and G. Hansda's *kaki* (FyBW) had become *saki* when they were young.

192 For the relevance of the aspect of similarity in bringing about a ritual relation see above Desai (2010: 118) and Skoda (2004: 170).

reciprocally and irrespective of gender *gungu*[193] (yBCh, ms, or HyBCh, ws) to them and *gungu* to us, were often around listening, leaving, and returning. Time and again, the brothers or their wives also came around for a short chat and a good laugh, which started instantly as soon as they spotted me.[194] From the very beginning, the developing *saki* relation was no socially isolated affair. It could not have been, because wherever and whenever we met, others were there, and continuously so. When we met at our *saki*'s house, these others were usually, but not only, their kin living there. They addressed us and introduced their children to us in quite a matter-of-fact way, just as we were told how to address them. The *saki* relation was never meant as or limited to an indoor activity but was displayed in public as a value to be proud of. That way we learned about kinship relations, about how they are lived, and about linkages between *saki* and kinship relations.

It turned out that the agnatic and affinal kin of my male *saki* became included in the *saki* relationship as follows: while my husband was obviously becoming identified with his *saki*, the *munda*, I was becoming identified with my *saki*, the *munda*'s wife. In other words, whoever was agnatic kin to my male *saki* became agnatic kin to my husband and affinal kin to me. This was reflected in the relationship terms. Whereas my husband and his *saki* addressed the *munda*'s younger brothers as *undi*, my *saki* and I addressed them as HyB or *iril*. Both of us were *hili* (eBW) to them. The *hili-iril* relation is a joking relation, and the rela-

---

193 *Gungu* in the sense of parallel nephews and nieces here refers to my male *saki*'s younger brothers' children. Otherwise, in the same generation, a woman's/wife's younger sisters' children are also addressed as *gungu*, but not others that according to the German nomenclature are classified as nephews and nieces such as a man's sisters' children (*ge-kowa, ge-kui*) or his elder brothers' children (*hon-sed, hon-era*) or a woman's brothers' children (*homon-kowa, homon-kui*) or her elder sisters' children (*hon-kowa, hon-era*).

My *saki*'s daughter's six children, their grandchildren, on the other hand were *jai-hon* to them and us, while we were *jiyan* ('my' grandmother) or *tatan* ('my' grandfather) to them. Although analytically one generation below the level of *gungu* as elaborated above, empirically the distinction in relationship terminology of almost equally old children was hard for me to remember since it presupposed that I was able to exactly trace the relation between any child and my *saki*/ me.

194 This kind of roaring laughter was exclusively directed towards me and not towards my husband (who reacted with a note of jealousy). It was immediately to be sensed that there was some cultural reasoning and social grounding to it in that the immediacy of the response when seeing me was confidently, selectively, and regularly acted out. Not denying the possibility of a 'genuine' display of 'spontaneity' among two individuals, this extrovert behaviour seemed to reveal something else; see also Vitebsky (1993: 9), who treats feelings – given the sociocultural context of his fieldwork among the Sora – not as innate, but as socially informed exterior states and hence observable.

tion I had with the *munda*'s brothers – different from that of my husband, who was elder brother (*bau*) to them – was my introduction into the sphere and character of joking relationships, which until then I had encountered only in my anthropology textbooks, and rather disbelievingly so. On the other hand, while my *saki* and I by identification addressed her husband's younger brothers' wives as *undi-kui* and had joking relations with their husbands (*iril-hili*), my husband inherited by identification his *saki*'s respect or avoidance relations with his younger brothers' wives (*kimin–bau-honyar*).

Plate 21: *Saki* and kin relations
The web of agnatic and affinal kin relations is given as a gift along with the *saki* relation. In generations -1 and -2 this invites relations such as *gungu*, *ge-kowa*, *ge-kui*, *homon*, *boronja*, *kowa-hon*, *kui-hon*, *hon-kui*, *hon-kowa*, *hon-era*, *hon-sed*, *jai-kowa*, and *jai-kui*.

The avoidance between a man and his younger brothers' wives is such that not even the address term *kimin* may be expressed or spoken aloud. It created some difficulty when we worked through my male *saki*'s pedigree and he was unable to pronounce the proper relationship term for his yBW. He whispered something into my assistant's ear and spelt the term into his palm with his right finger instead. It also showed in a situation that was already outlined above, when my husband and I were offered *jowar* (formal welcome) by the same physical person in different ways: while my *undi-kui* (HyBW) gave me a warm smile and used both hands to put the pot of water (*muta*) into my two hands for me to wash my hands and feet (*abun*), the same pot, refilled, was put on the floor for my husband in front of his feet, while his *kimin* (yBW) carefully avoided any eye contact.

Distinctions in identification

Ours is a case of two married couples, the *saki* relation hence embracing four persons of mixed gender. The fact that we address each other reciprocally by one identical term seems to linguistically suggest notions of identification and equality that also bridge gender distinctions. As I will argue and illustrate in this section, however, the idea of identification takes material form in different ways and at various layers within and beyond the *saki* relation. The examples given in this paragraph will show that the degree of identification is context- and gender-sensitive. It is not identical for and among the four *saki* persons.

In my interpretation, my structural identification with my female *saki* is more complete and comprehensive than that with my male *saki*. The preceding section argued that the kinship relations – agnatic and affinal – that I have adopted are those of my female *saki*, while I conceive of my male *saki*'s kinship relations exclusively through my female *saki*'s perspective. Thus, whereas notions of near total identification, equality, and sameness are lived out by and, as my fieldwork data show, restricted to the two persons related as same-sex *saki*, hierarchical distinctions are relevant to and continue to exist outside the very same *saki* structures, as soon as the *saki* relations become accommodated within existing and affiliated kinship relations, as the mentioned examples of my husband and I being grouped into opposite relationships have shown.

Gender distinctions within the *saki* relation keep being relevant. The gender divide may even contribute to and intensify the notion of total identification between same-sex *saki* within a wider ritual context. Two examples will illustrate this.

The first example concerns my participation in a secondary burial (*diri dulsunum*) at Pathan Sai in 2006, relevant aspects of which in terms of my relative *haga*-ness have already been outlined above to illustrate the cultural fluidity of the category *haga*. I argued there that due to being related to my same-sex *saki*, I was invited to participate and classified as *haga* as she was, though with a difference. The analysis of the same situation is continued here, focussing on how gender distinctions and the issue of graded identification played a role. The complex of raw-food exchanges, the technicalities of which was given above in chapter 3, was an utterly female affair. Moreover, the rite of *jom-mid* (to become one by eating) in the course of which the food I cooked was exchanged, fed, and eaten was a strictly female affair. As plate 22 shows, it was one including my *saki*, the widow, and myself. As we performed the rite, different roles were distinguished and became "paired" (Desai 2010: 12). By acting out my role as hostess in the temporary hut that was assigned to my husband and me, serving the food that I had prepared to the widow and me without eating herself, my *saki* underpinned the total identification between herself and me as *saki* in *this* situation. To underpin the total identification in *this* situation between the widow and me, the two of us – as two differently distinguished *haga* persons – were made one in a rite of the same name (*jom-mid*). The total identification between my *saki* and the widow was underpinned by the two of them being related as members of the same *kili*, being ranked as full *haga*, staying in the same (main) house together, and jointly visiting and attending to their spatially separated *bala*.

This example of *saki* and *haga* (and *bala*) participating in a secondary burial is another instance of how the *saki* relation may immediately become relationally accommodated within a specific socioritual context and of how the same-sex *saki* relation between two women may become dominant to the exclusion of the opposite-sex *saki* relation in a specific situation. My husband, invited as I was to the funerary rites and present as I was, played no part *in this*. He remained the observer (and photographer) and hence outside – as did his *saki*, who remained physically absent throughout this part of the proceedings. While identification between my *saki* and me was obtained by both of us being included in the process of food exchanges and commensality, identification between my husband and his *saki* took the opposite form and was obtained by their being excluded from this phase of the funerary rites.

Plate 22: Distinctions in identification: *haga* and *saki*
Jom-mid (ritual commensality: to 'become one' in eating) at *diri dulsunum* (secondary burial) in Pathan Sai, February 2006. My *saki* (left) is preparing plates from sal leaves after serving the food that I had prepared to the deceased's widow (centre) and me (right). We exchanged the food three times before we started to eat.

The second example will illustrate the reverse situation. It relates to *ba porob* (flower festival), the great annual village festival in February/March, following *mage porob* in the month before. March 1, 2010, was the day after the full moon in Pathan Sai. I was able to observe the rituals performed by the *diuri* and his men from outside the sacred grove (*desauli*) without any difficulty. Many hours later, my male *saki* and one of his younger brothers, my *iril*, arrived. I followed them into the *desauli* when it had become too dark to take photographs without using the flash, when the ritual chanting had come to an end and the sacrificing was done. Over the years, I had become used to my assistant not turning up for an appointment at all or only doing so many hours later, and this could also easily happen with my *saki*, who as *munda* had to live up to many fellow villagers' expectations. In the long run, this being left to myself over and over again strengthened my independence and autonomy, and I became accustomed to being allowed to observe almost anything at any time and to participate in almost everything (or so I thought), accompanied or unaccompanied. I had translated the concept of identification implied in the *saki* relation into the unlimited and unhampered possibility of being allowed – as the *alter ego* of my two *saki* – to be (physically present) wherever and whenever they were (physically present). Depending on context and situation, however, the value of identification could become graded, a matter of degrees, as the continuation will show.

This time, joining my (male) *saki* and his younger brother, felt quite different, almost uncomfortable and hostile. I wondered whether I had unduly trespassed onto the sacred site. My presence before had been tolerated for many hours, but all of that time I had been outside the *desauli*. The moment came when the sacrificial meat was ready to be eaten. It was wrapped up in sal leaves (*sarjom sakam*). It had been prepared by the *diuri* and his men (*diuriteko*), roasted over fires made from logs of a sal tree, and eventually distributed to the various parties sitting in individual sacrificial sites enclosed by rings of stones to mark their boundaries, just as the *desauli* as such was circled by stones. The atmosphere became increasingly tense after the distribution of the meat. My *saki* and his brother were quarrelling, complaining about the *diuri*'s portion being larger than theirs, about their portions being too small, the *diuri*'s too big, and where were their two other brothers? Something seemed to be awfully wrong – and then I was instructed: didn't I see that the sacrificial animal was a *kowa ni:* (a male living being), a *boda* (an uncastrated he-goat), all the people in attendance were *kowako* (males), the *bonga* meat was *kowa jilu* (male meat), it was prepared by *kowako* (men) for *kowako* (men), hence it would be eaten by *kowako* (men) and not by *kuiko* (women)? It was true: while otherwise rituals are publicly performed and observed from outside the sacred grove by women and children of both sexes over long periods of time, for *ba porob* there were no more females around as soon as it got dark. They had been there before, and they would be back again later to dance all through the night. But I had not realized. Should I leave? My *saki* seemed deeply relieved that I asked of my own accord and that he therefore did not have to send me off. My husband, on the other hand, had been invited four years previously to stay on and participate until late at night (while I had not been present at all). So the restriction for me four years later came unexpectedly.

It does make cultural sense, however, in several respects: on the one hand, it opened my eyes to the predominantly male character of some, not all, phases of *ba porob*. This is the Ho's hunting festival, which includes a shooting competition in the course of which the excellence of the most competent person to hit a target with bow and arrow during complete darkness is rewarded by decorating him behind his ears with the white flowers of the sal tree picked from the *desauli*.

It also revealed, on the other hand, that a *bonga* performed at village level and witnessed by the highest (male) god, Sinbonga, also ideologically ranks highest. In a *bonga* at village level, the *desauli* is the sacred meeting ground where representatives of the Ho are the ritual hosts of their gods and spirit world, who are not only invited but assumed to physically be present and who hence must be addressed in a state of utmost purity. Representatives chosen for this purpose, such as the ritual guide and his men (*diuritekin*), enjoy divine recognition, as the gods have publicly signalled consent to their election in a specific ritual called *mad pata:* (entwining of bamboo). Hence they are trusted to have mastery of the rules and norms of purity. These have not been defined by humans for humans. They are conceived to be rooted in Ho mythology, anchored in Ho elders' memory, and demanded and in fact dictated by the rituals themselves. As I have mentioned several times, Ho people do not say that a *bonga* is performed but that they 'obey a ritual's orders' (*bongareya: kaji manatin*), thus attributing ontological qualities to rituals. Of course, the supra-individual sociocosmic values that are celebrated in the course of their great village festivals outrank considerations of a *saki* relation that is man-made and acted out at an individual level.

Lastly, this restriction taught me a lesson about the mentioned different degrees of identification. As I became fully identified with my (female) *saki* by being excluded from parts of the ritual and the sacrificial food, my husband had become fully identified with his male *saki* by being included all of the time, inside the *desauli*, and by being offered a share of the sacrificial meat.

As I have experienced the *saki* relation, it is complemented by social relations surrounding it horizontally and vertically. It is conceptualized as one that transgresses generational, local, and tribal boundaries in time. While I was initially convinced that being offered the *saki* relation meant that something quite exceptional, exclusive, and unique was happening to me in a given locality in the present, I eventually came to realize that there was a historical and trans-local dimension structurally attached to the *saki* relation and in which it was embedded. Unaware of it at the time, I had become linked to a web of *saki* relations that had existed for at least two generations among Ho and Santal people and stretched as far as Tatanagar, affording me *saki* relations there. The process of inclusion is a continuous one. Even after so many years, I am not sure whether I can represent it in its entirety.

Doing the *saki* relation: Content and meaning

Over the course of time, my husband and I were constructed by our *saki* into Ho whose ancestors had left Ho country long ago, who had forgotten all about their cultural background, and who had eventually come back to learn from scratch. In our country we would be the only Ho. There would not be any other Ho. We were introduced as such when we accompanied especially our male *saki* on his numerous errands. There is a gate between us and them, he would say, but so far only these two have gone through. As our *saki* it was his duty (*man* – literally: 'respect'), pleasure (*suku*), and pride (*mamaran*), he continued, to reintroduce us into Ho culture (*Ho-reya: kaji* – matters of/related to the Ho). It was as if he was "grafting," in R. Hertz's understanding (1960: 77), the *saki* relation onto us, as if the *saki* relationship itself was an accomplishment – for him and for us – transforming us into more accomplished, more complete social beings. He explained to others (without ever having talked to us about it) that our lack of knowledge concerning Ho language and culture was due to our lack of interaction. That way the idea was conveyed that Ho culture is what you *do*,[195] that it is something that is *done*, and that learning (about) and acquiring Ho culture is the result of *doing* it, of *practicing* it *along with others*. The *saki* relation itself is a way of *being* and *doing* rather than of *having*. It then makes sense that in the first encounter, when we expected to be introduced to the concept of the *saki* relation, its content and meaning, we were instead told what to *do* and in what order.

In the process of our Ho identity construction as we interpreted it, it was my male *saki* who set the agenda for our necessary education and did most of the instructional work (*jagar paiti*). It was he who decided that we needed to

---

195 Verardo (2003b: 40) similarly refers to a ritual that she translates as "Doing the clan ceremony".

know about the history of the Purty settlement, because it was to become our history, and the Holon Purty myth of origin (see chapter 4), because it was to become our myth of origin. We learnt about Ho ancestry and the social dimension of death. The Holon Purty *miyad mandi chaturenko* was unfolded to us in several time-consuming sittings (Reichel 2009). We learnt about Ho cosmology, which he liked to enlarge upon, along with his brothers and other fellow villagers, in the evenings when the cultivation work was done for the day, and about the Ho version of the creation of the world. He was continuously involved in marriage and *gonon* (bridewealth) negotiations which he was asked to moderate and mediate. Indeed, marriage and the value of affinal ties were a constant topic of some relevance. The section "Diachronic affinity and synchronic affinal symmetry" below is about Ho marriage patterns and the sub-section "Diachronic affinity: the case of our *saki*" is our *saki*'s matrimonial relations over three generations.

Doing the *saki* relation: the female sphere

As was confirmed later in the course of the *saki* ceremonies, this ritual relation constitutes ties of mutual support in all circumstances of life. While my male *saki* introduced us into the Ho's universe by explaining to us what he considered essential for us to know, his wife introduced me into the female sphere by doing things with me. Contrary to Ho understandings of hospitality, according to which a guest is spoiled with food, drink, friendliness, and company, she did not mind me participating once in a while in larger parts of her days and her everyday duties, as she became aware that I considered this a form of much-appreciated female support by my *saki*. Examples of this will be given next. Her husband was usually outside cultivating the fields during these times, weeding and irrigating the gardens in collaboration with his brothers, or seeing to their goats in the jungle.

This was how I learned how to mix fresh cow dung (*guri:*)[196] and water, achieve the appropriate consistency, and treat the floor of the courtyard with it, thus hardening its surface and turning its colour a light grey when dry. This is a procedure that is done on all festive occasions. In most Ho households it is also done daily early in the morning, as a norm by women, after the courtyard has been cleaned of animal excrement (*ii:*) and the dried leaves that have come

---

196 Ho make a distinction between fresh cowdung (*guri:*) which is collected from one's own or one's neighbours' cattle and dried out cow-dung (*gŭsi*) which is used for burning if people are short of firewood.

down during the night. All of this organic waste is carried to the fields and dumped there. Here also the ashes (*toroe:*) from the various fireplaces (*chula*)[197] are discarded, while the remaining embers (*hangar*) that are still glowing are kept in a tile (*ketcho:*). They will be re-used to ignite a new fire (*sengel tin*) or passed on to the (female) head of the household (*owa:rini:*) next door. This female neighbour is often addressed and related as *aji* (HeBW; eZ) or *undi-kui* (HyBW; yZ).[198] In the case of my *saki*, embers are continually exchanged between her and her husband's three younger brothers' wives, who are classified as her *undi-kui* and to whom she is *aji*, both of which are terms that are otherwise used to address one's 'own' younger or older sister.

I also learned to carry water from the well on my head (*dupil*) without spilling it, which I began to be able to do only when I succeeded in placing the vessel (*dikshi*) precisely on the crown of my head. But I was never strong enough to lift the *dikshi* or take it down on my own, which, however, was never a problem, since Ho women are used to reciprocally supporting each other without much ado. In their honour it should be mentioned, though, that they often leave the well carrying two pots of water, and larger ones, too: one on their heads and one on one hip while balancing a baby on the other.

The dark, aubergine-coloured liquid obtained by boiling bark from a particular kind of tree for hours was applied inside the house almost daily to polish and dye the mud floor that my *saki* decorated by hand with flower motifs, as is the responsibility and skill of the female head of the household (*owa:rini:*). I have seen handdrawn graphic or abstract patterns on the floors of a number of Ho houses, most of them showing some idiosyncratic features. Only once did I have the opportunity to recognize almost identical patterns in two different houses, one of which turned out to be a woman's parental home, and the other her home after having married virilocally into another village.[199] This was no coincidence, as the daughter confirmed that she had copied her mother's pattern.

---

197 *Chula* is the Hindi term that is used by both Ho and Santal in the area replacing the Ho term *itu:l/ itu:lad*. *Chula* are usually hand-made by women, often in a combination of bricks and mud.
198 The category spsibsp that Pfeffer characterizes as 'quasi-consanguines' (2004: 393), its members' non-affinal status and their partial terminological identification with the category *haga* (brothers) has been introduced above. It will be analysed below in the third part of this chapter.

The reference here to the category spsibsp is not meant as a digression, but rather as an illustration of how participatory involvement beyond the more distant observation may lead during fieldwork to perceiving hidden cultural structures by doing simple everyday chores.
199 Unfortunately, I could not observe in other houses if there is a regularity in a daughter on marriage continuing (her mother's floor) patterns and if that allowed to assume other cultural continuities.

The roofed (unpatterned) veranda (*pindigi*) running around Ho houses was also regularly attended to and darkened by applying the same liquid several times a week.

While women usually went to the jungle in larger groups, announcing their willingness to take me along, many times, though not always, I was left waiting in vain when they vanished all of a sudden without informing me and were gone. I was glad, then, when my *saki* took me to collect firewood (*san*), leaves (*sakam*), berries, edible herbs, tubers, and mushrooms (*a:-ud*), all of which we carried home on our heads, while I was never able safely to rope up the load with vines from the jungle myself. More than once, I collapsed, losing my balance and sending the load on my head tumbling down. My *saki*, however, as well as all the other women I accompanied, walked quickly and elegantly, almost running, with a twist of their hips to counterbalance their heavy loads when moving across level ground. They needed to slow down on their risky way down steep hills in order not to lose their footing on the slippery rocks while often simultaneously gossiping, joking, laughing, and singing.

Quite independent of the *saki* relation, all of the above activities are female duties done in every Ho household, but they are not done independent of the social and hierarchical kin relations within the household. As a rule, they will not be done by just any female living in a household. In my assistant's house, his wife was constructed as my daughter-in-law (*kimin*), and I reciprocally as her mother-in-law (*hanar*), and as such, in terms of seniority, I was excluded from doing these activities as a matter of cultural principle. In contrast, in another household in which I was hierarchically included as (classificatory) daughter (*mai*) to my mother (*kaki, kaki-ma*), who was biologically younger than I was, I was expected and taught to do all these activities and a lot more. The *saki* relation, as elaborated above, constitutes yet another social space beyond kinship relations, as it is about mutual support between equals. In this understanding, it was conceptually possible for my *saki* to have me assist her with these activities, as they contributed to my becoming a more qualified female Ho person. Still, she did so rather hesitantly and reluctantly.

But she was quite intent on my acquiring the skill of making rice flour (*holon*), as she was determined to teach me how to produce rice-beer (*diyan*). In the context of rice-beer production, *holon* is needed to prepare *ranu* (see plate 23). I would learn in the course of time that rice-related activities are ideologically charged in Ho country and that rice is more than a mere food item providing a certain number of calories. It attains its social meaning in a given sociocultural context. Rice is conceptually linked to people's forebears and ancestry, and serving rice-beer to guests (*kupulko*) is at the core of Ho understandings of hospitality (*em-ched*), a key value in their society. In fact, as elaborated above, members of the Purty clan were (among) the first to settle in the area and make the land cultivable to grow rice there, and the Holon Purty in particular represent one of the forms rice takes in their (subclan) name. This, however, was never given to me as a (functionalist) reason why our joint production of rice flour (*holon*) seemed so important to my *saki*.

Helping to produce rice flour (*holon*) initially scared me a lot for fear of crushing my *saki*'s hands in the process of husking paddy by hand (*run*). The process ran as follows: while my *saki* used both hands to shuffle small portions of initially unhusked paddy (*baba*) and after that of the husked uncooked rice (*chauli*) in a hole in the ground (*sel*), I pulverized the grains into flour by crushing them with a wooden husking pole (*tuku*) attached to the wooden post (*kuntu*) of a mechanical apparatus (*denki*) that I pushed up and down in a fast and regular rhythm with one of my feet. I needed to stand in an upright position in perfect balance on one foot while moving the wooden post with the other foot. This required complete bodily control. The procedure as such was quite efficient, as an iron ring (*sambe*) was fastened around the bottom of the husking pole, but potentially quite risky in the event that I was unable to fully manage the appropriate rhythm. Then the pole might crash down early with my *saki*'s hands still in the hole. To my amazement, I realized that not only does the activity presuppose rapport, but the act of doing it contributed to striking up closer rapport. When we had finished, she would get up and say in a matter-of-fact way to those who were watching, *runkedalin* (she and I were husking paddy to prepare *chauli*), making use of the dual first-person exclusive pronoun (*alin* – we, s/he and I, not you).

Where the process of preparing rice-beer (*diyan*) is concerned, I was not only introduced into the technicalities of producing a locally popular brew but also acquired some elementary knowledge from scratch, from collecting herbs and tubers in the jungle for the fermentation process to serving the product to guests in the manner culturally required, which I was asked to demonstrate in the course of the second *saki* ceremony. A few words on rice-beer (*diyan*) and the process of preparing rice-beer under my *saki*'s supervision follow.

Plate 23: Participant observation – participatory research
My *saki* supervises the process of my preparing small balls of *ranu* ('yeast'), which will be covered with straw and left to dry.

Rice-beer is a social drink that is present in most Ho households all of the time. For some, it replaces food in the daytime, when in the midst of physically strenuous cultivation work under a scorching hot sun people feel like a nourishing and refreshing drink and a good chat during a break in the shade. Children help themselves to a large portion before going to school in the morning, long before the time for breakfast at around ten in the morning (*basiyam singi*), when the cattle have been attended to, the house and courtyard have been cleaned, water has been fetched from the well, and the dishes from the evening meal have been washed (see the prologue). Rice-beer is usually homemade and served or drunk at home, preferably in the company of kin and friends. On market days a bowl (*bela*) or two of *diyan* – sold for two rupees in 2006, for five in 2016 – is welcome, and the stalls under whose leafy roofs rice-beer is offered at the market or next to the road on the way home from the market are usually crowded sites where people meet, socialize, and exchange the latest news. Rice-beer is consumed by males, females, and children alike. Only women carry rice-beer in big pots, often two on top of each other, to the market on their heads, just as only women carry things on their heads in general among the Ho, and only women sell rice-beer in the market. Also, preparing rice-beer for secular purposes at home (*owa: diyan* – rice-beer of/for the house) and for ritual occasions at the household level – such as the *saki* ceremony – is a purely female activity, as well as one that presupposes that the females involved are fully married and entitled to enter the *adin*, where the tools to prepare *diyan* are kept.

Things are different when it comes to performing rituals at village level. On the eve of the grand village festivals *mage porob*, *ba porob*, and *jomnama porob*, it is men – after having fasted and taken a ritual bath – who prepare ritual rice-beer brew (*ti chipa rasi*) at the household level, where it is first offered to Sinbonga[200] before being consumed by members of the household only, in honour of the dead of the house. On the occasions of *mage porob* (with its obvious notions of fertility and fecundity) and of *ba porob*, however, the ritual rice-beer to be offered to Sinbonga at the *desauli* (sacred grove) and consumed there by the *diuri* and his men (*diuriteko*) is prepared by the *diuri*'s wife. To do so in a pure state, she – along with the other women of the household – will fast, too, take a bath (*oran*), and wash her hair by applying a special greyish soil (*naka hasa*) as a kind of shampoo, (something regularly done in a ritual context, also by men). On their return home, the women will leave their hair down (plate 24). It is assumed that the deities and spirits of the village that are invited to witness the process of preparing ritual rice-beer will settle down in the women's unbound hair as long as they are present. This class of ritual rice-beer – here prepared by women, in other contexts by men – is referred to as *bonga diyan*. To my knowledge there are altogether four categories of rice-beer that Ho people distinguish depending on the sociocultural context, determined by when, where, and by whom the rice-beer is drunk, to whom it is offered or addressed, and by whom it is prepared.[201]

---

200 This has been described in the subsection *Mmc – a metaphor of commensality* and illustrated by plate 7.

201 Apart from *owa: diyan* and *bonga diyan dili diyan* (*dili* – to set a date; to invite) and *harom diyan* are classified differently although both are drunk in the various stages in the process of two people getting married. When representatives of the groom's party go to the bride's (father's) village in order to set a date for the wedding *dili diyan* is taken along to the girl's place. It is made from contributions by the villagers of the groom's village. Contrasting to this *diyan* which is brought from outside, *harom diyan* is made from contributions by villagers within a given village (*harom* – "a contribution or collection, esp. in kind; to collect this [...]" (Deeney 2005: 144).

Plate 24: Return from the ritual bath
Before preparing *bonga diyan* on the occasion of *mage porob*, the *diuri*'s wife takes a ritual bath and returns home with her hair down. She is at the head of the queue, followed by her *hanar* (HM), who is looking after her *jaitadi* (grandchild), and the other women of the house.

Ranu – similar to yeast in its effect – is a fermentation agent that transforms cooked rice kept in a pot filled with water into rice-beer. It is a mixture of rice flour (*holon*), dried herbs, and roots that have been collected in the jungle. Neither my *saki* nor anybody else wanted to say too much about the exact plant names, the composition, and the measurements of the ingredients, as if to keep that constituent of rice-beer a secret. Even Deeney, who is otherwise very precise, does not give Ho or botanical names of the plants that *ranu* is made from. His classification of *ranu* as medicine was, however, echoed by many Ho and Santal who refused to label *diyan*, and especially *rasi*, which is the liquid skimmed off the top of the fermented rice-beer brew, an intoxicating alcoholic drink. Components of *ranu*[202] may be from the *pithraj daru* tree (the rohituka tree in English or *Aphanamixis polystachya* by its botanical name) and the

---

[202] "*ranu* – ferment for rice-beer [...]; yeast for bread; medicine; [...]; to bring a woman under the influence of a man by giving her some (aphrodisiac) medicine" (Deeney 2005: 305). The botanical names of the components were given to me by G. Hansda (see chapter 7, 2nd portrait), whose father seemed to have had a good knowledge of the medicinal use of regional plants and a book about it. His son claimed to have inherited this knowledge and the book which was kept with other family valuables in the *bhitar*, the Santali word for their ancestral abode.

false pareira brava root (*Cissampelos pareira*). These are considered medicinal plants and valued for their manifold medicinal uses in contemporary homeopathy and in ayurvedic medicine, although homeopathy and ayurvedic medicine were never mentioned to me by my informants. Deeney's attributing aphrodisiac qualities to *ranu* is also interesting, as *satavari* (Sanskrit) or *Asparagus racemosus* (the botanical name for wild or Indian asparagus) is said to be a component of *ranu* and have exactly this effect.

Small balls of *ranu* are formed by mixing the chopped ingredients with water and rice flour. After a process of drying amid rice straw, as shown in plate 23, the *ranu* balls are crushed and mixed with rice (*kosowa chauli*) which has previously been boiled and spread on a mat (*jaṭi*) in order to cool down. The fire to boil the rice for rice-beer is fed by rice straw only, which requires some expertise to keep the fire going continuously. The mixture then is put back into an earthen pot (*mandi chatu*). Cold water from the well is added to cover the rice mixture and start the process of fermentation. The pot is covered with leaves from the sal tree (*sarjom daru*). The mixture is not stirred or touched as it ferments, but time and again the leaves are lifted, and the tiny bubbles that rise to the surface are scrutinized and listened to as they produce much-awaited soft gurgling sounds. Depending on the outside temperature, the process of fermentation will take three to four days (*diyan unupudre* or *unupud*). The procedure reminded me a lot of the stages of preparing sourdough for baking bread at home, including the very specific, quite intense smell of flour during fermentation.

The *saki* ceremonies

Invitation

While we were dancing on the *akara* (the dancing ground, the meeting place of males for the political discussion of village affairs and decision making, the arena for a cockfight) on February 14, 2006, the first day of *mage porob* in Pathan Sai, we were requested (*asi*) by the *munda* to see him at his house. There we were informed that the first of the two *saki* ceremonies was to be held at ten o'clock in the morning two days later, which coincided with the last day of *mage porob*, also called *mage moroe:* (sour, acid) or *har* (to chase) *mage*. Apart from *saki-lija* and flower garlands, we were asked to also bring salt and rice (*chauli*). Our assistant, his wife, and his *wife's female* relatives from Bagrai Sai (see map 5) were invited, too. At that point I was already beginning to wonder whether there was a female bias implied in the *saki* relation or whether there was another objective, rational reason that I did not understand.

Purifying the scene for the first ceremony

In the morning of the day of the ceremony, I was decorated by my assistant's wife, who dressed me up in a newly bought *saree* (I had been clearly told that only a new one would be appropriate for the occasion), forced both my hands through some of her own bangles, and applied *sinduri* to my hair as married Santal women do, saying this is an utterly tribal thing to do, and most married Ho women refuse to do, saying this is no tribal thing at all. She was unhappy about my short haircut, as she unsuccessfully tried to produce some kind of a knot, as married Santal and Ho women have. She, her relatives, and her children would set off only four hours later.

When my husband and I arrived, both *saki* – as usual before inviting us to wash hands and feet (*abun*) – ignored us completely. They leisurely and with full concentration continued the work they were busy doing inside the house, while outside in the courtyard two helpers were busy cutting up a goat (*merom*) for the ceremony into three equal parts. One part was meant to be prepared by my husband and me (it would eventually be taken over by our assistant's wife), another part by our *saki* (it would eventually be taken over by our *saki*'s daughter). Both parties would work separately but side by side, using the two cooking sites facing east in our *saki*'s open kitchen. The third part would be cooked by my (female) *saki* inside the *adin* (secluded, sacred part of the kitchen), which neither I nor my husband was allowed to enter, as already noted. The *adin*, in fact, was the site that strongly relativized any illusion of complete identification.

After quite some time, our *saki* finished their work. As it turned out, it had been preparatory work for the *saki* ceremony. Goats and rabbits sheltered by the same roof as our *saki* were attended to, and the room where they were usually kept (*merom kulae owa:* – goats' and rabbits' house) was emptied completely and purified by carefully plastering the floor with a mixture of cow dung and water (*guri: sapa*). This was to become the room where the ritual meal (*jommid*) would take place later. The floor in the reception area, usually the living-cum-sleeping room, had been beautified by applying the dark dye obtained by boiling bark, as explained above. Two earthen pots with *diyan* and *rasi* were placed in a corner of this room, where first the ritual exchange of rice-beer (*nui-mid*) and later the third part of the *saki* ceremony were to take place. Here two mats (*jaṭi*) were spread out. Already at this point it becomes obvious – when taking all these preparations into consideration – that there is more to the *saki* ceremony in its entirety than those inconspicuous five minutes that Desai (2010: 118) cuts it down to in his description.

Eventually, my *saki* offered us water from a brass pot (*muta, lota*) to wash our hands and feet (*abun*). This welcoming process – from *abun* to *jowar* – was done as described above, only that this time the pot was lifted upwards as far as the forehead before being handed over and received back. Not only was the procedure done to my husband and myself, but *I* was taught how to do it reciprocally to our two *saki*. Immediately after this purification procedure and as if caused by it, a metamorphosis took place in our *saki*'s attentiveness and posture. Whereas upon arriving we were practically treated as physically not present, and the atmosphere was still slightly distanced and casual when we were offered the jar (*lota*) for *abun*, our *saki*'s behaviour completely and visibly changed for the *jowar* procedure and after. Such sudden changes, literally from one extreme to the other, kept taking me by surprise. They are, however, most usual among Ho people. In the case of death, for example, visiting females are used to beginning their intense ritual wailing with 'authentic' tears flowing down their cheeks the very instant they enter the deceased's compound – and they are able to stop crying just as instantaneously as soon as they leave (see "Prologue" in Reichel 2009).

There was nothing casual or informal about it when we performed the *jowar* at last. This was done in the friendliest and most elegant Ho manner, with our heads visibly bent towards our *saki* standing opposite us while simultaneously sucking in breath and saliva noisily.

Nui-mid [203]

After that we were invited to sit down on a ritual mat (*jaṭi*),[204] with the same-sex *saki* opposite each other and next to us our assistant and another male person from Manbir he had asked to come along as one more witness, who was classified as *haga* to us. It fell to our *saki*'s daughter to serve all of us during the ceremony. Thus from the beginning of the day the ritual relation was embedded in a frame of kinship or *haga*-ness to formalize it. While the four *saki* were first served *rasi* (rice liquor) in cups (*pu:*) made from sal leaves by my *saki*, the others were served *diyan* (rice-beer), all taken from earthen pots covered with sal leaves. In the second round we were all served *diyan*, but only the four *saki* performed the *nui-mid* (to become one by drinking) ritual as follows: my husband and his *saki* each drank a sip from their respective glasses, then each one poured a sip into the other one's glass to fill it up. This was repeated once. After the second exchange of *diyan*, both drained their glasses. My *saki* and I did basically the same, except that we exchanged the *diyan* three times before drinking it up,

---

203 (*nu* – to drink; *mid* – one; to become one; to have sexual intercourse)

204 A ritual mat is exclusively used in ritual situations. Otherwise it is rolled up and hung to the wall. A mat (*jaṭi*) used in ritual is usually made from *buru kita*, which is a dwarf palm tree growing locally in the hills and mountains (*buru*).

something which, as pointed out above, may be seen as yet another expression of the female bias implied in the *saki* relation. The witnesses were served *diyan*, but they did not participate in any exchange procedure.

Our male *saki*'s younger brothers and their wives and children suddenly turned up during the *nui-mid* ritual, which itself lasts only as long as it takes to drink a glass of *rasi* and a bowl of *diyan*. These relatives became included in the process of establishing the *saki* relation, as they were introduced to us – and we to them – by giving the respective relationship terms. Within a few minutes we were 'officially' taught – and expected to remember – our *kinship* relations, agnatic and affinal, across the three generations that the *saki* relation was linking us to. While it was dawning on my husband and me that it was going to be hard work to remember the terms, recognize the people, and relate both, some of our *gungu* came to us, took our hands, pressed them, and tried to get really cuddly with us (see plate 21 above), while especially the youngest of my *iril* (HyB), in contrast to the other two, who were also present but markedly reserved, became impressively extroverted, cracking one joke after the other, none of which we understood. It was he who would be present later in the day for the ritual food exchange (*jom-mid*), while his two brothers were not. It was only he who would accompany us some weeks later, along with our two *saki*, to a wedding in the village of his elder brother's daughter, his *hon-era*. He was also the one who accompanied his elder brother, my *saki*, to the *desauli* at *ba porob* in 2010, while his brothers stayed away.

Besides the male witnesses and the *saki*'s *haga* and affinal relations, I will argue, the village and the villagers became included in the next stage of the proceedings, when the new relation was symbolically announced by living it out publicly and embedding it in a wider social and ritual context. After all, it was the time of *mage porob*, one of the great village festivals. After the *nui-mid* ritual, which took place inside our *saki*'s house, our *saki*'s youngest brother almost kidnapped us by jokingly dragging us behind him, thus forcing us to follow him outside. He showed us around his compound and house next door, in whose courtyard the main *diuri*, his successor, their helpers, and their wives and other women were singing and dancing. While the women were moving fairly slowly and with some discretion, the men acted in openly sexual ways. Their dancing was rather wild and provocative; they pretended to fall against the women and rolled on the ground. A man was playing the village violin (*banam*). All were in high spirits. They sang about *Ho disum* (Ho country), that they were living in a world of plenty, that there was everything they needed to live a good life, that although their parents had died, they had brothers, and that they were happy. I was immediately incorporated into the line of dancing women. Between dances, the two *diuri* (ritual guides) had their feet washed and anointed with oil by a woman who then also washed and anointed my feet. After that, the dancing resumed. We needed to go back to our *saki.*

Jom-mid[205]

There were duties waiting for us. We had to light the fire in the hearth and feed it with firewood (*san*) from the sal tree, we had to cook rice, prepare a vegetable curry and the meat – it was going to be an all-day affair, and we were glad when our assistant's wife arrived and took over; that is, she inconspicuously taught us what to do and how to go about it and helped us practice the relationship terms, because she knew not only how everybody was related to her, but how everybody was reciprocally related to my husband and, differently from him, to me. She did not take over completely, though, making sure that my husband and I remained involved in the preparations, as if the later act of commensality (*jom-mid* – to become one by eating) included the process of jointly preparing the meal as part of the *saki* ceremony. The plates for the meal were made from sal leaves picked in the jungle the day before by the women present. This does not mean that the men are ignorant, because whenever I wanted to be creative and make a plate or drinking cup in a deviating style, I kept being corrected by men (and children), who kept watching me closely. We produced large plates (*tareko*) for rice and *dali* (green lentils) and small bowls for the meat (*jilu*).

The *jom-mid* took place in the goats' and rabbits' house (*merom kulae owa:*) that our *saki* had emptied and purified with cow dung and water for the occasion. The structure of the *jom-mid* ritual was as follows:

– *Jom-mid* began with the two male *saki* sitting next to each other on one side of the room and my *saki* and I sitting next to each other on the other side of the room. The four of us sat on ritual mats (*jaṭi*), while the two male witnesses sat on the floor without a mat, facing the male *saki*. The witnesses joined us in eating, but only the *saki* exchanged food from their plates, both rice (and *dali*) and meat. Every *saki* exchanged rice and meat with every other *saki*, meaning that I exchanged rice and meat with my female and my male *saki*, and so did my husband. In this phase of the ceremony the witnesses were one with us by sharing the identical meal and room, but they were at the same time distinguished by not sitting on a ritual mat and by not exchanging their food.

---

205 (*jom* – to eat; *mid* – one; to become one; to have sexual intercourse).

- The next step of *jom-mid* was about serving rice, *dali*, and meat to our *gungu* (HyBCh, yBCh) children in the part of the house where we had been received in the morning and where the *nui-mid* ceremony had been performed. The children were one with us by eating the identical meal prepared by us, but they were distinguished from us by eating it in a different room and facing north, while my husband and his *saki* had been facing west, my *saki* and I had been facing south, and the witnesses had been facing east.
- When the children finished, it was the men's turn to be served in the same room.
- The women eventually had their meal in the same room where the *saki* had their *jom-mid* before. This is the goats' and rabbits' house.

In this *jom-mid* ceremony the four *saki*'s relation became formalized among each other, and my husband and I became related in commensality to our (male) *saki*'s agnatic and affinal kin. I also argue that in the collective dancing, purifying, and anointing intermezzo with the village's ritual guides (*diuri*) described above, at the time of *mage porob*, which unites the whole village with its spirit world and which celebrates Mother Earth and notions of sexuality, fecundity, and fertility, the *saki* relation as such and the individual *saki* persons became embedded in the Ho's sociocosmic order.

Sunum em[206]

The last step of the first *saki* ceremony consisted in the four *saki* washing each other with water and anointing each other with oil in the following way:
- My *saki* and I washed our hands and feet outside, but this time we did it reciprocally to each other. My husband and his *saki* then did the same.
- In the reception area, where we had begun the day by drinking *rasi*, we sat down on ceremonial mats opposite the *munda* and his wife, who were facing east.
- While I applied oil to my *saki*'s feet, hands, arms, hair, forehead, and cheeks, my husband was instructed to do the same to his *saki*.
- The anointing was reciprocally done to me and my husband.
- We then hung the garlands that we had brought along in the morning around our *saki*'s necks. By now, after a day's wait, the hibiscus blossoms had utterly withered away. While this did not seem to matter at all, obviously

---

206 to rub with oil; Deeney adds (2005: 357): "[...] *sunum* is used with the meaning 'to make well' (by anointing with oil)".

the symbolic status and value of a flower as a constituent element in forging the relationship matters. It alludes to the ritual relation, which in Odiya is also referred to as *phulo* (flower; *pulo, pulu* in Ho are used in prayers as poetic parallel to *ba*) by some. In Santali a person will refer to his parents' *saki* as *phul-ma* and *phul-baba* (flower mother, flower father).

− We were asked to hand over our gifts: the *dhoti* and (Sambalpuri) *saree* which my two *saki* wore later that day when dancing on the *akara* (dancing ground in every village).

− To conclude the *jom-mid* ritual, we were once again anointed, but this time we did not do this reciprocally with our *saki*, but it was instead done to all of us by a young girl. Only in 2016 did I realize when showing a photo taken of this last part of the first ceremony in 2006 that this girl was the daughter of my/our Santal *saki* living in Jamshedpur. The web of *saki* relations linking Santal and Ho people will be illustrated below in the section "Relatedness across tribal boundaries."

Now the first *saki* ceremony had almost come to an end. *Nui-mid, jom-mid,* and *sunum em* had been completed. The *munda* explained that by becoming *saki* to each other we had turned two families (*owa:renko* – the people of the house) into one. From now on, we should exchange all important information, we should invite each other to all family get-togethers, and their door would be open to us at all times. He reminded us that the second ceremony would take place at our place.

It was five o'clock in the afternoon. Preparing and performing the *saki* ceremonies had kept us busy from the morning. While the *munda* stayed at home, my *saki*, my husband, and I went to the *akara* to participate in the dancing that had been going on there for some time. Both my *saki* and I were wearing our new *sarees*. Men had been drumming for many hours; other men and women had been dancing for many hours. People were in a hilarious mood and seemed to be enjoying themselves tremendously. Many of them had drunk so much that they could not keep the rhythm. But they kept dancing, although more than a few of them were mixing up the steps. Women took turns as to who was going to lead the line, sometimes uniting forty to sixty people, in which case it is understandably almost impossible to stick to one identical rhythm. At *mage porob* women, men, and children do not dance in separate lines as they do at *ba porob*. When I was offered an opportunity to take the lead, I did not refuse. I enjoyed the challenge thoroughly. That eventually up to eighty women followed my lead is to this day, even after more than ten years, remembered by many.

After an hour or so, when it was getting dark, we left to have a farewell drink of *diyan* with our *saki* at his home. He gave a brief farewell speech looking back at the day and the relevance of the ceremony: "We have invited you. We have given you what we have. Are you happy (*rasate*)? We do not have money, but we have what we need to lead a good life." He reminded us of the social obligations implied in the *saki* relation. The second ceremony, we were told, was to take place shortly before our departure from the field to return to Germany. More immediately, he added, "if I do not send you home now, you will reproach me for it." It was the time of the new moon and pitch-dark outside, and we would have to cross the rice fields to get home.

The second *saki* ceremony

The decision on the proper location for the second *saki* ceremony, which my husband and I were to host, was the subject of several serious debates. In terms of reciprocity, it should have been our turn in Manbir. But more than mere practical or technical aspects had to be considered: in our house in Manbir, as it was a *diku* house originally built for *diku* people, there was no *adin*, the hearth did not face east, as Ho norms require,[207] but south, there was only one cooking site instead of the two or more that are needed to prepare meat, vegetables, and rice to be offered to about forty people, and the house as such was small and lacked a proper courtyard where so many people could be served decently and safe from the village's gaze. Obviously, the choice of the place, which needed to be related to us as one party to the *saki* relation, was of ritual importance. The decision was made by our *saki* in collaboration with our assistant, who meanwhile had transformed into my son and I into his mother. The ceremony was to take place at his home in Santal Sai, about six weeks after the first ceremony and about two weeks before our departure.[208] At that time, none of the village festivals was going on, as had been the case with the first ceremony. Another exceptional and auspicious[209] day, however, had been chosen, since on March 29, 2006, a solar eclipse was expected to take place in India between 3:00 and 3:30

---

207 In Ho houses the fireplace (*chula*) inside the separate *adin* always points towards east. More fireplaces outside the *adin*, but inside the house or outside in the courtyard point east- or westward.

208 Although this was not given as a reason, I suspect that not only the spatial closeness mattered in this decision as Santal Sai was a lot nearer to Pathan Sai, our *saki*'s residence, but that perhaps primarily the relational closeness between our assistant and our *saki* mattered with our Santal assistant's *kaki* (FyBW) and my Ho *saki* being related as *saki*.

209 I assume this day to be considered auspicious since people went to the jungle in order to pick herbs whose healing powers were said to be particularly strong when collected during the period of the eclipse.

in the afternoon. We would not be able to see it, but during that particular period there was considerable thunder and lightning, and rain was falling.

The appointment for us in Santal Sai was for 9:00 a.m. to get started with the preparations. Our *saki* and their relations were supposed to arrive by noon. Instead, they came at around 3:30 p.m. (coincidentally the exact time of the eclipse?), the ceremony of reciprocally washing hands and feet (*abun*), anointing with oil (*sunum em*), and exchanging *diyan* (*nui-mid*) and food (*jom-mid*) started about an hour and a half later, and by the time everybody was served a meal and rice-beer, it was 9:00 p.m.

When we arrived, my *kimin* (SW) had already been busy purifying the site for the ceremony: the kitchen, which in this Santal house is an extra room and accessible to me and my husband,[210] had been cleaned; the floor of the courtyard had been swept and purified with cow dung (*guri: sapa*); a wall marking off the courtyard from the garden space had been coloured with a red-brownish colour made from earth that my *kimin* had carried all the way from the jungle along with other women of Santal Sai. There were also others who were inconspicuously contributing to the ceremony: our assistant's FyBS, Champai, came from Tatanagar for the occasion and would be the ritual cook preparing inside the kitchen the ingredients that, as was our duty, we had bought in the market for the meals (*mandi*) and the *chakara* (small spicy edibles served along with *rasi* and *diyan*); our assistant's FFyBSS, his 'brother' and neighbour, 'son' (*babu*) to me, shaman (*dewa*) of Santal Sai at village level, and *diuri* (ritual guide) at the household level, had already killed the goat and was cutting it up behind his house.

We did not know what to expect, but by now we knew that there is a known script concerning the setting, the work to be done, and the structure of the *saki* ceremony. My husband was not allowed to give any help. He was made to sit, drink, and socialize. As the hostess of the ceremony to come, I felt responsible to do my share. This was not easy, for the reason that the ceremony took place at the home of my (classificatory) daughter-in-law (*kimin*). She was very clear that as my *kimin* she was obliged to do the work for her *hanar* (mother-in-law) and instead expected me not just to tell her what to do but rather to give her orders.[211] I had made up my mind not to oblige in this and instead help-

---

210 The sacred part of a Santal house is the *bhitar* which is an area inside the house facing East that is separate but not separated by a wall as is the case with the *adin* in a Ho house. A household's valuables are kept in the *bhitar,* often also rice or at least part of a year's rice harvest; the cooking is done elsewhere which is the reason why I could trespass into the kitchen.

211 Three years later, when I stay with her for my long-term fieldwork, she insists on me ordering her around, and when she realizes that I refuse to comply, she lectures me by imitating a *hanar's* voice and intonation that is required in a situation like this. She seems really despaired.

ed wherever I could. But this was not really appreciated. Of course, I was surprised, as in the course of the first *saki* ceremony my *kimin* had made sure, as
mentioned above, that both my husband and I kept being involved in the process
of preparing the meal for *jom-mid*, as if helping (*denga em*) was a constituent
part of the ritual itself. Here, obviously, within the space of her own house,
the relationship between mother-in-law (*hanar*) and daughter-in-law (*kimin*) became the dominant determinant and impacted her behaviour. I was welcome,
though, to do what a hostess is expected to do: welcome the visitors who kept
coming and going, offering *abun* to them before serving them *rasi* or *diyan*
and *chakara*. This in fact kept me busy all day, and this was indeed appreciated
by all.

Apart from a few villagers from Santal Sai and the *majhi* (Santali: secular
head of Santal Sai), most of the visitors came from up to three generations of
our assistant's *alerenko* ('our people' in Santali and Ho) or *gusti*, agnatic and affinal kin comparable to the Ho's *owa:renko* (people of the house) and *miyad
mandi chaturenko* (people of one rice pot; see chapter 3). In the ritual situation
of the second *saki* ceremony, the *gusti* representatives were our assistant's immediate neighbours, all related to him as the offspring of his FF or FFB, along with
their wives. Our *saki* were accompanied by their/'our' daughter from K., their/
'our' only male grandchild (*jai-kowa*), and several of his five elder sisters.

The core elements of the second *saki* ceremony were basically similar to
those of the first ceremony (*nui-mid, sunum em, jom-mid*), but some elements
were performed differently or in a different order:
– After reciprocally washing hands and feet (*abun*), as in the first ceremony,
  we and our *saki* were asked to sit down inside the house by the eldest
  woman present, an in-law of our assistant's living in the compound next
  door. She was in charge of the procedures to follow. She taught me to address her as *dai*[212] and addressed me as *mai* (young girl, younger woman).
  She has a *gungu* relation with our assistant (FeBW-HyBS), an *aji–undi kui* relation with me (HeBW-HyBW), a *hili-iril* relation with our male *saki* (eBW-

---

Only in 2016, when I am so busy doing other things that I am unable to give her a hand in the
household, she seems to be really satisfied. So it has taken me almost ten years to learn the lesson that specific relationship positions require a specific behaviour which not only consists in
what to do but also in what not to do.

212 When two Ho or Santal women meet it is a common practice that the elder of the two is
addressed as *dai* and the younger as *mai*. I have not come across these two terms as formal kinship terms, and also Deeney does not list them as such. However, informally, elder sisters are
colloquially addressed as *dai* instead of *aji* just as elder brothers are often addressed informally
as *dada* instead of *bau*.

HyB), and, of course, an *aji–undi kui* relation with my *saki*. It was she who performed the ritual by anointing the feet, cheeks, forehead, hair, and arms of all four of us, one by one, while we remained seated.

– In the *nui-mid* ritual following the anointing, she observed how the same-sex *saki* exchanged *diyan* three times with each other, while they did so only twice with the opposite-sex *saki*. She witnessed this part but did not interfere in the exchange of *diyan*. She accompanied us outside for the next step to follow and would stay till the end.

– Outside in the courtyard she was witness to our *saki* putting the flower garlands around our necks. They were made from hibiscus, which is the identical flower that we had chosen for their garland. After that, a *dhoti* was presented to my husband and a *saree* to me. We sat and drank *diyan* served in *pu:*, cups made from the leaves of the sal tree. My *dai* and witness joined us in drinking, but she did not sit on the ritual mat as the *saki* did. Earlier in the day, my *kimin* had inconspicuously been busy producing *pu:* and *tanre* (plates made from the leaves of the sal tree), like so many other things.

– Before the *jom-mid* ritual was performed among the *saki*, *haga* and *bala* were served their meals outside in the courtyard. They sat in separate lines for women, men, and children, and the children were served first. Meals for forty people had been cooked and were eaten. After the meals, *diyan* was offered to all, including children, and cigarettes (*bidi*) were offered to the men and tobacco (*sukul*) to men and women.

– Only after that was the *jom-mid* ritual performed among the *saki*. As in the anointing ceremony, my *dai* was in charge and did the ritual work for the four of us. She first exchanged portions of rice between the plates, then the meat, which had been ladled out into separate bowls. In between, she was given advice about how to perform the exchange properly, and sometimes the advice itself was negotiated. My daughter-in-law (*kimin*) would be the last to have her meal served to her, when everybody else had finished. Maybe in this context, in this situation on this particular occasion, this reveals more than anything else that she not only was the *owa:rini:* (woman/wife/female head of the house) but had in fact been the hostess of the day and the ceremony and that my husband and I were the guests given the gift of Ho-Santal hospitality.

– By this time, it had become dark. Time to leave. As at the end of the first ceremony, our male *saki* again took the initiative for a short formal farewell chat. In the special voice of his that he "switches on"[213] whenever we are to-

---

213 The quality of someone's voice or speech behaviour in certain ritual situations can be mark-

gether as *saki* and especially in situations where Ho hospitality is to be acted out, he invited us to sit down under the stars over a final *pu:* of *diyan*, along with our assistant. He and his wife wondered how we would be able to exchange important family news once we had left. My *saki* wanted to know whether we would ever meet again, when, and how, in the absence of post offices, telephones, and mobile phones.

To conclude the ceremony, we performed *jowar* to each other. When we left two weeks later, as already mentioned, a jeep was organized for us by our *saki* without our knowing about it beforehand – a gift that we would not be able to reciprocate. When the vehicle was about to drive off, my *saki* flung her arms behind her head as women do when they start their immediate wailing in the event of someone's death.

Relatedness across tribal boundaries

The web of relations accommodating the particular *saki* relation that we experienced in the field transgresses tribal boundaries between Ho and Santal by linking members of the Ho clans (*kili*) Purty and Sinku with members of the Santal clans (*paris*) Murmu, Hansda, and Tudu.

---

edly different from that displayed in secular contexts. I have mentioned above the immediacy with which people in the context of death rituals can 'switch on/off' their tears or 'switch on/ off' their laughter and show some sudden extrovert behaviour in the case that two people meet who have a joking relationship. I argue that this is a culturally acquired skill that Ho people have at their disposal. Similarly, my ♂*saki* who is a grandfather (joking relationship to his grand-children), husband, elder brother, father, mediator, matchmaker (*dutam*) and *munda*, can change the quality of his voice depending on the situation. Desai to my knowledge is the only one who has emphasized this by pointing out the "requisite tenderness" (Desai 2010: 131) of the voice as required in the conversation between *saki*. In my memory this has always added a significant note of lightness to any encounter that is characteristic of the *saki* relation. This note of tenderness, I argue, is fed by elements of affection and distance, politeness, warmth, dignity, deference, respect, commitment and formality, and to my Western mind these components were initially difficult to think together. In fact, one of the few situations when my assistant was really cross with me concerned my initial inability to command this skill. When, e.g., inviting our *saki* for the second ceremony (*dili-ura*) to his place, I was quite happy with the correctness of my grammar and the appropriateness of my vocabulary, whereas he would not stop complaining about the lack of tenderness in my voice. Desai also reports an instance when he was scolded off by someone else outside the *mahaprasad* relation for not expressing the required softness in his syntax adequately.

While so far I have argued that by two individuals establishing a *saki* relation, the respective and already existing agnatic and affinal kin immediately and structurally become included in or affiliated to the ritual relation, my argument here suggests the reverse process as well. My data reveal that *saki* relations constitute a social resource indeed by opening up new 'roads' (*hora*), by inviting or notionally initiating prospective future relations by marriage (*bala*) to come into being *after* the *saki* relation between certain individuals – across the tribal divide of Ho and Santal – has been sealed. This reads as follows in the case of Ho and Santal interrelatedness:

- In the research area, Kisku, a Santal *paris*, and Sinku, a Ho *kili*, are considered brother *kili* or one clan (*miyad kili, haga kili*). As elaborated above, intermarriage between brother clans is prohibited, commensality is practised, and notions of *denga em* (to give monetarily unpaid help) prevail.
- In figure 1, my assistant's wife's father (a Santal, person 1) from *paris* Kisku addresses my (female) *saki* (a Ho, person 2) from *kili* Sinku as younger sister (*misi-era*), while she addresses him as elder brother (*bau*). In other words: the two of them – one Santal, the other Ho – have a brother-sister relationship and grow up as such within a close vicinity. They have addressed each other as *bau* and *misi-era* ever since.

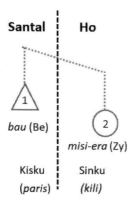

Figure 1: Transtribal brother-sister relationship

- In figure 2, after their respective marriages, which made my (female) *saki*, before marriage S. Sinku, adopt her husband's *kili* Purty, they have retained this brother-sister relationship in address and reference.

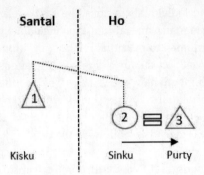

Figure 2: Relations of (classificatory) kinship and marriage

–   In figure 3, my assistant's wife addresses her father's younger sister as *hatom* or *ji*, as is usual in the area for both Santal and Ho people, while her *hatom* addresses her elder brother's daughter as *mai* (young girl, 'daughter'). In the area of research, I often heard Santal people make use of Ho relationship terminology. Here, with a gap of one generation, *mai* carries the meaning of 'girl child', while within the same generation Ho and Santal women often address each other as *mai* or *dai* (younger woman/older woman) according to their relative ages, so that the terms then express a relation between (classificatory) sisters in terms of seniority. This was seen above in the second *saki* ceremony when I addressed the most senior female and witness as *dai* and she addressed me as *mai*.

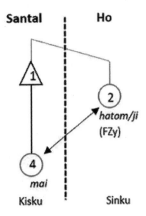

Figure 3: Relations and relationship terms across tribal boundaries

– A social relation (*bau–misi era*) like the one illustrated in figure 1, between two people across the clan and tribal divide and outside someone's *miyad mandi chaturenko*, is what Ho people call a village relation (*hatu-sairenko* – villagers, as opposed to *eta:renko* – other people, people from outside the village). Such terminologically identified social relations are usual where villages are multiclan villages and include hamlets with members from non-Ho tribes and nontribal service castes. This is frequently found in northern Mayurbhanj, in the region of research, where Ho villages are interspersed with Santal hamlets, and in the Lupungutu region near Chaibasa, where Ho people live in multiclan villages alongside Munda, Oraon, and Kharia.

– It should also be noted for analytical purposes that in the example represented in figure 1 of a village relation between two individuals, one Santal, one Ho, born to two clans that are classified as brother clans or *miyad kili* (one clan), the constellation of the relations of a girl, her father, and his (classificatory) younger sister as shown in figure 3 is to this point operative independent of any *saki* relation.

– In figure 4, according to the information I was given, S. Sinku (Ho), who was later to become my *saki*, was provided with two *saki* relations when all three persons involved were very young. Of the three *saki*, two were Santal. They had been chosen by their parents from Gara Sai and Santal Sai, both hamlets of villages in the immediate vicinity and within walking distance from each other across the rice fields, as map 5 shows. One of the girls was from *paris* Tudu, the other one from *paris* Murmu. By identification, the *saki* relation came about between three individual girls, all three of them as yet unmarried and in terms of kinship, to my knowledge, unrelated to each other before becoming *saki*.

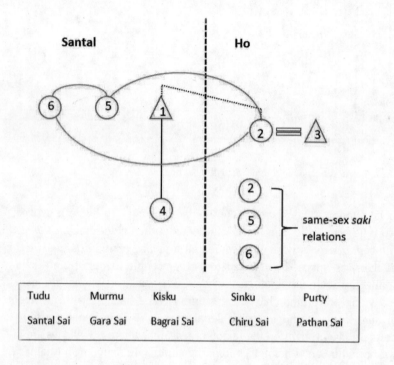

Figure 4: Before marriage
Saki relations between same-sex individuals from different clans and hamlets/villages.

– In figure 5, eventually, upon the girls – related as *saki* – growing up and marrying, their husbands become *saki* to each other, too. The *saki* relation initially linking three individual females has turned into a relation linking three couples. The husbands represent the Ho *kili* Purty and the Santal *paris* Hansda (twice).

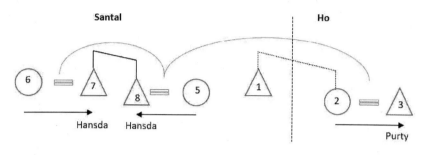

3 couples of *saki* relations:

persons 2 and 3, 5 and 8, 6 and 7

Figure 5: After marriage
Same-sex *saki* relations continue and include the respective spouses.

This is the moment when the structure or frame that a *saki* relation offers may be said to invite future and new marriage relations, as suggested above. This is not meant as a kind of functionalist reasoning implying that marriages are brought about *because of* the parties being linked in one way or another to already-existing *saki* relations. Instead, when exploring the choreography of the chronology of establishing social relations, my data show that an interdependence between marriage and *saki* relations may suggest itself.[214] The argument is developed as follows:

–   The two Santal *saki* females of *paris* Tudu and *paris* Murmu married two (actual) brothers of Hansda *paris* (figure 5). In the process of marrying, the women adopted their husbands' *paris* title Hansda. They remained *saki* as before marriage, while their husbands newly became *saki* to each other after marriage. Also, after marriage, the two female Santal *saki* became related to each other as HyBW/HeBW (*undi kui/aji*), but they continued to address each other as *saki*. At least I was told so, but I cannot confirm this for myself, as both women had died when I entered the scene.

–   In figure 6, about one generation *after* the *saki* relations under discussion had been sealed, a marriage (by elopement) is sparked by or rather embeds itself within the existing web of *saki* relations.

---

214 More data won in fieldwork will be needed to generalize this hypothesis.

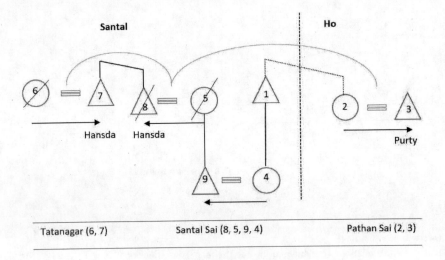

Figure 6: *Saki* relations inviting and embedding marital relations

This is the marriage of the female person from Kisku *paris* (person 4 in figures 3 and 4). She got married, that is, she decided to run away (*nir*) with G. Hansda (person 9) to live with him in his and his mother's house in Santal Sai.[215] G.'s mother is person 5, one of the three *saki* discussed above.

– In figure 7, G. Hansda refers to his mother as *enga* or *ma* (in figure 7 rendered more precisely as *mã*), as is usual in the area for Ho[216] and Santal people. Since he identifies his mother with her two female *saki*, he consequently also addresses them as he addresses his own mother. He addresses their husbands as he addresses his own father, *pa* (a colloquial vocative in the region) or *ba*, short for *baba*.[217] He is *babu* to them.

---

215 The process of their run-away marriage as an example of a marriage by elopement is given in the second portrait in chapter 7.

216 Mothers are interchangeably addressed as *ma, eyan, or kaki ma* (vocative).

217 Deeney gives 'father' for *baba* in address "used in affection" (2005: 21). I often heard male children and their fathers reciprocally addressing each other as *babu* or *babu/ babu hon. Apun* (my father) is less common in the area.

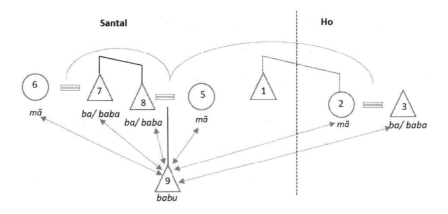

Figure 7: *Saki* relations and relationship terms

In marriage, G. Hansda's wife became *kimin* (SW) to both of his parents (persons 5 and 8). By analogy, she is identified and addressed as *kimin* by G. Hansda's father's two male *saki* (persons 7 and 3). She addresses them as *ba* or *baba*. When she was asked how she feels about her husband's mother's *saki* (person 2) who is also her father's younger sister (*hatom* or *ji*), the answer was that *mã* had been a serious option, but that she had decided to address her as *hatom*, thus defining the relation not via her husband but via *her* natal Kisku *kili/paris* links, in other words via her father (person 1). Accordingly, she is addressed by her *hatom* (person 2) as *mai* (see figure 2 above).

My argument about ritual friendship and especially about the Ho's *saki* relation so far has been that by two or more individuals establishing a ritual relation, their respective already-existing agnatic and affinal kin will immediately become included, thus turning even a relation of the individual type into a collective venture. This last section on relatedness across tribal boundaries is intended to complement these findings by illustrating how two or more already-existing *saki* links (between persons 2, 5, and 6) structurally contribute to bringing about new roads (*nama hora*) as culturally sustained options for two individuals to marry (persons 4 and 9 in figure 6). Figures 1–7 have illustrated that after marriage, both will continue their former ritual and social relations. In this regard, same-sex ritual relations or the *saki* relation may be interpreted as a hinge, a "lived-in" (Lévi-Strauss 1953: 548) transtribal empirical option that is complementary to the kinship and opposite-sex ties established by marriage. Just as marriage contributes to perfecting a Ho and Santal person's state and status, so does her or his becoming accommodated within a larger web of social relations. Notionally free from cost-benefit calculations, ritual relations crosslink members of these tribal societies, thus contributing a valued ontological quality to social cohesion in their own right.

To conclude: ritual friendship is just one instance of the ordered interrelatedness of distinct ethnic communities that works at different layers and across tribal boundaries. It is characteristic of the tribal societies in Middle India which have been outlined in general terms in the introductory chapter. Ritual relations among initially unrelated individuals are a known and empirical sociocultural reality in this region. In fact, apart from the ties created by ritual friendship, the ethnographic description of the ritual, social, and economic collaboration of Ho, Santal, and distinct nontribal communities highlighted in chapter 5 already revealed that the artificiality and rigidity of substantialist boundaries ideologically isolating those social units from each other are colonial, postcolonial, and anthropological constructs.

Diachronic affinity and synchronic affinal symmetry

I am proud to say that we have been able to establish matrimonial relations with Chiru Sai
over three generations.
(Ch. Purty, Tarana, Odisha, 2010, personal communication)

Introduction

Marriage and the value of affinal ties proved to be a topic of great ideological and empirical, ever-present relevance during my fieldwork. Especially towards the end of the harvest, it became a subject of attention, given momentum by young men leaving their villages in the afternoon to visit other villages to drum there all through the nights while the young women danced. The following section is about Ho ways of getting married, about marital practices and social norms, and about Ho relationship terminology accommodating and structuring relations of and between Ho individuals and Ho social categories. It is included in this chapter on the long-lasting social ties created by the *saki* relation as ritual friendship because it was my *saki* who as *munda* and competent mediator was frequently asked to conduct marriage and *gonon* (bridewealth) negotiations. By having me accompany him to different hamlets at different stages of those negotiations, he paved the way for me to explore the field of diachronic affinity and synchronic affinal symmetry through participant observation. Passing on his knowledge concerning Ho ways of getting married was as important to him as passing on the Holon Purty myth of origin and the narration of settlement in the area given above in chapter 4.

Hospitality and affinity

Hospitality – facets of the social relevance of which have been outlined above – and affinity are interlinked key values in Ho society. In fact, hospitality is lived out especially towards affines as a matter of cultural principle. Ho understandings of hospitality (*em-ched*) linguistically imply repeated giving, as the denotation of the word reveals, literally 'to give-give' (*em* – to give; *ched* is a poetic parallel of *em*). This holds true for profane as well as ritual situations. Hospitality towards affinal relations expresses that affinity as such constitutes an underlying, structurally ever-present value which continuously needs to be enacted and re-enacted. Comparable to the *saki* relation that was characterized above as a piece of processual culture that is *done*, affinal relations (*bala*) are not static givens that one *has* or accumulates in terms of quantity, but an ongoing process that has to be permanently enlivened in specific ways in order to keep it notionally and empirically alive. Of course, these ways differ from the behaviour displayed towards one's 'brothers' (*haga*), as the following two examples will illustrate.

In quite a secular context, hospitality towards and among affinal relations was demonstrated towards me whenever my *kimin*'s[218] (SW) parents were visiting. Evening meals at their daughter's place were usually served very late, well into the night, when children and not seldom I were fast asleep. As it is believed that only after having eaten can one have good dreams, the children were woken up, had their meals first, individually and separate from the rest, and went back to sleep. Things were different with me. I was regularly woken up, as I was told that my *bala-era* (SWM) would not be allowed to start eating without having exchanged food with me as her *bala-era* (DHM) first. This was done three times. Sitting next to each other and following the exchange of food from our plates, the two of us would exclaim, "*balatadi!*" (vocative of *bala-era*), pronouncing the final vowel by prolonging it softly and ingesting our saliva with a mildly hissing sound before we started to eat. Nobody minded me failing to continue to eat after the first bite if I was too tired – as long as structural homage had been paid beforehand to the value of affinity and to its gender bias, as the food exchange

---

218 *Kimin* is the relationship term for one's son's wife (SW) and a younger brother's wife (yBW) both implying strong, though not identical respect connotations.

was not done between me and my *kimin*'s father, who also falls in the category of *balatadi*.

The second example concerns the ritual context of the secondary funerary rite (*diri dulsunum*) which has been discussed above for the group of affinal relations participating in food exchanges during the rite called *jom-mid* (to become one in commensality). The focus here is on the spectacular hospitality that is addressed to those who are classified as *bala*. *Bala* are afforded not only separate huts in a separate space, separate cooking sites, plenty of firewood, separate water tanks, and a separate dancing ground, but also a grand farewell ceremony and farewell gifts before leaving the scene and returning home.

Affinity and marriage

It is, of course, L. Dumont who famously focussed on "affinity as a value" (Dumont 1983) by contrasting the secondary and subordinate status attributed to affinity in what he calls modern Western societies with the equal status it commands with consanguinity in the South Indian kinship system. As values are permanent and durable by definition, Dumont argues that by affinal relations (and terminology) being transmitted there from generation to generation, affinity is recognized and valued as just as permanent and durable as consanguinity (ibid.: vii). According to him, the social whole in nontribal South India is projected as constituted by the binary opposition between consanguineal and affinal categories and maintained by affinal exchange relations between them. I will show that Dumont's statement on the diachronic nature of affinal relations and their perpetuity may be considered true for Ho society also, despite the fact that Dravidian kinship terminology and Middle Indian relationship terminologies differ widely, as do affinal exchange patterns and terminological prescriptions and proscriptions.[219] Although these distinctions are relevant, they do not touch upon the overall value attached to affinity in tribal Middle India in general and in Ho country in particular.

It is in the ways of getting and being married in Ho country that the value of affinal relations becomes prominently emphasized. Being married contributes to completing the social maturing of a Ho person, and so does his or her becoming furnished with and accommodated in a web of affinal relations. This is a compre-

---

[219] Continuing his life-long immersion in things Middle Indian Pfeffer has analysed and contextualized the structural principles of Highland Middle Indian relationship terminologies including those of the Munda system (Pfeffer 2019: 83–102). His ideas unfolded there have greatly inspired my discussion of Ho relationship terminology in this section.

hensive process indeed, as a Ho person on marriage not only acquires new *affinal* relations via his or her spouse, but in terms of terminology *consanguineal* ones, too, as structurally *ego*'s affines' affines are terminologically classified as consanguines. In an aside when discussing joking relationships, marriageability, and age groups, Dhan (1961: 72) confirms the character of consanguinity attributed to those related to *ego* as spouse's siblings' spouse(s). In Ho this category of sp(sib)sp is referred to by the Santali-Ho term *pera chetan perako*.[220]

In the course of fieldwork, I was invited to participate in a number of collective negotiations in the drawn-out process of two Ho individuals getting married, as it is widely acknowledged that a relationship forged by marriage is not "purely individual but essentially collective" (Dumont 1983: 148). Most of these usually time-consuming negotiations concerned quite practical steps in a marriage under way, and hospitality required treating the respective visiting parties of the spouses-to-be with attention and respect, *diyan* and food, before and after the talks, in a clear tripartite structure. Representatives of the bride's and groom's sides were usually quite prepared to come up with all kinds of information, as it sometimes offered the opportunity of reconsidering their decisions and of making sure everything would be done correctly (*bugin*, literally 'good'). But they were focussed on the immediate next steps of the upcoming marriage to be *done* rather than on verbalizing the diachronic dimension of the relationship in question. Surely, the important issue of the affinal compatibility of the future spouses' clan affiliations[221] had been clarified beforehand.

Only once, then, and over several sittings, was I given the chance to trace the consecutive continuation of a pattern of intermarriage which was communicated to me as one between two *kili* from two villages, or more precisely, between two localized segments of two subclans from two hamlets of two distinct villages, over several generations (see figure 8). It is the empirical case of our *saki*'s pattern of diachronic intermarriage, as I will call it. It is given from his perspective and as he presented the case. He did so, as he pointed out, to illustrate a matter of some general relevance and public concern and not just an isolated individual affair. He circumstantiated what he said by giving names and detailed genealogical information. Always interested in learning more, our *saki*'s *gungu* (yBCh, HyBCh) of generation -1 living next door also joined us in listening to their *gungu* (FeB, FeBW) of generation +1. They thus would learn what was recognized

---

220 In Santali pera/ *perako* carries the meaning of affinal relation(s): *pera*, sg./- ko, pl. marker; *chetan* in Ho denotes 'above, on top'. Literally *pera chetan perako* may be understood as 'affinal relations on top of (one's) affinal relations', in anthropological jargon denoting the category of *ego*'s spouse's siblings' spouses (*see* below for Consanguineal Line 2 in figures 15,16).
221 *See* above "Subclans, brother clans, and marriage".

as an ideal, a good and proper (*bugin*) Ho way of establishing and perpetuating matrimonial relations. This is in line with Bouez (1979: 87) and Verardo (2003b: 80, 81) emphasizing the continuity of affinal relations and the repetition of alliance relations between localized groups for three to four generations. For this reason, our *saki*'s case of matrimonial exchange is documented in some detail in this section. This is also done for the reason that his marriage pattern and praxis runs structurally against the logic of the terminological system, which linguistically prohibits exactly that particular type or kind of marriage. How the tension arising from this discrepancy is resolved will be developed in the final part of the section.

Diachronic affinity: the case of our *saki*

> *You should keep trying the fruit of the tree that you have once eaten from.*
> *Where your cows once loved to graze, there you should send them again.*
> *(Ch. Purty, 2010, personal communication)*

To our (male) *saki* it was an accomplishment and a matter of pride (*mamaran*) to have continued and repeated affinal relations with the same village over three generations (*manatin-uju* – to obey or observe from some time in the past until the present; Deeney 2005: 241) and to pass on this knowledge.[222] The diachronic nature of perpetuated, stable, and enduring relations between the localized groups affiliated to affinal clans[223] in Ho marriages is a social norm that is much appreciated and a highly valued factor. Our *saki* softly and in a low voice[224] mentioned the term *niyam* (a law, rule; Deeney 2005: 267) in this context,

---

222 Again, as remarked above, the verbalization of what follows was primarily done by our male *saki*.

223 The characterization as 'affinal clans' is to be understood in contradistinction to brother clans intermarriage between members of which is prohibited.

224 This suprasegmental feature is worth mentioning because of its phonemic character: as concerns the *saki* relation the required *tenderness in the voice* has been noted above. When referring to their highest god, Ho people point their thumb upwards rather than pronouncing the name Sinbonga *aloud*. Indeed, over the years in the field I have heard the name of the Ho's supreme god only very rarely. I have interpreted this as the expression of an attitude to keep the very concept and the value as such untainted, immaculate, free from any potentially polluting interference. Likewise, although Ho people have a keen awareness of how things should and should not be done, they prefer to refrain from voicing terms of the highest order such as *niyam* at all or, if the *saki* relation socially obliges them to do so, it is done in a low and soft voice as described above.

as if to stress that his own conservative marital praxis coincided with the Ho rules, norms, or laws of marrying that are rooted in a suprahuman moral order[225] and are thus of high status. Of course, most informants freely admitted that there are different ways of Ho people getting married, with runaway marriage (*nir andi*) the most frequent. While I have never come across this modality assessed negatively, there seems to be a generally recognized hierarchy of valuing some ways of getting married over others. In our *saki*'s case, connecting his marital state in the present with social norms and aspirations that are believed to have come into being in the distant past added an air of timelessness, a quality of permanence to his performance. It increased the prestige of all those linked by and linking two hamlets of two villages in long-established alliance relations. This is comparable to the relevance conveyed in the accounts of the Holon Purty subclan's origin and its history of migration given above, which award a note of superiority and seniority in status to this subclan by linking it to some mythological past. As they included more than three generations, the details of the alliance relations were delivered with a similar note of severity.

The model of figure 8 is based on my *saki*'s data. The construction of the statistical information into a model of elementary, restricted, and symmetric affinal exchange suggesting bilateral cross-cousin marriage along the lines of Lévi-Strauss (1969: xxiii), Barnard and Good (1984: 95), Dumont (1983: 14), and Barnard and Spencer (2002: 313–15) is mine. It tries to capture my understanding of my *saki*'s indigenous perception of marriage as a perpetuated transaction between affinally related and localized corporate groups[226] involving two distinct exchanging categories only.[227]

---

225 For the relevance of *niam* (in Ho *niyam*) as encompassing the sociocosmic divine order in tribal Middle India and beyond *see* Pfeffer (2016: 287, 295); Berger (2007: 529); Hardenberg (2005: 609); Fuhrmann (2013: 304); de Maaker (2006: 9).

226 These 'localized corporate groups' are the local segments of what has been discussed above as *miyad mandi chaturenko*. As this is an unnamed institution Ho people in terms of arranging marriages relate to the sociocentric affinal category of clan and the respective localities of residence instead.

227 The analytical shortcomings of a model operating with two exchange units only will be outlined below in "Affinal exchange and Ho relationship terminology" where an alternative model will be suggested.

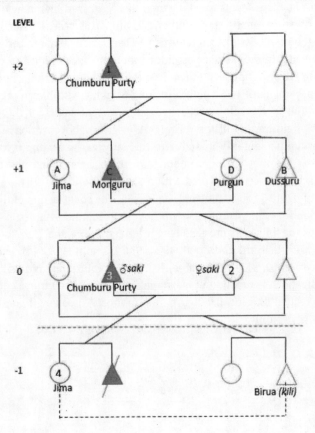

Figure 8: Affinal exchange over three generations
Preliminary model. Our *saki* are persons 2 (♀) and 3 (♂), as in figures 2–7 above.

The model and the data

- Our *saki*'s type of marriage is qualified as *bapala andi*, a "properly arranged marriage [...], as distinct from an elopement" (Deeney 2005: 30), including preliminary visits and negotiations between the groom's and the bride's parties on behalf of and before the marriage. *Ba-pa-la* is the reciprocal form of *bala* (affines, in-laws), literally meaning 'becoming affinally related to each other'.

- Jima/Dussuru (A/B) and Purgun/Monguru (C/D) of generation +1 were given as our *saki*'s (2, 3) respective in-laws, whom they simultaneously conceived of as their own parents' cross siblings.
- My ♂*saki*'s parents Purgun and Monguru addressed their cross niece, my ♀*saki*, *before* marriage as *homon* (BCh, ws) and *ge* (ZCh, WBCh). *After* marriage she became *kimin* (SW) to both. *Ge*, *homon*, and *kimin* are address and reference terms. The same terms are used by my ♀*saki*'s parents Jima and Dussuru when addressing their cross nephew, my ♂*saki*.
- *Before* marriage *each* of our *saki* referred to the parents of his or her spouse-to-be as *mamu*[228] and *hatom*, just as these had addressed the respective parents of their own prospective spouses *before* their marriage as *mamu* and *hatom* one generation before.[229]
- A terminological prescription exists in the first ascending generation (+1) in that *mamu* equates FZH and MB, *hatom* FZ and MBW. Seen from *ego*'s perspective in generation 0, a cultural specificity lies in the *lack* of terminology distinguishing the relative age of *ego*'s parents' cross siblings (FZ – e, y, *hatom*; MB – e, y, *mamu*), which otherwise is a structural requirement in the case of *ego*'s parents' same-sex siblings (FeB – *gungu*; FyB – *kaka*; MeZ – *gungu*; MyZ – *kaki*).
- Only *after* marriage, then, were our *saki* referred to as *mamu-hatom honko* (*honko* – children; here MBD/FZD–MBS/FZS). This is a composite term that is used in its singular or plural form as a reference term when reconstructing people's relationships *before* marriage. I have not come across this term as address term.[230] By linking in one composite term the basic terms related to two ascending generations and thus documenting the

---

228 In the region of research and in Porahat (Verardo 2003b: 69) Ho refer to the category MB as *mamu* more often than *kuma*, which they seem to do in the Chaibasa area according to Deeney (2002: 131). Deeney has *mamu* exclusively as address term.

229 Although the doubled reference to *mamu* and *hatom* may seem unnecessary to the outsider as the context and the 'message' have already become clear, Ho people in fact tend to double the contents of their information in certain situations that they consider especially important. Sometimes this doubling is done in a word by word fashion, sometimes by making use of poetic parallels as outlined above.

230 For Porahat in Jharkhand Verardo records *mamu-hon* as distinct from *hatom-hon* (2003b: 71), but finds it "surprising that MBCh are distinguished from FZCh given that MB=FZH" (ibid.)

depth of their reciprocal relatedness *before* marriage, *mamu-hatom honko* is a term to characterize a specific type of bilateral alliance pattern: a ♀ *mamu-hatom hon* marrying another ♂ *mamu-hatom hon*. Though not a lexically distinct, separate basic relationship term, *mamu-hatom honko* is a term to classify and characterize two categories as affinal or marriageable "on the grounds that people recognize the relationships involved" (Barnard and Good 1984: 39). *Mamu-hatom honko* constitutes a linguistic discrimination at the behavioural level. It allows for terminologically marked conceptual distinctions in generation 0 within the encompassing pool of (terms denoting) *ego*'s 'siblings'.

– Unspecified by relative age and sex, the composite term *mamu-hatom honko* by its identical morphological form highlights the value of the equality of the social categories that the spouses-to-be belong to. This equality is otherwise terminologically excluded by the distinction of relative age classing *all* males and females in *ego*'s generation (0) as either senior or junior 'siblings', thus suggesting hierarchical relationships.[231]

– In the social universe of nonmarriageable 'siblings' in *ego*'s generation the term *mamu-hatom honko* resorted to in retrospect represents a transgenerational option to qualify and linguistically set apart categories as affinal, as the case of our *saki* confirms. It is, as will be seen next, one of several options.

– Complementarily, the type of marriage arranged for a boy and a (younger) girl of two different *kili* who are related as *misi-era* or *undi-kui* (yZ, ms) and *bau* (eB) or *bare*[232] (B) *before* marriage is identified and known as *mis-iya-bariya bapala*. This expression lexically implies gender and age qualifications, as *misi(-era)* presupposes an older male speaker, *bare* a younger female one. A male Ho's older 'brother' is his *bau*, not his *bare*. While his younger 'sisters' are his *misi-ko* or equally his *undi-kui(ko)*, a woman addresses her younger 'sisters' exclusively as *undi-kuiko*.[233] *Misi-era/undi-kui* and *bare/bau* are relationship terms frequently used as synonyms to denote a Ho's younger female and older male siblings. However, when a marriage between cross cousins is arranged, the invariable collocation is between

---

231 *See* above subsections on 'Equality, hierarchy, and identification' and 'Ritual friendship and kinship'.

232 Female Ho use *bare* as a general term for a girl's 'brother' in contexts in which age in terms of seniority does not matter as long as both belong to the same generation. *Bare* is heard less often than *bau/dada* (eB) or *undi* (yB). In the context of marriage, the collocation *bare-misi* presupposes an older 'brother' and a younger 'sister'.

233 see figure 9.

misi and *bare* and definitely not between *undi-kui* and *bau*. Thus *misiya-bariya bapala* constitutes a terminological discrimination and an implied opposition in its own right, going beyond the concept of siblingship. Linguistically, the combination of *misi-bare* alludes to the semantic field of marriage and marriageable categories.

- *Misiya-bariya bapala* is used synonymously with marriage between *mamu-hatom honko*. In both cases the parents of the spouse-to-be are referred to as *mamu* and *hatom* before marriage (personal communications with Deeney, 2007, and D. S. Purty, 2010).

- The distinction between *mamu-hatom honko bapala* and *misiya-bariya bapala* is one of perspective. In the first expression *ego*'s affinal relations in the adjacent generation (+1) are included, thus linking two levels and highlighting a marriage pattern that *ego* continues. The perspective in the second expression remains with(in) generation 0, focussing in contrast on sex distinction and connecting male seniority with female junior status, congruent with the fact that within *ego*'s generation relative age and sex terminologically distinguish *all* relations.

- Our *saki* emphasized the value of the diachronic nature of his and his forefathers' marital norms and practices, while knowing that other forms exist at the same time. By interrelating and linguistically merging the cross-cousin type of marriage of his father's (and forefathers') generation(s) into one composite expression, *mamu-hatom honko bapala* represents the value attached to a maintained pattern of intermarriage decided on by "reference to [his] ascendants' marriages [...] reproducing the marriage of [his] father and [...] grandfather," as Dumont put it for South India (Dumont 1983: 72; Barraud 2015: 237),[234] thus passing on affinal ties from one generation to the next. Majumdar similarly observes for the Ho that a man's children will marry "into the family or *kili* of his father-in-law" (Majumdar 1950: 125; Parkin 1992: 154). My *saki*'s and other Ho informants' cases, however, reveal that

---

234 The point of departure in Dumont and Barraud is the cultural logic whereby in South India affinal ties *and* bonds of consanguinity are diachronically transmitted and equally valued. In contradistinction, Western understandings attribute this diachronic nature to consanguineous relations only. Dumont defines for South India alliance relationship as a "relationship between two persons of the same sex" (ibid.: 74) and consequently categorizes the children of affines (who are about to marry) as "*ipso facto* affines" (ibid.: 72) themselves rather than labelling them as cross cousins with its individualizing air of consanguinity attached to the term. Parkin 1992 when referring to Majumdar 1950 contrastingly focusses on Ho "marriage choice" (ibid.: 150) differentiating between prohibited actual first-cousin and preferred classificatory MBD marriages such as MFBSD which indeed is one form that I have come across during fieldwork.

the permanence of what Dumont calls marriage alliance or simply alliance, which is lastingly engraved in Dravidian kinship terminology and sustained by Dravidian marriage regulations as a structuring principle, works out differently in Ho country. By "repeating marriage alliance between groups" (Trautmann 2000: 566), the Ho system, as part of the Munda system of kinship, clearly resembles the Dravidian one in its appreciation of diachronic affinal ties and affinity as such.[235] In contrast, however, never have continuous marriage relations over more than three to four generations been pointed out to me, neither in praxis nor as an ideal. Moreover, this has never been considered any kind of a deficiency. Going back three to four generations is almost synonymous with going back to the beginning of the world, as the Purty myth of origin in chapter 4 has shown.

- The character of relationships *after* marriage changes, and so do the relationship terms. The respective spouse's actual parents, cross uncles, and cross aunts transform in reference and address from *mamu* and *hatom* to *hanar* (HM, WM) and *honyar* (HF, WF).
- While the basic terms *hanar, honyar, mamu,* and *hatom* are terminologically distinguished by sex only, the composite term *mamu-hatom honko* terminologically differentiates neither relative age nor sex.
- Terminologically, *ego*'s parallel and cross cousins are not distinguished from *ego*'s actual or classificatory siblings. In address and reference they are comprehensively classed linguistically as 'siblings'. Like *ego*'s siblings, parallel and cross cousins are distinguished by relative age and sex as *bau/undi* (e, yB) and *aji/undi-kui* (e, yZ). These terms are used by female and male speakers alike.
- This constitutes a cognitive paradox, as implied conceptual distinctions between affinal and consanguineal relations within generation 0 become linguistically camouflaged. This absence of distinction matters socially and conceptually, however, because it affects the core of Ho ways of (not) marry-

---

235 Trautmann (2000: 559–572) has relevant details of a systematic comparison of North-Indian, Dravidian, and Munda kinship systems in "India and the Study of Kinship Terminologies". The "crystalline beauty of the mutual entailment of the Dravidian rule of marriage [...] and the Dravidian terminology" is juxtaposed to the terminological requirements in North India implying the "non-relatedness of bride and groom, and the non-reciprocity of the marriage transaction" (ibid.: 564–566). While Trautmann in former publications commented on the lack of a "distinctive Munda kinship terminology and a set of kinship norms" (1981: 136 as quoted in Verardo 2003b: 68), he speaks of the Munda system of kinship as the third of the Indian systems in (2000: 566). Here Trautmann mainly relies on Parkin (1992) for the Munda system, who in his turn relied almost exclusively, as concerns Ho and Santal, on Bouez (1985). I have discussed controversial aspects in Parkin/Bouez above in chapter 1.

ing. Figure 8 may illustrate the case in point: Purgun, my ♂*saki*'s mother and female *ego* (D) in the +1 generation, her elder brother Dussuru (B), and her husband Monguru (C) were reciprocally related in address and reference as *bau* or *bare* and *misi-era* (yZ) before her marriage. In other words, Purgun – like my *saki* and other Ho – married someone who used to be classified as her 'sibling' but was obviously *also* perceived as someone belonging to yet another category of 'nonsiblings', while others within their generation would remain related as 'siblings' all their lives. As outlined above, the collocation *misi-bare* seems to matter in terms of marriageability.

–   In the case of considering marriage, additional orientation is required. As a rule, marriage between *ego* and his or her parents' actual same-sex siblings' children is considered incest and followed by severe punishments. This norm is known and socially recognized even by those who break it. Marrying a (first) cross cousin is considered less unambiguously incest, and its social acceptance regionally varies greatly. While it is conceived of as inappropriate by some, though not excluded as a matter of principle, it is favoured and valued by others. Figure 8 suggests that our *saki*'s type of marriage falls into this category.

–   To linguistically express that the boy and girl about to marry are not brother and sister in a genealogical sense despite the terminological system classifying them as such, Ho people resort to a number of complementary specifications. They say that the two being married are not *mid lai:ren* (born of the same mother),[236] that they are not *miyad apurenko* (born to one father and his 'people'), that they are not *boko-boya* or *undi-boya* (children of the same parents). Marrying into the categories MBD/FZD and MBS/FZS as *mamu-hatom honko* also meets the requirement that the two are of different *kili* (clans), which was often pointed out by informants as the most important norm. Referring to figure 8, then, and to illustrate: Purgun (D) may marry Monguru (C), her elder 'brother' (*bare*), as he is in a *mamu-hatom* relation

---

236 When enquiring into the relationship between two people, I was often given the answer that they are related as brother and sister (*misi-barekin*). When I continued enquiring into the nature of the 'siblingship' I was either given the negated answer *mid lai:ren do kage!* excluding any genealogical link or I was given any of the above expressions. As in patrilateral Ho society membership in a clan (*kili*) is inherited from the father's side, *miyad apurenko* (my emphasis) probably emphasizes the aspect that the two about to marry are from different clans. These two expressions are used almost synonymously, but they highlight different aspects of relatedness: while in *miyad apurenko* a father is identified with his respective *kili*, in *mid lai:ren* the maternal side is identified by the respective part of her female body, as *lai:* literally means womb, stomach.

to her but not *undi-boya*; she may not marry Dussuru (B), her elder brother (*bau*), as he is *undi-boya* to her but not in a *mamu-hatom* relation.
– Marriage into the categories F/FB or M/MZ is ruled out, as these are conceived of as *mid lai:ren*.

In terms of actual empirical relatedness and the diachronic dimension of our *saki*'s marriage pattern, figure 8 illustrates that:
– My male *saki* and his grandfather are namesakes: Chumburu Purty in generation 0 and Chumburu Purty in generation +2. Both were born and lived in the house in Pathan Sai which my *saki*'s great-grandfather Kirsai (not in figure 8) built (Reichel 2009: 108).
– The relations depicted were conveyed as genealogically traceable ones, the knowledge of which was substantiated by the names of those living and dead family members involved in affinal exchange and by the respective relationship terms.
– Also, my ♂*saki*'s father Monguru was born in the same house as my ♂*saki*, but so was, of course, Monguru's sister Jima (A, +1), as both were *undi boya* or *mid lai:ren* (see above: born of the same parents/mother).
– Jima (+1) became my ♂*saki*'s mother-in-law (*hanar*). She is my ♀*saki*'s mother (*ma*).
– Of course, my ♂*saki* continued to live in the house of his birth after marriage, as his F and FF had done in their time and as his son would have done had he not died young. To repeat: my ♀*saki*'s mother (person A) and my ♂*saki*'s father Monguru (person C) are remembered and presented as cross siblings and *undi boya* to each other.
– My ♀*saki*'s mother's natal *kili* is Purty. On marriage into Sinku *kili* she moved to live virilocally with her husband Dussuru (person B) in Chiru Sai, where my ♀*saki* was born, her natal *kili* being Sinku.
– Upon marriage, my ♀*saki* became Purty and – again following the social rule of virilocal residence – moved to Pathan Sai just as her MM (*jiya*, +2) had done two generations before her. So my ♀*saki* *after* marriage moved to the village and into the house where her own mother Jima (+1) had been born and where she herself gave birth to Jima (-1), her own and only daughter. Thus, Jima of generation +1 and Jima of generation -1 grew up in physically the same place *before* their marriages in alternating generations.
– In three consecutive generations (+2, +1, 0) presented as consanguineously related (*hagako* – 'brothers'; of one *miyad mandi chaturenko*), as illustrated in figure 8, my ♂*saki*, his F (*miyad apurenko*), and his FF of *kili* Purty, sub-*kili* Holon Purty, claim to have given sisters to and received wives from *kili* Sinku of village Chiru Sai in immediate repetition of affinal exchange. Giving

sisters and taking wives was claimed to have been repeated diachronically between two localized groups of two localized subclans in two hamlets without any interval of two or more generations, in a process in which each of the two categories involved were equally givers and receivers. The concept of the principled North Indian or Indo-Aryan distinction of wife-giving from wife-taking affinal categories is absent among the Ho and, as Pfeffer argues, in all of tribal Middle India, thus confirming that "the Munda system occupies a structural middle way between the Indo-Aryan and the Dravidian system" (Trautmann 2000: 566). Whether and how the regular pattern of giving and taking implies, demands, or allows for symmetric exchange will be considered later in this section.

– The organization of alliance in a system consisting of only two categories linked in affinal exchange is not a closed system but open to variation, though not arbitrarily so. The continuation of our *saki*'s perpetuated affinal relations ended after three generations. As the dotted line in figure 8 shows, our *saki*'s daughter Jima (-1) married into a different affinal place and into another *kili* (Birua), as did their granddaughter (*jaitadi*), who married into *kili* Alda and moved virilocally to Simlipal (not in figure 8). These deviations in their turn were *bapala andi*, too, fully arranged marriages in Ho terms. As such, they were welcomed and reassessed as new roads (*nama hora*) contributing to social cohesion in their way by following or strengthening a complementary alliance concept of dispersed affinity. 'New roads' are often synonymous with roads leading some distance away, and marriages following that path command a high reputation for the opportunities they offer to constitute new alliances in the future. Simlipal – the area my/my *saki*'s granddaughter (*jaitadi*) married into – almost defined the end of Ho country to the southeast in that Ho spirits' and Ho deities' power and protective capacities were said not to be able to reach out beyond that area.

– Given the large number of more than 132 Ho clans, the supercategory of affines comprising basically all those who are not constructed as consanguines lends itself to being subdivided into a large number of distinct localized affinal categories that are defined in relation to *ego* as those from which to choose spouses.

To sum up and conclude: the ideological relevance attributed to these particular affinal exchange patterns hints at something that provides status by reaching out beyond the limited factual fate of two empirical beings in the present. Affinal exchange over generations is *done* in the awareness of complying with social norms and rules (*niyam*) that have stood the test of time and Ho forefathers. Affinity is a value, and diachronic affinity is created and re-created in ordered, predictable, transparent, reliable, and systematic ways. It is *one* of several known ways of marrying (properly).[237] The repetition as well as the *immediacy* of the repetition of what formally equals "sister exchange" between two moieties (Barnard and Good 1984: 96) figures prominently in my ♂*saki*'s type of perpetuated intermarriage pattern. According to the information given, this coincides with diachronic relations between territorial units that constitute kin places (*haga jaga*) and affinal places (*bala jaga*).[238] Structuring the physical landscape linguistically along kinship perceptions underlines the social prevalence of the domain of kinship in the Ho's ideational universe.

While my *saki* focussed in his account on the regularity and the immediacy of repetition, the metalanguage of symmetric and diachronic exchange, of course, was not his way of talking about it. It is mine in order to make sense of the data obtained in long talks. Confronting the data of symmetric affinal exchange as projected in figure 8 with Ho relationship terminology from an analytical perspective, as I will next go on to do, gives rise to questions and reveals discrepancies. Such discrepancies were not evident as long as our *saki*'s affinal exchange was documented by giving concrete names of actual persons involved and by resorting to composite terms to clarify the relationships – all of which, of course, is relevant at the empirical and jural level where marriages are planned, arranged, and lived.

In order to make it easier to follow the argument and accommodate the contradictions that unfold between the levels of prescription, preference, and practice,[239] a survey of Ho relationship terminology is given first, placing the terms already mentioned within a systematic arrangement (see figure 9).

---

237 Deeney has listed four different ways (2005: 9); see chapter 7.

238 Dumont coined the terms "kin place" and "affinal place" when discussing for Southern India the Dravidian terminological dichotomy of kin and affines and the opposition between the two taking on "a spatial aspect" (Dumont 1983: 77).

239 Analytical distinctions and potential or necessary correlations between these three levels have been debated at length. Barnard and Good (1984: 100f) have an outline of the hotly discussed issue in kinship theory by referring a.o.to Lévi-Strauss (1949/1969), Homans and Schneider (1955), Leach (1971 [1961], 1991[1970]), Needham (1962, 1973). Broadly speaking, the debate is informed by tensions between linguistic *invariance* at the terminological or categorical level and cultural *variability* at the level of preferential rules and marital behaviour.

A criticism of the shortcomings of portraying systematic links between alliance units by using the genealogical format in diagrams is also summarized there (Barnard and Good 1984: 98).

Digression: Ho expressions of relationship

In an effort to order and structure the multiplicity of Ho expressions of relationship and to pay tribute to *ego*'s empirical social relations from generation +2 all
the way through to generation -2 at the same time, Deeney (2002: 130) worked out
a visualization in which he arranges in a nonlinear way five generations of *ego*'s
consanguineous and affinal relations in *one* diagram. Nowhere else have I come
across a more inclusive or a better structured survey of Ho relationship terms. It
is systematic and comprehensive in that it takes into account the principles of
relative age, generation, and sex and refrains from artificially separating *ego*'s
affinal relations. Except for Pfeffer, however, who in his studies of social organization and kinship in tribal Middle India introduced Deeney and his list of Ho
designata (in Pfeffer 1982: 79 f.; 2004: 404) more than three decades ago, this author has as yet been ignored by those working on Munda and Ho relationship
terminology[240] and Ho alliance patterns. For this reason, and also as Deeney successfully avoids making use of a conventional mechanistic genealogical format,
his diagram of Ho relationship terminology is reproduced directly here (figure 9).
In the course of my fieldwork, this diagram proved a true survival kit when prob-
ing my way through the jungle of Ho social relations.

Deeney's diagram is graphically organized as a mind map around the following four focal centres in generation 0: a male *ego* (*kowa*) and his wife (*era*) and a
female *ego* (*kui*) and her husband (*herel*). Each of the four central positions is
systematically assigned its share of more than fifty corresponding Ho relation-

---

240 Both Bouez (1985, 1990) and Verardo 2003b were personally in touch with Deeney (personal communication) in the course of their fieldwork, but they do not refer to his publications in
their discussing Munda/ Ho kinship and terminology. Verardo comes up with an incomplete
table of 'Munda kinship terminology' in which affinal terms are included, however not systematically so, so an air of selectiveness and arbitrariness is unfortunately lingering around this effort (Verardo 2003b: 69). Deeney is also missing in Parkin (1992), but perhaps he did not have
access to Deeney's books, as these are circulated only regionally, and Parkin was not in the area
himself. Yorke 1976 met Deeney and discussed Ho matters with him (see above: *miyad mandi
chaturenko*). Deeney's grammar containing the list of Ho clans and relationship terms had
just been published in 1975. Yorke, indeed, has it in the list of the references of his thesis, but
then kinship, marriage, and terminology was not his topic.

Majumdar (1950: 175 – 176) offers a non-structured, non-annotated and incomplete collection of 92 terms many of them overlapping, others missing altogether (e.g. WeBW, HyZ) and
quite a few that seem quite questionable to me when compared to my own data (i.e. apart
from the general problematic of unequivocal transcription). Majumdar re-published a former
monograph on the Ho in 1950, which is the year after Deeney arrived in India for the first
time. To my knowledge there has never been any intellectual collaboration between the two.

ship terms. The central four persons are positioned in the midst of the web of their social relations, consisting of their

- siblings (lines slanted to the upper and lower left give elder and younger brothers, and lines slanted to the upper and lower right give elder and younger sisters),
- siblings' spouses (whose terms are given in parentheses right next to the siblings),
- spouse's siblings (following the identical pattern, lines slanted to the upper and lower left give the spouse's elder and younger brothers, and lines slanted to the upper and lower right give the spouse's elder and younger sisters), and lastly
- spouse's siblings' spouses (given next to the spouse's siblings in parentheses).

The diagram differentiates between the relations of a man and those of a woman by dividing the grid horizontally into two correlating parts based on gender. Thus the relationship terms related to a male *ego* (*kowa*) and his wife (*era*) are given above the horizontal axis, and the respective terms for a female *ego*'s (*kui*) relations and those of her husband (*herel*) are given below the horizontal axis. Relative age (sibling seniority bias) is differentiated along with gender throughout the three medial generations and has been systematically accounted for in the model. All in all, Deeney's diagram is arranged *ego*-centrically, introducing on five levels those terms that constitute a male and a female *ego*'s terminological universe.

Cutting across the horizontal separation based on gender, the diagram vertically opposes on all levels the terms for *ego* and those related to her or him consanguineously on the left-hand side to the respective terms for *ego*'s affines on the right-hand side.[241] Considering the great number of terms on the righthand side, roughly representing the body of a Ho's affinal relations and hence constituting almost half of a Ho's social cosmos, Deeney's visual arrangement of Ho

---

241 This clear-cut description is simplified in that it seems to mechanically separate and juxtapose consanguineal terms on the left-hand side of the diagram from affinal ones on the right. Figure 9 has been given to introduce the overall structure of Deeney's model. However, when studying the model in detail, it will be seen that also on the left-hand side affinal terms are included concerning e.g. *ego*'s siblings' spouses, while on the right-hand side terms denoting the categories of *ego*'s spouse's siblings' spouses (spsibsp) terminologically turn out to be assessed as consanguineal (*see* also figure 15 and the section on *mmc*, *hagako* and *mid mayom* in chapter 3 above).

relationship terminology graphically highlights the value attributed to affinity in Ho country.

Figure 9

According to my informants and compared with my own field data, Deeney's survey given in figure 9 is accurate and complete[242] as concerns the categories inquired into. This qualification is necessary, as probably no published list of relationship terms will ever be complete. Terminological and regional variations in address and reference exist. When collecting data on individual pedigrees, in fact, I refrained – in order not to grate on my hosts' nerves too excessively – from enquiring into categories going beyond those represented in Deeney's grid and recommended by Barnard and Good (1984: 26 f.).

A few technical remarks concerning the noninflected forms of the reference terms given in figure 9 are necessary:

– In Deeney's diagram, two lines are missing: one horizontally connecting a female *ego*'s son, *kowa-hon*, with her daughter, *kui-hon* (bottom left), and one vertically connecting son and daughter with their mother, *kui*, as is done correctly on top in the case of a male *ego*.

– I presume by now that in accordance with the cultural logic that the system of Ho relationship terminology conveys, a wife's elder brother's wife (WeBW) is *aji* and not *aji-hanar*, as Deeney's model suggests. Maybe it is a misprint which I could not clarify in the field, as I detected the possible error – if it is one – only after my return home. It goes without saying that this is more than a technical matter, since *aji-hanar* would be an affinal category, as opposed to *aji*, the consanguineal relation which the system requires, as figure 16 will show.

– Deeney's data confirm what has already been said in a different context, that all of *ego*'s cousins, the children of *ego*'s parents' siblings (ss and os), are terminologically not differentiated from *ego*'s siblings.[243] For this reason, only the four basic terms for ♂♀ *ego*'s siblings (elder and younger) are given, which do not reappear separately for *ego*'s cousins *in* the diagram. Not only are *ego*'s cousins terminologically equated with *ego*'s siblings and hence linguistically and semantically void of any affinal connotations;

---

242 The semantics of the term *sango* representing more than one specific kintype and missing in Deeney's diagram is discussed in the following subsection.

243 The 'Cheyenne' variety reveals the same feature according to F. Eggan's presentation of (male) *ego*'s relations on level 0 (Eggan 1970: 43, quoted in Pfeffer 2016: 350). It will be elaborated in more detail with figures 15 and 16 below.

their children (MBChCh/FZChCh) are also terminologically equated with *ego*'s siblings' children. They appear in the diagram as *ego*'s parallel (*hon-sed/hon-era, gungu*) or cross nieces and nephews (*gekowa/-kui,* ms; *homon,* ws).

Several relationship terms in the research area deviate in reference and address from those in Deeney's diagram. A few examples have already been mentioned.

Kuma/mamu: in the research area in Mayurbhanj *mamu* was used in both reference *and* address to refer to a mother's brother and a father's sister's husband. *Kuma* is preferred in the Chaibasa area.

Hatom: people were aware of this term in Mayurbhanj, but *ji* was used more often in reference and address, though never in the collocation *mamu-hatom honko.*

Apu/enga (F/M): these terms were used as reference terms only, in address replaced by *babu* and *ma* or *kaki-ma.*

Aji/bau (eZ/eB): my informants preferred *dai* and *dada* instead.

Era/herel: these terms were understood but were hardly ever used as reference terms and never as address terms and were replaced once children had arrived by the respective teknonyms *mai engate* and *mai apute* (mother/father of the young girl).

Undi (younger brother) and *undi-kui* (younger sister): these terms were used by many, female and male alike, but *boko* (younger brother/sister)[244] by others.

Someone's 'son' was usually referred to as *hon* and addressed most of the time as *babu,* whereas a daughter was more often referred to and addressed as *mai* or by the Hindi term *beti.*

I infrequently came across *ge-kowa/ge-kui,* which is the term for a man's cross nephew or cross niece (sister's child, ms) as well as both spouses' cross nieces/nephews (WBCh, HZCh). I heard the terms *boronja* (male form) and, less often, *banji* (female form) instead.

In all cases *gaun* was replaced by *kaki* (MyZ, FyBW).

Sango: the semantics of an enigmatic term

I came across the self-reciprocal relationship term *sango* many times during fieldwork and afforded it prominence at the beginning of chapter 3 in the section "How to establish a relationship." It was introduced there as a category on demand, a terminological option in the context of Ho people negotiating their re-

---

244 Deeney gives *boko* as yB/yZ in his dictionary, but only yB in his grammar. In Mayurbhanj it was commonly used to relate to someone's younger brother *and* younger sister.

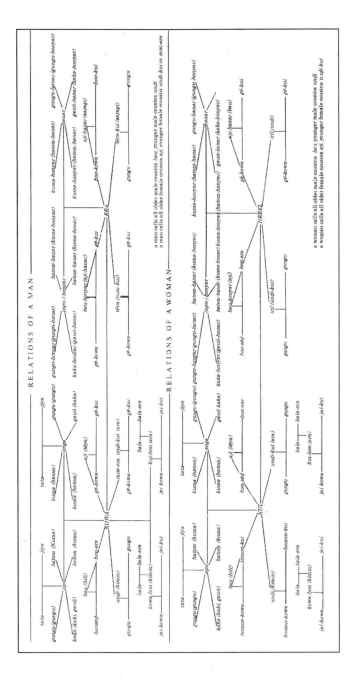

Figure 9: Ho expressions of relationship
The relationship terms of male Ho are given in the upper half, those of female Ho in the lower half of the diagram (reproduced from Deeney 2002: 130–31).

lationship when meeting for the first time. It is a multifaceted term, since it may carry different meanings for different people in different – and even in the same – regions. Of Hindi origin, it obviously lends itself to becoming accommodated in a number of Middle Indian terminologies, in the process changing its meaning, as the following examples show.

For the Juang, for example, *sango* has been reported to link members of the categories of ♀ sibling's spouse (yZH) and ♀ spouse's sibling (WeB) (McDougal 1963: 447). This relation formally complies with the equation WB = ZH and may therefore suggest symmetric affinal exchange. As the diagram reveals, however, the relation implies a doubled distance of relative age between a husband and his wife. As Juang members of any generation are assumed to marry in order of relative age (ibid.: 157), the term *sango* only hypothetically constitutes a symmetric affinal relationship, because of the formal distance of seniority. Consequently, McDougal does not point out *sango* as a category for *ego* to choose a spouse from.

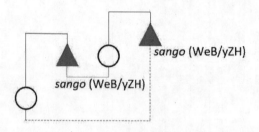

Figure 10: *Sango*, a Juang relationship term
In Juang cultural logic the term denotes a hypothetical symmetric affinal relationship.

Skoda reports different types of *sangat* marriages among the Aghria of Bonai in Sundergarh district when discussing their marriage preferences. He refers to ZHZ and BWZ as *sangat* categories. He also points out that marrying a *sangat* or BWZ may imply a repetition of the marriage direction, while marrying a *sangat* or ZHZ may hint at reciprocal exchange relations (Skoda 2005: 297). This last type of marriage is known among Ho people, who also call it a marriage of two related as *sango* (see figure 13).

Judging from his research site bordering on Keonjhar district, Bouez (1985: 59) lists *sango* exclusively as a Ho husband's address term for his wife before she gives birth to their first child. This is a usage that I have not heard at all in my field area less than fifty kilometres north. Only for Santal does Bouez (ibid.: 101) classify *sangat* in address and reference as a self-reciprocal relationship term. He defines eBWyZ, eZHyZ as the two forms of *sangat* relations as seen from the perspective of a male speaker and eBWyB, eZHyB from the perspective of a female speaker. This, however, comes very close to how *sango* relations among Ho people were conveyed to me in Mayurbhanj, as I will show.

Interestingly, *sango* is missing in Deeney's publications altogether.[245] Figure 11 is an aside that D. S. Purty, Deeney's assistant, sketched in my notepad while discussing with me the fieldnotes I had taken on the term.

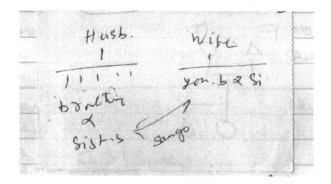

Figure 11: *Sango*, a Ho relation (as represented by D. S. Purty)
"A husband's brothers and sisters have a *sango* relation with his wife's brothers and sisters who – as such – are classified as younger brothers and sisters. If you have a married brother or sister, all of his/her spouse's siblings are your *sango* and marriageable." Chaibasa, October 3, 2010, personal communication. The term *sango* next to the arrow is my addition and my handwriting.

He confirmed that *sango* among the Ho refers to the category of *ego*'s siblings' spouses' siblings (ZHZ, BWB, ZHB, BWZ). If we try to locate or position *sango* within the relational logic and graphical arrangement of Deeney's diagram (figure 9), it turns out to be a category of actual or classificatory siblings of *ego*'s *hili* (eBW), *kimin* (yBW), *teya* (eZH), and *ara* (yZH). It thus concerns the lateral aspects of *ego*'s social relations within generation 0, as depicted in figure 12.

---

245 He was utterly unaware of the term as he frankly admitted. – I thank Uwe Skoda who drew my attention to the category *sango* in 2006 when paying us a visit in the field at a time when I was quite unaware of the relevance of this category. I then asked Deeney, who then asked D. S. Purty, his *pandit*. Deeney returned from his discussion with D. S. Purty really thrilled to have learned something new and planned to have the term listed in the next edition of his Ho-English Dictionary (personal communication). This, unfortunately, did not happen due to Deeney's death in 2010.

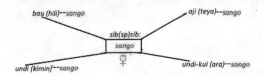

Figure 12: *Sango*, a self-reciprocal Ho category of *ego*'s siblings' spouses' siblings
Depending on context, the semantics of the term *sango* oscillate between denoting the genealogical position of a specific kintype and denoting an optional category implying marriageability. Here the perspective of a female *ego* (*kui*) as *sango* is given. (Adapted from figure 9. *KUI*, a woman, at the bottom left in Deeney's diagram, has been specified as *sango*).

A total of five examples will illustrate how the term is used by Ho people and how it changes in meaning depending on social context.

Example 1: when I enquired into the pedigree of G. Bage, Ho village elder (*munda*) of Manbir, I was given the relationship terms for eighty-six relations from generation +2 to generation -2. In his own generation, he remembered thirty-nine people, *haga* ('brothers') and *bala* (affinal relations). The wife (*kimin*, yBW) of one of his two younger brothers (*undi*, yB) had one actual younger brother and one actual younger sister. Only these two persons were reciprocally related as *sango* (yBWyB, yBWyZ) to G. Bage as eZHeB in reference and address. Their respective spouses were linguistically referred to as G. Bage's younger 'siblings': *misi-kui* (yBWyBW) and *undi* (yBWyZH). In G. Bage's case the *sango* relation is one across two age steps, which rules out marriageability and affinal symmetry in terms of seniority – apart from those *sango* relations that exist between persons of the same sex.[246]

Example 2: when clarifying details concerning his pedigree, L. Barda, another villager and informant from Manbir, came up with forty-nine persons in his generation 0. He enumerated altogether nine *sango*, female and male, to whom he is reciprocally related via his elder brother's wife (*hili*) as eBWyB, eBWyZ/eZHyB and via his younger sister's husband (*ara*) as yZHsib/yBWeB.

In these two examples, *sango* has been referred to as a distinct kintype. The term was unequivocally accommodated within the respective pedigrees, comparable to all the other genealogical positions that were given. All *sango* positions were identified via G. Bage's and L. Barda's siblings and siblings' spouses within

---

246 Lea Schulte-Droesch conducted fieldwork among Santal in Dhalbhum, approximately 50 km to the east from where I had stationed myself among Ho people. She defines the *sangat* relation as a joking relationship restricted to a pair of the spouses' opposite-sex siblings (Schulte-Droesch 2018: 164).

generation 0. No recourse was taken to tracing the *sango* relation by going back to the ascending generation +1. While the term *sango* distinguishes neither relative age nor sex, *sango*'s spouses are so distinguished, and the latter as a rule are classified as *ego*'s senior or junior 'siblings'. There are *sango* relations between Ho of the same and the opposite sex, between married and unmarried Ho, and across the tribal divide. Irrespective of their own marital status and that of those reciprocally related to them as *sango*, *sango* keep referring to and addressing each other as *sango* for a lifetime. However, addressing each other as *sango* is discontinued in the case that two individuals so related marry each other.

A *sango* relation implies marriageability, symmetry, and symmetric exchange if the categories involved conform to the rules of seniority, as illustrated in figure 13. In line with D. S. Purty's definition and illustration rendered in figure 11, my classificatory 'mother' (*kaki-mã*) from Boja Sai claimed to have married her *sango*, her classificatory elder brother's wife's actual younger brother (eBWyB) who, when asked how he was related to my *kaki* before they married (*chikaiyam andi ayer?*) confirmed she was his *sango*, reciprocally, as she was his eZHyZ.

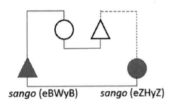

sango (eBWyB)   sango (eZHyZ)

Figure 13: *Sango,* an affinal Ho category on demand
The relation between the categories eBWyB and eZHyZ conforms to the order of seniority.

Structurally, this marriage pattern (and quite generally any marriage into the category ZHZ) indicates symmetric affinal exchange if the order of relative age is observed. In contradistinction to the Juang system, however, where affinal symmetry between two persons related as *sango* (W₂B = yZH) is precluded due to the distance of seniority, *sango* relations among the Ho may indicate symmetric affinal relationships when they agree with the demands of seniority, that is, when they are anchored on the same age level. When they are not, as in the above examples of G. Bage and L. Barda, affinal exchange and symmetry between those related as *sango* is precluded[247] – but they do remain *sango* to each other, they continue to address and refer to each other as *sango*, and, as such, they continue to joke with each other.

Sango as presented so far is an ambiguous term and relation: apart from it being a relationship term to identify the precise genealogical position of a specific kintype surrounded and embedded in an empirical Ho's social universe next to others agnatically and affinally related to her or him, it complementarily represents a more general category that is strictly nonconsanguineal in character and signifies marriageability. In fact, among the Ho people of Mayurbhanj *sango* was used almost generically to refer to someone defined as being of a marriageable, in any case affinal category, turning *sango* into a category on demand, as it were, without necessarily pinning down the position to a specific kintype. This, however, was also frequently done, and in my field experience especially so in the case of a Ho *ego* when referring to a father's sister's children. This adds to the term's semantic and contextual adaptability. Again, examples will illustrate the point.

Example 3: initially I became quite irritated when some informants insisted on referring to their actual bilateral cross cousins as *sango* with some regularity. S. Kondangkel, for example, *munda* (village elder) of Gara Sai (see chapter 7 below), was a committed, serious informant and my 'younger brother'. He referred to the two daughters and two sons of his father's elder sister (FeZD, FeZS) as his *sango* and refused to classify them as 'siblings' as others did. On further inquiry, he specified his four cross cousins as *hatominya: honko* (children of my father's sister) to whom he is related as their *mamuya: hon* (MBS) or, he said, as *sango*. As often, composite terms were resorted to in order to clarify the relational context. While S. Kondangkel terminologically discriminated his cross cousins from his siblings as *sango*, the respective spouses of his cross-cousin *sango* were given as his elder or younger siblings. Neither with S. Kondangkel nor with any other informant was there any ambiguity as concerned this point.

Example 4: I stayed in Boja Sai so long that eventually everybody living in that hamlet was introduced to me. I learnt that a young man who could have been my son and I were reciprocally related as *sango*. The age difference of pos-

---

247 Being related to someone as *sango* within one age level represents an option in terms of marriageability though not necessarily a privileged one and by no means the only one. L. Barda, of the second example given above, despite his having also female *sango* his age, was in the process of getting married – to his MFBSD. The negotiations concerning his marriage were under way. When those representing his side (*haga*) and that of his spouse-to-be (*bala*) met at his parents' place to negotiate the details as was their responsibility, L. played football with his friends first and then left for the market to return fairly drunk.

sibly thirty-five years kept irritating me as long as I tried to sort out the *sango* relation within generation 0. It only began to make sense when I realized that his mother was my classificatory father's elder sister, and hence the young man and I structurally belonged to the same age level. This meant that we might as well have been constructed as 'siblings'. In fact, he occasionally addressed me as *dai* (eZ), which I immediately returned as *undin* (my younger brother), but whenever he felt like joking, as he usually did, he addressed me by the term *sango*. After his father's death, I was told, his mother had moved back with her son to Boja Sai. This was her natal village, in which her *jonom owa:*, the house where she was born as an only daughter, was left deserted after her parents' death. Here she lived together with her son, my *sango* (FeZS to whom I was reciprocally MyBD), and his wife, my *sango era* (*sango*'s wife) or younger sister (*undi-kui*). This was a *sango* relation between two married persons whose relation as classificatory cross cousins was traced by moving back to the parental generation (+1).

Example 5: similarly, by moving back to the parental generation (+1) and without mentioning the term *sango*, Dhan, herself a Ho, is straightforward and outspoken in stating that a "man may have joking relationship with his mother's brother's daughters, all of them the elder as well as the younger, because he can marry any of them" (Dhan 1961: 72).[248] When discussing the possibility of cross-cousin marriage, especially among first-degree cousins, as Dhan suggests, my Santal informants agreed, but immediately added, "Yes, Ho people do that, but we don't, never (*ale do kage*)." Among Ho people, however, things were usually hotly debated and not as unambiguously obvious as it seems to be for Santal people and Dhan. For instance, a Ho student[249] who was attending a college in Bhubaneswar and spoke English well had come to attend a secondary burial (*diri dulsunum*) in the area. He volunteered to emphasize that marrying one's MBD was out of the question among Ho. In this he was strongly supported by others who had joined in the debate. Marrying one's MFBSD, he added, however, would be a much-appreciated option which he classified as marrying one's *sango*. To underline the relevance of the point the young man then managed to draw the following diagram:

---

248 Structural tensions arising from marrying into a category that terminologically is proscribed for marriage will be discussed in the following subsection *Affinal exchange and Ho relationship terminology*.
249 It should go without saying that I am not interested in coming up with individual statements. Such clarifying discussions took place most of the time in public and usually involved committed combatants as well as keen listeners.

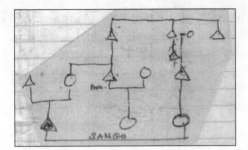

Figure 14: *Sango,* a reciprocal Ho relation between MFBSD and FFBDS
The diagram was sketched by D. Kondangkel from Katbaria in my notebook after he had spotted some pedigrees there and immediately grasped the logic. Additions in red are mine.

He referred to his mother as his reliable source of knowledge and authorization, and all of those who were present agreed that it was a mother's task to brief her children and teach them the proper codes of conduct. In fact, I, too, found that women were often a most reliable source of knowledge, and it happened quite frequently that men referred me to their wives for clarification.

The composite term *mamu-hatom hon(ko)* was described above as a surrogate label to linguistically mark the genealogical position of marriageable cross cousins furnished with an air of intergenerational temporality within an otherwise unmarked category of nonmarriageable 'siblings'. While both my *saki* made use of that option to specify in retrospect their relation before marriage, other Ho informants who were likewise related confirmed that they had addressed and referred to each other reciprocally as *sango* before marrying. Only in that respect is there an overlap between the two terms, one which is recognized by some but not by all.

Depending on context, however, *sango* is even more multifaceted and polysemous, as has been elaborated above. *Sango* is unambiguously affinal in character. By representing the category of *ego*'s siblings' spouses' siblings, for which there is no other basic term and no alternative composite term, it is a category that strongly suggests marriageability – presupposing that the rule of seniority is complied with. This corresponds to D. S. Purty's understanding of *sango* among Ho people in figure 11. As such, *sango* comes close to signalling marriage preference.

Relationship terminology is no isolated issue restricted to the terminological level only. It bears on the levels of marriage regulations and marriage behaviour. A few relationship terms are debatable, and *sango* is one of them. In any case, it is a term with strong joking connotations, and it may make a world of difference if two as yet unrelated young people negotiate and decide in a specific context whether to establish a relation as 'siblings' or reciprocally as *sango*. Both options are there, kindling different expectations. Ho people have a choice. The details of such a decision-making process have been rendered above in chapter 3's "How to establish a relationship," where I introduced the character of *sango* as an enigmatic affinal category on demand.

Affinal exchange and Ho relationship terminology

In the previous section, Deeney's systematic overview of Ho relationship terms (figure 9) was supplemented by a discussion of the affinal category *sango*, which does not lend itself to becoming accommodated in a formalized grid because of its oscillating character. Following next is the step-by-step confrontation announced above between our *saki*'s empirical data of symmetric affinal exchange projected into the two-line model of figure 8 and the system of Ho relationship terminology, without intending to offer a formal analysis in the strict sense.

Empirical and jural level: Referring to their lived experience, Ho people will classify both of their parents (F, M) as their consanguines. In a society with a patrilateral bias such as Ho society, a male Ho – and a female Ho *before* marriage – will be considered agnatically related to their respective F's and FF's side, while they are considered affinally related to their MB's (and MF's) side, who represent a category and *kili* different from that of their F. Following from this and depicted in figure 8, FZ (person A, Jima, +1) *after* marrying MB (person B, Dussuru, +1) eventually becomes integrated into MB's *kili* Sinku as MBW and thus changes her status from that of a consanguine to that of an affine. She changes sides in terms of clan membership and residence (and ancestors), just as *ego*'s M changed sides when she married F, whom she could marry only because she was an affine in relation to F before marriage.

Given the specific characteristics of relationship terminology in tribal Middle India, it becomes obvious that empirical reality is not as static and one-dimensional as figure 8 suggests if we assume it to portray *diachronic* affinity in its structural overall complexity. It is one of the shortcomings of this model – but not the only one – that it is a segment cut out from a diachronic process, and even as a segment it is structurally inconsistent and incomplete, as I will show. While figure 8 juxtaposes – according to my intention – two opposing *empirical pairs* in terms of territoriality (Pathan Sai vs. Chiru Sai) and clanship (Purty vs. Sinku), it masks or at least blurs the opposition(s: plural) between consanguineal and affinal categories (plural) involved in the process of affinal exchanges and the temporal dimension (change in status before and after marriage and the specificities of affinal exchange(s) in generation 0).[250]

Figure 8 suggests bilateral cross-cousin marriage, which is indeed one form of Ho alliance that is confirmed by Ho informants as one option alongside others and that is supported by ethnographic data for the Ho reported by Verardo (2003b: 68), Bouez (1985: 66–70), Parkin, following Bouez 1985 (1992: 154f.), and Majumdar (1950: 125, 162).[251] That abstracted model, however, was not enlivened here by biographic detail in order to represent the single case of my *saki*'s actual marriage pattern over several generations, but rather in order to make use of his practised and recognized form of Ho alliance as an instance of some general relevance. The specific form of systematic symmetric affinal exchange involving *two* exogamous categories only, as illustrated in the model of figure 8, suggests and presupposes in generation 0 the equations ZH = WB and HZ = BW. While these equations correlate with the Dravidian system in nontribal South India, they do not apply in tribal Middle India, where they constitute nonequations at the terminological level. The following argument is about this paradox. By looking in some detail at the terminological level, I will argue that the Ho alliance pattern of symmetric affinal exchange requires another modified and enlarged model to be adequately represented.

Terminological level: What results would we get if we translated the constituents of the equations ZH = WB and HZ = BW, as suggested by figure 8, into the respective expressions of Ho relationship terminology? We would certainly expect to find lexically distinct Ho terms for each of the categories ZH, WB, HZ, BW. The problem arises, however, that the above equations ignore relative age distinctions, but relationship terminology does not and cannot. Lexically, there are no unifying basic Ho terms to denote a sister or a brother as such, which means that there are no terms to denote ZH or BW, but only yZH, eZH, yBW, eBW etc. (see figure 9 above). In short, ZH ≠ WB, and HZ ≠ BW; that is, Z(e/y)H and WB(e/y) belong to linguistically marked different affinal categories, just as HZ(e/y) and B(e/y)W belong to terminologically distinct affinal categories. The categories of WB/HZ accommodating ♀♂spouse's siblings (spsib) are terminologically and structurally not identical with the categories ZH/BW housing ♂♀siblings' spouses (sibsp). Hence spsib ≠ sibsp. If, then, ZH/BW (elder and younger: sibsp) cannot be equated with WB/HZ (elder and younger: spsib), it log-

---

250 Figure 15 attempts to make up for these deficiencies suggesting four distinct affinal categories involved in symmetric affinal exchange.

251 For cross-cousin marriage among the Aghria of Bonai Skoda has the details in (Skoda 2005: 294), Berger for the Gadaba of Koraput in (Berger 2007:170).

ically follows that *symmetric* exchange between *these* categories is linguistically precluded.

Also, by the same linguistic and analytic logic it appears in generation -1 that SW (*kimin*) ≠ BD (*homon*, ws) ≠ HZD (*ge*), and DH (*ara*) ≠ ZS (*ge-kowa*, ms) ≠ WBS (*ge-kowa*). Hence, the categories of *ego*'s children's spouses (♂*ara*, ♀*kimin*) are also not equated terminologically with those of *ego*'s cross nephews and cross nieces (♂*ge-kowa*, ♀*ge-kui*, ms; ♀♂*homon*, ws), as figure 8 structurally suggests as a relational regularity.

It then follows – again in contrast to what figure 8 implies – that formally more than two exchanging units must be involved in generation 0. Given this un-ambiguous terminological explicitness and the necessity of more than two categories, the question arises of whether and how the model can be adjusted to still portray *symmetric* affinal exchange, which is the message implied in figure 8, on the one hand, and which – more importantly – correlates with Ho narrations of the value of diachronic affinity, on the other hand, independent of and beyond the structural implications of a two-line terminology conventionally associated with Dravidian patterns and nomenclature in nontribal South India.

Figures 15 and 16

Figure 15 below attempts to *linguistically* order this structural complexity on the terminological level. Excluding from the grid for this purpose all composite terms whose social relevance has been discussed above, it organizes the basic[252] affinal *and* consanguineal terms by opposing them within one diagram and by representing them as seen from *ego*'s perspective. It visualizes the change from generation to generation in alliance relationships over the three medial generations +1, 0, and -1.

---

252 By comparison Deeney's list of relationship terms contains the whole complex of affinal *composite* terms operative on the first ascending level. This concerns the categories of *ego*'s spouse's parents, i.e. the e/y siblings and e/y siblings' spouses of *ego*'s spouse's parents. In other words, Deeney's diagram shows clearly that on level +1 *ego*'s affinal relations are equally differentiated in terms of gender and relative age, though by composite terms. To give two exam-ples: ♂*ego*'s FeBW is *gungu*, while ♂*ego*'s WFeBW is *gungu-hanar*, his WMeZH is *gungu-honyar*. Like this *ego* 'affinalizes' the basic terms on level +1 of W/H's respective consanguineal relations by adding *hanar* for female, *honyar* for male persons. The lexical structure results in a body of composite terms on level +1 and linguistically emphasizes the value of affinity. This applies also to a Ho spouse's *elder* siblings on level 0, *bau-honyar* (WeB, HeB) and *aji-hanar* (WeZ, HeZ)) thus emphasizing their senior sibling status.

In contradistinction, Pfeffer's formal analysis of Middle Indian terminologies (Pfeffer 2019) is concerned with basic terms only.

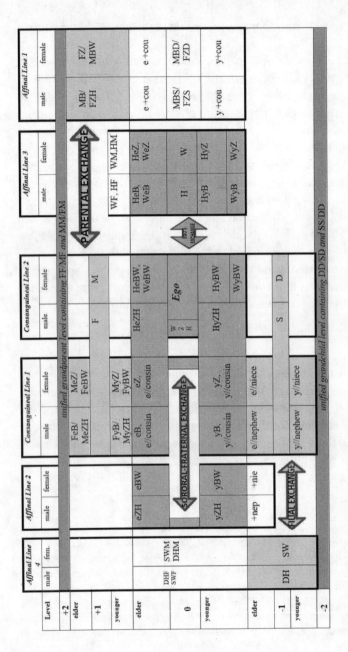

Figure 15: Ho relationship terminology I
The structural logic of Ho denotata and the pattern of synchronic affinal symmetry. (Adaptation of Kharia relationship terminology as ordered by Pfeffer 2019: 89)

Figure 15 is my adaptation of a model of Kharia relationship terminology which Pfeffer has developed for affinal *proscriptions* as mapped out in Highland Middle Indian terminologies (Pfeffer 2019: 83). With reference to proscriptive Seneca Iroquois terminology, Pfeffer identifies the terminological patterns in this region "as semi-complex, non-prescriptive structures." He highlights the relevance of classifying relative age as the decisive principle of relationship terminologies in tribal Middle India, distinguishing the area from the terminological givens in both North and South India.[253]

I have made use of this model to accommodate Ho relationship terminology, as it successfully manages to terminologically answer the questions raised by the shortcomings of figure 8. In particular, by classifying relative age and discriminating between lineal and collateral relations and terms, it offers a structural solution that accounts for the symmetric affinal exchange patterns prevailing in Ho country, especially for *synchronic* affinal symmetry in each of the three medial generations and the *doubling* of the affinal exchange relationship in generation 0. This doubling, visualized by two distinct arrows in generation 0, appears in a situation in which *ego* marries into a category (in figure 15 arbitrarily called Affinal Line 3) other than his e/y siblings, who in marriage are assigned to Affinal Line 2. In other words, *ego*'s spouse is not the sibling of a spouse of *ego*'s sibling. So the model considers and comes to grips with the terminological nonequations ZH ≠ WB and BW ≠ HZ, which conventionally suggest asymmetric exchange patterns which require a minimum of three exchange units and systematically separate the categories of 'wife-takers' and 'wife-givers' (Barnard and Good 1984: 96–97). Also, the model provides a lexically based understanding of the tensions that are characteristic in "semi-complex"[254] systems and conceptually

---

253 Drawing centrally from Trautmann and Whiteley (2012), Whiteley (2016) and going back as far as Morgan's model of 'encompassed' affinal symmetry (Morgan 1871: 169) and Lévi-Strauss 1969, Pfeffer discusses definitions, relevance and applicability of semi-complex systems for *all* of Highland Middle India or the "proximity and transformations of Dravidian, [Seneca] Iroquois, and Crow-Omaha structures" (Pfeffer 2019: 84) there. Following the logic of diverse terminological systems in this region his focus are the lexically invariant affinal relations between the given categories and lines which are changing from level to level and which ultimately underpin notions of symmetry and seniority as value-ideas in the region. The doubling of the " 'encompassed' affinal exchange relationship in *ego*'s generation is the unique feature of Highland Middle Indian terminologies" (ibid.: 94).

254 I agree with Pfeffer in criticizing the evolutionist tinge expressed in sequencing structures as 'elementary', 'semi-complex', and 'complex'. I also agree with his and Barnard and Good's principled criticism of the continued use in anthropological debate of labels such as 'Dravidian' and 'Iroquois' for formal types of terminological structure. Barnard and Good call this practice "unfortunate", the labels "pseudo-ethnographic", the terms "inherently ambiguous" (1984:59).

arise between specific forms of alliances that are discontinued and those that are regularly reproduced though terminologically proscribed.

An instance of this is Ho cross-cousin marriage constituting an empirical possibility of considerable prestige and a terminological impossibility at the same time. As elaborated above, Ho cross cousins are terminological siblings, as figure 16 shows.[255] As such, they belong to a category that is formally nonaffinal in character and as such proscribed for marriage. But Ho people marry – though not as a norm – into exactly that category, repeatedly and immediately over several generations. The dilemma is sorted out on two levels. First, by terminologically resorting to the doublet *bare/misi* Ho people transform the same empirical persons from nonmarriageable 'siblings' into members of a marriageable category, only to rearrange the configuration after marriage in line with the logic of the terminological system. Second, as argued above, by deciding on an option such as *sango* that does not distinguish relative age, as the basic terms for *ego*'s siblings do, Ho people maintain the implied *conceptual* discrimination between siblings and cross cousins.

In order not to analytically confuse the structure of a given terminology and actual kinship configurations, Dumont suggested in this context a distinction between "terminological affines" and "terminological kin" (1983: 75). He emphasized these categories' character as categories "abstracted by us from the [...] terminological system" (ibid.). The denotata in figure 15 and the Ho relationship terms in figure 16 are to be understood in this sense.

Accordingly, Pfeffer's model presupposes six terminological lines, two collaterally linked consanguineal lines (Consanguineal Line 1 and 2) and four distinct, genealogically and otherwise unrelated affinal ones (Affinal Lines 1–4). The scheme and its extent comply with the particular cultural twist of Consanguineal Line 2, which – apart from *ego* – represents the affines of *ego*'s affines (*pera chetan perako*), a category that has been introduced above. The assumption of the classification of *ego*'s affines' affines as consanguineally related is based on ter-

---

For an overall criticism of Murdock's approach of statistically correlating and classifying social complexities into neat types of trans-cultural data sets see Barnard (2003: 41), Petermann (2004: 755), Barnard and Good (1984: 60 f.).

255 In an essay on transformations of 'Dravidian', 'Iroquois' and 'Generational' systems Tjon Sie Fat has identified the "Merging of All First Cousins" as "Iroquois-Generational Pattern of Crossness for Male Ego: Variant 1" (1998: 75). Like the terminological system of the Ho variant 1 of the "Iroquois-Generational Pattern of Crossness" is characterized on level 0 by the equations B=FBS=MZS=FZS=MBS and Z=FBD=MZD=MBD resulting on level -1 in terminologically equating also the children of *ego*'s siblings and those of *ego*'s (parallel and) cross cousins. *Ego*'s own children, however, are lexically discriminated, since in Ho and in other Middle Indian terminologies lineals are distinguished from collaterals as mentioned above.

minological equations such as B = HZH (e, y, *bau, undi)* and Z = WBW, HBW *(aji)*. This is in line with Ho and other Middle Indian relationship terminologies. Ho relationship terms for Consanguineal Lines 1 and 2 are identical – except for *saragi* (WZH). This is the one terminological exception that is not a constituent element of Consanguineal Line 1 and that is indicative of the conceptual distinction between the two lines. The category *saragi* (spsibsp, ms) not only necessitates a second consanguineal line in a pragmatic technical sense. Consanguineal Line 2 is required for structural reasons, because despite otherwise identical basic terms for *ego*'s siblings and parallel and cross cousins in generation 0, affinal exchange relations and patterns of the two consanguineal lines are *not* identical, as figures 15 and 16 illustrate. This constitutes a key characteristic of the Middle Indian as distinct from the Dravidian system with only one consanguineal line (Dumont 1983: 10, 75) and two terminological lines altogether.

As in Deeney's arrangement of terms (2002; see figure 9), generations +1, 0, and -1 constitute the core of the model. Generations +2 and -2 are differentiated by sex only, not by relative age or by their consanguineal or affinal character.[256] Due to the lack of terminological specification, the horizontal lines in the diagram representing generations +2 and -2 in figures 15 and 16 remain undifferentiated as well, thus connecting all of the six terminological lines in *this* respect.

Terminological distinctions apply in the three central generations due to the linguistic discrimination of relative age. The diagram, which has been adapted to the structural requirements of Ho terminology in figure 15 and complemented by the specific Ho relationship terms in figure 16, reveals:

- that affinal exchange takes place in each generation between those categories and lines that have been shaded grey (lighter grey in generations +1 and -1);
- that the immediate repetition of affinal exchange between the terminological lines involved in the exchange is excluded in the subsequent generation(s), which is indicated in the diagram by discontinuing the shading of the respective affinal boxes;
- that the terminological exclusion of immediate repetition leads to a terminological dispersal of affinal relations;
- that affinal exchange is symmetric on each level, as illustrated by the double arrows specifying parental exchange in generation +1, *ego*'s exchange and

---

256 The respective relationship terms on the generational levels +2/-2 are given in Deeney's model on *ego*'s (left-hand) side, but not (repeated) for +2 on *ego*'s spouse's (right-hand) side. It should be remembered that Deeney's concern is the compilation of the collectivity of Ho relationship terms and not necessarily the specification of their structural relatedness or the formal repetition of identical terms such as *tata* for FF, MF ms, ws, and ♀, ♂spouse's FF, MF.

ego's sororal and fraternal exchange in generation 0, and filial exchange in generation -1;

– that symmetric exchange between consanguineal and affinal categories differs from Dravidian patterns of affinal prescription in that affinal categories in generation +1 differ terminologically from those in generation 0, and affinal categories involved in exchange in generation 0 differ from those in generation -1;

– that – in other words – *ego*'s affinal exchange relations vertically differ from those of *ego*'s parents, siblings, and children;

– that in generation 0 *ego* (Consanguineal Line 2) is horizontally classified differently from his or her siblings (Consanguineal Line 1) and marries into a category (Affinal Line 3 in the diagram: spouse's siblings) other than his or her siblings (Affinal Line 2: siblings' spouses); and

– that the terminological distinction in generation 0 between the categories of *ego*'s spouse's siblings (Affinal Line 3) on the one hand and *ego*'s siblings' spouses (Affinal Line 2) on the other is another "unique aspect of Middle Indian terminologies" (Pfeffer 2019).

While the more focussed two-line model of figure 8 embraces the continued interrelations of a limited number of intermarrying local agnatic groups or sides, the six-line model of figures 15 and 16 conversely accounts for the dispersal of affinal relations proscribing continued intermarriage between the same two lines in consecutive generations. Both alliance strategies – neither initiated nor determined on the terminological level, given the autonomy of the terminological realm – coexist side by side and contribute to strengthening social cohesion in their opposite ways.

In the lives of our *saki* both options have materialized. They have been exemplified in this section: while our *saki*'s strategy of marrying was applauded for reproducing existing alliances over several generations, their grandchild's contrasting strategy of walking a new, as yet unknown road (*nama hora*) was applauded for marrying a 'distant' husband from a distant *kili* and a distant terrain, thus following the path of dispersal.

Conclusion: marital practices, social norms, and terminological prescription

The empirical case of our *saki*'s pattern of alliance put forward by him and translated and presented by me as restricted to two sides involved in immediate and symmetric affinal exchange over three generations was indigenously argued as one in which marital practice and social norms fully coincided. Moreover, it

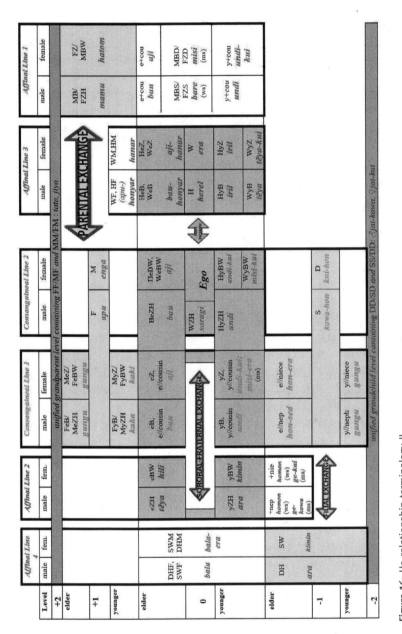

Figure 16: Ho relationship terminology II

Discrimination between lineal and collateral terms, nondiscrimination between parallel and cross cousins, merging of all first cousins and siblings.

was conveyed as terminologically safeguarded and embedded in *niyam*, the Ho's understanding of the perfect order of things. This order is considered sacred, as it is associated with Sinbonga, and *niyam* – a concept rather than a term – is expressed with awe. The diachronic element and the symmetry of the exchange were highlighted as the key values that took concrete form in my *saki*'s alliance pattern. In contradistinction to the Dravidian system, however, diachronic affinity from the Ho's perspective is a concept that is aspired to for three or four generations. This is also confirmed by Bouez (1979: 87). Even ideally, it is not a pattern characterized by permanence, as the Dravidian system suggests, and it is therefore significantly distinct in this respect also.

In retrospect, figure 8 did preliminary justice to our *saki*'s concern by visualizing a formula that formally indicates this exact idea of two (localized) alliance units diachronically intermarrying. However, the concept of diachronic symmetric alliance is conventionally expressed by the terminological equations ZH = WB and BW = HZ and structurally connotes the Dravidian system. This is where discrepancies with Ho and quite generally tribal Middle Indian alliance patterns and terminology show up.

The discussion in this section has grappled with sorting out these inconsistencies, which as a matter of principle emerge in the first place when making use in figures and diagrams of the genealogical format to grasp systematic relations between exchange units and treat them as if they were close genealogical links between individual persons. Consequently, by avoiding this individualizing and genealogical bias, figures 15 and 16 offer a systematic survey of Ho relationship terms with a difference. These two figures claim to capture the logic of the terminological system, requiring six terminological lines and accounting for the ideology of dispersal structurally built into Ho terminology by distinguishing terms assigned to and necessitating four distinct affinal lines. Figures 15 and 16 introduce the principle of seniority throughout the three medial generations and make sense of the nonequations ZH ≠ WB, BW ≠ HZ without questioning the notion of symmetry implied in the equation. They thus reconcile the contradictions that have been pointed out above *and* terminologically accommodate and account for the diversity and empirical variability of marital practices at the same time.

To conclude, I will test the plausibility of the *ego*-centric model represented in figures 15 and 16. I will illustrate how this model complies with and can be identified in the empirical case of our two *saki*. To begin with, EGO is my ♂*saki*. In the diagram, he is assigned to Consanguineal Line 2 and related in affinal exchange with Affinal Line 3, the line of his wife (W), *era*, my ♀*saki*, who is on the same age level as her husband. As argued above, his three younger brothers (*undi*) belong to a terminological line different from that of their elder brother, in the diagram Consanguineal Line 1. Their respective wives (yBW) are from Affinal Line 2. They are *kimin* to him; he is *bau-honyar* (HeB) to them. The relation between *kimin* and *bau-honyar* is one formally linking Affinal Lines 2 and 3 and structurally connecting the categories of siblings' spouses' (sibsp, here yBW) and spouses' siblings (spsib, here HeB). The children born to my ♂*saki*'s younger brothers are his younger parallel nephews and nieces (yBCh, ms), *gungu* in reciprocal relation to their father's elder brother (FeB, *gungu*) and classified as members of Consanguineal Line 1. His only son (*kowa-hon*) of Consanguineal Line 2 has been taken care of in the *adin*, where he has been invited to stay along with his forefathers ever since his early death. He is assigned to the same terminological line as his father. His only daughter, like her brother of Consanguineal Line 2, married into Affinal Line 4, which is the line of her husband (DH) and her husband's parents (DHF, DHM). His daughter's husband (*ara*) is my ♂*saki*'s son-in-law, and his parents and my ♂*saki* are reciprocally related as *bala* (DHF, SWF) and *bala-era* (DHM). His daughter's children in generation -2 are all *jai-tadi* (vocative form) to him, undifferentiated by relative age and their consanguineal or affinal character unmarked.

In the second case, EGO is my ♀*saki* from Consanguineal Line 2, and her husband (H, *herel*) is from Affinal Line 3, as the terminological system has it that these two lines and not any other two are invariantly related in symmetric affinal exchange. At the same time, this reversal of the respective assignments illustrates that the model orders *relations* between categories within a given abstracted structure. It is not about allocating to substantial units a predetermined fixed position within a rigid system. To continue, ♀ ego's husband's three younger brothers (HyB, *iril*) are also classified in relation to her as members of Affinal Line 3, which assembles and orders her husband's siblings according to gender and relative age. To her *iril* of the category spouse's siblings (spsib) she is related as their eBW (*hili*). It makes sense that in the diagram *hili* is assigned to Affinal Line 2, as this line represents the category of sibling's spouse (sibsp). Her husband's younger brothers' wives (HyBW, *undi-kui*) fall into the category *pera chetan perako*, her affines' affines, and in the logic of the terminological system are her terminological *kin* of Consanguineal Line 2. Their children are *gungu* (HyBCh) in relation to her, as they are *gungu* (yBCh) to her husband. The relations between her and her daughter's husband (DH), his parents, and their children involve Affinal Line 4 and generation -2. They are terminologically identical with those of her own husband. Altogether, all of her social relations involve as many terminological lines as his do.

Considering the wide range of Ho terminology, two Consanguineal Lines (1 and 2) are linked by my ♂*saki* having siblings; another two *distinct* Affinal Lines (2 and 3) become included in generation 0 by all of them being married;

and *another* distinct Affinal Line (4) becomes affiliated in generation -1 by all of them having married children. In only two generations (0 and -1) of my *saki*, his siblings, their spouses, and their children, five of the six terminological lines are interrelated *and* separated in affinal symmetric exchange according to the pattern offered in figures 15 and 16. The same model equally works for my ♀ *saki* by systematically accommodating her relations as defined from her *ego*-centric perspective.[257]

How does the model account for deviations and what is indigenously considered a deviation? How does the model account for the specific type of our *saki*'s marriage deviating, as argued above, from the unambiguous exchange pattern between Consanguineal Line 2 and Affinal Line 3 suggested by the terminology? Clearly, their respective parents' marriages were classified as being in line with the terminological prescription (MB = FZH, FZ = MBW) in generation +1. This corresponds with the model. The deviation from the model comes in generation 0. Here terminology *proscribes* alliance between Consanguineal Lines 1 and 2 and Affinal Line 1, but at the same time *ego*'s cross cousins are assembled here as preferred spouses *alongside others*.

The solution, I argue, consists in socially contextualizing empirical affinal exchange and marital practices. Instead of blurring a situation that may be confusing for the anthropologist, figures 15 and 16 contribute to sorting it out and provide terminological orientation. Given that my ♀ *saki* has married her *mamu-hatom hon*, she refers – *after* marriage – to his younger brothers no longer as *undi* (yB, Affinal Line 1), as she did *before* marriage, but as *iril* (HyB, Affinal Line 3). Likewise, my ♂ *saki* no longer addressed his wife's elder sister as *aji*, who was also *aji* to him before marriage, but as *aji-hanar*, marking unequivocally the formal change in relationship to one between affines. In his case and quite generally, the transition in status from *aji* to *aji-hanar* is linguistically emphasized by a parallel term resorted to in marriage negotiations, which is *upuniya katani:* (literally 'a four-footed animate being'). This term is usually said in jest when referring to a goat asked for as part of the bridewealth to be handed over to the future wife's elder sister (*aji-hanar*). Speaking to the husband-to-be, some even use this term as veiled language to directly refer to a wife's eZ in remarks like "Are you really serious about marrying this woman? You know that an *upuniya katani:* is waiting for you!" The point I want to make is that independent of the specific type of marriage, social relations *after* marriage are ter-

---

257 Deviating from the Ho's six-line terminology presented here and given the very same relations under nontribal South Indian circumstances the respective terms would have had to be arranged within the Dravidian two-line terminology distinguishing ♀/♂ consanguineal relations from ♀/♂ affinal ones.

minologically unambiguously rearranged and reliably ordered as in the model. Marriage will not only enrich and add new relations and relationship terms to *ego*'s life but may also bring with it a change in the character of already-existing relations as concerns responsibilities, rights, and duties. The case between two males, where this is indigenously reflected and negotiated as a *bau-undi* relation changing into a self-reciprocal *teya* relation, will be elaborated in the following chapter in the portrait of G. Hansda, who dramatically pointed it out to me as part of his biography.

While in generation 0 a major part of *ego*'s social relations before marriage are linguistically labelled as relations of siblings, they are not comprehensively and indiscriminately conceptualized as such, as analysed above in detail. The terminological classification then does in fact seem ambiguous in terms of legitimizing marriage choices, especially in the absence of unambiguous marriage regulations. The sociocultural acceptance of a marriage is the result of embedding it socially by linguistically elevating in retrospect the *known* relations *before* marriage of two persons about to marry as relations between *mamu-hatom honko, bare* and *misi-era,* or *sango. Sango* is sometimes used as the most unspecific, quite vague, almost generic term of all, sometimes synonymously with *mamu-hatom honko.* In this analysis, originally proscribed marriage relations are terminologically reframed and obviously no longer considered an unacceptable deviation. They instantly become integrated by being swapped from one *affinal* line (e. g., 1) to another *affinal* line (3), thus proving as a side effect that the categories of MB and FZ are clearly conceived of as affinal and hence beyond *ego*'s local agnatic group, outside *ego*'s consanguineal line (2) and (sub-)clan boundaries. In the course of fieldwork, I observed a number of times that marrying within one's own clan is the one deviation that is considered unambiguously unacceptable and has in no case been tolerated. The exogamy rule is mandatory, and it is enforced – in terminology, as social norm, and in marital practices.

7 Two portraits as conclusion

It does not matter to take a poem apart as long as you do not forget to put it together again.
(Personal communication with a Welsh poet about what to do when the work of analysing and
interpreting a poem has been completed)

This last chapter differs from the preceding ones in its methodological approach, perspective, and presentation. Instead of highlighting, generalizing, and comparing relevant arguments and results in a conventional conclusion, it will offer a conclusion with a difference.

In analogy to the epigraph above, this chapter is meant to put together the tribal society that has been taken apart in the preceding chapters. So the portraits of the two protagonists that follow do not aim in any way at offering a comprehensive and ordered or systematic picture. But they do aim at presenting dimensions of the subjective-individual and the social-collective and combining both. If Durkheim (1976: 107) is right that the social body of any society enforces its culture-specific givens on the individual, this is a powerful statement about an objective process independent of an individual person's free will and awareness of this process and despite the individual's possibly being convinced of the opposite. So, following Durkheim, there is no nonsocial sphere apart from, beyond, or outside this process, and any individual life will be impacted by prevailing social values, norms, and rules – if in varying degrees. Certainly, Durkheim's statement is not aimed at mechanically defining social beings as cultural clones. It should be complemented rather than contradicted by Weber's notion of *agency*, which in contrast focusses on the individual working out strategies to make sense of and disposing of options to lead a meaningful life – within a given framework (Weber 1976: 1). These strategies and options, though culturally and socially informed, may display enormous variations and a high degree of individuation, and they will always tell a story that is larger and more comprehensive than an isolated private life.

Two individual protagonists, one Ho, one Santal, have been singled out and will be portrayed here within the sociocultural setting of the region of research to illustrate this dialectic: to show the social encapsulated within the private and to simultaneously reveal the individual construction of meaning-making within social, collective, or communal performances. Also, the idea of portraying 'authentic', that is, real-life protagonists is to unsystematically and fragmentarily bring together, as happens in real life, institutions, issues, and aspects that had to be taken apart in this book for analytical reasons: marriage and affinity, kinship and ritual relations, precedence and seniority, ancestors and the spirit world, land and inheritance, sacrifice and ritual, purity and reciprocity. If tribal values

https://doi.org/10.1515/9783110666199-011

and norms, as I argue, exist in their specificity as well as in their interrelatedness, they must matter and be alive notwithstanding contradictions and strategic distortions of different kinds at the empirical level where individuals plan and live their lives.

Portrait of a Ho: S. Kondangkel, *munda* and landowner

Hard work, rituals (*bongako*), and witchcraft

"I believe in hard work rather than in spirits, sacrifices, and rituals (*bongako*)." This is what S. Kondangkel, henceforth referred to as Sadurgon, answered in December 2012 when asked whether he, too, was about to perform a particular paddy ritual (*ked bonga*), as Ho and Santal households in the area did on the occasion of the final harvesting of the paddy plant (*baba*) in the fields, before the threshing on the threshing floor (*kolom*) would begin.

Of course, I had gotten to know Sadurgon as a hard worker, and I knew from Dhan that Ho believe "that hard work makes the crops grow" (Dhan 1962: 24). Still, his answer came as an unexpected statement, since I had myself participated in rituals regularly performed in the courtyard of Sadurgon's house every year by members of the Gau community. In rituals such as *ote ili* and *gau o:l* (see plates 15 and 19) the *diuri* of the Gau had been respectfully assisted by Sadurgon. Also, on the vigil of *ba porob*, one of the major village feasts that is addressed to the village deities, a ritual called *gram bonga* or *guri: bonga* (*guri:* – cowdung; to clean with cow dung) is performed in his courtyard and presided over by the local Ho shaman (*dewa*) and his men. A white cock, one goat (*boda* – uncastrated he-goat), one red and one black chicken, two pigeons, and one duck are sacrificed inside a walled enclosure facing east. This is the sacrificial site (*sare*) that is attached to the back of Sadurgon's house and thus protected from potentially defiling gazes from outside. The *sare* is strictly used for ritual purposes only.

When I learnt about the prominent role that young boys are assigned in *ked bonga*, I wondered whether the absence of a son (of his own and of his elder brother's wife who lives on his compound) was the reason for Sadurgon's being so reticent about the ritual. In this particular paddy ritual (*ked bonga*), the rice mother (*baba enga*) is honoured. She is invoked as the original source from which all paddy is believed to have come. She is personified in the last sheaves of rice stalks that are left in the centre of each rice field while all the paddy around them is harvested. In support, the rice stalks are tied to a branch for *baba enga* to lean against. Ho people say that in the act of harvesting, *baba enga* gets killed and hurt. Eventually, in order to propitiate her and make good all the maltreatment that she has had to endure, the last sheaves of rice stalks are ritually cut, and *baba enga* is ceremoniously carried home to the threshing floor (*kolom*). This is done towards dusk by one of the sons or grandsons of the landowner (*gusiya*). He carries *baba enga*, that is, the stalks, on his head, while other children, boys and girls, escort them in a queue. They are, however, unaccompanied by adults, who are not involved in this part of the ritual. On their arrival, the boy and *baba enga* are ritually greeted (*jowar*) near the threshing floor. Constructed as representing *baba enga*, the boy has his feet washed and his legs anointed with oil up to his knees by the *female* head of the household (*owa:rini:*). By approaching *baba enga* with an air of respect, the participants also implicitly honour and propitiate Sinbonga, who gave *baba enga* to the world of the living as a gift when he created the earth. No other or separate offering or sacrifice is made to the rice mother, however, which documents that *baba enga* is not assigned the definite status of a spirit (*bonga*). Towards the end of the ritual, *baba enga* is asked to forgive any disrespect shown to her and to guarantee future fertility and the growth of the rice grains to be sown in the months to come.

Symbolically, rice grains referred to in the course of this ritual are also personified. They are constructed as offspring of their mother (*baba enga*) and consequently called *babako* (plural of *baba*). This is not only a striking phonetic parallel to *balako*, the term to denote a Ho's affines, but also a conceptual one, since the category of *balako* represents a key value and symbolically guarantees the continuity of Ho society as such. The association of *babako* and *balako*, of course, exists in the anthropologist's mind only. For Santal and some more sophisticated Ho, *baba enga* is identified as Lakshmi, who, even if considered an alien (*diku*) goddess, after all is a goddess. Linguistically this ritual, which is also termed *baba keya ader* (calling back the rice [mother]), is related to the *umbul keya ader* ritual in which the soul (*umbul* – shadow; soul) after a person's death is ceremoniously called back into the sacred part of the kitchen (*adin*) in order to be ritually taken care of there. Notions of life, continuity, and reproduction link both rituals – conceptually and linguistically – and reveal at the same time in terms of reciprocity that only if proper ritual treatment is offered can the continuation of life and reproduction be expected.

"You know, Eva," Sadurgon had confided in me in 2010, "Ho people may be innocent and pure, but sometimes they know so little; they are so ignorant, and they have forgotten so much about our Ho traditions." Was there a note of despair in his voice? "They easily believe what others tell them. That is why many believe in witchcraft and witches. I think this is blind faith, and there is no proof for it. I believe only in what can be proved. So I believe in our Ho spirits and deities."

Plate 25: *Ked bonga*
Baba enga, the rice mother, is personified in the last sheaves of the paddy stalks that are left in the centre of each rice field. While all the paddy around her is harvested, she holds onto a branch, before she is ceremoniously led to the threshing floor.

Sadurgon

Sadurgon is a Ho, a husband and a father, a village headman (*munda*), someone who owns land, a house, and cattle (*gusiya*), who is a cultivator of his own fields (*taso ho*), and who sometimes works for wages (*nalatani:*); he is my younger brother *(undi)* and has become a friend *(juri)*. I met him for the first time in January 2006 when he was asked to mediate a discussion of some significance concerning a widow's and her four young children's future following the first burial of her husband. He invited me to participate. Ever since then, I could rely on him as an informant and, if his scarce time allowed, as an assistant. I became his *aji* (elder sister), and he and my husband were *teya* (elder sister's husband–wife's younger brother) to each other, which is a joking relationship. Sadurgon's clan (*kili*) is Kondangkel, whose members claim and are acknowledged, also by non-Ho, to be senior, a status ascribed to the *munurenko*, the descendants of the original settlers of a village, and one of the founding clans of Tarana, including Gara Sai. It was their forefathers who cleared the jungle in that area. This high status is not a passive attribute attached to a person once and for all. Indeed, it needs to be re-enacted, maintained, deserved, and actively achieved by performing one's publicly known social duties: "It has been enjoined on us as first settlers since time immemorial to exercise our duties as ritual guide (*diuri*) and headman (*munda*)," Sadurgon explained. Sadurgon's sphere of responsibility, of course, is not an administrative unit as outlined above or listed in the written records of the village council. It is the secular and ritual space that is recognized by the villagers, within which and beyond whose boundaries they organize and structure their kinship and marriage relations. As a member of his *miyad mandi chaturenko*, his relations reach well beyond Gara Sai.

Sadurgon is an educated person, although he himself would never admit to that. He can speak and write Hindi, English, and Odiya, he can understand and converse in Santali, and, of course, he is fluent in Ho. One day I went to see him at 5:30 a.m. in his courtyard, as he used to say, "This is a good time to meet because I am not yet working in the rice fields." He was reading a book about Ho traditions written in Waran Chiti, a script that was invented for the Ho language by Lako Bodra. Many usually well-informed Ho people whom I met in that area were either unfamiliar with it or uninterested. Those who had heard about it labelled it as the business of some intellectuals in the Chaibasa area. It was certainly none of their business. Sadurgon, however, wrote down the whole alphabet for me in Waran Chiti without the slightest difficulty.

As a wage labourer (*nalatani:*) he had been in Gujarat, Kashmir, and Bhutan for extended periods of his life. Here he picked up his English. In 2008 he worked underground with dynamite and other explosives in the course of a construction scheme for the Indian railway in Kashmir. He earned more than 4,000 rupees a month, which equalled 156 rupees a day and was more than double the official minimum wage for unskilled labour at that time. But, he said, he worked twelve hours a day. He was interested in and informed about the sociopolitical situation outside Ho society. He also knew about the legalization and institutionalization of the *manki-munda* system in Jharkhand, euphemistically asserted to have been designed to give the tribal population a legal voice. But Sadurgon warned against the danger of *manki* and *munda* turning corrupt, losing their independence, integrity, and tribal identity by accepting government salaries for fulfilling their customary obligations. He knew that it was government policy to seek tribal support for tribal land alienation and that economic progress in terms of mining the mineral-rich areas in Jharkhand often spelt destruction of the sacred landscape of tribals and a status at the very bottom of the social hierarchy. He was aware of the determination of the Indian government to assimilate members of the Scheduled Tribes into the Indian Hindu mainstream. More than anything else, perhaps, he knew about and had himself been exposed to mainstream India's contempt for the tribal world and its values.

Sadurgon did not drink rice-beer (*diyan*), usually a must in Ho society – especially for a ritual elder – and he did not smoke, typically another cultural must for males in ritual situations. But he did not proselytize about this. He did not avoid rice-beer in order to distance himself ideologically from his Ho fellow-villagers. Verardo (2003b) makes exactly this point about conceptual disintegration expressed in contrasting attitudes towards the jungle, ancestors, and the consumption of rice-beer as markers of Ho-ness. She writes that those Ho who began to feel ashamed of these core Ho values and label them as backward and primitive would turn into Munda, that is, swap Ho clan membership for Munda caste membership. They would begin to cremate their dead instead of burying them; they would change their marriage patterns and their commensality rules; they would stop eating meat and drinking any kind of alcohol.

If a ritual situation within the compound of his house so demanded, Sadurgon saw to it that rice-beer was there. Some people, though to me amazingly few, were regularly and heavily drunk, which led to their neglecting their duties and their families at times. What Sadurgon deplored was the weakness of mind, the lack of socially adequate behaviour, rather than the lack of physical control. But he would not despise others for drinking or make them feel ashamed. Maybe it was also because of this attitude that Sadurgon was a respected man.

The protagonist as village headman (*munda*)

Sadurgon became *munda* of Gara Sai when he was still young, inexperienced, and ignorant, as he says. "Too many of our elders who knew have died." One of the knowledgeable elders was his father, who had taught and passed on the office of *munda* to his elder brother, who then died quite unexpectedly, while Sadurgon was away in Bhutan, and long before his time. As a matter of cultural logic, it then became Sadurgon's turn despite his age, "because the villagers insisted."

When asked about his duties as a *munda*, Sadurgon explained: "I don't act as *munda*, you know. Nowadays the law has changed. The government does not recognize these institutions in Odisha. There is the village council (*panchayat*) that is in charge. So acting as *diuri*, *munda*, or *sadar* [the headman of a confederation of villages, who in Jharkhand is called *manki*] is not a legally recognized activity." This may be a politically correct statement, but it tells only part of Sadurgon's ambivalent story, because, as I realized in the course of my fieldwork, he did act as *munda* but was downplaying his role, as becomes a village elder in Ho society. Also, when in 2010 a *diuri* for the Ho community of a neighbouring hamlet needed to be elected by invoking the pantheon of Ho deities, it was Sadurgon who opened and moderated the meeting of all male representatives at the *akara*, a site within a village where males discuss village politics. "Well, people continue to come to me seeking my advice. They address and keep approaching me as their *munda*. And if people ask you for help, you comply with their demands, don't you?" When my perception had developed the necessary sensitivity, I became aware that someone's wishes were quite often interpreted as demands, almost commands, that were obeyed where possible, thus constituting and strengthening a net of reciprocal social obligations, often within a known kinship framework.

The protagonist as landowner (*gusiya*) and cultivator of his fields (*taso ho*)

As a *gusiya* Sadurgon owns and lives in a house that was built by his great-grandfather's father, his FFFF, in Gara Sai. He claims to have been told so by his father. Even though this house has sheltered generations of *munda*, it is not any different in size, style, and structure from other villagers' houses. It is constructed according to similar principles, which are kinship principles above and beyond architectural or aesthetic reasons, which are not neglected. What I mean is that in Ho society, brothers live together all their lives. After marriage, their wives will move in, too. Residence is virilocal. As his grandfather had a (younger) brother, another house was built facing the first and sharing the same courtyard. And, of course, with two houses constituting two independent yet interrelated working units, there are two separate threshing floors (*kolom*), a number of separate hearths, and separate *adin*. Sadurgon's grandfather's younger brother (FFyB) had three sons, all of whom married. There was sufficient land for all within their *miyad mandi chaturenko* (illustrated in figure 17) and enough space for more houses to be built around the rice fields in nearby hamlets. These are not always easily recognizable as independent hamlets, which in fact not all of them are, since many of them are socially interrelated, as this narration also shows. So Kondangkel brothers – and their forefathers (*ham hoko–dum hoko*) – could continue living and working together on ancestral land cleared by the Kondangkel.

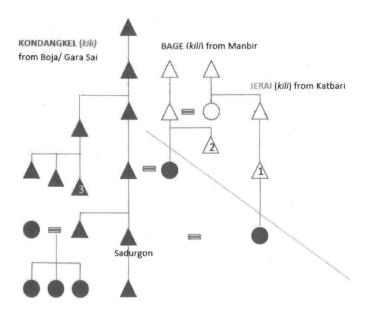

Figure 17: Sadurgon's *miyad mandi chaturenko*
The members of Sadurgon's *mmc* are represented by solid blue circles for female members and solid blue triangles for male members. Persons 1 and 2 are Sadurgon's *honyar* (WF) and *mamu* (MB). Neither belongs to his *mmc*, but they are the two main people with whom he discusses relevant family matters such as marrying a second wife. Person 3 is Sadurgon's *kaka*, his FyB, whose two elder brothers died long ago. It is between Sadurgon and his *kaka* from Boja Sai that ritual interaction and economic collaboration are very close.

Sadurgon was born and grew up in Gara Sai. He lives with his wife in the house in which he was born and in which his elder brother used to live with his wife. Sadurgon is *iril* to his elder brother's wife, who is his *hili*, which is a joking relationship. According to Ho customary reasoning, after Sadurgon's elder brother's death his wife and her three daughters were entitled to continue living there, which they do. Everything that a husband owns is passed on to his wife after his death, but whatever a wife owns is passed on in the case of her death to her sons – her male children only.

As a *gusiya* of cattle Sadurgon owns two bullocks for ploughing and threshing, eighteen or more goats for sacrificing, sale, and consumption, and a number of chicks and hens for the same purposes. Each different category of livestock is housed in its own permanent and separate shed, sometimes as spacious as the houses for the human beings and immediately attached to those houses, sharing the same roof, which, however, turns from one of tiles over the human houses into one of thatched grass over the animal sheds.

As a *gusiya* of land Sadurgon owns 7.41 acres that are registered in his own name and those of his father and brother but are not separated or divided in the land register. This is a common Ho practice, and quite generally Ho will avoid the written, legal partitioning of corporate land. An official paper folded, signed, and stamped many times shows that Sadurgon yearly pays 16.45 rupees instead of 39 rupees in property taxes according to Schedule XIV. "Government discount for BPL [Below Poverty Line] people," Sadurgon jokes.

As a cultivator (*taso ho*) Sadurgon works in his own rice fields and helps in the rice fields of the members of his *mandi chaturenko* also living in Gara Sai, Boja Sai, and the vicinity. This cultivation work is linked to the original ancestors of the specific *mandi chaturenko*, whose membership is continually re-established in such corporate activities. In terms of status, this kind of work is qualitatively different from wage labour, which always means work for others and as such is considered polluting though not always avoidable. Giving help (*denga em*), however, is not considered impure, since it is work done reciprocally among notional equals as a matter of principle, and as such it is never paid. Sadurgon grows rice and, after the rice harvest, a cultivated pulse (*kansari*), linseed (*unchi*), and a kind of field pea (*kalae*). But his specific situation is difficult, as there are no brothers with whom he can organize mutual help right in front of his house door, as it were. His *hili* is busy working in her rice fields, meaning those of her deceased husband, herding the cattle, getting firewood from the jungle, and doing the cooking on the hearths assigned to her household. There is a division of duties between her and her *iril* fixing separate and shared responsibilities and an internal division of land. Sadurgon and his wife cannot do without wage labourers, whom they employ and pay daily, sometimes in kind, sometimes in money.

Death, polygyny, and the continuity of ancestral land

Sadurgon encountered death early in his life. Both parents died when he was a young boy. His father had no brothers in the sense of *mid lai:ren* (born of *one* mother). His two elder sisters (FeZ) had married into the Alda *kili* and lived in Jharkhand with their husbands. In reference and address Sadurgon called their offspring *sango* (FeZD, FeZS).

Sadurgon's own elder brother died at perhaps the age of thirty-five, he thinks, and his elder sister when she was about fourteen or fifteen, when he was still small. He is uncertain of their absolute biological age and does not recollect the exact year, but he recollects their ages in relation to his in terms of seniority. In both cases medical doctors had been involved and had come to their home, so he is acquainted with healing concepts beyond the indigenous ones. "There is a paper with all the details in the *adin*," he said.

Sadurgon lost his only son in July 2011. He had shown symptoms of some undiagnosed neurophysiological malfunctioning (my diagnosis) ever since 2006. By 2009/2010 his situation had progressively deteriorated. He had become paralyzed and needed permanent care. Both parents took turns. By then Sadurgon was deeply worried, and so was I.[258] Sadurgon's son was my younger brother's son, *homon*, to me – was that a relationship term or a living relation? Were my responsibilities abstract and academic or real? When I returned in 2012, the death of Sadurgon's son was one of the first pieces of news that reached me.

In the two preceding years, when consulting and making sense of my field notes, I had begun to realize in hindsight on how many different planes and in how many different ways Sadurgon had been active on behalf of his son without my being aware of it at the time.[259] While performing different kinds of rituals addressed to different kinds of spirits was his ritual duty as the ritual head of the house and the secular head of the village, this was not unrelated to taking care of his son. All the steps were negotiated within the frame of kinship and the ritual specialists of Gara Sai. This seems more than a model of extreme interpersonal solidarity, which it may also be. In the concept of a Ho person defined as a social category, an individual opens up into the outside, comprised of the collectivity of his *mandi chaturenko*, the cosmos of influential spirits, ancestors, deities, and the residential site of his hamlet. The successful treatment of a disease or a diseased person requires all components to be considered adequately on the household and village levels.

---

258 So far, I had been the anthropologist observing from a relative distance, although in the course of six years I had become emotionally involved. However, this chapter's focus is on Sadurgon and is meant to remain there -and not on the state of the anthropologist's mixed feelings. For this reason, these are not enlarged upon here. At the same time, it goes without saying that an anthropologist's necessarily subjective perception, interpretation and selection of data will bear on the representation of the protagonist's portrait. (see also Reichel 2014b: 32–46). Having said this, an anthropologist's understanding of her/his responsibilities (and his/her confusion about them) does affect her/his research in the field, but this will not be discussed here.

259 One way of supporting his son was not to commit himself to be my permanent assistant although he appreciated my work and began seriously considering writing a book on Ho traditions himself – in *Waran Chiti*.

Tellingly, this was revealed in a *bonga*[260] called *red topa* (burying of medi-cine), in the course of which medicine was administered or rather buried (*topa*) in the soil of the hamlet at five different spots where different spirits were invoked along the ritual boundary surrounding Gara Sai, which until then had not been known to me. That way a ritual fence was constituted around the village in order to ward off malign spirits and evil influences. The *bonga* was not directed towards Sadurgon's son as an autonomous individual, but towards a human being as someone related to an encompassing social whole. The ritual itself was witnessed and accompanied by eighteen male Ho representing the complete ritual village. It was carried out by five male village specialists chosen for their divining qualifications. Women and children were not present and not supposed to watch – save for the female anthropologist under Sadurgon's spe-cial protection. The procedure took thirty-five minutes, from 10:30 p.m. to 11:05 p.m. during the new moon in March 2010. It was a duty to be performed by known actors in known ways developed through trial and error. There was noth-ing secret or mysterious about it. I was informed about the names and specific qualities of the sixteen spirits and deities, all of them male,[261] that were invoked in the course of the rituals, about the ingredients of the medicine administered to the village, which I was allowed to photograph, and about the *bichar* (judgment; to pass judgment) procedure the night before.

As a sort of complementary measure Sadurgon had made an appointment with the medical doctor in the nearest town, only to find out that the doctor had left for a conference. His assistant asked him to go to Cuttack for an X-ray and then charged 100 rupees for this consultation. The trip to the doctor had been an ordeal for the son. Sadurgon, however, paid and did not complain. He then asked me to get in touch with a renowned hospital in Jamshedpur. When I did, the receptionist remarked, in a very friendly, very clear way, "You'll see. We may make an appointment, no problem, but he will not come. Tribals don't come." She was right; in the end, he did not go. But it was not at all an easy decision. He discussed it beforehand with his son's *mamu*, his wife's brother – as matters of disease are as a matter of course also kinship mat-ters. How to get his son there, who was going to accompany and stay with him, where to stay, how to prepare the meals, and how to pay. By no means was money the main concern. Sadurgon gave his son costly, special food that had

---

260 Actually, these were at least three interrelated *bonga*. Here only one part of *red topa* will be given.

261 *Pat* in Ho denotes "a *guru bonga* type of spirit, usually found in mountains and called upon by shamans for help in discerning what spirit is causing some sickness, etc." (Deeney 2005: 284). The distinction between *bonga* and *pat* has been given above.

been recommended to him; he gave him medication. He kept trying to find out the cause of the disease – inside and outside the physical boundaries of his son's body. In Ho reasoning there is strong causal thinking: no effect without cause. Were relations, were spirits negatively affecting his son? Were they adversely affecting the whole hamlet and had chosen to punish his son? Sadurgon had become a wage labourer outside Ho territory in order to cover the expenses for his son. He is aware that this might have offended his ancestors. In other words, he himself might have offended the ancestors, who were now punishing his son for it. In that way, he might be the source of their anger and the cause of his son's disease. Maybe he had imported some pollution from outside, and he considered it his duty to purify the dwelling site and become purified himself.[262] He had been in touch with medical doctors, he had had meals prepared and eaten outside his home – all this was possibly polluting behaviour. Ancestors, whenever annoyed, need to be propitiated. This is the job of the shaman (*dewa*). He was sent for, not only once, not always the same one. After a *bonga* Sadurgon was always quite optimistic. "The correct thing has been done. Everything will be all right now." In between the *bonga* he carefully watched his son for a few days. If he could not observe any improvement, he would try something else, he would try someone else. He also tried a Ho *dewa* who claimed to be in touch with Hindu gods and goddesses and thus be extraordinarily powerful. During all this time Sadurgon's son was fed, washed, and anointed regularly; he was spoken to and entertained; he lay on a bed on the threshing floor in the shade surrounded by *baba*, ancestors, and people working; his maternal uncle (*mamu*) came to visit frequently – after all, it was a three-hour ride on his bicycle one way.

In December 2012, I talked with Sadurgon about his future. What would happen to his land now that his son had died and that his *hili* has no sons? He was prepared for that question. "I think of marrying a second time. I have already spoken to my wife, my father-in-law, and my *mamu* about it. They all agree." What about the process of finding a second wife? "I will leave that to my relatives according to Ho customary law. They will look. I am not doing that myself. If I have another son, he will take all of the land." Of course, he is very interested in what advice his *teya*, my husband, has for him.

---

262 This was not really exceptional. Other Ho, who had been outside Ho territory for the same purpose of earning money, had to undergo purification rituals on their return, too. One Ho told me he was almost treated as an outcast by his own brothers (*hagako*). He was not allowed to touch the *mandi chatu*, and commensality was interrupted. He had to make special offerings to his ancestors in order to become re-integrated into his clan.

When we returned to the field in 2014, we were of course very interested in catching up on the situation. "No," said Sadurgon, "I have not married. You know, my wife has agreed, my *honyar* [father-in-law], too, but, you know, there may be so much quarrelling, so much haggling. The situation may become really nasty."

In a comparable situation in 2019, many years after the death of his only son, my male *saki* from Pathan Sai had made the decision to adopt a young man, one of his younger brothers' sons. That way the land would remain within the *mmc*. My *saki*'s younger brother had already agreed to the adoption; his son did not yet know about it. But he helped to completely renovate my *saki*'s house, which would become his house following the adoption. Sadurgon, on the other hand, a lot younger than my *saki*, did not seem to be impatient with the situation. His *kaka*'s son (*kaka*: position 3 in figure 17), about ten years old, might be an option for a possible adoption, but it is one that has not yet been mentioned.

Plate 26: Negotiating life: Sadurgon and his *teya*
Teya – a self-reciprocal relationship between WyB and eZH.

Epilogue

January 31, 2018. For the first time in more than ten years, Sadurgon answers the phone. Obviously, a cell tower has been built near his hamlet of Gara Sai. The news we received after two years' absence from the field:

Your *saki* has passed away. Last year's harvest was excellent. *En sirma doe: sumukikeda* (that year there was abundance/plenty/prosperity)! No, he hasn't married another time. Yes, he is still hoping for a son. No, he is not worried about his land. It will surely remain within his *miyad mandi chaturenko*. He mentions his *kaka* (FyB) from Boja Sai and his *kaka*'s son. "When are you coming?"

Portrait of a Santal: G. Hansda in his domestic environment

While I was initially intent on doing fieldwork exclusively among Ho people in order not to dissipate my efforts and get distracted, my staying with a Santal family in a Santal hamlet for many months over many years meant that I came to observe local life there intensely, though unsystematically and not seeking to continuously participate in it actively for the sake of research. Unexpectedly, then, I found myself right in the midst of Ho-Santal interrelatedness – only to learn that this is a lived empirical reality rather than an exception to the socio-cultural fabric of Middle India. I learned that the *saki* relation (see chapter 6) not only connected my (female) Ho *saki* and me as two individuals but cut across tribal boundaries by relating the households of my Ho *saki*, G. Hansda, and other Santal people (see figures 4–7 and 13). I also learned that the concept of brother clans (see chapter 3) included Santal clans, and I found that the construct of a Santal *gusti* that I will outline in this chapter was indigenously explained to me in terms of the Ho's *miyad mandi chaturenko* (see chapter 3).

G. Hansda, henceforth called Guru, was known in the region as a learned person, a tribal who had been outside in the *diku* world, who had experience of how to deal with *diku* people, and who had decided to leave that world and return to his tribal 'brothers'. He was frequently consulted, including by Ho people when they needed support in their interactions with local *diku* representatives such as the police, the forest department, teachers, the bank, and local government institutions.

Gradually, I would become included in the Santal web of kinship. The head of the household, Guru, volunteered as my assistant and classified himself as my son (*babu*), which not only transformed me into his classificatory mother (*ma*) and his wife into my daughter-in-law (*kimin*) but also transformed me into the 'mother' of several adult males previously unknown to me and into the *hanar* (mother-in-law) of a number of female villagers who introduced themselves as my *kimin*. I realized it was high time that I made sense of the relational chaos, as it appeared to me at the outset, of people living or temporarily staying as immediate neighbours in several houses in a closed compound and cooperating in what were to me nontransparent ways. The result is given in the following sections of this chapter. It is based on the empirical data I continuously collected over more than a decade, and still, this data may be incomplete or may have changed.

The portrait centres around Guru and, as seen from his and other Santal consultants' perspectives, aspects of Santal sociocultural life that have been discussed earlier for the Ho: the localized corporate grouping called *gusti* as a key element of Santal social organization, the empirical dimension of selected relationship terms in the context of seniority, and (the case of Guru's runaway) marriage.

Gusti, alerenko, mit orak hor – miyad mandi chaturenko?

Solidarity and ritual and economic collaboration within the localized corporate grouping of the *miyad mandi chaturenko* (*mmc*) have been discussed in some detail in chapter 3 for the Ho community in the research area. Interestingly, Santal informants there made use of the Ho term to denote a specific Santal social unit within and related to one of the twelve Santal clans (*paris*). Figure 18 portrays Guru Hansda's *gusti*, whose members are all linked to or members of the Hansda *paris*. These units are corporate in character, although they may be locally dispersed. Synonymously with *mmc* I was given the terms *gusti* and *alehor/alerenko* (Santali/Ho: our people) or, in a mix of Santali and Ho, *mid owa: hor* (the people of one 'house'). This term is to be distinguished from *orak hor/owa:renko* (Santali/Ho: the people of the house) which refers to those – including the dead – who live in a concrete house defined and conceived of in a physical sense. In this limited sense, Santal people in the research area, however, preferred to speak of *hagako* (brothers) or (also) *alerenko*. *Gusti* was explained to me as a localized group of people whose genealogical ties are remembered for three generations, maybe four. This is a relevant piece of information, as the dead male members are commemorated by name in rituals performed at the household level by the most senior member in his role as ritual guide (Dhano in figure 18) – or his son should his father fail to do so. Wives and unmarried daughters are included in this unit, the distinction being that daughters are born into their father's *gusti* and will leave it on marriage, while wives only adopt full membership by being fully married, which may be a process taking some years. In Guru's case, the process took thirteen years between his elopement in 1996 and the final ceremony of inviting the village and putting vermillion on his wife's head in 2009. Only after the final step of a wedding has been completed is a Santal wife allowed to enter the sacred corner (*bhitar*) of her husband's house and to be buried in her husband's ancestral territory.

Schulte-Droesch, who has recently completed fieldwork among Santal people in Dhalbhum, identifies the "people of one house" (Santali: *mit orak hor*) as *gusti* and defines both, following Leach, as a "local line" (Leach 1971: 57; Schulte-Droesch 2018: 106, 112–20). The members consider each other notionally united by the idea of a "common origin in one house in the past [...] reflected in the fact that today members of one *gusti* have the right to enter each other's ancestral shrine (*bhitar*)" (Schulte-Droesch 2018: 119).[263] Eligibility to enter each other's *adin* (sacred part of a Ho house) has also been emphasized in this book as a key determinant indicating and presupposing a Ho's membership in a specific *mmc* including all those who may claim a common origin traced back to a common, if putative forefather – plus their wives and unmarried daughters. In that respect, the Ho's *mmc* has not been classified here as a "local line", in accordance with Leach's restrictive focus on males only.

Due to the characteristics that I was given, I assume that the categories 'people of one house' (*mit orak hor* in Santali) and 'people of one rice pot' (*miyad mandi chaturenko* in Ho) are rooted in analogous concepts of relatedness and genealogical depth and refer to corresponding parallel social institutions in this area. I do not argue that these traits reveal sufficient family resemblances to assume *identical* social institutions among Ho and Santal, because apart from recording the pedigree of the locally dispersed segments of Guru Hansda's *gusti* in Tarana, Tatanagar, Rairanpur, and Lucknow (see figure 18), I have not explored this social unit in more depth. Also, Leach's construct of the "local descent group" or "local line" includes the co-resident *males* of three genealogically related generations of members of localized corporate groups of the same clan, but

---

263 Offering rich ethnographic material, Schulte-Droesch presents *gusti* as a named unit and its members united in common sacrificial action meeting regularly for that purpose. Both characteristics are shown in her book to be relevant identity markers. Both were not confirmed to me by Santal consultants in my research area. Also, those Santal rituals such as *sohrae*, *magh*, and the cattle ritual (*uri: bonga*) that I participated in, were rituals at the level of the hamlet and not restricted to the boundaries as marked by membership in a specific *gusti*. Neither was a name for the particular *gusti* offered to me nor a narrative about the name's origin as Schulte-Droesch reports from East Singhbhum. For the Ho, names and myths about the origin of the names (see chapter 4) are assigned to those *categories* that I have called *subclans* (see chapter 3), while the corporate *group* of people united within an *mmc* remains unnamed. Schulte-Droesch presents *gusti* as both a group and a category.

the respective wives are excluded in the formation of a "local line" as Leach defines it. Following that definition, a Santal *gusti* in my understanding cannot be identified as a "local line," since women would be excluded. Rather, *gusti* as it was explained to me can possibly be identified with the Ho's *mmc* in that married women and unmarried daughters are included.

Plate 27: A Santal house for 'the people of the house' (*orak hor*)
Orak hor constitute one segment within a larger corporate social unit called *gusti* or 'the people of one house' (*mit orak hor*).

The physical house in its social environment

Guru lives with his wife and two sons in a fairly large mud house of about a hundred square metres (twenty metres long, five metres wide; see plate 27) in a Santal hamlet which is part of the village of Tarana near Jamda.[264] The house was built by Guru's grandfather Antu. It opens north into a courtyard (*racha:*) which is approximately the same size as the house and is fenced in (*bakai*) towards the road. Typically, houses and courtyards behind the houses are shaded and sheltered by huge trees, mainly tamarind trees (*jojo daru*), mango trees (*uli daru*), and village bamboo (*hatu mad*). Running water is supplied twice a day for an hour via pipes for those who pay for the installation. The pipe can be spotted in plate 27 at the foot of the lush green bushes. In addition, a well offers unlim-

---

264 For locations see chapter 2, maps 5 and 6.

ited water to all and, for women, the possibility to exchange news and discuss relevant matters.

Like most other work related to building, repairing, renovating, and decorating a Santal house (except for making tiles and roofing the house), building fences is a job done by women. Social life is centred in the courtyard: it is here where guests are welcomed, children play, and meals are prepared and eaten, with people often eating separately from each other. Paddy is boiled (*tiki baba*) on one of several hearths and spread on the ground to dry (*tasi*) before being husked (*run*). Chicks are continuously and patiently scolded (*simko har*) when they eat more than their share of the paddy. In the evening, at least in the dry season, Santal like to socialize and relax over a bowl or more of rice-beer while sitting in the courtyard or on the *pindigi*, a kind of roofed veranda running around Santal (and Ho) houses (see plate 28). At night in the dry season, men more often than women or children sleep outside in the courtyard beneath the starry sky. Some have a mosquito net and use it as such. The courtyard is brushed immaculately clean at dawn and regularly purified with a mixture of cow dung and water (*guri:*). While the muezzin is heard at 5:00 a.m. sharp, it is usually a few minutes later that the people of the house (*orak hor*) will wake to the sound of the broom as the female head of the household (*owa: rini:*) begins to sweep.

Opposite the long side of the house and enclosing the courtyard is the cattle shed. It is used to house a pair of bullocks and plenty of chickens and as a storage room for bicycles and rope beds (*karkom*), which are offered to all visitors dropping by and which otherwise accommodate drying vegetables and dishes and people taking a nap. The cattle shed also stores sacks filled with differently coloured soil. In the company of a group of women from Santal Sai, Guru's wife has carried these sacks home on her head (*dupil*) from various distant parts of the jungle. Such an expedition may take up to three days. When the women return they are giggling, gossiping, and singing – and they are physically exhausted. My *kimin* would not get up for two or three days, lying as if in a coma and in between complaining about a severe headache. But, of course, she – and the other women – would go again. I could neither move nor lift any of the sacks, not even a tiny bit. Going to the jungle for this purpose is usually done every or every second year to have the houses regularly repaired and beautified before *magh*, which is the Santal equivalent of the Ho's *mage* feast. Sometimes, the layers of many years covering the walls of a house are knocked off completely before a new coating made manually from pulverized mud and water is applied and painted anew, often in an utterly different fashion. As with Ho houses, this work is done exclusively by women. But while Ho houses are as solid as Santal houses, they look rather plain and uniform from outside. The outside of the main part of the house is usually coloured white with black around the bottom, and sophisticated patterns show perhaps on the floor inside the house, if at all. In contrast, Santal women are known for their skill and creativity in ornamenting the outside walls of their houses, turning them into idiosyncratic handmade masterpieces.

Behind the cattle shed is the threshing floor (*kolom*), which out of respect for the rice mother (*baba enga*) may never be entered with shoes on, and an attached garden. The *kolom* is about the size of the courtyard. This was large enough in 2009 to store the paddy stacks piled up there waiting to be threshed (*hasa*). The harvest was so rich that it lasted for almost two years, which was most welcome, as in 2010, due to a severe drought in the region, the harvest was poor.

The house itself has one undivided, roofed living space, with the *bhitar*, the sacred corner, in the east, not separated from the rest of the large room by a wall as the Ho's *adin* is. Here the valuables of the people of the house are stored, and attention is paid to the forefathers. Attached to the house are another two rooms sheltered by the same roof. The three-roomed house is part of a compound with three other equally large houses right adjacent to Guru's where three of his younger brothers and their families are living. Their houses are built around the three sides of another courtyard that the human and animal members of the three houses share and that opens on the west, on its fourth side, behind another threshing floor, towards the rice fields, the grazing grounds for the cattle, and the hills.

Plate 28: Paying tribute to female Santal skills
A house where former exterior layers have been knocked off completely in order to plaster the walls anew (1). Soil is manually pulverized by working it through a sieve before mixing it with water and kneading it into a smooth material (2). Before the veranda (*pindigi*) is coloured, it is plastered (*jalom*) and straightened with smooth wet mud (3). A Santal house worked on without any mechanical assistance to obtain the dead straight lines (4). Various patterns and designs handmade by Santal women (5–8.) A typical Ho house with white, unpatterned, windowless walls, a dark-coloured and fully roofed veranda, and burial stones in the courtyard (9).

Diku paiti (government jobs)

The dirt road in front of Guru's house runs through the hamlet from north to south. It was built only in 2008. A new government scheme had offered work related to building roads through the villages. Guru was one of the contractors. His work was *jagar paiti* (talking work) and getting the labour force organized. For his wife and other women of the hamlet, it was hard physical labour and paid work which was done in groups for a few hours (*nala paiti*) every day. After a day's or a week's labour, women were paid in cash according to the time or working hours needed to complete the work. Only since 2016 have things changed. Day labourers are now paid according to the volume (*tika paiti*) of heavy soil dug out, irrespective of the time they need to do that. One person is supposed to be able to earn 226 rupees in eight hours by digging a ten-by-ten-foot square to a depth of 7.5 inches. This is classified as unskilled labour offered to BPL people in the region for a hundred days per year. Relatively speaking, the pay as such is not too bad, considering that strong young male persons are used to working for as little as 50 rupees a day, despite the official minimum wage being 75 rupees for unskilled labour and 150 rupees for skilled labour. Throughout all my years of fieldwork, I saw young men waiting next to the road between 6:00 and 7:00 a.m. to be picked up by some lorry and driven to some unknown building site and some unknown boss. By 5:00 or 6:00 p.m. they would be transported back and receive their day's pay. This is referred to as *nala asul* (to support, e.g., one's family by day labour). Maybe they would work somewhere else for someone else the next day and be paid by yet another *diku* employer: alienated capitalist wage labour (*nala paiti*) trespassing on tribal terrain.[265] But at least they were paid for the work they did, and this on the very day itself.

---

265 *Nala paiti* is to be distinguished from the concept *achu* (to employ someone to do some work). My *kimin's* neighbour's work who produces the soil to repair the house and who plasters the walls with it (as shown in plate 28/ 2nd photo) falls in the category *achu*. In exchange for her work she will not be given money. She will be reciprocated in kind such as a pair of earrings (for doing the *pindigi)* or a saree (for plastering the courtyard – *jalom*). Both *nala* and *achu* are concepts related to work done *for others* outside one's *mmc, gusti, hagako, alerenko*.

    Within these social units, notions of *asul* (to help, to support) or *denga* (help) prevail. When in the preparation of *mage* and *ba porob* my *kaki-ma* from Boja Sai had no *ramba* (sacrificial pulse) it would not do to buy this from the local market. As the ancestors to whom *ramba* is offered in sacrifice would expect to be served pulses that have grown on ancestral ground the arrangement of *denga em* (help) in this case was as follows: my *kaki-ma* was given the necessary amount of pulses by someone *within* her *mmc* and in exchange spent a day's work harvesting one of that person's rice fields (see Prologue). *Asul* (to help, to support) was explained to me in yet another context among members of the same *mmc*: some of Sadurgon's chicken had

So, while the idea of earning some extra money was generally welcome, the conditions since 2016, euphemistically characterized as modernization, were not, for two reasons: while government contractors preferred to employ single persons to work for eight hours a day, tribal people preferred to work no more than two to three hours a day and in groups, especially at the time of harvest, but also when the harvest work was completed. On the whole, though, contractors – usually *diku* people from outside – were quite unprepared to offer or allow such part-time jobs. In any case, modernization was accompanied by bureaucracy. Henceforth, people had to submit a written application to be given work. When eventually their application was considered, after several weeks or more, the agricultural season and cultivation work might have begun, leaving no spare time to do extra work for extra money. Also, since 2016 wages are no longer paid in cash but transferred into individual accounts set up for that purpose in a bank in Jamda. While nobody offered positive feedback concerning this practice, many deplored its demoralizing effect. People have access to their accounts only two days a week. It not too seldom happens, I was told, that people have to queue up and wait long hours, only to find the counter closed for the rest of the day when it was their turn or closing down for the clerk's extended lunch break. On such days, then, people will not receive their salary for work already done, and they will also miss out on another day's work. People are utterly frustrated by this experience that they are exposed to without their consent. Some complained that in March they were still waiting for their pay earned in January.

The structure of a Santal *gusti*

The data concerning the 'people of one house' (*gusti/ mit orak hor*) as arranged in figure 18 were collected and checked in collaboration with Guru and counterchecked with Dhano's eldest son Ragu (both generation 0), who assisted his aged father in the rituals performed at the household level. Since in some of these rituals the names of the dead members of the *gusti* are regularly called out, he seemed a most reliable source, whereas I have never observed Guru involved in performing any ritual.

<u>Generation +3</u>: Bima is recognized by the male persons of Guru's generation (0) as their common forefather. He is said to have acquired but not cleared in his

---

caught some disease, and my *kaki-ma* offered to shelter those not yet infected by it. The food for his chicken was *chauli* (husked, home-grown paddy) and supplied by S.

lifetime the cultivable land in Tarana that they cultivate today. At that time Ho people had been in the area for a long time, were recognized as constituting the dominant category there, and in terms of precedence enjoyed a high status as first settlers (*munu: hoko*). Santal people in the region of research readily subscribe to that assumption (see chapter 1).

Bima had three sons and two daughters, all of whom are remembered by name. No further information is given about Bima's brother Dhano, whose name is passed down in every alternate generation. The same logic applies in the case of Bima (+3), whose name was given to Guru's father (+1) and the elder of Guru's two sons (-1). His second son (-1) was given the name of the boy's mother's father (+1).[266] Thus alternating generations become identified by the names of forefathers being repeated systematically. Bima's elder daughter died unmarried. She thus remains a member of her father's *gusti* and is remembered in ritual. Her younger sister married. As a consequence, she adopted her husband's *gusti* and left her natal one. Although this happened two generations ago, as seen from generation 0, she is remembered by name in the pedigree, as is the village that she married into. Bima's youngest son K. was married but had no children. As mentioned above, the chart is incomplete in some respects. Daughter's names were always given, while wives' names almost as a rule were not. As wives, they belong to their husbands' *gusti* and, if fully married at death, will be remembered in rituals at the household level. Their namelessness perhaps indicates that they are collectively referred to and that only men are named in ritual. At least, this is the case among the Ho (Deeney 2008: 41; Reichel 2009: 91). On the other hand, the chart is also 'overcomplete' in other respects, as in terms of *gusti* one of Bima's daughters would no longer be reckoned a member *after* her marriage.

---

266 Judging from those Ho and Santal pedigrees that I took in the field I can confirm as a rule that a first son is given the name of his FF. That the second son is named after his MF is a matter of negotiation I was told.

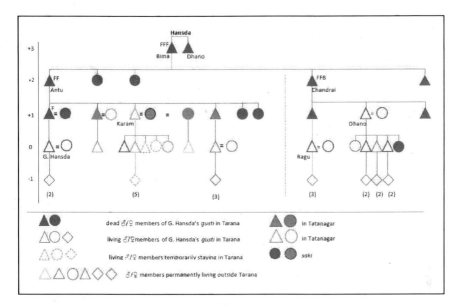

Figure 18: G. Hansda's *gusti*

Generation +2: Guru's grandfather Antu (FF) was the eldest of the three brothers. Within the *gusti* seniority is passed down the generations as a structuring principle ordering the relations among its male members. As a consequence, Guru's father Bima (F) is considered elder brother (*bau*) to his three younger brothers and also to Chandrai's (FFB) three sons. Following the same logic of interrelatedness to this day, Guru is reckoned elder brother (*bau*) to all (ten) male persons of his *gusti* within his generation (0), irrespective of their absolute ages, of which they are not aware.

Following the death of their youngest brother, Antu (FF) and Chandrai (FFB) split up the land that they had inherited from their father Bima. While ritual interaction continued, economic collaboration between the two sides ended (indicated by the vertical orange line), although the 'brothers' kept living right next to each other in Tarana. In the process of splitting up the land Antu (FF) was left with twenty-seven acres which he eventually divided into four shares (*hatin*) for his four sons (+1), without the division being officially registered by the local *panchayat* to this day. Registration is usually avoided in order to continue jointly cultivating the land corporately. Proceeding like this reflects a key feature of Santal and Ho people's relation to their land to the extent that the term 'brothers' (Ho: *hagako*; Santali: *alerenko*) in certain contexts may become coterminous with *mid ote hapatinrenko* (the people so related that if one of them dies, the land will be divided among the others) and *mid mayom hapatinko* (those who reciprocally share one blood). These are Ho terms. The infix -pa- in ha-pa-tinko expresses mutuality and reciprocity. The concept implied in these terms has been elaborated for Ho people in chapter 3, and in the research area it is talked about by Santal people discussing Santal affairs by resorting to the identical Ho expressions.

Generation +1: In the generation of Guru's father (F) economic collaboration between the two sides (Antu and Chandrai) had come to an end, but, of course, it continued among Antu's sons and among Chandrai's sons. Each side had its own threshing floor (*kolom*) and its separate hearths.

Chandrai's three sons remained in Tarana and cultivated their respective shares of land corporately. Dhano (of generation +1) and his wife live in their eldest son's house. They are both actively involved in the economic activities of the household. Dhano is also respected by Guru from the other side as the eldest "who knows all," thus highlighting the principle of seniority as a superior value linking the two sides of the pedigree in the absence of economic collaboration. As the only brother in his generation living in Tarana and in the absence of Karam (green triangle, +1), who lives in Tata, Dhano is in charge of performing the rituals at the household level. Whenever he is not available or too ill, his eldest son replaces him as ritual guide. Apart from this, Dhano's son is a much-requested shaman (*dewa*). In the second *saki* ceremony, which took place in Tarana and which was argued in chapter 6 to primarily be a female affair, it was Dhano's wife Salgae who was the female witness and who led me through the ceremony. She is the eldest member of the *gusti* alive in Tarana. Before she became active in her role as witness, she made sure that I understood that she was *dai* (older sister/woman) to me, and I *mai* (young girl) to her. It was the distinction in relative age that mattered, not the absolute age difference, with her being perhaps a little over sixty, and me a little under sixty. As this shows, the principle of seniority contributes to structuring social relations as well as ritual life within the *gusti* and beyond tribal boundaries.

On Antu's (FF) side after splitting up the land, things developed quite differently for his offspring in generation +1, his four sons and two daughters. For reasons not further explained, Guru's father (+1) made a living by working in the steel plant in Rourkela, where Guru was born. He grew up as an only son and received his education at St. Xavier's High School in Lupungutu near Chaibasa.[267] Three of his father's brothers migrated to Jamshedpur, today Tatanagar, and remained there (green triangles in figure 18). Two of them died there.

---

267 St. Xavier addresses tribal children and is run by the Jesuits. Deeney (see chapter 2) was one of Guru's teachers and headmaster for seven years.

Karam (+1) continues to live in Tatanagar, as do two of his sons and one unmarried daughter. One of Guru's father's younger sisters (+1) married virilocally but is remembered by name and village. She left the *gusti*, as Santal cultural logic has it, and is buried in her husband's territory. Sauri, his father's other younger sister, remained unmarried. She is *hatom* (FyZ) to Guru, but Santal and Ho people in the region prefer the term *ji* (Ho) or *jhi* (Santali) instead of *hatom*.

Since her four elder brothers were in Rourkela and Tatanagar and her elder sister married in Ulidih, Sauri remained in Tarana and took care of everything. She must have been an amazing woman. Guru raves even today about the efficiency of his *jhi*. She looked after Guru's severely ill mother, the house, the animals, and those twenty-seven acres of land that though assigned to four brothers had remained undivided and needed to be cultivated. Today someone owning and cultivating twenty acres or more is considered a rich person, while someone owning ten acres is said to have sufficient land, and someone who has five or fewer acres is considered poor. So Sauri had plenty of land and plenty of work. Obviously, she managed it extremely well until she died. She is buried in the shade of a tree near a tank close to the fields she cultivated. Guru had difficulty finding the burial stone commemorating her, as it is inconspicuously small and hardly visible – quite unlike the Ho's eye-catching flat burial stones. The sociality of the Ho's dead, lived out inside the *adin*, is permanently present, as are the *sasan diri* (burial stones) collectively covering the ground of the courtyard or the burial site.

Karam (+1) from Tata had two wives. His first wife – elder sister to his second wife – turned out to have been *saki* to Guru's mother (blue and green circles, both red-rimmed), by identification also to me, and to my Ho *saki* from Pathan Sai (see chapter 6). Karam has addressed me as *saki* ever since we first met – instead of *hili* (eBW), which constitutes another logical option. Obviously, the *saki* relation (and its concept of implied equality?) ranks superior.

<u>Generation 0:</u> After his *jhi*'s (FyZ) death in Tarana, with his father's three younger brothers (FyB, *kaka*) living in Tatanagar, Guru decided to settle in Tarana, get married there, and take over. Fluent in English, Hindi, Odiya, Ho, and Santali and with some knowledge of Sanskrit and Pali, he left his teaching job in Rourkela after a history of humiliations that he was exposed to as a tribal person. This was an experience that he has never forgotten.

In his generation (0) and within his *gusti* Guru is elder brother (*bau*) to all of his five *kaka*'s (FyB) sons. On his or rather his grandfather Antu's side of figure 18 they are the individuals identified as living in Tata, in Chaibasa (orange-rimmed triangle), and in Rairanpur (red-rimmed triangle/circle), leaving no male person his age to support him in getting the cultivation work done. For this reason, one of Karam's (+1) sons decided in 2015 to move from Tata to Tarana for good (blue-rimmed triangle). Physically unfit to do hard manual labour and work in the fields due to illness, he is eager to offer support and be useful to his people. He occasionally works as a local contractor and is an efficient organizer. He was able to buy a tractor which may be hired out by others in the vicinity. The subsidies that he was entitled to as a BPL person, though, were cancelled, as happens to everybody who owns any kind of a four-wheeled vehicle (or a motorbike or a *pakka* house with three or more rooms).

The main work in the fields, however, was done by one of his brothers and his unmarried sister (green triangle and circle, dotted rim). Over the years they were always there for long periods until the work was done: helping in the house with the cooking, getting firewood from the jungle, and busy with the rice-related work at home and in the fields during the harvesting and the sowing season. These two were extremely hardworking, dynamic, and very pleasant people indeed.

Once, after a hard day's work in the fields, Ch. (green triangle, dotted rim) collapsed and fell into a coma-like state, in which he remained for two continuous days (*goe: anjed* – to become unconscious). For long periods, his body was rigid. He did not wake up once in this time and did not respond to any address from outside. This passive state was interrupted by energetic phases in which he was wildly delirious, mumbling incomprehensibly, screaming as if he was fighting his way through a different world. With his eyes wide open and yet not reacting to anything around him, he murmured mantras in tone and intonation quite similar to those sung by the ritual guide (Santali: *naeke*) and his men during the village festivals in the sacred grove. While Guru could not have cared less, it fell to Ch.'s *hili* (eBW), Guru's wife, to keep vigil at the side of her *iril* (HyB) day and night. As mentioned above, the *hili-iril* relation is a joking relationship.[268] She shook him, sang to him, shouted at him, whispered to him, told him stories and jokes, caressed his face, threw water on him, slapped his cheeks repeatedly and fiercely, massaged his feet, legs, and arms intensely and patiently, covered him with a blanket, and unsuccessfully offered him food and water. After two long days, he returned to his senses, got up from his bed, and immediately start-

---

[268] see above chapters 3,5,6. Guru reported another situation in which his wife had fallen victim to continued sexual harassment by a co-villager with whom she was in a (classificatory) *iril-hili* relation. Guru commented that the joking character of this relation may have contributed to bringing about the problematic situation. This judgment hints at the possibility that the *iril-hili* relation as such is one that is not free of sexual connotations and possibly even allowing for or even inviting sexual behaviour.

ed joking with his *hili* as before.[269] She welcomed him back into life by scrutinizing his head closely, delousing him (*siku*) skilfully, and expertly pulling out single white hairs from his otherwise thick black hair. He then resumed work as intensely as before his collapse. While I was amazed at the suddenness of both collapse and recovery in this and other cases, nobody else was.

On Chandrai's (+2) side there are – apart from Dhano and his wife (+1) – four brothers (generation 0), one of whom lives permanently in Lucknow and only very seldom comes for a visit (Chandrai, red-rimmed triangle). But he is known to have two sons and be married to a woman of the Soren *paris/kili*. The other three brothers and Dhano constitute an active branch of economic and ritual interaction, organizing their collaboration independently of Guru's side. They live with their families in the complex of three houses immediately adjacent to Guru's house, as mentioned at the outset of this section.

When I first met Guru in 2006, I was impressed by the beauty and size of his house and the extent of the cultivable land that I thought was assigned to him. He was one of the few in the hamlet to grow basmati, which was sold in the market for a good price, as he emphasized. He could even afford to refuse an offer by the mobile-phone company BSNL, which was interested in acquiring a plot of land in order to place a cell tower there. At that time, I did not understand why he was classed as poor and belonged to the category BPL. Only when I began collecting data about Guru Hansda's *gusti* in and after 2010 did things begin to connect. I learnt that those undivided twenty-seven acres were administered and managed by Guru, not owned by him. Instead, they were assigned to Guru's father's three brothers (+1) and their offspring (generation 0), independent of their physical absence from Tarana.

The same holds true for the 'house' in a physical and social sense. I learnt that the offspring of his father's three brothers and Karam as the only living person in that generation (+1) on Antu's side are entitled to use the house whenever they want, live there for good and may claim access to the land and its products. Guru, fond of dramatizing things, theatrically emphasized that his father's brothers' six sons and their wives and children would not even have to ask beforehand if they decided to move to Tarana! From one day to the next, they can come and stay and stay on! Wouldn't the place be totally cramped then? Eventually, in fact, in 2010, the male representatives of the village community jointly decided in one of their nightly meetings on the *akara* (the village's meeting and dancing

---

269 Their enjoying each other's company so outspokenly and in public without any attempt at hiding its intimate character encouraged me to enquire Guru how he felt about his wife joking so intensely and continuously with her *iril*. Well, it is an *iril-hili* relationship, he answered, so what can one do?

ground) to give priority to extended living space to be attached to Guru's house should government money be offered to the community of Santal Sai to be spent for that purpose.[270]

So the corporate ownership of the 'house' constitutes a joint venture indeed, related to a multitude of people – according to figure 18, more than twenty individuals on Antu's side. As a social unit within Guru Hansda's *gusti*, it is composed of the four distinct 'houses' of Guru's father and his father's three brothers. This division of the unit is known in the hamlet, recognized, recollected, and publicly confirmed in ritual at village level. On the occasion of the cattle sacrifice (*uri: bonga*)[271] the sacrificial meat of one cow and one ox is redistributed in equal shares to the exact number of Santal 'houses' in the hamlet, thus reproducing the Santal community of Santal Sai in its entirety and equalizing in ritual its component elements: the ritual guide (*naeke*), the secular headman (*majhi*), and the cultivators and landowners, those present and those absent. The leaf cups containing an identical number of pieces of sacrificial raw meat are examined several times to make sure the number, size, and composition are correct. Guru receives two shares for the two households (*orak hor*, people of the house) that he represents: his own and that of his FyB Karam from Tatanagar (see figure 18 and Schulte-Droesch 2018: 121).

Economic collaboration is strong within Guru's half of his *gusti*, though it does not primarily take the form of corporate fieldwork. Rather, sacks full of husked paddy and firewood are transported to Tata, from where kitchen utensils, a pressure cooker, plastic chairs, and a television set are sent in return. Village bamboo is cut for building purposes and transported to Rairanpur by those of the *gusti* who permanently live there, which is reciprocated in kind by clothes for the children staying in Tarana. A major part of the cultivation work is done in Tarana by family members coming temporarily from Tata for that purpose, but they cannot manage it all by themselves. Guru never lifted a finger once. Those who were aware of this complained, at the same time that – as younger brothers – they were not in a position to give orders to an elder brother.

---

270 This extension was attached to the front of the house in 2012 occupying that space that had formerly sheltered the cattle by a thatched roof (see plate 27). In 2016, another room was to be attached to the back side of the house looking west.

271 In more than ten years that I spent in the area I have been able to observe the cattle *bonga* only once at full moon in December 2009. Informants were quite hesitant to pass on any knowledge concerning this specific ritual which was surrounded by an air of conspiracy. It was agreed that it was considered illegal and should the police find out about a cow and an ox battered to death by two men whose names were kept a secret all the men of the hamlet would be severely punished.

Additional helpers needed to be recruited (*achu* – to employ) to do the cultivation work, for which they were paid from the money received by selling paddy and vegetables in the local markets and by the occasional paperwork that Guru was asked to help with. In 2010, males could expect to receive 70 rupees a day for work done in the fields, women 50. For two oxen needed to plough the soil and the manpower to see the work done, 120 rupees was the price for four hours.

The young children of generation -1 from Tata live in Tarana either permanently or for long periods. Some attend classes in the local school or stay in the hostel until they run off to return home, where they are scolded but never sent back. The fluidity and variability of these arrangements on the compound, involving more than ten active young children and notionally and economically connecting people from several dispersed localities, account for the situation which initially seemed so chaotic and nontransparent to me. Apart from those who came to visit and stayed for extended chats in the daytime, up to eight persons and often more quite regularly lived, worked, ate, and stayed overnight at Guru's place, though not always the same persons.

On Guru's FFB's side of the *gusti*, economic collaboration was structurally not too dissimilar in that most of the crop and soil cultivation and animal husbandry was managed by Dhano's eldest son, Dhano himself, and their competent wives only, while Ragu was busy for the larger part of the day doing semi-skilled work on a construction site, and Dhano's younger son Bisa did unskilled work as a messenger. As a result, complementary paid labour was a regular mandatory feature to cope with the amount of cultivation work, although both Ragu and Bisa were busy in the fields, too, as soon as they returned home from their wage labour.

The unity of the *gusti* as depicted in figure 18 is primarily tied to and rooted in the corporately owned land in Santal Sai and comes alive in ritual at the household level, performed by Dhano as the eldest in his role as ritual guide or by his son. Among Ho people I have nowhere come across a situation characterized to such a degree by outsourcing cultivation work to paid labour (*nala paiti* – work for wages) as a rule. In the five localities where I did fieldwork (Manbir, Boja Sai, Gara Sai, Pathan Sai, and Jamda; see maps 4 and 5), Ho landowners were fully involved in corporate cultivation work on their own fields and those of the localized segment within their *mmc* or in their at times large gardens.[272]

---

272 G. Bage, *munda* in Manbir, spent a lot of time in his garden where he was tending 50 lemon trees.

Relationship terms and behaviour

In the previous section, aspects of a *hili-iril* (eBW-HyB) relation were examined in terms of its character as a joking relation between a woman and a man and the empirical behaviour related to it. Next, two more same-sex relationships within Guru's domestic environment will be looked into. The *dada-undi* and the self-reciprocal *teya* relations are between two male individuals, the first nonjoking in character, the second joking, although the same two persons are concerned. The final relationship to be highlighted here is a respect relation between two females, for which I will discuss the notion of respect and how it affects the relationship.

dada (eB)–*teya* (eZH)

Guru reported an empirical situation illustrating how specific relationship terms may become an issue of negotiation between two male persons of the same generation.

Guru grew up in a neighbourhood where he had become used to addressing a girl of his generation as his elder sister (*dai,* eZ). He was her younger brother (*undi* – yB). A *dai-undi* relation is typically one within the same generation, and Santal people, just like Ho people in the area, prefer the term *dai* instead of *aji*. When eventually the girl married a man of the Hansda clan, the question arose for the two men of how to define and verbalize the potential and the risks implied in the relation between them which had come into existence as a result of the marriage. They saw two options. One was to establish a reciprocal *teya* relation (eZH-WyB), which is a joking relationship. The other option was a *dada-undi* (eB-yB) relationship. In the *dada-undi* construction Guru would maintain the principle of seniority by addressing his elder sister's husband after her marriage as *dada*. Obviously, seniority is considered a relevant element. Also, since the husband was from the Hansda clan, Guru felt towards him as a 'brother' in the first place, more precisely as an elder brother, as he would address all male Santal of his generation as his younger or elder 'brothers'. Thus the definition of the relationship between the two males became a matter of negotiation.

His *dada-teya* then suggested a solution that Guru Hansda agreed to. When he met his elder sister (*dai*) and her husband at his *dai*'s (natal) place, they would address each other reciprocally as *teya* (eZH-WyB). When they met at the husband's place, Guru would address his eZH as *dada*, which is often preferred to using the term *bau* with the same meaning (eB). Hence, as the couple would live at the husband's place, in line with Santal women marrying virilocally, Guru would address his eZH as *dada* most of the time.

The explanation given was as follows: as *dada* his eZH would feel secure and would not have to expect any complications (*muskil* – difficult; difficulty; to meet difficulties). No risk was to be feared, and he would be safe from any unexpected demands. As *dada* he could rely on being paid respect. A reciprocal *teya* relation, however, is fundamentally different in the behaviour implied. A *teya* relation is a joking relation. As a result, despite its containing an element of seniority, seniority does not constitute the determining feature, as the age distinction within this particular relation is equalized. While the joking becomes the dominant characteristic, such a relation is about more than just having fun or jesting with each other (*argae* – a jest; to jest; joke; *argae: apargae* – mutual jesting; a joking relationship).[273] A *teya* relation implies the obligation to comply with any of your *teya*'s demands. A *teya* may feel free to demand just anything, and even if something is demanded in jest, the demand should never be refused. This is the obligation implied in the relation, which contributes to its erratic character, as one never knows what one may be jokingly asked to give. Hence, in subtle ways a *teya* relation is not free of risks. It may involve social obligations and formal requirements that cannot be clearly defined in advance. Guru gave a concrete and yet unspecific example from his own experience to illustrate the point:

In his wife's natal village, all those of his generation to whom his wife was and remains after marriage related as elder sister (*dai*) have reciprocally become related to him as *teya*. This otherwise dormant relationship is brought to life on each visit that Guru and his wife pay to her parents in Bagrai Sai (see map 5). This happens not infrequently, as Santal and Ho people tend to entertain and maintain close relations between a wife and her parents also after marriage. On any such visit to his in-laws' place, something that as a rule will attract more in-laws (Santali: *perako*), neighbours, friends, and also his *teya*, one of their demands could be "You have taken / we have given you our sister in marriage; now, please give us your sister." Knowing that he has no sister in the sense of *mid lai:ren* (born of the same mother), they still might make the demand, jok-

---

273 *argae:* is often collocated with *baiyo:* (D. S. Purty, personal communication). *baiyo:* "(passive participial form) with whom something is allowed, e. g. one with whom one has a joking relationship and therefore one with whom one could dance, etc." (Deeney 2005: 24). The passive form of *baiyo:* emphasizes that jesting is an action that is done on you, that happens to you, that cannot be escaped (personal communication with D. S. Purty).

Bouez (1985: 63) instead of *apargae:* gives a pronounced form of jesting as *belen* – "to playfully clown around [e.g. wrestling] with someone. Often used in the recip. *bepelen*" (Deeney 2005: 37) which I have not heard in the context of a joking relation in my research area further north.

ingly, obliging him to look for a classificatory sister in exchange. For that reason, Guru explained, he would never stay late in his wife's village and would leave as early as possible. At home, he would be on safe ground in that respect: no *teya* waiting for him in Santal Sai. *Teya* usually live elsewhere, outside: they are affinal relations acquired via a man's or a woman's elder sisters (who marry outside) or, for a man (only), via his wife's natal hamlet, which is also outside – most of the time.

The *undi-dada* relation as elaborated here is a computable kin relation signalling safe ground,[274] while the reciprocal *teya* relation is a joking relation between affinally related persons, erratic and not risk-free. The examples given show that where choice is possible in terms of terminology, relationships and relationship terms may be negotiated, and flexible solutions may be reached.

hanar (HM)–*kimin* (SW)

The relation between a husband's mother, *hanar* (or his elder sister, *aji-hanar*) and her son's wife (or a younger brother's wife), *kimin*, is a respect relation which has been linguistically characterized by expressions such as *man-manatin* (respect; *manatin* – to obey; to observe; to respect; obedience, respect) or *man-mapan* (a generic term for respect, including mutual respect).[275] Neither Ho nor Santal people ever used these abstract nouns in the research area, nor does Bouez, who defines the relation *hanar-kimin* as characterized by "conflit, hostilité" (Bouez 1985: 65).

Conflict and hostility may be inappropriate characteristics in my empirical case, but surely there was a fairly strong note of respect, formality, obedience, and a certain distance involved in the relation between Guru's wife and me, as the two of us were *kimin-hanar* to each other. I was initially quite unaware of the expected behaviour implied in this specific relationship at the time I was given the gift of entering into it. As soon as Guru had decided to become my assistant and my son, his wife became my *kimin*, and I her husband's mother, *hanar*. Unlike in the *dada-teya* situation above, there was nothing to negotiate in this case, although I tried hard. The structural distance implied in the respect relation had a negative impact on the quality of our daily collaboration in the long run in my understanding and contributed to my looking for another place to stay,

---

274 Tensions arising among 'brothers' due to hierarchically connoted age distinctions have been discussed in chapter 3.

275 These terms were given to me by D. S. Purty 2010 (personal communication). Deeney 2005 has the denotations of the terms, but does not translate any of them as respect or avoidance relation.

although my *kimin* was a very pleasant and active person who had a fine sense of humour. The following scene will illustrate how my wrong and inadequate behaviour as *hanar* kept irritating my *kimin*.

Several times I had asked my *kimin* to take me with her to harvest the basmati paddy (*baba ir* – to reap; to cut with a sickle; to harvest) and to teach me how to do it properly, how to use the sickle (*datarom*), but to no avail. Only when I asked her in what I considered a polite and modest tone why she continuously evaded my offer to assist (*denga em*) did she state a clear position, without any shyness. She was friendly and polite as usual, but also determined. Due to our relation, she explained, it was impossible for her to allow me to work. As *hanar* I should not ask questions, I should not help her, I should not speak to her in a modest tone or in a soft voice. All of this was out of place within a *kimin-hanar* relation. As my *kimin* she was the one to do the work; I as her *hanar* should give the orders, and this in a harsh voice. Her husband's mother would have done exactly that, and their relationship had been a really good one. She then suggested I begin by practicing the proper tone. I was supposed to order her to do something. I tried hard, several times, yet so reluctantly that my performance must have been awfully poor. It was utterly contrary to my idea of how people should communicate with each other, and my *kimin* was not at all happy with my effort. "You know," she said, "when you speak in that harsh voice and in that tone, I will become frightened. I will fear you (*boro*). Then I will obey (*manatin*), and I will say to you in a low voice: yes, *ma*."[276] Guru confirmed that a mother gives orders and sees to it that they are carried out; she does not politely ask. According to Guru, his wife is a good mother to her son, because "he fears her."

Fear (*boro*) is an element embedded in a more comprehensive and lived concept among Ho and Santal people that in my perception has overall positive connotations within certain relationships involving age differences of one generation, like that between parents and their children. It is considered a necessary element in order to acquire, learn, and internalize a desired behaviour such as obedience or respect and also contributes to gaining knowledge[277] or developing desired insights, such as that it never pays to rebel against the principle of seniority by not obeying one's elders. When my *kimin* scolded or slapped her sons (six and eight years old), which happened not infrequently, she was hardly

---

276 see chapter 6 for a person's soft or low voice as suprasegmental feature and its phonemic quality.

277 *Ada* – to experience; to feel; *adana* is the reflexive form suffixing -*ana* to the verb root *ada* denoting "to experience for oneself, to know" (Deeney 1991: 22; 2002: 77).

Similarly, *eto* carries the meaning "to teach, to know", while the reflexive form *eton* suffixing -n, literally means "to learn" in the sense of "to teach oneself".

in an angry mood, furious about what they had done or ill-tempered in any way observable to me. She showed the behaviour expected in specific situations, which was explained to me as teaching (*eto*), not as punishing (*saja*) her sons. The contradistinction of teaching and punishing had been explained to me by analogy during *sohrae* (in Ho: *karika*),[278] a feast celebrated in honour of the cattle of the house. On that occasion, during new moon (*mulu:*), a tall wooden post (*kuntu*) was set up in front of Guru's house in the middle of the dirt road (plate 27). Two cows were tied to the post. Before being fed, caressed, and having their horns anointed with oil, they had to pass through an ordeal. They were teased, hit, kicked, and scolded while simultaneously the onlookers cajoled them into walking around the pole in a disciplined way. This the cows initially and forcefully refused to do. They went wild, which was expected, but they could not escape. It was a violent, physical affair which continued until after quite some time the cows gave in and behaved. While observing the cattle trying to break away from the post, those present commented on the scenario agitatedly, confidently, and expertly, as if they were fully aware and in control of the process, its choreography, and its meaning.

Towards the end of this rite, my *kimin* breathed out with a loud sigh[279] and said *na:do adanako* (now they know/understand/have learned). In other comments, I made out repeated expressions such as *patarsin* and *itu-muli*. Deeney defines *patarsin* as "to slap or scold so as to make one smart (physically or in spirit)" (2005: 284) and *itu-muli* (ibid.: 168) as "to train; to discipline (*itu* is used mainly of training an animal [e.g. a bullock for ploughing], figuratively it may be used of training a person; *muli* – 'straight' also has a figurative meaning of straightening out someone morally, setting him on a straight path)." *Saja-muli* is yet another term-cum-concept denoting "by punishing to straighten someone out (correct someone's behaviour)" (ibid.: 323). These terms, I argue, linguistically coincide with Ho and Santal people's convictions and attitudes when interacting within a known and unquestioned concept. In this, the focus is on the de-

---

278 *Sohrae* is a Santal feast. It is known to Ho people, but not celebrated by them. In the research area, however, *karika-sorae* was celebrated in Jamda by the (dominant) *Bage kili* of the Ho community there– though during full moon (*ponai*).

279 This sigh of relief in my interpretation relates to the fact that the ritual or some superior order had been obeyed (*bonga manatin*) rather than the empirical people responsible for the set-up of the arrangement. When at the end of the first *saki* ceremony I was oiling my *saki*'s legs, arms, and hair my *saki* gave a similarly pronounced sigh of relief signalling: all is well now, the right thing has been done.

sired result. The means to achieve this result and people's unshaken confidence in their ability to bring it about are not questioned.[280]

Runaway marriage

> *In a runaway marriage you run away, but you don't just run anywhere! There are steps to follow, rules to observe, and this in a strict order!*
>
> *(G. Hansda when discussing with me a form of marriage, like his own, in which the couple elopes by mutual consent; Tarana, Odisha, 2016)*
>
> *We have grown a flower. We have watered it. We have given it attention. So now that it is in blossom, we surely want a price for it when we give it to you.*
>
> *(Ch. Purty commencing in the Ho's veiled language the bridewealth negotiations during a fully arranged marriage,* bapala andi, *in which he mediated the demands of the bridal side. This formalized negotiation is absent in a runaway marriage.)*

There are various ways of getting married that are distinguished in the research area by Ho and Santal alike, as follows: *Bapala andi* is a fully arranged marriage including bridewealth (*gonon*) to be given to the bride's side, a mediator or go-between (*dutam*), preliminary arrangements and activities, and a feast usually held at the house of the groom. *Diku andi* is an arranged marriage held at the bride's house and officiated by a Brahmin. *Sasaṅ andi* is a marriage that comes about by a boy putting a wet *sasaṅ* mixture on a girl, thus claiming her as his wife. *Sasaṅ andi* is the only way of getting married that I never observed, but in 2012 I came across *opor-tipi:* (marriage by capture; reciprocal of *or-ti: –* to pull by the hand), which refers to a boy bringing a girl to his village without her previous consent. Like many other Ho and Santal persons' empirical marriages, Guru's marriage was an elopement by mutual consent, more commonly referred

---

280 I will refrain here from commenting on the link between slapping, teasing, and provoking a child (or animal) and the assumption of being able to correct, 'straightening out' or improve someone's behaviour that way. In my perhaps limited (Western) insight of matters psychological or psychiatric this comes close to what is conventionally and critically classed as *double bind*. The awareness that the Ho's language accommodates this very link or concept in its vocabulary positively and is no biased interpretation arbitrarily impressed from outside rather came as a shock to me.

In the absence of the "impossible fiction of the idea of a universal child" (Montgomery 2009: 1) an analysis of concepts coming to the fore in Ho 'childhood' within a comprehensive and comparative Anthropology of Childhood (Lancy 2008) will surely be worth considering in depth. The essay on *Concepts of Children and Childhood* (*see* appendix) is my preliminary attempt at tracing notions and concepts of young Ho persons guided towards maturity in the sociocultural context of tribal Middle India.

to as *nir andi* (runaway marriage) than as *kepeya andi* (*keya* – to call or invite; *kepeya,* reciprocal – to call and invite one another), which is an expression that Deeney provides.[281]

The following report sheds light on a very brief moment extracted from the drawn-out process of getting married. It is about Guru engineering the initial steps, the few hours at night of physically abducting his wife and formally introducing her into the social web of his village. It is in large part Guru's narration and presented from his perspective. From other runaway marriages that I was lucky enough to participate in and observe (this step never takes more than a night and is never announced beforehand), I can confirm the standardized structure that comes to the fore in Guru's presentation. Guru eloped with his wife in 1996 (his information), and the final step in order to be recognized as a fully married couple was performed in 2009 (my participant observation).[282]

When Guru decided to leave Rourkela (see above), settle in Santal Sai, and find a wife there, his father had already died, and his mother was seriously ill, although she was well enough to be the first to be informed by her son about his wish to marry and whom, to give him permission to go ahead by himself, and to eventually welcome his wife and introduce her into the secular and ritual affairs of the house. So he had to do without the parental support a Santal or Ho may usually rely on when intent on getting married.

The second person to be informed about the girl and his plan of eloping with her was his *nana buri*, a classificatory grandmother with whom he entertained a joking relationship. She lived not too far away from his future wife's parents' house and in the same hamlet. She was prepared to conspire with him. He bribed her, he said, by promising her a *saree* and a *sim* (chicken) if she complied with his request to act as his matchmaker (*dutam*), which she did. He talked his idea over with her on a Thursday and announced his planned elopement for two days later. In the meantime, she was supposed to think things over, get in touch with his future wife, make the necessary arrangements, and organize and prepare extra food for Saturday evening.

An appointment was arranged for Saturday evening in his future wife's natal hamlet, but not at her parents' house. The *dutam* surprised him by suggesting to

---

281 *Kepeya* – "of a man and woman, to arrange a marriage by mutual consent (a 'love-marriage'); to elope" (Deeney 2005: 202). Although I have no statistical data on the matter those who volunteered to talk about their run-away marriages – always with a smile in their faces – conveyed the impression that this kind of marriage is quite common and, in their perception, the most numerous.

282 In fact, Guru requested me (as his mother) to be in charge of the final ceremony, as his own mother had died in the meantime. This was my duty, I was told (and not asked politely).

him to elope not with his prospective wife but instead with her elder sister, who was to be married first.[283] He refused and insisted, he said, on his original choice, knowing that this was absolutely beyond the pale. This news was then broken to his future wife. Guru had to wait for four endless hours, as he melodramatically complained. The worst hours in his life! He was accompanied by Ragu, eldest son of Dhano (see figure 18).[284] His future wife remained inside the house to negotiate and contemplate the situation with her two girlfriends and the *dutam*. She finally agreed to the elopement and to accompany her husband-to-be to his house in Santal Sai. It was one o'clock in the morning. Her parents were not informed. "I have stolen my wife, so it was a case of theft (*kumbu* – to steal; a thief; theft). And the proper time for thieves to move around is the night," Guru said, and he again emphasized, "It took her four hours to consent to being stolen!"

Tellingly, a jeep had been hired beforehand, which took the group to Santal Sai: Guru, his one-man escort, the mediator, his bride and her two friends, and the driver. From the very beginning, this type of getting married also revealed a structured and collective character. The bride had her head completely covered by a *saree*. She had to stay in the courtyard and wait. She was not allowed to enter the house. The headman of Santal Sai, the *majhi*, was to be informed first about the elopement. The *majhi* then requested two of his helpers (*dakuwa-kin*)[285] to immediately inform the villagers, as is their duty, also in the middle of the night. Shortly afterwards, the villagers assembled in the courtyard of the house, where Guru and his mother lived. Sitting informally on the ground of the courtyard, men were offered cigarettes and tobacco. The first person to be served was, of course, the *majhi*. Obviously, this nighttime meeting was of great significance and an indispensable part of the script dictating the chronology of how to graft a collective and social character onto a seemingly individual matter. It revealed the standardized tripartite structure of such get-togethers: first the participants socialize informally, chatting, drinking, and smoking, which is followed by serious, often formalized talk (*jagar*) concerning the purpose of the meeting. When the couple have thus become reintegrated into the communi-

---

283 In Ho marriage negotiations veiled language is resorted to. Of two or more sisters the older or oldest is referred to as *suba sakam* (low leaf: the lower leaves coming out first), the youngest one as *sirma sakam* (*sirma* – sky), and a sister between (*tala*) them in age would be *tala sakam*.
284 The wives of Guru and Ragu, Guru's younger brother, are those two sisters (*mid lai:ren* – born of one womb). Figure 18 does not show that in these two marriages the principle of seniority has been violated: Guru, elder brother to Ragu, is married to the younger sister, while Ragu as younger brother is married to the elder sister.
285 This is the Ho expression, *jog-manjhi* is the Santali term.

ty in their new status, there will again be extended socializing, dancing, singing, and drumming.

Introducing the second step with an air of gravity, still outside in the yard, the *majhi* told Guru and his bride to sit in front of him. Taking turns, he addressed both of them. She was to state her name, her parents' name, the name of her father's *paris/kili*, the name of her natal village's *majhi*, and whether she had been forced or had come of her own accord. These are some of the questions and answers as Guru remembers them:

- Question (addressing the bride): For what purpose have you come?
- Answer (expected and given): I have come to find my house.
- Question: Have you brought gold or other valuables?
- Answer: No.
- Question: Have you jumped across an *ari* (an embankment) before?
- Answer (expected and given): No.
- Question (addressing Guru): Were your horns (horns of an animal, *dirin*) broken previously?

The *majhi* is actually asking here in the veiled language that is usual during marriage negotiations whether either of them had had sexual intercourse before.

- Answer (expected and given): No.
- Question (addressing the two female friends accompanying the bride): Are you from the same village?
- Answer (expected and given): Yes.

This chronology sounds rather trite, as it does not reflect the humorous mood and welcoming atmosphere that usually prevails in such a situation, at least as I experienced it several times. The questions raised above have always been asked, but expressed in a language that is deliberately circumstantial and metaphorical without being cumbersome. Also, the villagers participate actively in interrogating the couple and jokingly tease them.

When the *majhi* confirmed aloud that the *paris* of Guru and his bride, Hansda and Kisku, were compatible in marriage, some old women instantly got up and began to sing and dance three rounds around the courtyard in an counterclockwise direction, and men played *dama-duman* (a collective noun for drums).

It was the mediator's turn next to tie Guru's shirt and his wife's *saree* into a knot and tell them never to untie this knot in their lives. Tied together, Guru prompted his wife for the next relevant act: she was to *jowar* everybody present in the courtyard. That way she would learn and was expected to remember who was who, how to address her new *owa:renko* (people of the house), and how she and the other villagers (*haturenko*) had become related to each other as a result of her marrying into the hamlet. For example, all male persons who were elder than the groom (his elder 'brothers') were expected from now on to address her not by name but by relationship term. Doing otherwise would be considered a sign of disrespect, as Guru's wife had become *kimin* to them (yBW). The *jowar* rite was a lengthy procedure and the final part of the standardized and formalized second step. Guru's wife repeatedly confirmed the relevance of this unique method of including her in the relational tapestry of the hamlet.

After this, singing, dancing, and drumming resumed in the courtyard while Guru and his wife were ceremoniously called inside the house by his mother in a rite called *tiril-tarob* (generic term for fruit trees that grow close to each other). Only towards dawn did the courtyard empty. Married life had begun for my *kimin* at her husband's place.

Two days later, the *majhi* and his two helpers went to Bagrai Sai to inform the parents about the theft of their daughter, that she was found in Santal Sai, and that she was safe. "No need to go to the police! A goat has been grazing on our ground and has been eating our grass, so we have tied her. Come and see if the goat that we have found is yours!" Before this was communicated to the parents in person, the group – without Guru – went to see the *majhi* of Bagrai Sai first. Along with him, they formed the delegation to break the news to the parents and discuss the next steps. A result of the discussion was that the blacksmith (*kamar*) was ordered to make an iron bracelet (*med sakom*) for my *kimin*, for which he was paid eleven rupees and given two *poyla* (measuring vessel) or roughly one kilogram of rice. Fixing the bracelet around her wrist confirmed the marriage two days later in yet another significant step – one of many more to come. Apart from the bracelet being a visible and public sign of being married, it meant more importantly that in the case of her death, from then on she was no longer eligible to be buried in her parents' burial ground in her natal hamlet. Also, without being married fully she was not eligible to be buried in her husband's *gusti*'s territory, as mentioned above. From 1996 to 2009 she was a woman in between: no longer a member of her father's *gusti*, not yet a full member of her husband's. This also meant that in all those years she was not allowed to enter the sacred part of the house, neither to clean it nor to paint it; she did not have access to the valuables of the house stored there but had to ask one of her sons instead. She was also not allowed to prepare *bonga diyan* for *sohrae*, which needed to be prepared in the *bhitar*, but had to call her *gungu* (HyBS) from Tata, who at that time was roughly ten years old, for that purpose. Should she have happened to die in those years in between, Guu would have had to apply *sinduri* (vermillion) to the face of her dead body, thus including her in his *gusti* for good and making her eligible to be buried in her husband's ancestral ground. It would also make his sons eligible to get married themselves one day, because, Guru exclaimed, how can our sons get married if their parents haven't been fully married? He added that the last phase of getting married implied inviting the village for a proper *jom-nu* (a feast, literally 'eat-drink') which may cost as much as twenty thousand rupees. This feast in which hospitality and generosity are displayed constitutes a social obligation and the final step in the process of getting married.

When in 2016 another runaway marriage in Santal Sai was underway in the middle of the night right next door to Guru's house, I heard the *dakuwa* give notice to the villagers late in the evening. Soon after, a crowd of women, men, and children excitedly assembled in the courtyard of the culprit's parents. In fact, news of the expected event had spread in the course of the day, and people were in a hilarious mood, looking forward to dancing, singing, and men drumming. Loudspeakers hired well in advance provided deafening Santal dance music all through the night, until ten in the morning when the loudspeakers had to be returned. In the morning, however, only the young children continued dancing, practising what they had learned the night before, while the adults resumed their daily chores.

Plate 29: After the elopement
Secular village life is resumed. Some children continue dancing until the loudspeakers placed between the pillars of the veranda have to be returned (Santal Sai, 2016).

Epilogue

February 11, 2018. After two years' absence from the field, we make a phone call. For the first time in more than ten years, Guru answers the phone. Obviously, a cell tower has been built near Santal Sai. In 2016, Guru had moved with his wife and two sons to the outskirts of Rairanpur (see map 4), where the boys attended school. The house where they lived was a *diku* building amidst other *diku* buildings. But Guru was very concerned about his sons' educational future. In the meantime, his younger brothers from Tata (see above and figure 18) were running the household in Santal Sai and busy doing the harvest work. Collaboration within 'the people of one house' (*mit orak hor, alerenko, gusti*) – as usual.

The news in February, 2018: "Your *saki* has passed away. Last year's harvest was excellent. We have all returned to Santal Sai. The boys go to school in Rairanpur by bus every day. They are naughty, but they do very well in school."

The news in August, 2019: "Maskal [Guru's eldest son] has passed his exams successfully. He wants to study science. When are you coming, *ma?*"

Appendices

Scholarly Commitment: John Deeney and the Ho of Kolhan[1]

[...]

When considering in faraway Europe research on the Ho in 2005 for the first time Deeney was pointed out to me as a Ho scholar and Jesuit of American origin having lived in Lupungutu (LPG) near Chaibasa in the state of Jharkhand right in the heart of Ho country in a community of Jesuits for more than sixty years. I thought this might be a good starting point, and I did not have any other. [...] At that initial stage I could not have the faintest clue that it would be the Jesuit John Deeney to introduce me, an atheist anthropologist, into the poetics of the Ho language and the intricacies of the Ho's universe.

My husband was able to accompany me. We had never been to this particular region so far, we had never before entered tribal Middle India. We were informed that the nights at the beginning of the year can be chilly and that the area is infested with cerebral malaria, that people die from it so we better take care. In a brochure with facts and figures of Mayurbhanj we later read that the region has been made out as one of the many "tribal-infested districts"[2] in Odisha which, on the contrary, was fine with us. We were told that there is a good library at the Tribal Research and Training Centre (TRTC), that Deeney was a very busy man and that we needed to respect that by all means.

Deeney and the Jesuit setting of Lupungutu

Nobody expected us, when we arrived in Lupungutu, but Deeney and other members of the Jesuit community were around. They were polite and friendly and busy as all of them were involved in some Ho related project or the other. They had a tight schedule every day leaving no spare time for two curious elderly Europeans to be looked after. Deeney himself was the most outspoken of all. "I have no time for you. I once allowed myself to become distracted from my work,

---

1 This article is a shortened version of Reichel (2018) related within this book to chapter 2. It concerns the relevance of Deeney's work for the study of the Ho.

2 The quotation by A. Samanta was published in a brochure on KISS, the Kalinga Institute of Social Sciences in Bhubaneswar/Odisha in 2012. Samanta is the founder and the head of KISS offering free education for more than 27000 tribal children.

https://doi.org/10.1515/9783110666199-012

so I better tell you straight away", he said when we met for the first time. He had just completed the revised and enlarged edition of the Ho-English Dictionary from 1978 whose publication was to be expected by autumn that year. His days now were completely absorbed by translating the Old Testament into Ho. He did this in collaboration with D. S. Purty, a Ho graduate and his co-worker for over 40 years about whose poor health he seemed more worried than about his own. He felt he could not afford to miss out on a single day's cooperation with his Ho *pandit*, as he called him. Of course, we accepted all of that. We were happy enough to be allowed to stay there, to be offered the safety of an ascetically furnished room with a mosquito net, three meals a day and the key to the library. At that time Deeney was 84.

So, at the beginning of our stay we spent a lot of time in the library in the daytime because most Fathers left in the morning and returned only for dinner. They worked in the vicinity and in what they call 'the interior' as priests, teachers, social workers, lawyers. Some were busy planning a scheme of night schools to be installed in villages in the jungle for Ho girls and boys who should be taught there in their mother tongue Ho, others were supervising the construction of a new TRTC complex offering non-formal and adult education programmes, computer cabinets and computer classes for *adivasi* of the surrounding and more remote villages in West Singhbhum district. A garden was to be attached to provide the vegetables, a hostel for tribal boys and one for tribal girls, and a repair shop for jeeps, bikes and bicycles. The new site was in Guira, in walking distance from LPG. While Deeney was not part of the outdoor activities of his Jesuit colleagues, he was part of much of it due to his published work on the Ho and his extensive research into the life of the Ho.

Over breakfast the Fathers talked about their plans for the day, over dinner they shared the experience of their days and discussed news. They did not mind us joining them for the meals, listening to their reports and eventually getting involved in the discussions. And they seemed not to mind that we were not affiliated to the catholic church although this was one of the first questions that we were asked. All were non-Ho, but fluent in the Ho language. They came from different parts of India, many from Kerala or from Tamil Nadu. All treated Deeney with that extra note of respect when he was around or when he was talking. There was an overall appreciative, undogmatic and non-patronizing atmosphere towards the Ho community and among each other. [...]

In 2008 when I attended a Ho language course for future Jesuit priests, use was made of the language material that Deeney had developed for grown-ups in which Ho is rendered in a modified Devanagari script. By then the construction work for the new TRTC in Guira was completed and the site had turned into a bustling place. The only place that was almost always deserted was the wonderful library that had been transferred from LPG.

The Fathers usually conversed in a mix of Hindi, English and Ho. But for the occasional female guest from outside and the (Ho) cook's wife it was an all-male lot. Almost all of them had been suffering from malaria more than once. One of them had caught the disease twelve times, but this may be no exception. They lived with it and kept going. As priests Jesuits live, often for decades, in remote tribal villages. When they catch malaria there, they sometimes go to Lupungutu to rest and recover, before they go back to their 'field'. These were no-nonsense people. Their days began with Mass at five.

Deeney concentrated on his work and confined himself to his study. [...] Quite of his own accord and contrary to his professed intention he eventually gave us some of his time and a number of articles written by him that had not yet been published and that dealt with different aspects of the Ho such as their spirit world, the relationship with their dead, their creation myths, their clan (*kili*) and totemic subclan nomenclature, their language and a comparison with the Munda's language. [...] We discussed Ho kinship matters and the Ho system of relationship terms of which he had collected 56 encompassing altogether five generations and brought into a graphic grid differentiating between the relationships of a man and a woman. [...]

Deeney died in January 2010. He had wished to be given a Ho burial in a Ho environment which he was promised. Also, a John Deeney Memorial Centre was to be erected in Chaibasa.

John Deeney: the scholar

"If anything is going to be remembered about me after death, it will be the Ho-English dictionary" (personal communication 2010). Between its publication in its revised and enlarged form in 2005 and Deeney's first appearance in the Chaibasa scene in the then state of Bihar half a century had passed.

Deeney was born in Philadelphia, USA in 1921. He joined the Society of Jesus when he was 18. He came to India in 1949. He stayed on and lived in the Jesuit community of Lupungutu most of the time. He was ordained a catholic priest in 1952 and received Indian citizenship only in 1991 after having unsuccessfully applied for it before. He was sure that his publications on the Ho had helped in this. Before going to India, he had acquired a thorough knowledge of the grammar of English, Latin, Greek, French and Gaelic. After his arrival in India he studied Hindi whose script he later modified to transliterate Ho vocabulary. He was not in favour of promoting and spreading a distinctive Ho script such as *Waran*

Chiti which already at Deeney's time had turned into a political issue. In 1952 he came to Chaibasa for a month and immediately began to learn Ho. When he was appointed headmaster of St. Xavier's High School/ Chaibasa in 1955, he already knew much Ho. He continued studying the language while he was headmaster of St. Xavier's High School/Lupungutu from 1957 until 1962. It was in the course of these seven years that he developed the habit of riding by bicycle to visit most of his pupils and their parents in their villages, one by one, to learn about their lives, their culture, their language. Initially meant for his own benefit he began to have index cards with him on these excursions on which he not only noted down Ho words and their denotations in English, but added other useful information in connection with that word (personal communication). The vocabulary collected on these cards plus the added notes containing information from the indigenous point of view constituted the foundation of the Ho-English dictionary to be published 50 years later. Maybe Deeney was inspired in his approach by Hoffman's *Encyclopaedia Mundarica* all the 16 volumes of which he had in his study in Lupungutu, as the added data turn the Ho-English dictionary into an anthropological encyclopaedia of the sociocosmic universe of the Ho in many respects. In it any references to sickness, spirits, rituals, 'folk beliefs' as he calls them are expressed as seen through the eyes of a Ho without Deeney himself holding such views as he points out in the introduction to the dictionary. After all, he is a scholar, not a 'going native' person. Deeney began publishing on the world of the Ho and their language in the mid-seventies after an extended period of extensive research. After hosting an anthropologist in Lupungutu and observing him interview elderly Ho informants while tape-recording their talks Deeney approached Dhanur Singh Purty, a Ho graduate and former student of his. Their collaboration had begun in the early sixties by Dhanur interviewing and tape-recording his own father. Deeney recollects how amazed Dhanur was about his father's memory and knowledge. The recordings plus Dhanur's follow-up research in a number of villages in the heart of Kolhan plus Deeney's own research led to the publication between 1978 and 1982 of a seven-volume encyclopaedia of more than 1000 pages on Ho village life, customs and culture entitled 'The Ho of the Ho Country' (*Ho disum Ho honko*). The process of writing up took almost twenty years. D. S. Purty is given as the author, Deeney writes the introduction. The text is written in the Ho language making use of the Devanagari script. Simultaneously Deeney and Dhanur began preparing the Ho-English dictionary containing the denotations in English of all Ho words that appear in the books of the series enriched by detailed ethnographic information (*see* Reichel 2009: 103–108 for the content of the seven volumes). The first edition of the Ho-English dictionary came out in 1978, the same year when the publication of the seven volumes began. Deeney claims that all 12000 entries of the dictionary plus those 900 added in the 2nd edition 2005 have been filtered through Dhanur. I do not know any of Deeney's publications in which he does not emphasize his complete dependence on Dhanur at every stage of their work. Also, when I sometimes got stuck at home while writing up my thesis and I consulted him via email, his answers were always carefully argued and would usually begin by: "I have discussed your mail with Dhanur".

Dhanur also collaborated in the preparation of the "Ho Grammar and Vocabulary" which was published in 1975. Deeney hoped that everybody who is familiar with the Devanagari script will be able to read and understand the seven volumes written by Dhanur by making use of the Ho-English dictionary and the Ho grammar. When the Jesuit language instructors realized that for teaching purposes there should be a faster, more effective and less theoretical approach than that conveyed in the "Ho Grammar and Vocabulary", Deeney wrote a condensed " Introduction to the Ho Language" which was published in 1991. This booklet is a jewel, a survival kit of no more than 50 pages. Although all of the language materials have been accompanying me throughout my fieldwork it was the "Introduction" of which I needed a second copy since my sweaty fingers due to the daily use in tropical climate had eaten up the letters. I still remember the first sentences: I drank rice-beer. She made/built a house. We ate cooked rice. The men sowed the seed. He ploughed the field.

Deeney's latest publication from 2008 is "The Spirit World of the Ho Tribals. And other glimpses into the Ho world." Deeney calls it a book about the Ho's religious attitudes representing their own perspectives. It is a revised and updated collection of hitherto unpublished essays. This publication written in English draws heavily from the seven volumes written by Dhanur. Deeney had originally considered to translate these volumes into English or to have them translated with Dhanur's help, but they never found the time. Also, Dhanur had fallen victim to moneylenders in the meantime and did only irregularly turn up for work in LPG, as he felt the lives of his wife and his ten children to be threatened in his village. Deeney himself was 87 years now and getting weaker. Before running the risk of the contents of the seven volumes getting lost to many because they are written in Ho and Devanagari, this publication from 2008 then is the condensed result of Deeney's effort to make available in English to others in one book the Ho's relationship towards their deities, their *bonga* (the body of tutelary and malignant spirits), and their ancestors.

Deeney was aware of the fact that outside Ho country little attention and even less published tribute was paid to his work about the world of the Ho as he portrayed it in his publications. And he was right: he had met and discussed with Serge Bouez, who published his book on the Ho's and Santal's alliance patterns in 1985 without reference to Deeney's material. He had enjoyed, he said, sitting with Michael Yorke and discuss aspects related to the Ho's *miyad mandi chaturenko* (*see* chapter 3). In fact, Yorke quotes him and lists him in his references, but then his thesis has never been published and at that time, in 1976, only Deeney's Ho grammar had been out. Barbara Verardo did long-term fieldwork among Ho and Munda people in the Ranchi area and was in touch with Yorke and M. Areeparampil from the Tribal Research and Training Centre in Lupungutu who helped her find her research site for fieldwork. There is no reference to Deeney's material in her unpublished thesis, though, but they met, if only briefly (personal communication). Eventually, Deeney's language books are listed in the bibliography of "The Munda Languages" (Anderson 2008: 253) which to my knowledge claims to be the most comprehensive and up-to-date publication on "Ho and the other Kherwarian languages" (Anderson, Osada, and Harrison, 2008: 195–256).[3] However, in the book's survey introducing relevant publications on Munda languages all through the 20th century, Deeney's works are missing altogether. While Sanjukta Das Gupta (2011) in her well-researched book on the socio-economic transition of the Ho lists Deeney's "Ho-English Dictionary" from 1978 (!), in her glossary of Ho terms (ibid.: 327–332) she does not stick with Deeney's transliteration suggestions and lexical options[4]. Pucilowski (2013), on the other hand, for her linguistic study in Ho morphophonology and morphosyntax makes extensive use of Deeney's grammar (2nd edition from 2002), but her dissertation was finished three years after his death.

Epilogue

Had Deeney been given a Ho burial as he had wished? I was wondering. My question was confirmed, though, even a film of the burial procedure had been made entitled "Fr John Deeney, S.J., The Apostle of the Ho", a copy of which I was given. It was irritating, then, to see that the stone to cover the grave was

---

3 The part on the Ho in this volume is not free of debatable information when the Ho speakers are said to be *mainly* located in the East Singhbhum district of Jharkhand (my emphasis). My own data and all of my informants confirm West Singhbhum to be the heartland of Ho speakers. Lea Schulte-Droesch did recent fieldwork in Dhalbum among Santal people there. According to her there is a small impoverished Ho population scattered in villages that are otherwise mainly inhabited by Santal (personal communication).

4 This is more than a formal context-free technicality as it affects the rendering of the semantics of tribal values. To give an example: according to Deeney a *děwa* is "a shaman, one who divines at times of sickness to discern what spirit has been offended and what offering should be made to appease that spirit [...]" (Deeney 2005: 91). A *deonwa* in Das Gupta's glossary is denoted as "witch-finder" (Das Gupta 2011: 328).

not a *sasan diri* which is one chosen and transported from the jungle as would have been the Ho tradition. It was polished black granite instead engraved with a large cross. It lay in a North-South direction as is mandatory with Ho people. D. S. Purty who I met in 2012 called it a *diku diri* (alien/ foreign stone) and complained about the burial site. When digging the grave, he said, water flushed inside and could not be redirected. Ho people always offer their dead a good 'site, he continued, which by all means is a dry grave. He and his wife are quite unhappy to know Deeney to be exposed to such humidity for good. Those in charge of choosing the burial site for Deeney just would not have listened when they were informed about the water leakage inside the grave. He and his wife could live with this knowledge only as they had done everything to prevent this from happening.

The John Deeney Memorial Centre in Chaibasa had been erected soon after Deeney's death. It had a library consisting of a few shelves with Deeney's and Dhanur's books that had been transferred from Deeney's study in LPG, and a larger room for seminars. When I was there in 2013 the place did not look used, some of the books and shelves were covered by cobwebs, others had been damaged by water or gnawed at by rats – an altogether poor sight as it conveyed the impression that there was no demand for the intellectual passion and precision encapsulated in Deeney's and Dhanur's material. Obviously the wonderful library at the TRTC in Guira was suffering a similar fate. It was closed and locked most of the time when I went there in 2013. So many books had been stolen in the course of the years that this seemed the most effective way of rescuing the rest. A charming, polite and educated Ho girl from the vicinity was in charge of the key, had regular office hours which, of course, were not kept, and books could only be read under her constant supervision. Unaccompanied individual entry was disallowed. She had learnt how to use a computer in one of the courses run by the TRTC especially for the advancement of tribal girls and had produced a modern, computer-typed inventory of the books.

In my interpretation the active role that Deeney played within the community of the Jesuits and the way he was included in their day-to-day activities very much revolved around Deeney's *personne* and his scholarly commitment. Although a Jesuit and as such a member of a large community and a world-wide social net, as a scholar of the writing profession he at the same time was an isolated single individual, especially when Dhanur withdrew from the scene. The Jesuits of LPG and Chaibasa were working hard, disciplined and efficiently in order to advance the Ho tribals' material and spiritual well-being. This to them spells constructing and running Hindi medium schools and colleges, initiating a number of agricultural development projects and irrigation schemes in the 'jungly' villages, and defending as lawyers free of charge Ho women and men when these are taken to court in cases of impending land dispossession. In my understanding Deeney's perspective on the Ho was different from that of his fellow Jesuits. He did not want to improve their lot, but to understand what constituted their Ho-ness and write about it, document it. He unconditionally respected Ho people, their tribalness, their religious beliefs, their tribal values for what they were, the way they were. He did not have this hidden developmental agenda.

[...]

Sunai Kondangkel: ethnography of a bad death[5]

During fieldwork 2009/2010 I stayed in the Jamda area of Mayurbhanj near Rairanpur. With respect to the tribal population this area is mainly inhabited by Ho and Santal, and very few Munda live also there. In order to improve my language skills in Ho I luckily succeeded towards the end of 2009 in moving to Boja Sai, which is a pure Ho hamlet in the very same area. All of its inhabitants are members of the Kondangkel *kili* or clan, but they do not belong to the same *mandi miyad chaturenko* or people of one rice pot. My younger classificatory brother (*undi*) there was Sadurgon Kondangkel, the *munda* or village elder living in an adjacent hamlet, Gara Sai[6]. He had helped me find this place to stay with his classificatory mother who had become my mother that way, too. It took me quite some time and was a real strain on my hosts' nerves until it was confirmed that she was the FFyBSW[7] to my *undi* (yB) who addressed her as *kaki, kaki ma* or father's younger brother's wife[8] just as I was supposed to do being his elder sister. On the other hand, I was not only addressed by my mother as *mai* or 'young girl', but also treated as such.[9] Of her five children Sunai was the eldest of her

---

5 This is an extract taken from an essay by Reichel about *The Ho and their language of mourning.* For the purpose of this book it has been slightly changed. For a photograph of the protagonist's grave *see* plate 8 in chapter 4. Under an altered title the complete text has been published as Reichel (2017: 107–135).

6 *Gara* – small river; *sai* – hamlet.

7 She was the wife of my (younger) brother's paternal grandfather's younger brother's younger son who became my *kaka* and father.

8 As a relationship term *kaki* refers to FyBW (the wife of a father's younger brother) and to MyZ (a mother's younger sister).

9 It did not matter much in this respect, when I told my classificatory parents that at home, in my culture, I would be mother of two daughters and grandmother of two grandchildren. First, they said that as the elder sister of the *munda*, who was their classificatory son, I would become their daughter and *mai* as a matter of cultural fact. Secondly as I knew so very little or almost

four daughters. In 2006 she was bitten in a toe by a snake and died a few days later. At that time, the girl was 16 years old.

Shortly after I had moved to Boja Sai where I was given a house all to myself the big metal box that contained all the family valuables and that was kept inside the *adin* of the main house was opened by my *kaki* and its contents presented to me. Of this daughter, there were a few photographs inside – a portrait, photos showing her in school uniform, together with her sisters, and together with her school mates. There were also her earrings which my *kaki* put into my palms and made me admire them. Weren't they the most beautiful earrings? She was very wordy about these earrings, and she used to wear them on special occasions, when she was singing and dancing herself. It was for the first time then that my *kaki* informed me about her daughter and her death. In the course of my stay I was told this story time and again- and always in an almost identical, clear, matter-of-fact way, emotional though non-sentimental, and free from fear, anger, or awkwardness. Two photos showing the daughter hung on the outside wall of the house above the entrance. A lot of people had been present for the funeral – this piece of information was also conveyed to me several times. I realised only in the morning of January 14th, 2010 and coincidentally so that Sunai's death had been classified as a bad death[10] and the consequences of this. It was the time of new moon, the rice harvest and necessary follow-up work had been completed, and huge lumps of brown sugar cane were sold in the streets and bazaars. On the occasion of *mokor porob*, the "*makar sankranti* feast of the Hindus held about January 14th [see also *diku porob*]" (Deeney 2005: 253) popped rice or *ata* and *lad* or sweet bread are homemade in most Ho households. This was done at night in the cow shed half of which had been whitened for this purpose, and the fireplace there was used for the first time. The food was prepared solely by the 13-year-old daughter and the 10-year-old son, no adults

---

nothing of almost everything this would even more turn me into their *mai*. In fact, my *kaki* was a brilliant and patient teacher, and a lot of what I have learnt, I owe to her.

10 The different ritual treatment of the *rowa* or soul is something that can be empirically witnessed in participant observation. For analytical reasons I make use here of Parry's (anthropological) construct of a bad death, although I have tried to show above that it is a simplifying classification when it comes to illustrating Ho understandings of death. In their language they speak about the different ways of dying, the various kinds of death in quite concrete and descriptive terms, e. g. of a death due to being bitten by a snake or tiger (*hab-goe:*) or by any other animal (*huwa:-goe:*), to being burnt (*urub-goe:*), by having fallen into the fire, by committing suicide (*goe:en/gojen*) etc. In another case when it was not clear whether a woman had been murdered or committed suicide, they called the death *tataka* ("stupefaction; amazement; to be stupefied, amazed", Deeney 2005: 371) or *roka* ("suddenly; sudden, fresh, for the first time", 2005: 313).

were around (apart from me) or assisting. They had finished their work before dawn.[11] While busy with the usual daily chores in the kitchen after that, I coincidentally overheard my *kaki* address her ancestors[12] in the *adin:*

> "I am offering/giving to you[13] *lad* of *mokor porob.* Today is *mokor porob.* I am giving you all *lad* of *mokor porob.* Today is *mokor porob. ham hoko – dum hoko,* I have not seen all of you. I do not know how many you are. This *lad* here, divide it and give each his share. This is how I am performing the *bonga.*"[14]

Having said that she disappeared outside. As I saw in each of her hands a portion of *ata* and *lad* filled into a cup made from leaves of the saltree (*pu:*) I followed her and observed this: behind the house there were about ten tall tamarind and mango trees below which, in the shade, a number of burial stones of enormous size lay. Right next to these stones was the *kolom* or threshing floor behind which, further away from the house, there was a tall bamboo tree. Houses, trees, gravestones, and threshing floor were surrounded by a fence running around most of Boja Sai and beyond which were the rice-fields. Now my *kaki* stood below this bamboo tree and addressed that very daughter who had been bitten by a snake. She did not address her as ancestress (*ham ho – dum ho*)[15], she did not call her by name either, but referred to her as *beti*, which is Hindi for 'daughter'[16]. This is what she said:

> "My daughter's soul has been called to this site and is still lingering around. That daughter's soul has been called to this site. I am offering/ giving *ata* and *lad* on behalf of that

---

11 There are a number of ritually important elements involved in this process which cannot be enlarged upon within the scope of this article. They concern questions of who prepares the food, who does not, what kinds of vessels are being used, where and how the food is kept, what kinds of ingredients are being used, what kind of firewood etc.

12 A Ho woman will gradually adopt her husband's ancestors after marriage.

13 She addressed her ancestors in the second person plural.

14 In terms of readability this is an approximate English version: "I am offering to you, our ancestors, sweet bread prepared on the occasion of today's festival, *mokor porob.* Today is *mokor porob.* I am giving to you all sweet bread of today's festival. Today is *mokor porob.* Old men, sleeping men, you, who are my ancestors, I have not seen all of you. I do not know how many you are. This sweet bread here, divide it and give each his share. This is how I am performing the ritual" (my translation).

15 In Ho gender is linguistically not differentiated.

16 It may be interesting in this context that in the area of my fieldwork a comparatively pure Ho was spoken with rather little Hindi mixed into it. It was, however, quite common in Boja Sai and the surrounding hamlets and villages to use *beti* and *beta* (son) as reference terms to their living children- alongside *kui hon* and *kowa hon* which are the equivalents in Ho.

daughter on the occasion of *mokor sankranti*. This is what I am giving her. That soul has not been called inside the house. It has been called to this site."

Next to the bamboo tree there was another burial stone separated from the other stones by the threshing floor and very near the enclosing fence, but still inside of it. Eventually I realized that this was my *kaki's* deceased daughter's grave. Contrary to the other graves covered by those massive slabs of stone (*sasan diri*) lying flat on the ground, this grave was lavishly maintained. Instead of a flat *sasan diri* covering the body there was a terraced cement construction sealing ground and body below. And, additionally, it had an upright burial stone informing about the girl's data (name, year of birth and death) in Oriya and English chiselled into the surface of the stone. I have never seen a double construction like this anywhere else in the area. My *kaki* had also planted a tree next to the grave which she would also regularly water to make sure that her daughter be comfortable in the shade. Concerning her daughter's soul, however, my *kaki* was convinced that it was floating and dwelling among the branches of the bamboo tree. I was also told with an air of pride that her daughter's cloths had neither been burned nor left inside the grave to cover the body (as would be the usual Ho way). They had been handed over to a river instead. This was expressed by the term *atu* meaning "to place something in flowing water so that it is carried away" (Deeney 2005: 18). Many people had participated in this ritual, she added, among whom were two of her daughter's teachers.[17] Inside the courtyard a ceremony had been performed. The daughter's body had been covered by a great many *sarees*, also newly bought ones. "She will not be cold," my *kaki* informed me. On the occasion of the following two seasonal feasts *mage porob*[18] and *ba porob*[19] the offerings were repeated in the same order and the same way.

By having been bitten by a snake my *kaki's* daughter's death was classified as a 'bad' death. Her on-going dependence on the living was revealed in the ritual and gustatory treatment by my *kaki*. She and the ancestors were materially given identical offerings; however, the ancestors were addressed differently, they were being served first and at a different location. Due to the identical

---

17 Teachers in the Jamda area were usually people from the plains speaking Oriya as their mother tongue and teaching the children in Oriya. There was no school in the vicinity in which Ho or Santali were spoken or taught. Similarly, in Jharkhand alphabetization was done in Hindi or in English, where parents could afford the school fees.

18 *mage porob* is the Ho feast observed in each village after the harvest work is done; in the course of this feast obscene language is used.

19 *ba* – flower; *ba porob* is the annual flower feast celebrated at the time when the flowers of the saltree (*sarjom daru*) blossom.

gift in the course of the ritual, I argue, Sunai remains conceptually related to her ancestors. She belongs. She is ceremoniously and materially taken care of, yet simultaneously a symbolic difference is established and made visible. The classification of a particular kind of death as 'bad' death is a mental assessment, a matter of evaluation and classification. It constitutes a formal degradation which is ritually seen to (*manatin* – to obey), but it does not result in any personal vilification. While the bonds of affection may continue, as the example has shown, it is an instance calling for action to comply with the unwritten order of things (*niyam*).

Concepts of Children and Childhood in Anthropology and in a Tribal Community of Middle India[20]

Abstract: The present paper takes a critical look at relevant discourses in anthropology of concepts of childhood as separate from concepts of adulthood in cross-cultural perspective. It challenges dominant Western notions of 'the universal child' and the focus on claims of its universal bio-physical and psychological needs. This limiting view is contrasted with and complemented by ethnographic illustrations emphasizing the unity of the child and adult social sphere in ritual that the author experienced in the course of recent long-term fieldwork among the Ho, a tribal community living on the Chota Nagpur Plateau in Central Eastern India, and especially among Ho children. The competent involvement of Ho children in a ritual at village level of paramount importance reveals them as knowing subjects and as intermediaries to the realm of the divine. Ho children experience early in their lives that their young age is considered a value and qualification that enables them to contribute to the recreation of the societal whole.

---

20 This is the title of a lecture held at the 2012 Inter-Congress of the IUAES Commission on Children, Childhood and Youth in Bhubaneswar, India. For the purpose of this book the complete text (Reichel 2014a) has been shortened and a photo (taken by author) added.

Text and photo are related to chapter 4 (the collaboration of young boys and the Ho's spirit world in selecting the community's ritual guide) and chapter 7, second portrait, on indigenous understandings of guiding young persons towards maturity.

Ho Children and Fieldwork

In my long-term fieldwork among the Ho, a tribal community in central eastern India, children were my best teachers many times – their acquired competence of socially interacting self – confidently within their Ho universe and their patience with the ignorant anthropologist were simply amazing. Often, when grown – up Ho interlocutors gave up because they had more urgent things to do, Ho children continued to spend their time with me. They taught me Ho, their mother tongue, made me repeat words time and again until they were satisfied with my pronunciation, often motivating me with a big sigh of relief when I got it right – just as the adults did. They shared fruits with me that they had plucked from high up in the tree tops. Often, they would take care of their younger 'siblings' by carrying them on their hips. They took me to the jungle where they knew their way around as if it was a second home to them. They would inform me when rituals were taking place somewhere, and they would take me along if they happened to be among the protagonists of these performances. They would run off, though, if there were duties waiting for them such as herding the cows which implied chasing them, beating them, calming them down, thus educating them. They demonstrated that they had the upper hand even in risky situations when the cows turned wild. Often, they would be busy for a full day.

[Ho] Children are 'not only important, in and of themselves, they are interesting'[21], and they can be so funny. The encounter with Ho children as knowing subjects has certainly been rewarding in every sense, but, of course, there is more to it than a personal, coincidental, and emotional experience. Since they are firmly entrenched in their Ho culture the encounter has also been revealing from an anthropological perspective. It has inspired this paper on children and childhood. [...]

Anthropology and Debates about the 'Universal' Child

Dominant Western discourses of 'normal' child development are quite frequently and centrally based on developmental psychology (Montgomery 2009: 3)[22] with

---

21 Margaret Trawick in her Position Paper for the 2012 Inter-Congress.

22 Montgomery points out the emphasis on psychology in American anthropology going back to the days of Franz Boas under whose aegis the Culture and Personality School was inaugurated, and LeVine (2007) remarks that to his knowledge Boas's assessment of this branch within anthropology has nowhere been documented. Montgomery further argues that British social an-

its unshaken claim of presenting universal facts about a supposed universal progression from childhood as a state of immaturity to adulthood as a state of being more complete and representing the norm. Ethnographically informed research literature on childhood, however, has confronted such generalizing assumptions ever since the 20th century, and continues to do so. Also, the applicability outside the West of standardized legal definitions of a child as any human being below the age of eighteen as reflected in the United Nations' Convention of the Rights of the Child (UNCRC)[23], its organic needs, its best interests, and its rights as a citizen is at stake. Not only within the context of human rights discourses it is D. Lancy who warns not only against the wholesale exportation of ethnocentric definitions, but also against the ethnocentric lens of a "wholesale exportation of culture–specific child-rearing practices" (quoted in Bluebond-Langner/Korbin 2007: 244) following from this. So, what and how should we study and examine, portray and represent, when we are doing research on children and childhood from an *anthropological* perspective or, more precisely, on culturally constructed concepts of children and childhood rather than biologically informed specific stages of life as static givens?

An anthropology of childhood will have to take into consideration that the very category of childhood has been claimed to be a recent invention in the West and a modern idea. Montgomery argues that the concept of adolescence has been travelling around a globalized world only since its 'discovery' in the 20th century (Montgomery 2009: 13, 15, 51). Such essentializing claims continue to be travelling to this day, sometimes supported by highly specialized discourses[24]. An anthropology of childhood would also have to account for those contemporary scholars who argue from a somewhat reverse anthropological point of view. They envisage children's *agency* as a dominant and unrelated factor to constitute a child-centred anthropology thereby recognizing children as active in-

---

thropology, on the other hand, has always been suspicious of this focus on psychology as a determining factor and the perspective resulting from this within anthropology.

23 This convention is also criticized within the West beyond anthropological discourses. It should be mentioned that the United States have signed, however not ratified this convention [...] One reason is that the convention legally binds the state to regularly check or control what is going on within the American family, another one is that the Convention's non-violence approach would disallow children's access to guns and rifles before the age of 18.

24 In a renowned national German journal for physicians, Deutsches Ärzteblatt (June 2013: 423), e. g., adolescence is the topical subject matter. It is presented from a neuroscientific perspective as an intrapersonal "developmental period" between the age of twelve to 24. In relation to a person's brain development and other somatic changes the focus includes psychological and legal consequences in terms of a youth's (age of) criminal responsibility, heightened risk behaviours, and emotional disorders.

formants, authentic voices and meaning-makers living in their own meaningful and autonomous culture, producing their own culture and shaping that of their peers as well as that of the adults (Hirschfeld 1999, Trawick 2012). On the other hand, this approach "to promote children's agency as a cornerstone of research" (Lancy 2012 in his blog) is sharply criticized by some as harmful to a scientific approach to the study of childhood. It marginalizes, the argument runs, anthropology because "it focuses attention on the traditional targets of psychology (the individual's mental state) and sociology (social position)" (ibid.) and denies the impact of a child's embeddedness within the tapestry of the surrounding culture. Lancy strongly emphasized this criticism in his key note at the IUAES congress in November 2012.

Indeed, some have only lately deplored the neglect of an empirically grounded anthropology of childhood due to anthropologists' hypothesized aversion to and professional ignorance of children (Hirschfeld 2002). At the same time others have begun to write out its very history (LeVine 2007, Montgomery 2009) and praise "the trove of scholarship" (Lancy 2012) that already exists. Referring to B. Malinowski, M. Mead, and R. Firth as pioneers – others even go back further to Boas 1911 (Montgomery 2009) or Spencer 1899 (Benthall 1992) – they claim there has been a well–established tradition ever since the 1920ies that was also critical of universal developmental markers as formulated in psychology and biology about *the* child. In fact, Margaret Mead's ethnographic reasoning contradicted the then mainstream assumptions by G.S. Hall (1904) of adolescence as a specific biologically informed stage in a person's life universally characterized by turmoil. They point to an already existing rich literature grounded in ethnographic fieldwork in diverse cultures and often discussing childhood in the context of kinship and ritual thus underpinning the unity of adult and child social spheres (LeVine 2007: 250, Benthall 1992: 1) and focussing on sociocultural aspects rather than a child's determining innate dispositions. It is exactly this line of argument that I will focus on and return to in my ethnographic examples later.

The debate is on – within anthropology as well as within the interdisciplinary field of childhood studies. Issues, methods, and perspectives on how to study children and childhood continue to be negotiated between the poles of "childhood is about health, vitality, and growth in order to produce a robust animal" (Charnov 2001) and "childhood is about culture acquisition" (Sapir 1993). Contemporary anthropological discourse has to come to grips with how to envisage children within a given society and cross-culturally. Do we conceive of them as innocent[25], weak, fragile, dependent, incomplete, immature, naturally good if

---

25 Seeing children as innocent is a view that Montgomery claims to be culture-specific in the

presocial, and vulnerable? Are they "cute cherubs, preternatural angelic beings" (Lancy 2008: X), individual isolates growing up in a *child-centred* neontocracy as opposed to those that are attributed social competence and maturity in varying degrees, reliability, trusted to assume responsibilities, growing up and into what has been called a *child-supported* society (ibid.: 11)?

To preliminarily sum up: assuming that generalizing views of *the* universal child are "antithetical to most anthropological thinking" (Bluebond-Langner and Korbin 2007: 244), anthropologists have resisted universal and essentializing definitions of children and of childhood as a matter of principle to this day. "There are no separate or autonomous categories of adult or child" (Montgomery 2009: 55), there is no domain of childhood that is notionally separate from a domain of adulthood the divide between both being complex, permeable, and culture-specific. However, how childhood is *conceptualized* has a direct impact on what 'equipment' they are believed to dispose of. Conceptualizations are cultural constructs: the innocent child, e. g., is one such cultural construct among many others; another contrasting one, e. g., is understanding infants as being ensouled by their dead kinsmen and having their "skills, knowledge, temperament and attributes" (Sahlins 2008: 100). The point I want to make is, "There is nothing *natural* in how children grow up" (Montgomery 2009: 236; my emphasis).

Human Nature, Children's Nature, and Personhood

This brings me back to the statement by Clifford Geertz which I quoted at the outset of this paper. Marshall Sahlins has embedded it in his reflections on Western and comparative notes on other conceptions of Human Nature – implying other cultural constructions of a child's 'nature'. Both Geertz and Sahlins have been largely ignored in most of the latest publications on childhood although in my view they offer some seminal insights into a child developing personhood – 'at home' and elsewhere, and also in Ho society. A similar neglect is true of Marilyn Strathern who finds highly sensitive and differentiating formulations concerning a child's social maturing processes in Melanesia[26]. In his essay Sahlins addresses Christianity and the Christian belief in the concept of Original Sin resulting in the assumption of Man as basically evil or inherently egoistic. In fact,

---

West. Moreover, she argues that the reifying concept of the innocent child can be "extremely dangerous to children" (2009: 236) in the case that children act as child soldiers, e. g., thus turning out to be aggressors rather than aggressed.

26 Montgomery, however, does draw from Strathern (1988) when discussing the Melanesian concept of the multiple person.

Sahlins develops in much detail, how the contemporary Western conceptualization of the individual, of human nature, of how a child and its needs is envisaged, has been informed over centuries by Christianity, by ancient philosophies, and, nowadays, by modern sciences. These assumptions have become materialized in the individualizing ideology prevailing in the West of the "selfish gene" (Dawkins 1989)[27], or what Sahlins labels the issue of 'biologism', i.e. the supremacy of the genetic imperatives ascribed to be operative, dominant and characteristic of human nature and also an infant's development. The cultural consequence resulting from this, he argues, is the narrowed conceptualization of a child's growth in the organic terms of its bodily achievements, desires, deficiencies, and needs.

Round the planet, in non – western societies, however, "the more common belief is simply that the infant is not yet a full person" (Sahlins 2008: 101). Children are treated as humanity – in – becoming or on their way from imperfect to perfected humanity. Children are trained into recognizing social obligations, and they are credited the confidence, sometimes at quite an early age as we would think in the West, in their capacity to perform social duties, and to perform them well. They are conceived to be born human whether incompletely so or fully so in the case of incarnation, but not from some pre-social state and not as an anti-person with inherent either agreeable or disagreeable dispositions. An infant in Hagen, Strathern remarks, is less trained than nurtured to personhood and certainly not considered wild or innately anti-social. A child's maturation is addressed towards developing the mental capacity of assuming social relationships or, in Strathern's words, the Hagen child grows into social maturity, becomes socially competent "through appreciation of what social relationships with others involve" (Strathern 1988). Sociality is conceived of as the normal human condition, Sahlins argues with reference to topical ethnographic evidence and with reference to contemporary anthropologists who also stress cultural and social aspects as the determining determinants in a child's development. Biological markers are neither denied nor ignored. But as they are always symbolically defined, they are expressions of cultural order and not of some 'irresistible', objectively existing, innate inclinations defined as universal human nature existing unrelated to the world around. Anthropology is about the social and cultural significance given to these inherent dispositions in culture-specific contexts. Children's maturing then may eventually turn out to be an issue of

---

27 "He argued that, in fact, living organisms are just the means by which genes replicate" (Lancy 2008: 8–9 on R. Dawkins).

"their progression of mind and soul rather than the regulation of bodily impulses. Person-hood is gradually achieved through social interactions, especially those involving reciproci-ty and interdependence, for these comprise and teach the child's social identities" (Sahlins 2008: 101).

I have shown in the representation of the anthropological debate that childhood is so much more than a set, separate, vulnerable, and physiologically deter-mined fixed stage in a person's life, an intrapersonal affair, as it were. It is also so much more than a space inhabited by rights-bearing citizens protected by much national and international legislation. In the next paragraph I will illus-trate how the Ho's alternative conceptualizations of children and childhood con-tribute to initiating mutual relationships, categories of behaviour, and, more generally, child – oriented practices. [...]

Unity of child and adult social sphere: a ritual to elect the *diuri*

[...] *Mage porob* is a feast that is observed in every Ho village after the harvest work is done. It usually takes place in the course of January or February, and the whole village is involved in singing, dancing, drinking, and, most important-ly, meeting kith and kin. In the process of fixing the very days of the feast the ritual guide of the village (*diuri*) has the decisive say. [...] The case that I want to elaborate here will shed some light on the ritual importance of quite young boys which came to the fore in the course of preparing *mage porob* in P.S., the site of my fieldwork.

The present *diuri* had decided to step down [...] from an otherwise hereditary post. So, in order to fix a day for *mage porob*, a new *diuri* had to be elected first in the course of a ritual designed to serve exactly this very purpose. For the pro-cedure itself, about 60 to 70 male adult persons assembled each household of the village being represented that way. Eventually everybody sat down on the ground next to the sacred grove of the village (*desauli*), whereas a few people stepped inside the sacred grove such as the former *diuri*, two village elders (*munda*) of two adjacent hamlets plus their helping hands. All were facing east when the ritual called *mad pata:* began.

Mad is a generic term for bamboo, and in this case, it became notionally im-portant that *buru mad*, i.e. bamboo growing in the jungle, was cut. This was the former ritual guide's task which he performed after he had taken a ritual bath in a pond near-by. *Pata:* on the other hand carries the meaning 'to entwine (e.g. two ropes, two branches), to interlace' (Deeney 2005: 284). The idea of the ritual is the following: the candidates willing to be elected as *diuri* needed to be suggested by any of the Ho villagers first and they needed to consent to standing as a candidate. The final say, however, was with the Ho spirits and gods. It was up to them to decide who was going to become *diuri* and who his helpers.

For this purpose, two boys, perhaps eight or nine years old, functioned as the intermediaries to the divine sphere. They had taken a bath and were dressed in a clean loin cloth (*dhoti*). A dot of vermillion (*sinduri*) and some rice grains were put into their palms by the *diuri* who was in charge of the ritual. They stood opposite each other, concentrated and calm, maybe three metres apart from each other, holding the bamboo branches that had been split into two halves, under their armpit, and throughout the ritual they did not move. When their positioning was considered correct, the *diuri* began chanting his sacrificial formulas thereby demanding of the deities to show consent or dissent whenever he called out the name of a candidate. It was interpreted as a sign of divine consent when immediately after a name was called out the bamboo halves that the boys were holding began to entwine or come closer to each other, visibly and publicly.

Indeed, this happened time and again. It was considered a sign of divine dissent on the other hand, if the split bamboo branches did not move. This also happened. That way not only the *diuri* got elected. Also, those two men (*oron sakowa*) were awarded divine distinction who would be entitled to blow the jungle bison horns on the occasion of all big village feasts just as those men (*da: go:*) entitled to carry on the shoulder the pots of water needed for the sacrifices to be performed at the village grove (*desauli*). *Desauli* refers to the sacred village locality and at the same time the main protective spirit of a village, to whom sacrificial offerings are made in the course of the main village feasts, of which there are quite a few. Finally, divine consent was demanded for those called *ramba rid* who are entitled to grind black lentils, a ritual pulse (*ramba*) for the same purpose. The success of the ritual had literally been in the two boys' hands. At last water was sprinkled on the ground by the preceding village *diuri* thus requesting the gods to leave.

Plate 30: Entwining of bamboo in ritual (*mad pata:*)
The ritual began, when two young boys' positioning was considered correct.

The complete ritual had lasted 35 minutes. When it was finished, the boys laid down the bamboo halves and left the scene in the same matter-of-fact way as they had entered it.

Coming back to my criticism of dominant Western discourses of child development: should I really call the two boys introduced in the ritual above children? Was there anything incomplete, incompetent, immature, imperfect, or deficient about them in this situation? Indeed, in terms of age they might clearly be considered deficient if being biologically adult was expected to serve as the norm.[28] However, the boys' integral involvement in this very ritual – and it is not the only one – reveals that their being so young turns out to be the very source of their value, of their purity, of their closeness to and their relatedness with the realm of the divine. As intermediaries, they are entitled to cross a bridge that is open to other boys their age, but certainly not to (male) adults. In this particular situation, I argue, their being a 'child' is not a deficiency, but rather a qualification, a marker of excellence, a constitutive prerequisite for the ritual to be performed adequately – or, more importantly, to be performed at all. The example illustrates that Ho children, in this case boys, are entrusted with ritual duties and they experience early in their lives that they are capable of contributing to the (recreation of the) societal whole. As Ho children are usually allowed to witness

---

28 The article critically questions the usefulness in anthropology of essentializing domains such as childhood versus adulthood. This debate constitutes the beginning of the article.

and participate in all kinds of cultural affairs that accompany the yearly crop cycle, they can perform as competent social actors and knowing subjects when it is their turn. Being junior in Ho country does not imply being inferior. Maybe Sahlins might have remarked that Ho childhood was a process of culturally informed growing into personhood or social adulthood.

Conclusion

There are many more rituals where Ho children figure in prominent ways which cannot be elaborated here. All of them would have revealed that although Ho persons may be quite young in biophysical terms, they may act in quite grown-up ways in sociocultural respect. Indeed, distinctions in age may turn out as a cultural resource and classificatory potential. In this vein, the paper has attempted to illustrate that the concept of childhood as opposed to that of adulthood is not a universal given, but narrowly culture – bound. It has at the same time attempted to illustrate, how due to some anthropologists' exclusive advocacy of the innocent child in need of legal protection and nutritional provisioning, a child's impressive abilities and cultural performances elsewhere may easily be underrated or even overlooked. Ho children develop not independently of or against Ho *samaj*, as far as I can tell from fieldwork among the Ho. It may well be that exactly their being socially and ritually competent and active, knowing subjects from an early age within an encompassing meaningful whole, makes them walk tall.

Gift exchanges between the living and the dead[29]

Reflexions on fieldwork in Highland Middle India

Introduction

EASA 2014 invites us to "explore *new* collaborative practices", approach "collaboration as relations of intimacy, as an intimate process" and study the "basic

---

29 This is a lecture held at the EASA congress in Tallin in August 2014. I have given it here, since Sinbonga and the dead of the house (*ham hoko-dum hoko*) collaborate in the process of a foetus growing inside a woman's womb and becoming ensouled there before birth. The respective rite of *rowa sarub* to bring this about has been addressed in the fourth chapter. The manuscript (Reichel 2014c) is unpublished.

terms of our contemporary interconnected world". The quotes from the position paper of the conference have been given here as they ask social scientists to focus on contexts suggesting revolutionary, if hidden dynamics, social networks and activism, and to allow for conceptual innovation. Against this backdrop the present paper may seem a provocation as it will take a different stance. I will challenge our contemporary modern obsession with change and innovation by confronting it with an equally contemporary and modern obsession not to change – elsewhere.

The paper takes a look at the Ho, a tribal community in Highland Middle India, who pride themselves of *continuing* time-tested intimate practices of gift giving in their mortuary rites relating the living and the dead rather than innovating or revolutionizing their ritual performances. In the classical Maussian understanding gift cycles engage persons in permanent commitments and compel them to make a return thus construing relations of dependence, of interdependence and solidarity. The dead in Ho country are 'routinely' transformed into protective ancestor – persons who are furnished with remarkable agency and who acquire added responsibilities as intermediaries between the world of the living and the Ho's spirit world. By gift exchanges Ho death rituals contribute to creating and reproducing a dynamic web of collaboration among the living and between the living and the dead. They illustrate the social character of death and the collective making of meaning in a holistic society.

Let me begin by making a few remarks on the nature of gifts and gift exchanges, about the Ho among whom I conducted long-term participatory research and their culture-specific concept of ancestry, before I'll conclude by discussing the role of gift exchanges as revealed in the course of the Ho's first and secondary funerals.

Gift, gift exchanges and the Ho

Anthropologically and sociologically the concept of the 'gift' has conveniently been defined vis-à-vis its relational counterpart, the 'commodity'. This division, of course, is an analytical and fictional one which cannot be found in every *language* as Marilyn Strathern explains in "The Gender of the Gift" (1988: 134). Referring to Marcel Mauss's famous essay from 1925 Chris Gregory points to the implications of a gift's inalienable character and its *social* properties. These contribute to creating qualitative relations between persons/subjects – as fundamentally opposed to quantitative relationships established between alienable objects/things (Gregory 1983: 104) in a commodity economy. The *social* property, Mauss says (1990 [1925]:1), is the force *in* the thing turning it into a gift and triggering off the accompanying mechanism of *obligatory* reciprocity. Since the Ho dead are made through subsequent ritual into ancestor–*persons*, they continue to remain an active part of this mechanism. To the Ho gift giving is no one way road guiding the living towards their dead. In the Ho language, a gift is '*enem*', a verbal noun built from the verb root '*em*': to give. By infixing –n- and repeating the initial vowel *em* becomes *enem*.

In her introduction to Mauss's text Mary Douglas adds that "gifts are given in a context of public drama, with nothing secret about them...gifts are visible and invite public scrutiny" (in Mauss 1990: XIV). This is spectacularly true among the Ho when the donour's clan name as well as the gifts of food, cloth and money that are given on the occasion of a first burial are meticulously listed by a village elder in a book. What is important about gift exchanges and the Ho's mortuary rites is that notions of price-formation such as purchase and sale are absent. It is Evans Pritchard who emphasizes that gift exchanges constitute a *moral* transaction between individuals and groups as opposed to a mechanic transfer of goods within a rational economically based commodity system (in Mauss 1990: 12). All this is elementary knowledge that we have acquired in the course of our first semesters and passed on to our students – despite the criticism of the general air of evolutionism lingering around the design of Mauss's essay. What began to make sense for me only in the course of my fieldwork among the Ho, though, is Strathern's statement in her discussion of the gift and the nature of gift exchanges: ..."if in a commodity economy things and persons assume the social form of *things*, then in a gift economy they assume the social form of *persons*" (Strathern 1988: 134, adapted from Gregory 1982: 41). Talking about gift exchange means considering the multicentric (Gregory 1982: 111) character that unfolds and gains meaning only within a social network connected by and connecting social actors.

The Ho

Here I'll give some very brief ethnographic background on the Ho to illustrate the scene. The Ho (denoting 'man, human') are a tribal category of roughly one million people according to the Indian census. Ho people live in villages, mainly on the plateaux and hills of the Middle Indian states of Jharkhand and Odisha – away from the more densely populated coastal plains inhabited by nontribal Hindu caste people. These two states are home to almost 100 out of more than altogether 460 tribes all of whom constitute the indigenous population of India. It is largely acknowledged, though probably not by India's recently elected Prime Minister Narendra Modi and the BJP, that they have inhabited

India since long. For this reason, they are known as *adivasi*, as original or first settlers. In terms of seniority this is a marker of excellence to the Ho – to the same extent as it is a marker of primitiveness and backwardness to the Indian government. An individual Ho today finds her-/himself in a social web of kin-ship-based relations. The membership by birth into a localized corporate group of one of altogether more than 132 Ho clans constitutes a meaningful source of Ho identity. In the Ho language, this institution is called *miyad mandi chaturenko* or 'people of *one* rice pot' that includes the agnatically linked dead ancestors and their living descendants including their womenfolk. Ho chil-dren are given as a gift the name of one of their ancestors, they grow up in exog-amous patrilineal clans where women rank high, girl children are most welcome and bridewealth is passed on by males to the affinal side at marriage. The caste system that surely knows different forms of gift exchanges is absent as are Hindu temples, Hindu gods and goddesses, and professional specialists such as Brah-man priests.

Contrastingly, Ho have their own sacred spaces, ritual guides at village level and a highly differentiated spirit world to which Sinbonga, their creator god, and their dead ancestors belong. Ho people are – this is the point here – interrelated with all of their spirit world in a system of reciprocal exchanges. Of the spirit world, I will focus here on Ho ancestry.

Ho ancestry

At the very beginning of my fieldwork when I entered a Ho house for the first time I immediately became aware of the continued presence of the dead in the Ho's everyday lives. Ho ancestors in their pure essence are spatially really close to the living – sheltered literally under the same roof. Inside every Ho house there is a secluded sacred part, the *adin* that faces east and that no out-sider is allowed to enter in order not to pollute it. This is the ancestral abode, the dwelling site of the collectivity of the ancestors. Ho assume that eventually the purified souls of those who die transform in the course of the mortuary rites into beneficial ancestors *of their living offspring* and continue to live with them inside their houses, though in a separate sacred space. In other words, they re-main, also after death, members of their patrilineally assigned social category consisting of those descended from a known or putative common male ancestor maybe 3 – 5 generations back. It is the sociality of this multigenerational ances-try inside the *adin* that a dead Ho person's soul is invited and assumed to share and enjoy as an ancestor. It is here where the meals are cooked, where gifts of rice-beer, rice, and meat are offered to the ancestors, where they are addressed, i.e. spoken to with the utmost respect, often in doublets and poetic parallels. In this way, the living offer and practice the gift of *remembering* their ancestors daily. In this, women are included who after their marriage will adopt their husbands' ancestors. To be forgotten means to become socially dead, i.e. dead for good, i.e. to leave the cycle of being reborn. Similarly, Vitebsky (personal communication 2014) has pointed out for the christianized Sora of his research area that elderly Sora grow timid towards death as in the process of conversion also the tribal concept of rebirth and the belief in the continuity of life after death is affected in that the living will stop talking to the dead who in turn fear to become forgotten[30]. In the Ho case, it is the *adin* that is associated with Ho ancestry, purity, continuity, fecundity and their protective presence, whereas graves are conceptualized as the sites assigned to a dead person's corpse left there to decay. I often observed that those huge slabs of stone that characteristically cover a Ho grave, gradually turn into a locus of the social, of life after the completion of the funerary rites. Ho construct their ancestors, although ethereal beings, in analogy to human beings and treat them as such. They are attributed human aspirations and feelings, also ill feelings, individual deficiencies and physical handicaps; they are treated as if they have a body that needs to be fed, sensual organs, and an awareness of their social role, their responsibilities, and a mind or consciousness that can be verbally addressed. In a ritualized language, Ho ancestors for whom there is no generic term in the Ho language are invoked as "old men, sleeping men, old women and mothers, crippled and blind grandmothers and grandfathers" depending on the specific ritual.

Gift exchanges between the living and the dead

Obligations towards their ancestors come as a result and return to the gifts made to the living by the dead. In the region of research most Ho people live in quite big mud houses that their forefathers have built a hundred years ago or so, and they make a living from the fields that their forefathers have cleared and in which the living grow rice as their main crop. *Hita* in Ho denotes both a seed (for propagation) and a progenitor or ancestor. The concept of ancestry encapsulating notions of growth and generating more of its kind is clearly given in the language. This notion is not at all abstract, but very concrete indeed. In a ritual

---

30 For the fear of old Sora people of becoming forgotten by their christianized descendants once they have died and for changes in the worldview of young christianized Sora see also Vitebsky 2017. His book was published after this lecture was held in 2014.

called *jom-sutam* a woman towards the beginning of her pregnancy fasts first, takes a bath, prepares cooked rice in the *adin* of which she offers to her husband's ancestors who in due time will become her own, inside the *adin*. Then she will eat a bit of this cooked rice herself and leave the rest in the *adin* for later. In this time Ho believe that the rice has become merged with the ancestors, i.e. their souls. By eating up the rice herself the following day also the woman's foetus will become en-souled. By eating, *jom*, a thread, *sutam*, is established between foetus and ancestral soul, hence *jom-sutam*. This process of the ancestral soul entering the foetus is also called *rowa sarub* which carries the meaning of "the soul (is) taking possession of" the foetus's body. This mechanism was explained to me as gift-exchange or *enem* between the dead and the living. This is just one of many rituals that reveals a kind of immediate gift return (feeding the ancestors – passing on their soul to a foetus).

As a soul immediately after death is considered restless, nervous, unpredictable and potentially dangerous to the living, in any case negatively affected by the fate of the decaying body left in the grave for good, the mourners attempt to socially appease it by continuous, often one-sided gift giving in the course of a first burial, but they will succeed only in the course of the secondary burial. Gifts offered by the living to the dead in the course of the first burial are rituals that contribute to separating the soul from the body, to purify it, to lure it into the company of its close relatives, in Ho *haga*, literally 'brothers', to offer it food and toothbrush and to offer it the sociality of its fellow souls inside the *adin*.

Only after the second burial, however, the souls will have fully transformed into protective ancestor persons prepared, able and willing to execute their social responsibilities and thus reciprocate the gifts that grafted them into the persons they painfully became after their physical death. In this context, I speak of a delayed gift return. The secondary burial was explained to me as *the* instance amalgamating and expressing core Ho values. "If you want to know what Ho-ness is all about, come and attend *diri dul sunum*, the Ho term for a dead person's secondary burial. *Diri dul sunum* is about hospitality and that is really important in our culture." Hospitality in Ho is *em ched*, a poetic parallel denoting give – give (back). *Diri dul sunum* may consist of up to three days, in the course of which affines and agnatic relations of a dead person meet, celebrate (*jom-nu:* eat- drink), and dance. Temporary huts are built indicating the relation between the affinal visiting party and the dead, and for each party one fire site for cooking; all invited are expected to stay overnight. The visiting parties bring along food, rice-beer and cloth. Food and cloth are exchanged among those present, which is understood as a gift exchange among the living. Kinship relations become re-established in food exchanges, where people become 'one' by feeding each other rice from their plates (*jom-mid*). Whereas the focus of the first burial is clearly on the dead and the painful processes of purification (*sabsi:*) in the course of which the whole village is involved, the focus of the second burial is on the dead person's agnatic kin (*haga*) and their affinal relations (*bala*). The dual gift giving at the end of a secondary burial is done by living female relatives related to the dead person's *mmc* distributing gifts of cloth and rice-beer to their affinal guests in a grand farewell ceremony. Secondly, the eldest married female member of the dead person's *mandi chaturenko* – accompanied by all other females of the *mmc*, married and unmarried, pours oil on the burial stones of the dead and of those related to him within that Ho kin category thus unifying and obliging the dead for yet another future return gift towards the living.

Glossary I: Notes on Ho history

This glossary may be resorted to independently of the main body of the text. It was written at an early stage while I was mind-mapping my way into historical, political, social, and anthropological issues although these issues were hardly ever discussed as isolated topics during fieldwork and some of them were not discussed at all.

It had become obvious during fieldwork that a powerful indigenous sense of history plays a crucial role in the Ho's self-portrayal as successful rebels and autochthonous people. Many Ho are aware that their way of being in the world has been exposed to continuous threats from outside and outsiders "since times immemorial" – and to this day. At the same time some Ho claim that they are a tribe that has been subdued not even once and that has resisted all *diku* onslaughts successfully. Therefore, although academic history is not the core concern of this book and knowing that much of it has to be classified as conjectural or speculative as concerns the region of research, I felt it desirable to delve into colonial and pre-colonial data, i.e. the written sources on Ho history – published or non-published or only regionally published – in order to explore if and how they contribute to developing an understanding of the overall ideational setting that today's Ho people find themselves in at the beginning of the 21st century.

The notes on Ho history draw from material written by British colonialists viz. scholar administrators, by American and European missionaries, by historians, lawyers, economists, sociologists, linguists, and, of course, anthropologists some of whom had access to archival sources, official settlement reports, gazetteers, and census publications.

For the transcription of Ho see *Annotations* at the beginning of the book. Terms that have been rendered in the entries in italics will be explained separately as headwords.

adivasi	(Hindi/ Sanskrit): generic, contested, and fairly recent term for the first settlers or "original inhabitant: a member of an indigenous tribe as opposed to later settlers" (McGregor 2011:85) of the Indian sub-continent. Created from Sanskritic roots the term originated as a concept in Chota Nagpur in the late 1920ies (Verardo 2003: 106) or 1930ies (Das Gupta 2011:11). *Adivasi* was to replace the designation "tribe" (Parkin 2000: 50, 60) with its pejorative connotations in order to suggest a more positive political identity (Shah 2010: 194). Ho intellectuals of the Chaibasa and Ranchi region use this term which then may have strong political overtones. My non-academic Ho informants in the field, however, did not use it, as they generally reject being labelled collectively by outsiders and feel Ho or *munurenko* (first inhab-

itants) more than anything else. There is no entry of *adivasi* in Deeney (2005) as he avoids Hindi vocabulary; he refers to *kunt-kati ho* instead which according to my informants is a Munda term used by Munda people. In today's political discourse in order to organize resistance against economic exploitation, land and forest dispossession, and political marginalization social activists have reframed the term. With them *adivasi* is meant to conceptually symbolize and represent a unified indigenous bloc directed against all *diku* aggression and encompassing all categories enlisted in the Indian constitution as Scheduled Tribes.

arkati   (Hindi): those recruiting foreign labour. In Chota Nagpur, for example, labourers were recruited for work in the tea gardens of Assam. Towards the end of the 19th century a yearly average of 30,000 to 45,000 workers got enlisted. In Mundari and Ho *arkati* were called *horo akarinko*, literally men-sellers. It is argued that a majority of the workers were recruited by fraud or violence or other kinds of abuse. Hoffman (2005) gives a number of instances indicating that this was done systematically or at least regularly.

Ashoka   304 – 232 BC: emperor of the Mauriya dynasty and "prominent figure of Oriya history" (Pfeffer 1982: 10). In the 13th Rock Inscription he warns the forest people – a term that may well refer to the tribal population of the hills – that he has the power to punish them should they fail to give up their resisting any kind of outside authority.

Asur(a)s   Areeparampil (2002: 39; S.C. Roy 1970: 23) calls them kinsmen of the Munda; Parkin (2000: 57, 59) speaks about the Munda-speaking low caste of Asur iron-workers, direct descendants of the ancient Asur(a)s. Deeney defines them as "an ancient race of iron-smelters and iron workers" (2005: 16). More than 100 Asura sites containing the slag heaps of iron-makers have been found in the Khunti area which is a region between Chaibasa and Ranchi. The famous *Asur legend* revolves around them. There is a theory of descent linking the Asur to the Indus Valley civilization and a reference to the Ho's creation myth.

Asurkowa: bankuri   Asur legend/myth. According to Deeney (2008: 15f.) a folk-tale is known to elder Ho people as follows: Asurs were iron smelters keeping their fires burning night and day thus causing a drought on earth which displeased Sinbonga. As they continued to do so and would not listen Sinbonga burnt the Asur men to death in a furnace which now displeased the Asur women. How should they be sustained? Sinbonga told them that they would be sustained by human beings who would offer them the blood of animals. He then took the women by the hair, threw them thus scattering them in all directions. Those who fell on hills and mountains became *buru* spirits, others falling into rivers became *gara kachui* (river spirits) etc. The myth shows that Sinbonga is supreme to these spirit – *bongako* who are referred to as the spirits of dead women. In the research area female spirits of water sites and low-lying places are preferably called *nage erako*.

begar

unpaid forced labour; "without [...]. This is a Sadri term, often heard in Mundari, but rare in Ho" (Deeney 2005: 37). In the course of time, especially due to and after the Permanent Settlement of 1793, *zamindar* or landlords became legally empowered to demand *begar* from their tenants to be done on their own lands in case these were unable to come up with the required rent in time. McGregor gives '*beg*' as "lord, master (Mughal title)" (McGregor 2011: 745).

bhuinar/bhuinhar

(Mundari) the original first settlers in a Chota Nagpur village, 'the breakers of the soil'. Dalton opposes the lands of the "Bhuinhari which was no doubt originally rent–free" (1973 [1872]: 167) to those of the "rajhas or rent–paying" (ibid). This changed later, and Rothermund (2001:6) defines the *bhuinar* as an occupancy *ryot* holding his land at a customary rent rate.

bhuinari ote

ancestral land which is legally recognized as such. Rothermund sees the *bhuinari* tenure as a degeneration of the *kunt-kati* system of tenure insofar as only "individual claims to land held due to ancient rights remained" (Rothermund 1978: 172).

bhuinari settlement

documents to officially register those lands that were claimed in each village as ancestral property by the *adivasi* and those that were claimed by the "newly intruded middlemen [...] brought into Chota Nagpur by Hinduised rajahs" (Hoffman 2005: 32–33). This process of individualizing the ownership of land as well as legally fixing the secular proprietorship of land that is considered communal or rather divine property and as such inalienable as a matter of concept by the indigenous people materialised in 1869 under the *bhuinari* settlement. Another major flaw of this settlement was that even if land was registered as *bhuinari* land, its alienation was not prohibited.

Birsa Munda

1872/74 – 1900. Birsa Munda is a household name among Munda and Ho today. Ranchi airport carried his name, and there are statues in several places commemorating him and his commitment. People link his name with the *ulgulan*, the armed rebellion of 1899/ 1900 which was directed against all kinds of European, especially British interference; in more general terms it was violently directed against all *diku* encroachments by *thikadar, jagirdar, mahajan, zamindar* and also missionaries. Birsa must have been a charismatic figure. He functioned both as a religious and political leader. Claiming that he had received his divine mission by Sinbonga, the Ho's and Munda's creator god, he blended elements of Vaishnavism, of Christianity and tribal ideas (Singh, K.S. 1966: 11). In order to establish a Munda Raj that was free of foreign influence and led by himself, he succeeded in mobilising and inspiring thousands of followers. Between 1890 and 1900 the Birsa Movement developed; Birsa himself became imprisoned from 1895 to 1897, but went on campaigning after his release. Finally, a violent revolt was decided on which began on December 24th, 1899. Birsa's field of activity was in present-day Jharkhand, especially in the area between Chaibasa and Ranchi and further to the West and North West. (see map in K.S. Singh 1966: 99). After a month of fierce fighting Birsa was again caught and arrested. The British treated the *ulgulan* as a criminal, not as a political movement and took more than four hundred prisoners to court. In June 1900 Birsa Munda died in prison in Ranchi under unclear circumstances (Areeparampil 2002: 210, K.S. Singh 1966: 130 – 132). Today the anti–colonial core of the Birsa Movement is officially reframed as an important contribution to the overall national struggle for India's independence.

bonga   (Ho): a spirit; to sacrifice. In Ho cosmology, in their rituals, in everyday life *bonga*-spirits play a significant role. In his Ho–English Dictionary Deeney lists 29 compounds with *bonga* as one of the elements, such as *bonga jid* "by a sacrifice to preserve the life of a man apparently dying", or *bonga tore* "a falling star (as though spirits are shooting arrows at one another)" (2005: 47, 48); see also glossary II

Captain Browne   In 1774 the representative of the East India Company became active in the area of the Rajmahal Hills in order to pacify the terrain. As in many other regions of Chota Nagpur the *Paharia* violently resisted the Company's attempts at extracting revenue. Instead of unsuccessfully opposing the indigenous population and continuously ignoring their set of values within which they made a tribal living Captain Browne worked out a scheme of divide and rule by co-operating with the *sadar* and *manki*. *Augustus Cleveland* was to become his successor.

Captain Camac   entered Jharkhand from the West in 1769 to make rajas and chiefs submit and agree to pay allegiance to the Company and comply to its monetary demands. The first contact between the Raja of Chota Nagpur and Captain Camac as the Company's representative is said to have resulted in an exchange of turbans in 1772 (Dalton 1973, S.C. Roy 1970).

caste   See *tribe* and *caste*

chanda   (Ho/ Hindi): subscription; quit rent or voluntary contribution. "A collection or subscription in cash made for some special purpose (for a subscription in kind the word *harom* would be used)" (Deeney 2005: 62). This was collected by the *munda* and the *manki* and eventually handed over with a/the Raja at the receiving end. Neither could the Raja become active in this process himself nor could he appoint any of his agents. The quality of *chanda* is conceptually different from rent which is paid by a tenant to his landlord, from a tax which is raised by a superior authority, from a tribute which is imposed by a ruler, and from other involuntary payments such as fees or fines (Rothermund 2001: 2). For the Ho the payment of *chanda*, however, neither implied recognizing the Raja as legitimate ruler nor their role as his subjects. The indirect character of the payment with the *munda/manki* functioning as intermediaries contributed to this.

Chota Nagpur

also Chotanagpur, Chutia Nagpur, Chota Nagpur Plateau. Chota Nagpur has variously been used synonymously with Jharkhand (Dalton 1973; Areeparampil 2002:15), literally meaning 'dense forest', 'forest region'.

Historically, the Chota Nagpur Division was an administrative unit of British India in the Province of Bengal (see *South West Front Agency*). After Independence Chota Nagpur (North and South) became an administrative division in the state of Bihar. Because of its long history of naming and re-naming, of partitioning and reorganization up to this day, of oppression and pacification schemes in colonial times Chotanagpur as Non-Regulation Province and Jharkhand have come to mean different things in different contexts. In administrative terms we find in contemporary India out of Jharkhand's five divisions next to the Santal Parganas and Palamau the two divisions of North Chota Nagpur and South Chota Nagpur, of which as a fifth unit the Kolhan division was carved out. It is constituted by the three districts of West Singhbhum, East Singhbhum, and Seraikela/ Kharsawan. My research among the Ho was carried out in this area.

Geographically the Chotanagpur plateau comprises uneven upland of 1000 feet up to more than 2000 feet in central eastern India that consists of a number of plateaux, hills, rivers, and valleys predominantly forested by the sal tree. The territory of the present-day state of Jharkhand on the Plateau is said to still have 27% of its land surface under forest cover (Areeparampil 2002: 245). The Plateau is extremely rich in minerals such as iron ore, coal, copper, bauxite, and uranium that have been exploited in open mines by different kinds of industries to this day ever since the middle of the nineteenth century. This development has contributed to the area being called the 'Ruhr of India' with Rourkela, Bokaro, and Jamshedpur, officially called Tatanagar, as internationally known industrial centres. It was as early as 1585 that Akbar became interested in Chota Nagpur when diamonds were found there (Das Gupta 2011: 65).

Politically, however, the tribal villages on Chota Nagpur terrain remained more or less autonomous under Muslim rule. Although formally under Moghul suzerainty, local authority remained in indigenous hands, and the tribute network was quite loose (ibid.) Chota Nagpur came under British suzerainty as part of Bihar in 1765; Bihar itself was at that time catalogued as part of Bengal with the seat of the British East India Company's government in Kolkata. As an almost immediate result after the British acquisition of the *diwani* rights (the right to collect revenue) in a terra incognita, its indigenous population that had hitherto effectively rejected any infiltration and outside control, became threatened by the Company's determination of crushing any resistance and imposing a new system of administration in order to extract revenue.

Historians suggest a Munda tradition or oral 'history' to exist concerning their history of migration. According to this they would have arrived at the Chota Nagpur Plateau at around 600 B.C. practising slash and burn cultivation techniques. 800 years later they would have finally settled in the Khunti area, right in the primeval forests of Jharkhand, with Omedanda as their first Munda settlement (Areeparampil 2002: 35).

The territory of the Chota Nagpur Plateau reaches into the adjacent present-day states of Bihar, Jharkhand, West Bengal, Odisha, Chhattisgarh, Madhya Pradesh, and Uttar Pradesh.

chowkidar
(Hindi): village policeman (see *thana*) or village watchman; according to Hoffman (1990) *chowkidar* constitute the lowest grade in the British Indian police.

Christian
missionaries arrived in Ranchi/ Jharkhand in 1845. German Lutherans from the Gossener Mission were followed by Anglicans 14 years later and Catholics in the same year. It took more than five years to have the first *adivasi* baptized.

chuar
This is a derogatory term meaning a barbarian or a robber. It was applied by the British in the course of the so–called Chuar Rebellions (1769 – 1784), when different groups of *adivasi* opposed any kind of violation of their communal rights and independence and began to fight back.

Cleveland, Augustus
1755 – 1784; collector, i.e. administrator since 1773 (Pfeffer 2017:49), legislator and commander-in-chief of Bhagalpur since 1779 (Dalton 1973, Bradley-Birt 1905, Areeparampil 2002). He established the Paharia Hill Archers and set up and presided the Hill Assembly of the Rajmahal Hills area. This was a tribunal of Paharia *sadars* in charge of the regional administration and jurisdiction that was thus withdrawn from the ordinary courts. For their cooperation with and submission to A. Cleveland the members of the Hill Assembly or *sadars* were granted pensions and given land. These measures were part of a pacification scheme sanctioned by the government of the East India Company in 1778 "to transform the Paharias into instruments of colonial administration" (Areeparampil 2002: 64). The *Rajmahal Hills'* territory was officially declared government property by the Company, and the Paharia were offered to cultivate this government land as tenants of the government without paying rent. No intermediaries were allowed to interfere. This was supposed to effectively stop land alienation by *zamindar* and turn the *Paharia* into settled agriculturalists in the course of time. Cleveland's strategy, realised in this area since 1782, is considered the precursor of the Non-Regulation system to come.

Damin–I–Koh
Skirt of the Hills; fertile territory south of the *Rajmahal Hills* demarcated by pillars erected by the Company government in order to protect the *Paharia* and make them settle and cultivate the lands free of rent and free of any outside interventions. The same privileges, however, were not extended to the Santal who had been invited to settle and cultivate the land, when the Company realised that the *Paharia*

	by and large proved to be unwilling. After the *Hul*, the massive Santal insurrection of 1855, this area was called the Santal Parganas and became a non–regulation district.
darogah	(Hindi): Inspector; Native Police Officer; the highest resident officials under the British Government (Dalton 1973: 168). Natives usually were Hindus from the plains who were considered foreigners or *diku* by the indigenous population of *Chota Nagpur*.
Deo, Juggernauth Sahi	became Raja of *Chota Nagpur* in 1822 at the age of 19.
diku	"a non-tribal; to act like a *diku*; to speak Hindi" (Deeney 2005: 92). This term carries plural meanings, and it means different things to different people. *Diku* was used by my Ho informants to relate to anything or anyone conceived as foreign or alien or strongly opposed to *adivasi*-ness. Das Gupta defines it as an indigenous "term of contempt for exploitative outsiders" (2011: 247) referring to subordinate right-holders within the bureaucratic apparatus of the Raj. However, beyond the politico-economic domain *diku* suggests a cultural, an ideological statement of in- and exclusion. With other non–Ho tribal categories as well as with other non-Ho nontribal long-term settlers and village service providers a long-established conviviality exists in the area of my fieldwork, and these 'others' are not considered *diku* by the Ho. Under British rule towards the end of the 19th century *diku* became an administrative term in official government records and acquired a legal meaning as revenue category. Non-Ho categories and nontribal tenants were listed indiscriminately and thus branded as aliens/*diku*, although Ho conceive of them as constituent members of a multi-faceted symbiosis (Das Gupta 2011: 26). see *kurmi, kumhar, tanti*.
diuri	ritual guide; "a village priest who performs sacrifices in the name of the whole village on certain occasions. His role is ritual and much different than that of the *dewa*, who is a shaman" (Deeney 2005: 95); in this book the translation as 'priest' has been avoided in order to avoid the connotations lingering around the priestly profession of Brahmans (and Jesuits) in an all pervading Indian context. see also glossary II
diwani	In 1765 the *diwani* or revenue administration of Bengal, Bihar, and Orissa was handed over to the British East India Company by Shah Alam II, the Mughal Emperor who had claimed to have had that right until then. Jharkhand at that time was part of Bihar. As these mountainous and forested areas were almost inaccessible for geographical reasons as well as because of the indigenous population evading and fighting any attempt at intrusion, this 'right' of revenue collection had so far hardly been materialised by the Muslim rulers. British attempts at the military and administrative control of Jharkhand for the purpose of efficient and maximised revenue collection began within two years after the acquisition of the *diwani*. In most areas they met fierce resistance, which was answered by military means and/or by a divide-and-rule policy. Some parts had to be de-

clared a non-regulation area and a special 'protective' policy was adopted.

Gau (Ho): a member of the Gaur or Gope community; the Ho's cow–herders.

ghatwal guardians of the jungle passes with service tenures.

gonon (Ho): cost; value; to set a price; bridewealth. Deeney uses the term "bride-price" (2005: 128); see glossary II

Ho language The Dravidian, the Indo-European and the Munda languages constitute the three major language families of India. Linguistically Ho – alongside Santali and Mundari – is classified as belonging to the Munda branch of the Austroasiatic language family that shelters languages spoken in Indonesia, Vietnam, Cambodia, Laos, Myanmar, and central and eastern India (Anderson 2008, Reichel 2009). According to Deeney (2002, 2005) the Ho language is close to Mundari especially in the field of grammar. However, in terms of vocabulary, semantics, usage, and register there may be considerable divergence.

Hul The Santal insurrection of 1855 – 56 was called the Santal Hul. The practices of the *mahajans* had contributed considerably to the bloody revolt.

ili rice-beer; my informants used the term *diyan*.

indigeneity The new transnational concept of 'indigeneity' and 'indigenous peoples' introduced in the 1980ies was meant to replace the terms 'tribal' and 'tribes' that had become discarded as derogatory and politically incorrect in political and anthropological discourses. This change in language and political intention was followed by heated debates over how best to develop and install equal (human) rights for people in a country such as India that is supposed to house the second largest indigenous population of the world who are accorded the right to consider themselves different and to be respected as such. The United Nations Working Group on Indigenous Populations (UNWGIP) was formed in 1982. The International Labour Organisation (ILO) adopted its Indigenous and Tribal Peoples' Convention in 1989 to become the world's first legal tool to internationally protect indigenous peoples, by definition a diverse and highly heterogeneous category (Shah 2010: 9, 194). Béteille (1974, 1998) has repeatedly criticized the applicability of the idea of indigenous peoples for India as a racist concept, since it would essentialize tribal culture on the one hand. On the other hand, due to the lack of precise data concerning the histories of migrations, indigeneity in terms of a priority of settlement, as the etymology of the term suggests, cannot be ascertained for any group or groups in India. (For a survey of the contesting perspectives around the issue see Shah 2010: 21 f). Although this is a valid assessment, Pfeffer warns against neglecting in the course of this debate the specific and separate social history of India's tribal population of roughly 100 million people (see Pfeffer 2014: 276; Gregory 2009); see *adivasi* above

jagir	originally a Moghul term for the grant of land, a village or the right of access to supplies from a village; the system of service grants. According to Hoffman the first ascertainable instance of a *jagir* took place in 1676, but the process probably started earlier – in any case well before the arrival of the British. By 1869 2482 villages had been legally expropriated in Chotanagpur.
jagirdar	(Hindi/ Persian): the owner of a *jagir* who was originally entitled to the "surplus of a certain area in lieu of a salary as well as for the support of troops which he had to supply in times of war" (Rothermund 1978: 12).
jagirdari	system of service grants introduced into Jharkhand for a number of reasons. One is the Rajas' inviting courtiers, attendants, servants, and Brahmins to be around as staff at their courts and their passing on to these their customary rights to supplies from the villages for their services, as they were not able to pay them otherwise. This created an explosive situation in the course of time, as these people were all nontribals, brought into the country from outside and utterly ignorant of and disinterested in the tribals' situation, their values, their sociocultural set up. It appears that economic exploitation and land alienation was one of their major incentives. To the indigenous population these were all people from outside who remained outside the village community and who constitute the category *diku*. According to K.S. Singh "in 1856 the number of new *jagirdars* had reached 600 and they came to own from a portion of a village to 150 villages" (1966: 2).
Jharkhand	(Hindi): a scrub or forest region; dense forest. Even today 27% of Jharkhand's territory are said to be forested. The first recorded reference to Jharkhand's name dates back to the 13th century (Areeparampil 2002: 15) and was used synonymously with the forested Chota Nagpur Plateau. Gond, Santal, Oraon, Munda, Ho, Kharia, Bhumij, Juang, Birhor and many more tribal categories conceive of themselves as the original settlers or *adivasi* of Jharkhand. They cleared the jungle by practicing "slash and burn" techniques. Eventually they turned into settled cultivators ploughing the land that had become theirs in this process, however without any notion of private ownership. Consequently, they were not inclined to individually pay anybody anything, neither rent nor tax nor revenue, fees and fines, and especially not to a foreign outsider.

In 1765, however, the East India Company not only obtained the right to extract regular revenues or *diwani* from this area as had been the rule in the Mughal era, but they were determined to see to it that it really happened. The entire Jharkhand area became included in the province of Bengal. It was directly administered by a Governor general until 1854 (see *South West Frontier Agency*), though from 1834 onwards as Non-Regulation Province. Jharkhand was in a strategically important position for the Company, but hardly accessible to lowlanders due to its thick upland jungles and a tribal population utterly and militantly adverse towards any kind of trespassing. The determination on both sides not to give in resulted in fierce atrocities. However, the Company was primarily and for quite some time interested and only interested in raising taxes thus guaranteeing fixed and regular revenues. So it aimed at pacifying the rebellious areas by penetrating Jharkhand from the Jungle Mahals and the Rajmahal Hills in the South East and North East and the Palamau territories in the (North) West. According to Areeparampil (2002) the Company's struggle to subdue the Paharia in the Rajmahal Hills proved especially violent and unsuccessful as seen from the Company's perspective. Also, in a great many other regions of Jharkhand the Company's attempt at bringing the country under administrative control by military means and other "ruthless methods" (2002: 55) immediately caused unrest, chaos, protests and revolts. Other reasons that disrupted tribal life were the Bengal famine of 1770, in the course of which 35% of the indigenous population died and for which the colonial government was held responsible, and the Permanent Settlement of 1793. Within a relatively short span of time it became obvious that the conventional strategies of military operations would not bring about the submission of both the indigenous population as well as the *zamindar* and the other foreign intermediaries. This category usually antagonistic towards the inhabitants of the hilly regions and quite relentless with them happened to side with the tribals and their chiefs in revolt against the colonial government when they had fallen into revenue arrears and became dispossessed themselves as a result. Then their land was auctioned and sold/acquired, since land had become a profitable commodity. All of this continuous unrest eventually led to a Company scheme of a Non – Regulation Policy for this particular area in 1834. This policy was installed by Captain *Wilkinson*, some of whose regulations are still operative today.

After independence the area of Jharkhand was split up between West Bengal, Orissa, Madhya Pradesh and Bihar. In 2000 the southern part of Bihar finally came into political existence as the independent state of Jharkhand.

kamar

(Hindi): iron worker, blacksmith; term used regionally in Bihar (McGregor 2011). see *lohar* glossary II

Karanpura

The Karanpura Valley is situated north of Ranchi. Several hundred megalithic monuments and rock art have been found there at least parts of which may date back to the Palaeolithic period. Also, near Isco, a new script containing 93 characters of the Indus Valley script has been found and may eventually turn out to be its parent script. These recent discoveries in Jharkhand might indicate – beyond diffusionist speculation – that pre–historic culture existed in this area (Areeparampil 2002, Parkin 2000). Today the site and its megaliths are threatened by coal–mining.

khunt

institution of "all the grand tribes of Chota Nagpur" (Pfeffer 1997: 19) to differentiate status within and beyond clan categories the membership of which is expressed in the language of seniority. The respective *khunt* titles indicate a person's place within a known and named status segment. They function as "agnatically assigned operational units for the ritual give and take within and beyond the village" (Pfeffer 2017: 63 – 64). These status categories are conceptually to be distinguished from sociocentric affinal units such as clans and matters of exogamy and marriage. In Ho *kuntu* is a wooden post; cf. below *kunt-kati ho*

Kokrah   designation for Chota Nagpur or Jharkhand under Muslim rule. S.C. Roy's spelling is Kokerah (1970:71).

Kol   contested generic term used by non-*adivasi* outsiders including colonial scholar administrators as a term of reference for all the "aboriginal tribes of Chota Nagpur including the Oraons who are Dravidians" (Hoffman 2005: 4). Like Dalton (1868, 1973) Singh relates the term to the Ho, Munda, and Bhumij. He adds that "the Hindus of the plains used it as a term of derision" (C.P. Singh 1978: 8). Also S.C. Roy (1970: 207) and Parkin (1992:23) call it an "insulting" term and suggest better not to use it any more. According to Majumdar Kol is an abusive epithet "by which the Hos are known to the outside world" (Majumdar 1950: 18; Das Gupta 2011: 28). Maybe it is for these reasons that the Ho have rejected the term as pejorative and contemptuous. They call themselves Ho which means 'man'. Ho also used to be labelled as *Larka Kol* (perhaps from Hindi *laraka*: warlike, quarrelsome, aggressive; militant; a fighter), *Larka Ho* or just *Larkas* by British colonialists. As such they fought alongside Munda and Oraon in the Kol insurrection of 1831 – 32 which Areeparampil calls the Ho's "first war of Independence" (2002: 91). Kol have perhaps impressed their name on that area of the Chota Nagpur plateau, where they eventually settled, and which may be known after them as *Kolhan* or land of the Kol (Das Gupta 2011: 28) viz. of the Larka Kol (Areeparampil 2002: 36,115).

Kolhan   a territory of 1919 square miles or 4970 square kilometres according to Majumdar (1950:1), Tuckey (1920: 1), Craven (1898), an extent when compared with topical data provided by Google Earth seems more reliable than the 7200 km² given by C.P. Singh (1978: 7). Kolhan is in the south-eastern part of the district of West – Singhbhum reaching into Mayurbhanj. It is the region on the Chota Nagpur Plateau where, according to their oral 'history' (Das Gupta 2011: 28), Ho had migrated from other parts of Chota Nagpur, especially from the north and northwest, perhaps along the river Koel (S.C. Roy 1970 [1912]: 70). They cleared the then densely forested jungles and took to settled cultivation based on the use of ploughs.

In the Final Report on the Resettlement of the Kolhan Government Estate Kolhan has been described by Tuckey (1920: 1) as naturally and conveniently falling into North Kolhan as separated from South Kolhan by ranges of hills and forests extending from the Singhasan Hill south-easterly towards the Mayurbhanj border and the mountainous forest area around Saranda in the southwest. By the 19th century North Kolhan is said to have become "pure Ho country" (Das Gupta

2011:28). South Kolhan extends into Mayurbhanj and Keonjhar, two districts within today's state of Odisha. Odisha became an independent province only in 1936 and was part of the state called 'Bihar and Orissa' before including the present state territory of Jharkhand.

Although not indigenous to the area in the sense of being the original settlers (Hardiman 1987: 13; Pfeffer 2014: 270), today's Ho consider themselves the autochthonous inhabitants of Kolhan (personal communication; Verardo 2003: 9). Before finally settling in the Kolhan region, the Ho had separated from their brother tribe, the Munda who either remained in or moved on into the central part of the plateau around Ranchi. Whereas the Ho retain an awareness of their having migrated from the country of the Munda (Deeney: personal communication), they do not share Munda traditions about the rise of the Nagbansi dynasty (Das Gupta 2011: 31; S.C. Roy 1970: 71; Tuckey 1920: 17) and the Chota Nagpur Raj. On the contrary, Areeparampil opines that the process of electing a Raja might have been the very reason for the Ho's breaking off from the Munda and their migrating southwards. For this he suggests some point in time between the 5th and the 13th century (Areeparampil 2002: 36, 43–46). Tuckey mentions a period of time "before about the tenth century (1920: 17). Das Gupta vaguely refers to a period before the 8th century, but at the same time warns that the Ho's early history is "purely conjectural" (2011: 31).

According to Dalton there was no contact between the indigenous population of Kolhan and representatives of the British East India Company before 1819, when Major Roughsedge entered the scene in order to pave the way for revenue collection. "Of the interior of their country, for years after the acquisition of all the surrounding districts, nothing whatever was known. The Hos would allow no strangers to settle in or even to pass through the Kolhan." (Dalton 1973: 178). Major Roughsedge was unable to gain the immediate support of either the Raja of Singhbhum or the *zamindar* in that area, as these claimed that for the last fifty years they had also been unable to establish any kind of control over the indigenous population of Kolhan and were 'in need' of British support against the Ho themselves. Due to widespread social unrest and a number of rebellions in the Kolhan (1819, 1820–21, 1830–32) the Kolhan Government Estate was established in 1837 as a non-regulation area, which came under the direct management of the Company government that became the direct landlord for all the land (Yorke 1976: 15). Until today Ho proudly claim to be the last tribe to have been forced to surrender vis-à-vis British military superiority, while still others insist on the Ho having never been defeated at all.

In today's India the Kolhan division is one of altogether five divisions of Jharkhand. It comprises the three districts of West Singhbhum, East Singhbhum, and Seraikela/ Kharsawan. see *Jharkhand*

kumhar (Hindi): a potter.

kunkal	(Ho): a potter; a man of the community that makes earthen pots. This community lives close to yet separate from the Ho settlements in the area of my fieldwork. These pots are produced for and sold at the local markets. My Ho informants used both terms, *kumhar* as well as *kunkal*.
kunt–kati	(Ho/Munda): "of land, to belong to the family of an original settler of a village" (Deeney 2005: 217).
kunt-kati hatu	(Ho/Munda): village of the descendants of the original founder. To the Ho this is more a cultural than a geographical space, since it houses also the ancestral spirits and village guardian deities. Like any Ho village it is surrounded by a religiously defined boundary.
kunt-kati ho	(Ho): "a descendant of the original settler of a village" (Deeney 2005: 217); Ho people int research area used *munurenko* instead; see *bhuin-hari*
Kurmi	and *Kumhar, Tanti, Tamaria*: these nontribal categories have been living together with the tribal people of Chota Nagpur for ages. *Kurmi* – a peasant community (Das Gupta 2011, Skoda 2005); agriculturalists (Parkin 2000); now enrolled in the OBC list – Other Backward Classes – , they were officially classified as tribe until 1931 (Parkin 2000); in one version of the Ho creation myth the "Koormees" figure as pork eaters along with the "Sontals" (Tickell 1840); *Tanti* – weavers; in the course of time they were able to acquire land, took to cultivation, performed as *dakuwa* (village watchmen) and legal advisors and were involved in the coolie trade as *arkati*; *Kumhar* – potters; *Tamaria* – cattle, oil, grain traders, middlemen or intermediaries. Das Gupta characterizes the relationship as "symbiotic, but asymmetrical" (2011: 52), and so did my informants. By being functionally distinctive and specific as musicians, potters, carpenters they are conceptually part of the indigenous communities and physically part of their villages. They share a number of cultural norms. Areeparampil draws a contra – distinction between the tribal patrons (Ho: *hatu hoko* or people from the village) and those landless 'others' (Ho: *eta: haturen-ko* or people from other villages) who he calls "professional service groups like blacksmiths, weavers and herdsmen of inferior status" (2002: 42; Rothermund 1978; Das Gupta 2011). K.S. Singh calls the village service providers who have lived in Kolhan since pre-colonial times, Sadans. These inside-outsiders (Das Gupta 2011) are constitutive of tribal society and not to be confused with those who indigenous people consider *diku* (K.S. Singh 1966, Areeparampil 2002, Pfeffer 1997, Dalton 1973, Niggemeyer 1964).
Land Acquisition Act	passed in 1894 under British rule and with minimal alterations still in use today (Moharana 2012: 10/11). It concedes to the state the supreme right to acquire, control and sell (tribal) land for 'public' purposes with or without the landowner's consent. In the mineral-rich tribal regions of Jharkhand and Odisha this act today functions as a tool to alienate otherwise inalienable tribal land for industrialization and large 'development' projects.

landlord	The very concept of agricultural landlordism or of a landlord, i.e. a person of superior status who owns the land as legally different from its cultivators of inferior status, was unknown to the indigenous population of Chota Nagpur. In various mother tongues such as Mundari or Ho there is no term to denote someone as landlord. Munda and Ho refer to landlords as *diku* or outsiders/ aliens instead. Likewise, *munda* and *manki* were not considered the villagers' landlords, but their chiefs, and as such did not command any superior (economic or political) rights. *Wilkinson* brought about the change: by conferring title deeds and granting official documents to both *manki* and *munda* he tried to win them as collaborators. Landlord property constituted the very basis of the *Permanent Settlement* (Areeparampil 2002: 104, 194), which notionally ran contrary to the very concept of a communal tribal set up and its overall social web. It can be seen as the immediate result of the introduction of colonial administration and its divide and rule policy that the influx of nontribal population into tribal regions was welcomed and accelerated. Communal property became transformed into individual tenures, and as *diku*-landlords were protected by a powerful colonial legislation, so were all their acts of tribal land dispossession legal(ized).
Madhu Singh	Raja of *Chotanagpur*; in 1585 he was made a tributary to the Mughal emperor. His successor to the *Nagbansi* throne, Raja Durjan Sal, refused cooperation with the Mughals and was sent to prison for 12 years.
mahajan	money lender
majhas	personal property
makar	the sign Capricorn of the zodiac
makar sankranti	(Hindi): entry of the sun into Capricorn; winter solstice; the Hindus' midwinter celebrations in Odisha and Uriya dominated areas, usually held about January 14th. In Ho it is called *mokor* or *diku porob*. Accompanied by their Odiya speaking school teachers Ho children are introduced into performing the *diku* rituals by taking a collective bath in the ponds.
malguzar	tributary: Raja *Madhu Singh*, e.g., was degraded and turned into a revenue paying *malguzar* or tributary chief by the Moghul emperor Akbar when diamonds were found in Jharkhand in 1585 and high revenues were to be expected.
manjihas	land in a village that a Raja claimed for himself and that he had cultivated for his own benefit (Dalton 1973/ 1872: 167).
manki	divisional headman. Representative of the Ho population of *pati*, *parha* or *pir*, a federation of a varying number of villages, maybe 12 or more (Das Gupta 2011: 331, Shah 2010: 43). Holds his 'office' in virtue of his election by the *munda*. According to Areeparampil a *munda*'s office became hereditary only in the course of time (2002: 43). It is important to note that both *manki* and *munda* were considered leaders and allies by the villagers rather than their (permanent) rulers or overlords. So this institution of village elders is compatible with

munda	the tribal concept of seniority, of political autonomy and social inter-dependence and incompatible with any notion of continuous political or economic supremacy or any kind of top – down power relations. "a village headman; wealthy [...]; a member of the Munda tribe" (Dee-ney 2005: 256). A Ho *munda* performs as the head in secular matters, in all probability one of the original setllers' clan who owns and cul-tivates his own land. As a matter of principle it was a constant source of conflict whenever the colonial administration made landless *diku* headmen in compensation for their collecting revenue from the recal-citrant Ho. Neither *munda*, *manki* nor *diuri* are liable to any rights or privileges superior to other descendants of the original founder.
Muslim rule in India	Under Muslim Rule the population in the mountains, hills and pla-teaux of Central Eastern India seems to have remained rather undis-turbed and the autonomy of the village communities unquestioned until the end of the 16th century. It was under Akbar's, i.e. the Mughal emperor's reign that, according to Areeparampil (2002) and Das Gupta (2011), diamonds were found, and a Mughal army set forth into Khukra or Kokhra, as *Chotanagpur* was called then. *Madhu Singh, Raja of Chotanagpur* at that time, became a tributary and was made to deliver regular payments which again he tried to squeeze out of the village(r)s. On the whole, however, the Mughal government had no control over this area and did not try to interfere with the trib-als' politics of independence and their social system as such.
Nagbansi dynasty	Dalton classifies the Nagbansis as "Hinduised Aborigines" who claim to be kinsmen of the *Raja of Chota Nagpur* (1973: 118 f). The *Raja of Chota Nagpur* is said to have constituted the Nagbansi dynasty. The Nagbansi origin myth, the ideological legitimization for claiming su-periority, was probably made up by Brahmins who became employed by the Rajas (Areeparampil 2002: 44). Dalton calls these origin myths "hazy fables which Hindus have invented" (Dalton 1973: 118) for the rulers. The Nagbansi Rule in Chota Nagpur, the so-called Chotanag-pur or Nagbansi Raj, was perhaps established in the 13th century, or later (K.S. Singh 1966, Areeparampil 2002: 43; according to S.C. Roy 1970 already in the 5th century, according to Das Gupta [2011: 31] eighth to twelfth centuries). The Raja of Chotanagpur applied and agreed to become tributary chief to the Company in 1772. He ob-viously hoped that way to gain the Company's military support against rebellious tribals refusing to comply with the raja's demands. He was deprived of that position in 1817, when Chota Nagpur came under the direct administration of the Company.
Non–Regulation districts	Districts in which the *Non – Regulation Policy* was operative. The 'Non-Regulation districts' were named 'Scheduled districts' in 1874, 'Backward Tracts' in 1919, 'Excluded' and 'Partially Excluded' areas in 1935, and 'Scheduled Areas' since 1950. Schedules of the new con-stitution after Independence suggest and implement policies of spe-cial protection to advance the tribes and castes living in the Sched-uled Areas.

Non–Regulation Policy   A system of administration based on indigenous notions of self-management and implying that the legislation related to other parts of British India was not to be executed in these areas. It was a policy of indirect rule and paternalistic in character; however, it guaranteed the realization of regular taxes, revenues and services and thus enabled financial long – term planning for the British East India Company.

pahan   a Munda village's ritual guide; in Ho this would be a *diuri*.

Paharia   Settling in and near the *Rajmahal Hills* this is a tribe of 'hillmen' over whom neither the Mughal government nor the *zamindar* had control. For example, it seemed impossible for the Company's 'runners' to make their way through the Rajmahal hills without risking their lives. "By the end of the 18th century the Paharias were engaged in open guerrilla warfare in order to resist encroachment on their territory and safeguard their independence" (Areeparampil 2002: 63). By a number of schemes initiated by *Captain Browne* since 1774, sanctioned by the Government in 1778 and carried out by *Augustus Cleveland* since 1779 the Paharia were eventually transformed into "instruments of colonial administration" (ibid.: 64). The Paharia were granted occupancy rights on their lands free of rent by the government to lure them into becoming settled agriculturalists and reliable tax payers. This privileged situation for the Paharia as the original inhabitants of the area was safeguarded within the *Damin–I–Koh* or skirt of the hills. It was not, however, granted and extended to the Santal who began settling in this area.

panchayat   'council of five' to settle village matters by consensus.

pargana   district, region, an administrative unit.

parha   Munda term for structure of intervillage governance for 12 to 21 villages (Shah 2010: 192) headed by a *pahan*. A *parha panchayat* exists analogous to a village *panchayat*. The Ho term for this system of *adivasi* self-governance would be *munda-manki*, the Santali term *manjhi-parganait*.

patta   lease (Hindi); system of service–grants imposed on the indigenous peoples. According to Hoffman the first leasing of a raja's rights in a number of villages to outsiders, e.g. *jagirdars*, is reported from 1676, which is almost a century before the British entered the Chota Nagpur area. "In 1869 as many as 2,482 villages had by the Ranchi and Lohardaga law courts been declared to be the property of Hindu and Mohammedan intruders" (Hoffman 2005: 17). Das Gupta defines *patta* as "title deeds executed by the government in favour of the village leaders and tenants" (2011: 331).

Permanent Settlement   of 1793; introduced in Bengal and extended to *Chotanagpur* a rigid, i.e. inflexible, and formal system of revenue collection was implemented by Lord Cornwallis in order to guarantee fixed payments for the Company to be raised from land (Pfeffer 2017: 49). However, the Company had neither the expertise nor the manpower to efficiently operate this settlement. So, in the course of time a growing set of non–*adivasi* outsiders, usually plains people from Bihar and Bengal, were invited and given legal status in the area as the Company's collaborators and responsible to its representatives only. "Against the payment of a fixed sum it gave the *zamindar* the lands from which they had till then collected revenue" (Areeparampil 2002: 75) and thus turned them into (intermediate) owners of land. The settlement constituted the legal basis for this massive alienation of ancestral land of the indigenous population. Beyond the technicalities of extracting revenue from land the opposition against this was fuelled by the foreign notion of the separation of land belonging to a landlord, a *zamindar* or the ruling government on the one hand and those cultivating it on the other hand. Basically and eventually, land with its status as a divine gift, a transaction within a process of reciprocal gift exchange, was to be transformed into a commodity that could be auctioned, sold and acquired at will. Since its coming into its non-successful existence the Permanent Settlement was opposed not only by the indigenous population, but also by a number of its native and indigenous collaborators who joined in revolts when it so happened that they themselves fell into revenue arrears because of a famine, a drought etc. After violent clashes, turmoils, and rebellions for more than four decades the Company came up with a new scheme of what has been coined non – regulation policy. As Governor-General Lord Cornwallis needed reliable resources, i.e. the revenue of Bengal, to finance the Mysorean war of the 1790ies (Rothermund 2001: 3).

Phani Mukut Rai   foster son of Madra Munda, a *manki* of Sutiambe village. He is claimed to be of Naga origin, no Munda, and, according to the Nagbansi origin myth, the founder of the Nagbansi dynasty and the 1st Raja of Chotanagpur. However, "a section of the Mundas, the Hos, did not subscribe to the idea of a Raja and left the parent tribe and moved over to Singhbhum where they lived an independent life" (Areeparampil 2002: 44). At least at the beginning the Raja did not seem to have commanded any special proprietary rights of land.

police, introduction of   In 1809 the Company demanded police wards to be established in Chota Nagpur in order to better come to grips with the situation of permanent unrest in the area. The new police officials were *zamindar* or police *darogahs*, all of them foreigners, non – *adivasi* agents, often plains people from Bihar and Bengal. Following their own agenda these *diku* were consequently opposed by the indigenous population. Also the Raja was against the institution of a police body as it contributed to minimising both his authority and his income. Eventually, with the formation of the South West Frontier Agency in 1834 and the end of indirect rule by the Company, a regular system of law and order and the *panchayat* system of administration were officially acknowledged and put into practice. Captain Wilkinson was the mastermind of these changes. The *zamindar* police was abolished in 1854.

Raja of Chota Nagpur   Rothermund (2001: 2) calls him a tribal king attempting to 'rule' the Munda who in their turn agreed to support him with contributions called *chanda*, but did not comply with the concept of performing as his subjects. – In the course of centuries various indigenous local kingdoms had come into being whose representatives tried to claim superior status and power due to their alleged royal descent. However, the accounts of the Jungle kings' Rajput origin seem to be mythical rather than historical. In order to legitimize their claims dynastic chronicles were made up, some tracing their descent back to the time of the Ramayana and the Mahabharata (Das Gupta 2011: 67); see *Nagbansi dynasty, Phani Mukat Rai.*

rajhas   (Hindi: *rajasva*): income from revenue, or revenue from taxation; in the political context of Jharkhand after 1793 Hoffman translates *rajhas* as "land leased out by landlords against payment of rent" (2005: 39).

Rajmahal Hills   mountainous territory to the North East of today's Jharkhand, home to the *Paharia* as the original settlers. see *Cleveland, Augustus, Damin – I – Koh.*

resistance   Although the indigenous communities of *Chota Nagpur/ Jharkhand* had been liable to taxation also under Mogul rule it was during British colonial presence in the area that the *diwani* rights were attempt- ed to be effectively imposed and carried through for the first time. This was resisted in a number of ways, from absconding into the jungle or leaving the area for the tea plantations in Assam to embarking upon open and fierce collective counter attacks. Such revolts and rebellions were the Chuar rebellions in the Jungle Mahals 1769–1784, 1799; the Chero revolt in Palamau 1800, 1817; the revolt in Silli 1773; the Tamar revolts 1782–83, 1789, 1793–98, 1807–08, 1810, 1812, 1820; the 1st Kol insurrection 1819 – 20; the Ho rebellion in Singhbhum 1820 – 21; the Ho uprising in South Kolhan 1830; the Great Kol Insurrection of 1831–32, 1837; the Bhumij revolt in Dalbhum and in the Jungle Mahals 1832 – 33; the Santal Hul 1855 – 56; revolts in and after 1857: the Singhbhum revolt 1857 – 59; the *Sardari Larai* since 1859, the Birsa Movement led by *Birsa Munda* since 1895 and the rebellion called *Ulgulan* in 1899. Over a period of 200 years about 70 uprisings are said to have taken place.

Roughsedge, Major   appointed in 1819 as the first political Agent to the Government of South Bihar. He was to install the Company's direct administration in Chotanagpur. He unsuccessfully attempted three times to penetrate the *Kolhan* by military means and subdue the indigenous population settling there whom he portrayed as criminals wreaking terror, as savages and a dreadful pest (Das Gupta 2011: 93). The first Kol insurrection of 1819–1820 was one result, the Ho rebellion in Singhbhum of 1820–1821 followed, which according to Areeparampil is labelled as the "Hos' first struggle for freedom" (2002: 89). The Ho who at that time had separated from the Munda had previously successfully resisted military attacks by the Maharaja of Chotanagpur and the Raja of Singhbhum. In their attempt at establishing themselves as the legal and lawful authority and making the Ho acknowledge their supremacy various competing royal families became regional collaborators of the Company hoping to crush the Ho that way in a joint effort. As late as 1821 the Ho had to submit, if only preliminarily for a period of ten years. Under Major Roughsedge they were made to pay eight *annas* for each plough, a regulation that was continued under Captain *Wilkinson*. It was also Captain *Wilkinson*, who was confronted by the next outbreak of indigenous dissatisfaction, the great Kol insurrection of 1831–1832.

ryot outsider settled in a village (Hoffman 2005: 11). They had to supply the food and clothing of the (*maha*) *raja*.

Sardari Larai In the 2nd half of the 19th century beginning in 1858, the Sardari Larai became a tribal movement to restore the adivasis' ancestral rights in their land and put an end to foreign encroachments and oppression by landlords, *zamindar*, *thikadar*, *jagirdar*, *mahajan*, and native policemen once and for all. The movement of "prayer, protest, and petition" was mainly legal and religious in character (K.S. Singh 1966: 26). In the course of their 40-year-long struggle, however, *adivasi* followers grew disillusioned and eventually turned against Christian missionaries and missions. In this the Sardari movement differed from the Birsa movement in that it was not primarily anti–British or anti–European at the beginning, but mainly 'anti- intermediary'. Petitions and appeals to the Viceroy, Parliament and the Queen, were directed against Ranchi officials and landlords, but proved unsuccessful. The Sardari Larai's experience informed the *Birsa (Munda)* movement that fought for an end of the British Raj altogether in order to install their own.

sepoy Indian native soldier in British service or: Hindu and Muslim soldiers.

SEZ The introduction in April 2000 (Shah 2010: 18; Moharana 2012: 14) of Special Economic Zones in otherwise legally protected Scheduled Areas invites private companies to legally acquire tribal land in order to exploit the rich mineral resources, such as iron ore, coal, copper, bauxite, chromium and uranium of the *Chota Nagpur Plateau* and elsewhere. As a result of large scale 'development' projects significant numbers of the landowning tribal population have been displaced and dispossessed of their ancestral lands, often not voluntarily. This also holds true for Ho people. In my research area in north-eastern Mayurbhanj/ Odisha news spread that 13 Ho were killed and more than 30 injured on January 2nd, 2006 in a collision with the state police who attempted to clear the path for the erection of a TATA steel plant near Kalinganagar by shooting into a group of Ho protesting against their involuntary displacement (Moharana 2012: 6, 24, 128; Shah 2010: 18). – Outside the SEZ-areas the Fifth and and Sixth Schedule to the Indian constitution though under constant threat of acts of amendment continue to exclude the Scheduled Areas from the legislation operative in nontribal India ever since the Scheduled

Districts Act of 1874 by disallowing the transfer of tribal lands into nontribal hands.

Shah Alam II Mughal Emperor who passed the *diwani* of Bengal, Bihar (including the present-day province of Jharkhand), and Odisha over to the British East India Company in 1765.

Sinbonga the creator God of the Ho and their supreme deity; see glossary II

Singh, Arjun He was the Raja of Porahat whose predecessors had not infrequently sided with the British against the indigenous population in former times. However, in the course of the revolts of 1857 – 1859 in Jharkhand he became a prominent figure as he turned not only against the Raja of Seraikela, but challenged the British troops in open revolt. In this he was supported by the *adivasi* of Southern Kolhan, especially the Ho. According to Areeparampil they contributed to converting "the rebellion of a Raja into a popular insurgency" (2002: 171). After the Ho's defeat in 1837 this was a way of rebelling once again against British rule in the Kolhan.

South-West Frontier Agency This was an administrative unit with an innovative legislation set up by British authorities in 1834 as a result of the *adivasi*'s obvious and continuous failing to submit to and comply with the Company's orders. A so-called Agent to the Governor General was in charge of introducing changes concerning revenue collection, supervising the police and jurisdiction in general. The Agency had its headquarters in Ranchi and included a.o. the tribal hotspots of Chotanagpur, Palamau, Ramgarh, most of the Jungle Mahals, Dhalbhum, and later also the entire district of Singhbhum. Finally, after the conquest of Kolhan in 1837, the Kolhan Government Estate was created and included in the SWFA. The SWFA was considered a Non – Regulation Area with Captain Thomas *Wilkinson* as its first Agent. According to Areeparampil the code of rules to guarantee civil justice and peace and bring an end to *adivasi* land alienation and other kinds of outside intrusion was developed by Captain *Wilkinson* and valid in the Kolhan area only, not so in Bihar and Bengal, and "is still operative in the Kolhan area today" (2002: 113). In 1854 the SWFA became the Chota Nagpur division, as non – regulation province to be ruled from Bengal.

swaraj (Hindi: *svarajya*): 1. own rule, sovereignty, independence; an independent state 2. (myth.) the heaven of Indra.

tenant a person who has occupancy rights and often has to pay rent to a landlord or land-owner for the use of land, for cultivating it, e.g. a farmer. A tenant as a matter of principle is someone who does not own the land he cultivates. The *Paharia* e.g. became government tenants and could cultivate the lands rent-free due to regulations implemented and controlled by A. *Cleveland*. On the whole, however, the Company was either ignorant of the indigenous notion of *adivasi* owning cum cultivating their own land or disinterested; in any case the concept of tenancy was an efficient instrument of guaranteeing revenues.

tenure	legal right to occupy property or land.
thana	(Hindi): police–station. In 1809 the *Raja of Chota Nagpur* was ordered to establish police–stations and appoint *thanadar* and *chowkidar* all over the country.
thikadar	(Hindi): contractor; revenue farmer; *tika* (Ho) – "a form of mortgage (the one who takes fields on *tika* cultivates them for a fixed number of years and then returns the field)" (Deeney 2005: 380). In the case of Chotanagpur Hoffman calls *thikadar* unmitigated robbers whose treatment of the indigenous population eventually led to the Kol revolt in 1831. After the Bhuinari survey *thikadar* succeeded in dissuading *bhuinar* from demanding *bhuinari* claims to which they would have been entitled following the Chotanagpur Tenures Act from 1869.
thikadari system	Following the Permanent Settlement this system began to "mushroom in Chotanagpur [...] in 1822 with the granting of indiscriminate rent-farming leases to a new set of middlemen [which led to] the gradual destruction of the *bhuinari* system" (Areeparampil 2002: 182).
title	a right or claim to the ownership of property, especially of land. "The only title Munda could conceive as giving a proprietary claim to lands, was the labour spent on their creation. That, in Chota Nagpur, belonged to them and could not be transferred from the original owner to anybody except by rightful inheritance in the male line" (Hoffman 2005: 17). So those who reclaim land, own it – as a gift.
title deed	"a legal document proving someone's right to a property" (ALD 1995: 1199). According to Hoffman the Munda claim that "the burial stones are our title deeds" (Hoffman 2005: 35); according to Das Gupta the sepulchral stone slabs are the exclusive title deeds of the original settlers and their descendants (2011: 31).
tribe and caste	recurrently and controversially debated dichotomous issue not only in Indian anthropology. Colonial ethnographers and administrators as well as the fathers of the Indian constitution have contributed to essentializing originally fluid social compositions into either caste or tribe and further into Scheduled Caste, Scheduled Tribe, and Other Backward Class according to criteria like backwardness, relative isolation, cultural distinctiveness, and primitiveness. Despite their differentiation in law both – tribal categories and a number of servicing castes – are equally indigenous to the area (Pfeffer 1997: 7f., Skoda 2005: 49–61, Parkin 2000). Das Gupta states for Ho, Munda, Oraon, Santal that the "primacy of settled cultivation [is] based on the use of ploughs" (2011: 27).
ulgulan	(Mundari): "a rebellion; to cause a rebellion" (EM 1990: 4804). It is the term that is attributed to the *Birsa* movement.
Wilkinson,Sir Thomas	First Agent to the Governor-General of the South Western Frontier Agency appointed to suppress the numerous rebellions and to implement the newly established policy of a more flexible system of non – regulation in 1833. Chotanagpur, Palamau, Kharakdiha, Ramgarh and Kunda, most of the Jungle Mahal territories and Dhalbhum constituted this so-called Non–Regulation area as South West Frontier Agency

with its headquarters in Ranchi. Wilkinson had far reaching powers and introduced a policy of patronage and isolation in and for this area. The indigenous *panchayat* system with its focus on consensus-based decision making was maintained and applied. Under Regulation XIII of 1833 the legal code to bring about an efficient system of justice and peace became known as "Wilkinson's Rules". His name is well remembered today and the administration of civil justice and law courts that he introduced in the area is still carried out in the present state of Jharkhand. However, his attempt at putting an end to *adivasi* land alienation and exploitation was not successful in so far as the Record of Rights which was to guarantee and legally fix *adivasis'* title deeds was never passed and recognized by the Company Government. So foreign encroachment did continue. Also, Wilkinson's resorting to the *zamindari* police's support plus his transforming *munda* and *manki* of this area into landlords which they had not been before by fixing land titles for them was opposed by the *adivasi* population and caused confusion and resentment. The institution of the *zamindari* police was abolished only in 1861 after the end of the Company's Rule in 1858. Also, of course, the Ho bitterly resented Wilkinson's waging war and the continuous police actions against them. After all, he had initially been called into the area to subdue the Ho by military means which he relentlessly did. In a number of revolts in 1820, 1821, 1830, 1831/32 (and later again in 1857 – 58 with *Arjun Singh*, the Raja of Porahat, as their leader) the Ho had rebelled against foreign infiltration and the imposition of British rule. No foreigner was allowed to trespass their country. Eventually they had to surrender in 1837, when Wilkinson in a summary trial insisted on five 'legal' death sentences according to which five rebel leaders were hanged. These were the first executions to be carried out in Singhbhum.

zamin (Hindi/ Persian): land; terrain; field(s); soil; the earth, world.

zamindar originally a Moghul term for landowner, landlord, samindar, intermediary; *dar* – *occupier, zamin* – *land; zamindar* are "rajas subdued by conquest, the high and mighty of locally dominant castes, adventurers who had established control over a local area by force and fraud, officials of previous regimes, who had managed to convert their official charge into a hereditary estate etc." (Rothermund 1978: 12). The *zamindar*'s control over an area was conceptualised as permanent.

zamindari (Hindi/ Persian): property, ownership of property, system of *zamindar* – ownership; "system of collecting land revenue through zamindars" (McGregor 2011: 359). The Permanent Settlement of 1793 legally turned the *zamindar* whose task it had formerly been to collect revenue from land, into landlords, into legitimate owners of hereditable land. As a matter of consequence, the tribal landowners became tenants on their own property, the headmen tenure holders. Payments to the *zamindar* became 'legal' rent. It happened that the *adivasi* absconded rather than make regular payments. In such cases the *zamin-*

dar were held responsible, and in a case of *zamindar* arrears their estates were confiscated, auctioned, and sold. *Zamindari* ownership was abolished in 1952 (Shah 2010: 80).

Glossary II: Ho terms

In the following section Ho terms have been selected and commented on that have appeared in the main body of the book and in the texts provided in the appendices. English denotations have been contextualized with notes from fieldwork where this was considered helpful for a better understanding of concepts, connotations, and ideas implied in expressions which have been listed alphabetically according to the English spelling order. The spelling and meaning of Ho terms have been checked with Deeney 2005, Hindi and Urdu terms with McGregor 2011 and Gatzlaff-Hälsig 2002.

Terms marked (*) below have an entry of their own with additional information. The Roman script is used neglecting diacritic marks except for those cases where they constitute a phonemic distinction (*jati**, *jaṭi**). The colon (:) indicates a glottalized vowel. The length of a vowel is given only when it is phonemic (*goe; goe:*; gōe:**). More notes on the transliteration of Ho have been provided in the annotations above.

a: sar	bow (*a:*) and arrow (*sar*); used by grown-up males when hunting in the jungle; used by boys to shoot at birds; a bow is put upright in the rope-bed (*karkom**) close to the head of a newly born male baby; used at night during shooting competition at *ba porob**
achu	to employ someone to do some work; work done for others; in the research region this work was not done for wages (see *nala**), but reciprocated in kind depending on the volume of work
adi (Hindi)	first; origin; prior
adivasi (Hindi)	original inhabitants; see glossary I
adin	in every Ho house there is an inner room which is portioned off and separated by a wall and which serves as the abode of the dead of the house (*ham hoko-dum hoko**). It is here where the cooking is done on ritual occasions and where the house valuables are kept. Only members of *miyad mandi chaturenko** may enter.
adowa chauli	rice used especially for ritual purposes; husked without previous boiling; sacred connotations
agom	promise made to one or more prominent spirits requesting some specified favour; from fieldwork: as an outward sign of this a new *mandi chatu** is put upside down on top of the roof; this was done in 2010, e. g. when a young girl showed a severely disbalanced state of mind; when after many months her situation had improved considerably sacrifices addressed to *maran bonga** and *desauli** were performed, a white cock offered to Sinbonga**, and the *chatu* was taken down.

https://doi.org/10.1515/9783110666199-014

aji	eZ; HeBW; WeBW
aji-hanar	WeZ; HeZ
akara	dancing ground, usually in or close to the centre of every Ho village and hamlet; meeting site for men to discuss village affairs when called by the *dakuwa**
amin	to clear land of trees, shrubs and grass to make it cultivable
amin-nam	to find/acquire land suitable for cultivation and settling purposes; used in parallel with *pu-nam** and *disum-nam** to refer to original clearing of the jungles
andi	marriage; to marry. Ho people distinguish four forms: 1. *bapala andi* – fully arranged marriage held at the house of the groom; *diku andi* – fully arranged marriage held at the bride's house and officiated over by a Brahmin. 2. *nir andi* or *kepeya andi*: elopement by mutual consent of the couple. 3. *sasan-ura andi* – marriage resulting from "a boy's sisters and friends holding back a girl" (Deeney 2005: 332) who is visiting their village by putting wet *sasan* on both. 4. *opor-tipi* – marriage by capture without the girl's previous consent.
apu	father
ara	DH; yZH; DHyB; SWyB
argae:	a jest; to jest, joke
argae:-apargae:	mutual jesting; a joking relationship
asul	to help, to support; to provide food for; help given within *mmc**; cf. *nala**
asul mail	a kind of reed usually found near villages and in jungle; see also *hatu mail**
Asurkowa: bankuri	myth about the Asur, an ancient iron-eating people; known to Ho, Munda, Santal; in this, after Sinbonga* had caused all Asur men to be burned to death, he scattered the Asur women all over the earth who thus became female spirits of the hills, mountains and water sites; see Glossary I: Asur(a)s*
ba porob	flower (*ba*) feast (*porob*) and sacrifice at village level; celebrated annually in the *desauli** of all Ho villages around full moon in the month *Pagun* (late February till early March), when the flowers of the sal (*sarjom**) and *mahua** tree blossom; addressed to village guardian spirits and ancestors; special focus in sacrifice on *jayer buri**; compulsory use of *ramba**
baba	1. vocative of father; in the research area, *babu* is preferred; 2. the rice plant; threshed unhusked paddy grains; unthreshed paddy stalks
baba enga	paddy (*baba**) personified as mother (*enga*); identified with original source from which all paddy has come; addressed in ritual (*her-mut**), but not constructed as *bonga**
baba keya-ader	calling back/inviting to the house on the *her-mut** feast paddy personified (*baba enga**)
baba tar	having cattle thresh paddy sheaves by walking on them

baba tela-ura	rice grains overflowing from a dead person's hand into the opened palms below of living members of the people of the house (*owa:renko*); *tela-ura* – to receive and return/pass on/ give back
baba tiki	to boil the paddy grains in water before husking in a pot that must not be used for anything else
babako	rice grains (plural ending *-ko*) of the paddy plant (*baba*) personified as offspring of their mother *baba enga**
babu	self-reciprocal relationship term for F and S; see also *baba*(1.)*
bala	(♂) in-law; DHF; DHeB; SWeB; SWF; to show respect, politeness, and hospitality as expected towards an affine; see *bala-saka**, *kutum**
bala-bundu	collective term for empirically existing relations established by marriage; to become related through marriage
bala-era	(♀) in-law: DHM; DHeZ; SWM; SWeZ; yZHyZ
bala jaṭi	mat on which the representatives of the groom's side are seated separate from those representing the girl's side seated on an opposite *haga jaṭi** during marriage negotiations at the girl's parents' home. Both mats are joined to form one large mat as soon as the negotiations have been successfully completed, and *bala** and *haga** sit mixed up.
balako	those going to the house of the groom's or bride's side for the purpose of marriage negotiations
bala-saka	affine(s): category of prospective relations classified as marriageable; colloquially abbreviated as *bala**; conceptually to be distinguished from *bala**, *bala-bundu**; cf. *haga**
bala-saka kimin era	reference made vis-à-vis a man's *ham hoko** concerning his newly wedded wife about to become included in her husband's *kili** in a rite called *jom-isin**
balatadi	vocative of *bala**, *bala-era**
bandi	container the outside of which is made from twisted straw ropes (*bor, boro*) tied together to store paddy usually kept close or inside the *adin**; to make such a container
baram bongako	dwarf-like malign spirits assumed to inflict epidemics and serious diseases, especially in animals; ritually driven out of the villages along with broken pots and dishes in an eastward direction twice every year: a task performed before dawn by young boys yelling, racing and creating a tumultuous scene; in the research region the spirits addressed in the *bonga** are considered female and old hence referred to as *baram buriko**
baram buriko	see *baram bongako**
bare	a girl's 'brother' (elder as well as younger)
batauli	one of the three main village feasts (*porob**) next to *mage** and *ba**; sacrifice and feast to obtain rain and protection for paddy when it starts to flower
bau	elder 'brother'; HeZH
bau-honyar	WeB; HeB

beja sim	chicken donated by individual households to be sacrificed by the *diuri** and then taken back and eaten by the members of the household. From fieldwork: only young boys each representing one household brought the chickens to an open field at the foot of a sacred mountain where a member of the Gau community, not the *diuri* sacrificed twenty chickens and returned them to twenty boys. This was done during *ba porob** and the *boro-bonji** sacrifice.
bid-diri	an upright memorial stone set in the ground in memory of a dead person, of someone considered dead or in commemoration of some relevant event; cf. *sasan diri**
bir	wild, undomesticated; jungle; forest
bisi:	social impurity; to contract social impurity by staying outside one's village too long; see also *bital**
bital	socially impure; in *bisi: bital* used in parallel to *bisi:**
boda	uncastrated he-goat
boko	yB; yZ
boko-boya	children of the same parents (also *undi-boya**)
bonga[1]	spirit: tutelary or malign; actively involved in people's lives protecting (or harming) them, their harvest, cattle, possessions; benevolent spirits ritually attended to by *diuri** and male head of household, harmful ones by *dewa**; nourished by animal sacrifices (*bonga*[2]*), they in return offer protection: reciprocal relation with the living; all principal yearly celebrations performed in honour of the tutelary spirits; see glossary I
bonga[2]	sacrifice; to sacrifice; from fieldwork: age, sex (female; male: castrated or uncastrated), kind (chicken, goat) and colour of sacrificed animals reveal which spirit/deity is addressed in ritual; a white *kaluti** or white *sandi** is offered (only) to Sinbonga; *ara: sandi sim* (cock of red-brown colour) to *desauli**; *suka kaluti** (chicken that have not yet hatched eggs, white-yellow) to *jayer buri*, ham hoko*, maran bonga**; *hende sim* (black hen) to *nage era*, gowa bonga**; *hende sandi* (small black cock that is stoned) to *mageya bonga**
bonga diyan	rice-beer made for sacrificial purposes; considered sacred and ensouled by ancestors; at the household level usually manufactured by males after having fasted and taken a ritual bath; drunk by males only; *bonga diyan* to be consumed during village festivals by the *diuri** and his men inside the *desauli** is prepared by the wife of the *diuri**
bonga-buru	generic term for sacrifices addressed to the spirits; *bonga*/ buru** – poetic parallels; see also *buru bonga**
bonga-nam	act of divination to discern what sacrifice should be offered and to whom in the case of a spirit afflicting some harm; frequently performed when someone had fallen ill or when something had got lost; done by either the *dewa** (shaman, diviner) or the head of the respective household, in any case by a male person.

bonga-tala	offering (*bonga**²) of a first meal consisting of *ramba**, *mandi** and *utu* (curry) to welcome and include a newly deceased's soul in the *adin** among (*tala**) her/his fellow *rowa**
boro-bonji	twice-yearly sacrifice to ward off malign *baram** spirits; picnic near or in the jungle
boronja	a cross nephew: ZCh (♂speaking); WBCh; HZCh; *ge** is the alternative Ho word for this; cf. *homon**
boyo	form of addressing a boy or young man (♀sp)
bui	form of addressing girl or young woman
bul	to make drunk; to become drunk
buru	hill, mountain, jungle; poetic parallel with *bonga** (a spirit; to sacrifice); (pass.) to become a spirit (addressing *ham hoko** in the *adin**)
buru bongako	powerful and benevolent spirits dwelling in the high hills near each village; servant spirits to and close collaboration with *desauli**; special powers to 'call' rain in times of drought; wealthy in grains and cattle; assumed to live in big houses; appear in the form of men; see *mageyako**, *jid bonga**
buru kita	the dwarf palm from whose leaves mats (*jaṭi**) are made. From fieldwork: at the time of the first burial a blade of grass from *buru kita* is stretched up from the corpse to the air above in support of the soul (*rowa**) on its way to leave the body.
buru mad	bamboo found in the jungle; used in rituals; see *hatu mad**
chacha:	to tear: cloth, paper, leaves
chacha:-bara	to tear into two equal parts
chacha:-bete:-bete:	to tear into many small pieces
chakara	small, well-seasoned, spicy and tasty snack served along with rice-beer (*diyan**) or rice liquor (*rasi**).
chala	strainer
chalu:	to hoe; to cut the ground with a *kudlam**
chandu:	moon; month; menstruation.
chandu: homol	a minor female spirit; in some stories said to be the wife of Sinbonga*, although in the research area all *diuri** confirmed that Sinbonga was not married. "Such stories are probably taken from other cultures and in them Sinbonga is substituted for e.g. Ram" (Deeney 2005: 63).
chatom	umbrella
chatom owa:	the inner part of a house raised higher and having a roof separate from that of its outer part (see plate 27)
da:	water
dabba (*Hindi*)	tin; container; term used by Gau *diuri's** wife for the tin holding the quantity of *chauli** given to her for a day's taking care of someone's cattle
dada	eB: vocative (colloquial); see also *bau**
da: go:	a *diuri's** two assistants carrying and supplying water for the main village feasts

dakuwa	village headman's helper who makes announcements to villagers, a messenger
desauli	prominent male spirit of the sacred grove; main guardian spirit of a village receiving sacrificial offerings – often a cock (*sandi**) of a red-brown colour (*ara:*) – on all main village feasts; husband of *jayer buri**; the sacred grove of a village; often pronounced as [*besauli*]
dewa	shaman, diviner; often no Ho, but requested by Ho at times of sickness; discerns what spirit has been offended, is causing the disease and what offerings have to be made to propitiate that spirit; drives out malicious spirits; performs *ere bonga** and *era: bonga**; pass. to become a *dewa*
diku	a nontribal; a notional outsider; foreign; alien; to speak Hindi or Odiya (see glossary II)
diku andi	marriage performed at bride's house with a Brahmin officiating
diku-bengaliko	nontribals; in the region of research the Ho's clients were not considered *diku** although they are nontribals and members of Scheduled Castes; the Muslim community, however, was referred to as *diku-bengaliko*, their mother tongue as *bengali kaji*
diku kaji	foreign language; the language of foreigners; from fieldwork: used when referring to Hindi or Odiya (*kaji* – to speak)
diku mage	*mokor sankranti**; from fieldwork: (Hindu) feast held by Hindu people of the plains about January 14th before the Ho's *mage porob**; talked about, but not celebrated by Ho community in research area
dinda	bachelor; unmarried man or woman; married man (with or without children) whose wife has left him
diuri	ritual guide: a highly respected *gusiya** usually from the *kili** recognized as *munu: hoko** (first settlers) of the village; a cultivator whose role as *diuri* is purely ritualistic: presides in principal yearly celebrations and performs sacrifices in the name of the whole village in *desauli**; addresses Sinbonga* and tutelary spirits by prescribed, orally commemorated invocations; assisted in rituals by *jomsimkin**; translation as 'village *priest*' avoided in this book in order to avoid conventional Brahmanic connotations
diyan	rice-beer; to make rice-beer; four kinds of *diyan* are distinguished: 1. *bonga diyan**; 2. *owa: diyan* (rice-beer of the house) to be drunk by people of the house in secular situations; 3. *dili diyan* (*dili* – to invite someone to come on a given date; to set a date): rice-beer 'from outside', brought from another village and made by other villagers on a specified date; 4. *harom diyan* (*harom* – contribution or collection, especially in kind): *diyan* 'from inside', brought on a set date and contributed by villagers of the same village
dukuila:	(*duku* – unhappy, sad); cf. *sukuila:**

dutam	to intercede; a go-between; the term *raibar* was preferred in the region of research by Ho and Santal when a marriage was to be mediated between the groom's and the bride's side
em	to give
enem	the gift (verbal noun of *em* – to give)
enga	mother; to mature, to develop; physical person and concept personifying as mother the original source from which comes all to sustain mankind such as *baba enga**, *ote enga**, *gowa enga**
era:	to throw out; to get rid of
era: bonga	rite usually performed by *dewa** to get rid of (*era:**) or ward off whatever causes or may cause any kind of harm, trouble, distress or calamity; directed against *nojor**; in the research area performed during first and secondary burials, in the course of marriage celebrations, in protection of newly acquired cattle; method: *sarjom pata chacha:**
ere	omen; to cause or show as an omen; capacity attributed to Sinbonga* as his means of communicating with men and requiring a person's skill in deciphering the omen
ere bonga	rite on request performed by an *ere panditi** (Deeney 2008: 13) to drive out or keep away malign spirits, discern unfavourable omens or get rid of any kind of potentially harmful impurity; in the research region *ere bonga* was often performed by a *dewa** in the context of marriage, death, sickness, or when cattle were newly acquired to ask for protection from the evil eye (*nojor**)
ere panditi	someone able to read and interpret omens
eyan	vocative of mother; *mã**
fufa (Urdu)	FZH
fufi (Urdu)	FZ, *hatom**
fufu (Urdu)	FZCh, *hatom hon** (Ho)
gara-hasa	mud-paste used in building houses, mortar
Gau	member of the Gaur or Gope community
gau o:l	major annual feast and sacrifice asking for protection of cattle; in the region of research it was the Gau* *diuri's** duty to perform the *bonga** at the Ho *munda's** and the Ho *diuri's** sacrificial sites; rice-beer fed to cowherders; see *gowa bonga** and *ote ili**
ge	cross nephew and/or cross niece: WBCh; HZCh; ZCh (♂sp.); see *boronja**
ge-kowa	cross nephew; HZS; WBS; ZS (♂sp.)
ge-kui	cross niece; HZD; WBD; ZD (♂sp.)
gōe:	to ladle out liquidy substance with one's hands
gōe: diyan	the *maya** of rice-beer ladled out with the hands by males on ceremonial occasions
goe:	to kill; to beat; dead
goe: anjed	unconscious; to faint
goe: en, gojen	(reflexive of *goe:**) to commit suicide; suicide

goe: – bage	to die and leave behind (sung in grief by a widow addressing her dead husband during first burial)
gonon	bridewealth; value; cost; to set a price. *Gonon* as a rule is given to the bride's parents' side (*gonon har*); *gonon* is usually settled in negotiations taking place at the bride's home (*gonon sid*) followed by a feasting there on the occasion (*gonon-sid bapala*). *Gonon* negotiations are about what the boy's side offer and/or what the girl's side request. This includes the number of heads of cattle (*gonon uri:ko*), cash given to the couple (*taka:* money, in the Ho's veiled language *sati-sati*, poetic parallel of *gonon* and conventionally understood as 101 rupees), expenses for meals and drinks offered to guests/ affinal relations (*pera gonon*). From fieldwork: the boy's side once handed over 501 rupees of which 400 rupees were returned by the girl's side. The couple thus, as is usual in the area, was left with 101 rupees. – In another case *lija: gonon** was additionally offered and distributed by the girl's side.
gonon har	driving the cattle/ taking the bridewealth from the groom's home to the home of a bride's parents
gonon sid	negotiations concerning the various components of bridewealth usually settled at the girl's parents' house
gonon uri:ko	cattle (*uri:ko*, pl.: more than two) given by the groom's side as part of the bridewealth to the benefit of the bride's parents' side. During bridewealth negotiations the number of heads of cattle demanded by the girl's side in the Ho's veiled language is indicated by a goat's droppings (*merom ii:**) handed over to the groom's representatives in a leaf-cup (*pu:**). Three droppings were usually understood as representing two bullocks (*hara*) and one cow (*gundi**). The cow will remain with the couple at the groom's house after marriage. If buffaloes are requested, this is indicated by the equivalent number of beans of *ramba** (black pulse).
gowa bonga	female spirit of the cattle-shed; spirit to protect the cattle of a house; ritually addressed at the household-level; a black hen (*hende sim*) and *ramba** offered exclusively to her – separately from other spirits – once a year; in the region of research celebrated on the day after *gau o:l**
gowa enga	the cattle 'mother' in the status of a *bonga** (*gowa bonga**);
gundi	a cow; as part of bridewealth requested by the bride's side to remain at the couple's residence, i.e. at the groom's side.
gungu	FeB/FeBW; MeZ/MeZH; HyBCh; WyZCh; great-grandchild; great-grandparent; parallel nephew: yZCh (♀sp.), yBCh (♂sp.)
gupi	to herd, e.g. cattle, sheep, goats
gupi ho, gupitani:	a herder
gusiya	landowner; cultivator of land usually corporately owned by the local segment of *mmc**
hab-goe:	to kill by biting (of snakes and tigers)

haga jaṭi see *bala jaṭi**

haga(ko) category of those classified as agnatically related or 'brothers'; inclusive social category with culturally defined fluid boundaries; idiom of social discrimination; category of those proscribed for marriage; coterminous with *mid mayom hapatinko** or *ale miyad hitaren honko**; notional opposite: *bala-saka**

ham ho(ko)-dum hoko *ham* – old; *ham ho* – old man; a forefather; to become an old man; *dum* – to sleep; *ham hoko* (pl.) and *dum hoko* are poetic parallels referring to those dead of the 'house' whose souls have been called into (*keya ader**) the *adin** and dwell there; invisible beings with agency; constructed as having entered the Ho's spirit world (*bonga buru**), but are not thought of as *bonga**; ritually transformed into almost human fellow inhabitants of their houses keeping their physical characteristics and deficiencies; ritually addressed and offerings made to them at village and household level; male forefathers remembered by name, female ones (wives and unmarried daughters) included, but not remembered by name; see also *tata-gunguko**

hanar HM; WM

hasi an adze: a tool to cut wood which is similar to an axe but with a smaller curved blade fixed at right angles to the handle; in the research area used as a ritual hatchet to kill a goat by beating it on the head with the back side of the adze and afterwards beheading the victim; also used in the *uri: bonga** to knock the bull and the cow dead and cut the sacrificial meat into equal portions; not used in ritual when chicken are sacrificed; cf. *kudlam**

hatin to divide, to distribute; to share

hatom FZ; MBW

hatom hon father's sister's child (FZCh)

hatu village; to establish a village (tr.)

haturenko villagers

hatu mad strong type of bamboo found in big clusters and growing high in villages (*hatu*); used for building houses; to be distinguished from *buru mad**

hatu mail kind of reed or tall grass found near villages and in jungle; see also *asul mail**

her to sow

herel husband; see also *ho**

her-mut	*her*; mut* (verbal affix) – to make a start; used synonymously with *baba mut, hon* ba** – feast and sacrifice at household level before the sowing of the main paddy crop; from fieldwork: rice seeds (*jan**) taken to field in a new basket (*tunki**) which is kept in the *adin**, used only once for this purpose and decorated with scented white flowers (of the *golanchi* tree) like a bride; ceremonious *jowar** as a sign of respect towards *ote enga** (Mother Earth) after working the seeds into the ground with a spade (*kudlam**) washed and similarly decorated like the basket; rite performed by the most successful landowner/ cultivator of the local segment of *miyad mandi chaturenko**
hero:	pass. form of *her**
hero: porob	feast and sacrifice of a goat in the field after sowing has been completed; in the field sacrificed meat, rice, and *diyan** are offered to village spirits and the dead of the house; from fieldwork: a goat was sacrificed every 3rd, 5th, 7th year; every year a sacrifice of *rasi*, sasan*, holon**, a white (*pundi*) and a red-brown chicken (*ara: sandi sim*) offered by the head of the 'house' to the spirits of the village and to Sinbonga first and then to *ham hoko** inside the *adin** before eating the sacrificial meal in the field
hili	eBW
ho	a man; a Ho; husband (in certain contexts); *herel**
ho andi	marriage taking place at groom's house according to Ho custom; cf. *diku andi**
ho mata	a living being (*mata* – to ripen; to grow to maturity)
holon	rice powder
homo	human body; human beings are constituted by their body (*homo*), *ji/jibon*, rowa**
homon	cross nephew and/or cross niece of a woman: BCh (♀ sp.)
homon-kui	a woman's cross niece
homon-kowa	a woman's cross nephew
hon	child; to give birth; small (if used before noun); expression of respect if used after the name of a spirit, e. g. *desauli* hon*, no notion of smallness implied, respectful address; also: Sinbonga *hon*
hon-era	parallel niece: eBD (♂sp.); eZD (♀sp.); HeBD; see *hon-kui**
hon-kimin	daughter-in-law: SW
hon-kowa	WeZS
hon-kui	WeZD
hon-sed	parallel nephew: eBS (♂sp.); eZS (♀sp.); HeBS; S
honyar	HF; WF
huwa:-goe:	to kill by biting (not of snake or tiger); see *hab goe:**
id	feast of breaking the fast; celebrated by males of the Muslim community in(side) the mosque
ii:	excrement; dung
iril	HyB; HyZ; joking relation with *hili**
jai	grandchild

jalom	to spread wet mud with the hand in order to plaster the walls of a house or the floor of the courtyard; female activity often performed before village festivals; cf. *lunda**
jan	a bone; a seed; a grain; the kernel of a fruit
janum	a thorn; to be pierced. by a thorn; from fieldwork: in the Ho's veiled language an allusion to a bride's elder sister (*aji-hanar*) in marriage negotiations; in the case of a 'bad' death a thorny branch covers the grave to prevent the soul from escaping
jate	to purify who/what has been defiled
jate bonga	rite of purification; from fieldwork: *jate bonga* became necessary to purify the *kili** (Kondangkel) of a woman who had eloped with a Pano in which case no bridewealth (*gonon**) was given to the woman's side; the rite was performed by *diuri** of the dominant Bage clan in woman's father's house in the presence of Kondangkel *haga**, in the absence of *bala**, groom and bride; state before *jate bonga* is called *bisi*:* – "social uncleanness" (Deeney 2005:43) or *bital* – "morally unclean" (ibid.: 44)
jate mandi	a meal to re-establish commensality with someone temporarily excluded (*jatite bar**) from her/his *kili** e.g. due to long absence from village or any other form of defilement
jate-ura	to re-purify anyone or anything after some defilement. From fieldwork: in case of trouble/ illness/ disbalance/ absence the head of household performs a *bonga** and sacrifices some animal to propitiate ancestors and clan-deity;
jati	"race; tribe; caste; type, kind" (Deeney 2005: 177)
jati ader	rite to ritually introduce a wife into her husband's local segment of the *miyad mandi chaturenko**; see *jom-isin** ceremony
jati-tala kili-tala	to include e.g. a daughter-in-law in her husband's tribe and clan; *tala* – to surround on all sides; among; between; expression used in a rite addressed to her husband's *ham hoko**
jatite bar	person excluded from *kili**; to exclude from one's *kili**
jaṭi	mat usually made from the leaves of a stemless dwarf palm growing in the jungle (*buru kita**). From fieldwork: *jaṭi* were exclusively used in ceremonious situations, e.g. during marriage negotiations as *bala jaṭi** and *haga jaṭi**, in death rituals to bid farewell to the *bala bundu**, or when making offerings to the dead of the house inside the *adin*. Otherwise the mat was rolled up and hung to the wall in order not to defile it by exposing it to impure gazes from outside.
jayer	generic term for the Ho's sacred groves including *desauli**
jayer buri	prominent female guardian spirit assigned her own sacred grove (*jayer**); the Ho's proto-mother and ancestress; wife to *desauli**

ji/jibon	vital essence, principle of life, 'breath' present in all beings considered animate: people, animals, god, spirits, sun, moon, stars (plants are not considered animate); non-material, non-individualizing concept as distinct from *rowa/ umbul** (soul): immortal, mobile, physical, individualizing attribute assigned to human beings only; a human being dies when *ji* leaves the physical body (*homo**); the *rowa** does not die: it can leave the body during dreams (and return); at death it is called into the *adin** in the *keya ader** or *umbul ader** rite.
jid bonga	a spirit, especially a *buru bonga** living in high hill; considered benevolent and wealthy in grains which he sometimes lends to people; appears in the form of a man; *jid* – to make live
jiya	FM, MM
jom	to eat; of a spirit: to kill someone
jom-isin	ceremony to initiate (*jati-tala kili-tala**) a newly married wife at her husband's place and include her into his *kili*;* only when introduced to her husband's forefathers she becomes eligible to enter the *adin**, touch the rice pot and cook the family meal inside (*isin* – to cook); sacrifice of a chicken and offering to the dead of the house dwelling in the *adin**
jom-nama	celebration of the ripening of the first fruits before the beginning of harvesting; each house offering separately
jom–nu	to eat and drink; to feast
jomsimkin	two assistants to the *diuri** prompting him in ritual at the *mage** and all other village festivals
jom–sutam	of a head of the household and/or his wife to eat but very little of a meal, leave the rest in the *adin** as an offering to the dead forefathers, wait for it to become ensouled by them and eat/ingest it after some time thus strengthening the link (*sutam* – thread) between the living and the dead
jowar	to greet; greeting; in ritual: gesture of showing respect to spirits, deities, guests, affinal relations, animals to be sacrificed etc.
juri	friend
kaka	FyB; MyZH
kaki	FyBW; MyZH; from fieldwork: children often addressed their mother as *kaki, kaki-mã or mã**
kalgi	large leaf-plate on which the meals prepared in the *adin** are served during village feasts
kamar	iron-worker; see *lohar**
kandan (Urdu)	*kili*, jati**
kanda	to set aside separate portions of rice, dal, meat, a place to cook, a place to stay; from the field: term referred to marriage or death ceremonies when 'brothers' (*haga**) cooked, stayed and ate separately from their affinal relations (*bala**); commands higher status than *panti**

kapi	"a battle or hunting axe" (Deeney 2005: 196); in the research area a *kapi* resembled a ceremonial adze (*hasi**) or knife rather than an axe when sacrificing animals (beheading them, slitting their throats) in ritual occasions; during the *uri:ko bonga** (cattle sacrifice) the cattle was hit on the head with the back side of the *kapi* or *hasi** in which case it was used as a ceremonial axe.
karkom	bed made from ropes tied diagonally between a wooden frame; men's duty to repair and renew the beds; kept outside the house in an upright position, if not used, and offered to visitors to sit on
karsa	to slit a goat's or chicken's throat in a sacrificial context by a *kapi**
kerai	frying pan of a concave shape
keya ader	ceremony to call the soul (*umbul, rowa*) of a dead person into the *adin**; also called *umbul ader* ceremony; (*keya* – to call, to invite to one's house; *ader* – to bring in/inside); see *baba keya ader**
khala (Urdu)	a mother's sister
kili	"a clan, sept, gotar, (now used as a family name); a type or variety" (Deeney 2005: 205); sociocentric affinal category; subdivided into subclans and localized segments; cf. *miyad mandi chaturenko**
kimin	SW; yBW; DHyZ; SWyZ
kita	palm tree; see *buru kita**
kowa-hon	S; cf. *hon-sed**
kudali (Hindi)	small hoe
kudlam	a hoe, a *kudali** kind of spade; Ho symbol of relatedness with their ancestors; used in cultivation work to hoe (*chalu:**) the ground; in the research area a newly deceased Ho's soul (*rowa**) is offered assistance by clinging to it on its way to the tank and, an uneven number of days later when purified in the water, is guided home towards its final destination in the *adin**; cf. *keya-ader**
kui-hon	daughter, D
kumbu	to steal; a thief; theft
kunt-kati	the land cleared by the original settlers of a village and passed on to their offspring
kunt-kati ho	offspring to the original settlers of a village; in the research area the expression *munurenko** was preferred, *kunti-kati ho* was said to be a Munda expression used by Munda speakers
kuntu	a wooden post

kutum	also *kutum-kupulko* – "relationship by marriage; a relation by marriage" (Deeney 2005: 219); *kupul* ('guest'); Ho language has numerous terms to refer to the category of affines. Verardo (2003) exclusively came across the term *kupulko* in the Porahat area of Northern Jharkhand; in southern Singhbhum and in the region of Mayurbhanj the terms *bala** (short form) or *bala-saka** were used as opposed to the category of agnates or *haga(ko)**, literally 'brothers'. Deeney also mentions *bala-bundu** as relations through marriage (2005: 25), a term my informants understood, but did not actively use themselves. McDougal holds that in Juang which is also a Munda language, *bondhu* is a "term applied to groups with which intermarriage is permissible", whereas *kutumb* is a "term applied to a group with which an agnatic relation is postulated, and intermarriage forbidden" (both quotes in McDougal 1963: 450, 453). Pano people in the region of research used the term *kutum* synonymously with *bala-bundu*.
lai:	stomach; womb
lama: jan	the seed (*jan*) inside the pods of the *lama: jo,* the edible fruit (*jo*) of a climber (*run daru**) which is referred to as tree (*daru*) because of its size. In the veiled language used during negotiations to settle the bridewealth (*gonon**) the number of seeds of the *lama: jo* refers to the amount of money that the representative of the bridal side claims. Example from fieldwork: one seed represented 1000 rupees. Two seeds, i.e. 2000 rupees, were demanded. Put into a leaf-cup (*pu:*) two seeds were handed over to the groom's side who either accepted the request or took out one seed thus continuing the negotiations accompanied by serious joking.
lija: gonon	part of bridewealth (*lija:* – cloth; clothing), optional number of pieces given by groom's side; from fieldwork: marriage negotiations concerning the *diuri*'s* elder brother's youngest daughter (eBD) included *lija: gonon*. The bride's side received 7 *sarees* and 23 *dhoti* which were passed on to the bride's *mamu**, *haturenko** (people of her village), *kakako* (FyB, MyZH), *balako** (those who go to the house of a girl and boy to arrange the marriage), her father (WF), her elder sister (*aji-hanar** to groom: WeZ), her younger sister (*teya-kui** to groom: WyZ), her father's younger brother (WFyB) and their wives (WFyBW: *kaki**), her younger brothers (*teya** to groom: WyB)
lohar	(Hindi): blacksmith; nontribal iron worker; clients of their tribal patrons; they produce arrow heads, ploughshares, iron ladles, knives, axes, and iron bracelets (*med sakom**).
Luku-ham Luku buri	in Ho creation myths the names of the first man and woman; also *Lutukum haram* and *Lutukum buri*
lunda	to spread a liquidy substance on to the floor by use of a cloth; cf. *jalom**
mã	vocative of mother; *eyan**

ma:-nam chalu:-nam	*ma:* – to cut, to slash; *chalu:* – to hoe; *nam* – to get, search, find; *ma: nam* and *chalu: nam* are poetic parallels; acquiring/finding land by cutting trees, shrubs, grass, and ground by hoeing/ by clearing the jungle
ma:-nam chalu:-nam bongako	the main body of the Ho's tutelary spirits having revealed themselves to the first settlers in the process of clearing the jungle; demanding continued offerings for their protection also from those leaving the area and able to inflict some harm if neglected or ritually forgotten
mad pata: bonga	ritual (*bonga*) to elect the ritual guide by branches from *buru mad** (bamboo growing in the jungle) entwining (*pata:*) as a sign of divine consent
mage kaji	obscene language used during *mage porob** by men, women, children
mage porob	sacrifice and feast (*mage* – meaning unknown) observed at village level in honour of the village *bongako;**; celebrated in the sacred grove after the harvest work has been completed; obscene language used; in the research region *desauli** is addressed in *mage* songs praising the male organ (*loe:*) and *jayer buri** in couplets celebrating female fertility; feast presided over by *diuri**; white cock sacrificed for Sinbonga for protecting and increasing children, cattle, harvest, rice-beer; red cock, black hen sacrificed for *desauli** and *jayer buri**, *suka kaluti** for ancestors; only after *mage* and before *ba porob** new fences (*bakai*) are built by women
mageyako	servant spirits to *buru bongako**; sacrifice of a black cock made to them in *mage**, *ba**, *batauli**; taking care of animals of the jungle, of hunt and hunters
mageya sim	small black chicken thrown into the air by *diuri** to be stoned by young boys on the main day of the *mage** sacrifice in the *desauli**; this hunting gesture is complemented by another one: the stoned cock is tied to a pole by its feet and carried on two boys' shoulders to the *diuri's* home – like a large animal killed in the jungle; *mageya sim* offered in the three main village feasts (*mage**, *ba**, *batauli**) to the tutelary *mageya bonga* or *mageyako** in their role as taking care of the jungle animals
mahua	a tree called *mahua* or *madkam daru;* from its white blossoms liquor is made; all blossoms are said to fall to the ground within a single night
mamu	relationship term of ego's MB and FZH; on ego's father's side there are only as many *mamu* as there are husbands to ego's father's sisters; on ego's mother's side all those males belong to the category *mamu* who are related to ego's mother as y/e 'brother', hence many more than on the father's side
man	respect
man-mapan	generic term for respect including mutual respect; respect relation; cf. *apargae**

manatin	to obey; to observe; to respect; obedience, respect
mandi chatu epera:	related to *miyad mandi chaturenko*;* referring to all those mutually getting rid of (*epera:* is reciprocal of *era:**) of their rice pots in the case of death of one of its members
manki	see *sadar* in glossary I
mansik	promise of delayed sacrifice: *sinduri** is dabbed on the wall to remind of the promise; cf. *agom**
manwa	a human being; man; mankind; see also *ho*, ho mata**
maran bonga	prominent tutelary spirit, sometimes called *disum maran bonga* (great or previous, i.e. ancient spirit of the country); protector of cattle and goats, of those going to the jungle, of work on threshing floor and of silkworm cultivation; served by different *kili** under different names as clan deity of their *kili*;* accepts promises (*agom**) of delayed offerings; periodic offerings made to him at household level by head of household. *Pangura bonga* is considered to be his wife and the female spirit of water places; *from* fieldwork: Ho referred to the female spirits of different kinds of water places or low-lying fields as *nage erako**.
masuri	a cultivated pulse used as an offering in ritual at *mage porob*;* cf. *ramba**
matiya	small earthen vessel used for ceremonial pouring of rice-beer (*diyan**) and rice liquor (*rasi**).
maulana (Hindi, Urdu)	spiritual dignitary of the Muslim community of Muslim Sai; "a title given to learned Muslims; lord, master; the Lord, God" (McGregor 2011: 839)
maya	fermented grains of rice-beer (*diyan**)
mayom	blood; pass. – to bleed
med	iron; *med sakom* is the bracelet for a wife provided by the *lohar** at marriage; at her death or at her husband's death taken off and broken
merom ii:	a goat's droppings; in the veiled language during marriage negotiations the number of the droppings relate to the heads of cattle requested by the bridal side.
mid	one; to be one with; to be united with; to have sexual intercourse
mid-lai:ren	born of one mother (*lai:* – stomach; womb)
mid mayom hapatinko	those who share one blood
misi, misi era	a man's younger 'sister'
misi-bareko	girls and their brothers
miyad kili	one *kili*; across tribal boundaries certain Ho and Santal clans are considered one clan or brother clans proscribing intermarriage. Sinku (Ho)/ Kisku (Santal), Birua (Ho)/ Tudu (Santal), Hembrom (Ho)/ Hemrom (Santal), Hasda: (Ho)/ Hansda (Santal) are such *miyad kili/paris.*
miyad apurenko	those (plural: *-renko*) born of one father

miyad mandi chaturenko	*mmc* is an exclusive, specified, and definitive unit within a sub-clan or clan. It is an empirical, egocentric, transgenerational unit. Membership is reckoned patrilaterally including a male *ego*'s unmarried sisters and daughters and – beyond agnatic linkages – his wife or wives.
mokor sankranti	see *diku mage**
mora	a corpse
mosani	separate burial site of the Gau community outside the village boundary
mufti	dignitary of the Muslim community superior to a *maulana**
munda	"a village headman; wealthy [...]; a member of the Munda tribe" (Deeney 2005: 256); his duties concern secular responsibilities; qualification either inherited from forefathers or acquired via election by villagers
munu	origin; original; first beginning; see also *sida**
munu hoko	first settlers (literally: original/ first men); also *munurenko;* used in the research area instead of *kunt-kati ho** which Deeney gives; as a rule (to which there are exceptions) the ritual guide (*diuri**) and the secular headman (*munda**) are related to a village's first settlers' *kili**
nage era(ko)	tutelary female spirit(s) (*era* – wife, woman; *-ko* – plural marker), numerous within the boundaries of each village at places where water gathers, low-lying places, pools, tanks, ravines; guarding the work on the threshing floor; offerings made to her are turmeric (*sasaṅ*), an egg, and a black chicken (*hende sim*)
naka hasa	a type of greyish soil used in the research area especially on ritual occasions for washing the hair
nala paiti	work for wages, work for others; cf. *tika paiti**, *asul**
niyam	universal sociocosmic order assumed to be operative in the world of the living as well as in that of the spirit world, its principles and values; a law, rule
niyar era:	to purify; purification ceremony after the birth of a baby, usually performed on the third day after birth; after this others may enter the room and the baby may be touched; cf. *tiki era:**
nojor	harm/spell inflicted by the evil eye
okowa	compartments at place of sacrifice directed towards specific spirits and deities containing heaps of rice grains and various condiments
or ti:	to pull, to drag
opor tipi:	reciprocal form of *or ti:**, marriage by capture, forcibly taking a woman to be one's wife without her previous consent; in *or tipi:* no mediator (*dutam**) is involved as in *nir andi**
oron sakowa	a *diuri's* two assistants authorized to blow the horns of the jungle bison on the main village feasts
ote	land, field

ote enga	Mother Earth; ritual rice-beer made from *adowa chauli** overflows into the earth (*ote*) in a sacrificial action (*ote ili**) as an offering addressed to Mother Earth (*enga* – mother)
ote ili	pouring rice-beer (here: *ili*) into a *matiya** to overflow into the earth (*ote*) in a sacrificial action; in the research area performed twice on the same day in the courtyards of both *munda** and *diuri** honouring Mother Earth
pal	ploughshare; two ploughshares are beaten against the roof by a male affine in the *keya ader** ceremony to lure the *rowa** of a deceased into the *adin**; from fieldwork: *bala sakom* was used to relate to the person (*bala* – affinal relation) beating the ploughshares (*sakom** – literally a bracelet) while shouting in *keya ader** ceremony *sukuila:*,* *dukuila:**
panji nam	by a shaman (*dewa**) finding out in an act of divining about a lost or stolen object
pankira	compensation of rice and/or money given to a village's messengers (*dakuwa**), blacksmiths (*lohar**), cow-herders (*gupitani:**) once a year
Pano	non-ST category of low social status, sometimes called Dombo; omnipresent in some regions of Odisha as weavers, musicians, traders, and messengers (Berger 2002; Niggemeyer 1964), though not in the research area
panti	in line; to be in line side by side; from fieldwork: *panti* was the term used by Ho e.g. in *diri dulsunum** to refer to *bala** and *haga** not being separated, who eat and sleep in one place: 'side by side'; cf. *kanda** which is attributed higher status
pat	mountain spirits usually called upon by shamans (*dewa**) for help in *bonga-nam**
pata:	to entwine, to interlace (two ropes, two branches); see *mad pata:* *
patarsin	"to slap or scold so as to make one smart (physically or in spirit)" (Deeney 2005: 284)
peyae	"member of a weaving caste; to become socially defiled, e.g. by child birth" (Deeney 2005: 288); Ho informants understood the term Pano*, but used the terms Tanti instead or insisted that *peyae* was the proper Ho term.
pindigi	veranda-type elevation built around one or more sides of a house; with Ho houses the *pindigi* is polished (*lunda**) in dark colours, often black
porob	feast; to observe a feast; major feasts and sacrifices observed in the region of research in this order at household and/or village level by Ho people: *gau o:l**, *gowa bonga**, *ote ili**; *mage porob**, *ba porob**, *her mut**, *hero: porob**, *batauli**, *jomnama**
poyla	vessel for measuring paddy grains, puffed rice (*ata*) etc.; measurement of approximately ½ kg *chauli**
pu	action when clearing the jungle: to uproot by hitting the stump of a shrub

pu:	leaf-cup used in ceremonial context; to make such a leaf-cup; depending on sacrificial purpose the leaves (*sakam*) must be taken from the sacred *sarjom daru** (saltree) or the *run daru**, a climber so immense that Ho people refer to it as tree (*daru**)
pu-nam	to find/acquire land by uprooting in order to start cultivation; used in parallel with *amin-nam**
punji	wealth; to increase in wealth; to increase in number (e.g. of animals); the heaps of *adowa chauli** in the compartments (*okowa**) at a sacrificial site; the capacity to increase is closely connoted with Sinbonga's* generative power; notions of wealth symbolized in the heaps of sacrificial food are reciprocated by men in ritual; see also *sumuki**
punji-nam	rite to find (*nam* – to get/find) a suitable site for building a house by burying a *punji**, i.e. rice grains; see *amin-nam**; *pu-nam**
ramba rid	a *diuri's** two assistants authorized to grind (*rid*) black lentils (*ramba**) needed at village festivals for sacrificial purposes
ramba	a coarse black pulse used for ritual purposes. During bridewealth (*gonon**) negotiations the black beans put into a leaf-cup (*pu:**) and handed over to the groom's side refer to the number of buffaloes (*kera*) demanded by the bridal side. – On the eve of the main feast of *ba porob** the use of *ramba* is compulsory in the meal eaten in honour of the dead of the house and offered to them in the *adin** (sacred part of the kitchen). Whenever *ramba* is eaten in ritual situations it is prepared without using *sasaṅ* (turmeric), *sunum* (oil), or any other condiments except salt; cf. *masuri**
ranu	(Ho) – balls made from rice flour and a variety of dried roots and herbs collected in the jungle functioning as ferment for rice-beer; "medicine; to apply medicine to; to bring a woman under the influence of a man by giving her some (aphrodisiac) medicine" (Deeney 2005: 305).
rasi	rice liquor, stronger than rice-beer; the liquid resulting from the fermentation on top of a rice-beer brew; juice; relevant component in ritual as sacred substance offered to Sinbonga, the spirits and ancestors; *ti chipa rasi**
roka	suddenly; sudden, fresh; often collocated with *goe:** meaning a sudden/fresh/unexpected death
rowa/umbul	soul; cf. *ji/jibon**
rowa sarub bonga	rite of a foetus becoming ensouled; by the pregnant mother eating a little rice inside the *adin** and leaving the rest there as an offering to the dead of the house; by the dead (*rowa**) accepting the offering, i.e. eating from it, the rice becomes ensouled; returning later the woman will eat up the rice ensouled with the *rowa** of the dead; hence the foetus inside her body becomes ensouled; see also *jom-sutam**; *sarub**
run daru	a climber so huge that it is called a tree (*daru**); its leaves used for sacrificial purposes

sadar (Hindi)	"chief, head of an organization; hist.: headman of a village" (McGregor 2011: 978); in Ho a *manki** is the headman of a confederation of villages; in the research area *sadar* is used in the compound *Sadar Sai* inhabited by members of the dominant Bage *kili** who are acknowledged to be the first settlers in that area and the founders of Manbir
saga:	grass with barbed seeds that break easily and get caught in one's clothes
sai	hamlet, separate section of a village
saki	namesake, to name after another; "a sponsorship [that] ends in unbroken friendship between the two, throughout after life" (Tickell 1840: 794).
sakom	bracelet; at marriage the *lohar** provides the bracelet made from iron (*med**) for the newly wedded wife
sakowa	horn made from the horn of a jungle bison (*sail*); carried and blown by men. From fieldwork: *sakowa* were blown from the top of the roof to announce the death of the *diuri*; during village festivals the *diuri** and his men blew them on their way to taking a bath before sacrificing in the sacred grove
sandi	male; a cock
saragi	a wife's sisters' husbands (WZH); relationship between two males whose wives are sisters to each other
sarjom daru	the sal tree (*shorea robusta*); connotations of the sacred: in the region of research in ritual situations leaf-cups and leaf-plates were made from the leaves of this tree; *diyan** in the process of fermenting was covered with sal leaves
sarjom pata chacha:-bete:  **Plate 31:** Getting rid of distress in *era: bonga*	of leaves (*pata*) of the sal tree (*sarjom daru**) to be shredded (*chacha:-bete:*); from fieldwork: during secondary burials (*diri dulsunum**) *pata chacha: bete:* constituted a regular ritual element of *era: bonga** (plate 31): two interlocked leaves of the *sarjom** or the *run** tree are first torn apart into two parts (*chacha: bara*) and after that shredded into small pieces; explanation by the performing *dewa**: anger, trouble, difficulties emphasized during first burial are projected onto those two leaves; torn into pieces/shredded/annihilated they are made to disintegrate during secondary funerary rites
sarub	to enter someone's body, to take possession of (of the soul/*rowa** entering the foetus, of a spirit to possess someone)
sarub bonga	any spirit taking possession of a person
sasan	burial site; to use as a burial site; from fieldwork: the bodies of the dead of the house are often buried close to the houses: inside the courtyard, behind the house within the fences
sasan diri	large burial stone covering a grave horizontally (cf. *bid-diri**); collected from the jungle by men each representing one household of the hamlet affected by the death of one of its members

sasań	turmeric; yellow; condiment in *sasań* mixture; to claim a girl as wife by smearing her with wet *sasań* mixture
sayu	grass used for thatching: the Spear Grass
sesen teya:	veiled language in marriage negotiations alluding to a vehicle; *sesen* (literally) – a habitual way of going; habitual form of *sen* – to go, to walk
shab-e-barat	grand feast and observances of the Muslim community with vigil and prayers celebrated all through the night; ancestors are commemorated in this night
shivratri	grand *Gau** feast celebrated once every year in the courtyard of the Gau *diuri* in honour of Shiva at a time before Ho people celebrate *mage**; ritual collaboration of Gau *diuri** and Ho *diuri* and participation of Ho *diuri* during the whole festival; Ho pronounce festival as [*sibrateri*]
shradho	the Pano's* term for their ancestors
sida	first; original; see also *munu**
sida kaji	"tales of the olden days" (Deeney 2005: 341)
sim	a chicken; *sim enga* – a mother hen
Sinbonga	the creator God of the Ho and their supreme deity; generative power personified, imagined and addressed as grandfather (*tata*); a bodiless spirit; offerings made to Sinbonga are animals of a white colour, and animals of a white colour are never made to any other spirits; as Creator of all beings and all things Sinbonga is assumed to have also created the sun and the moon, but is not imagined as sun-god or "in any way equated to the sun" (Deeney 2008: 14); unmarried; symbol and source of wealth, abundance, prosperity, increase; see *punji**, *sumuki**
sinduri	vermillion; applied in acts of divining, in ritual performances representing spirits of the village, but not the dead of the house or Sinbonga; used in marriages
somdi, somodi (Odiya)	*balatadi** (Ho)
suka kaluti	a hen which has not yet hatched eggs, its colour a mixture of white, yellow, brown; regularly sacrificed in rituals at village and household level; addressed to *jayer buri**, *ham hoko-dum hoko**, *maran bonga**
suku	joy and pleasure; to be pleased with
suku sumuki	joy and abundance, plenty, prosperity; see *punji**
sukuila:	denotation unknown: (*suku* – happy); expression shouted by male in-laws in *keya ader** ceremony along with *dukuila:** to find out if the soul of a dead has entered the house; ploughshares (*pal**) banged against each other and against tiles of the roof while shouting
sukul	tobacco; Ho women like to chew it
sumuki	plenty, abundance, prosperity; see *punji**

taka	a rupee; during bridewealth negotiations often 101 rupees were agreed upon to the benefit of the bridal's parents' side. From fieldwork: by the groom's representative 501 rupees were offered, by the bridal's representative 400 rupees were given back.
tala	among; between; middle, centre; to put among; to surround; *bonga tala**
tar	to spread out paddy sheaves and have the grains detached from their stalks by having cattle walk on and thus thresh them; from fieldwork: in the research area an activity taking place in the courtyards and mainly done by elderly people; some impatient young people replaced the buffaloes by a hired three-wheeler that they chased across the sheaves.
tata	FF, MF
tata-gunguko	ancestors; literally the collectivity of a Ho's grandfathers and great grandparents; an unnamed, but relevant body of 'human(-ized)' spirits; more distant in relation to the living than the immediate forefathers of a few generations back called *ham ho-dum hoko** who live in the *adin**
tataka	"stupefaction; amazement; to be stupefied, amazed" (Deeney 2005: 371). Related to classifying different kinds of death Ho people used this term when a person's death was diagnosed as sudden, unexpected, dangerous.
teya	eZH; WyB; self-reciprocal relationship term
teya-kui	WyZ
ti chipa rasi	liquidy ritual rice-beer brew notionally to be distinguished from *diyan** and *rasi** consumed on profane occasions; hand-made (*ti* – hand) by the *diuri** or the head of the household in his role as ritual guide by squeezing (*chipa*) fermented husked rice (*adowa chauli**) between the palms
tika paiti	work for fixed wages paid according to the volume of work that has been completed; *nala paiti**
tiki era:	final purification ceremony after birth of a baby; (*tiki* – to boil in water); after this the new mother may enter the *adin**, touch the *mandi chatu** and cook the family meal in it; baby is entitled to full burial if dying after this ceremony
tiril-tarob	collective noun for various fruit trees often growing next to each other. From fieldwork: in a Santal marriage the groom is addressed as *tiril*, the bride as *tarob*. The moment in the process of getting married when groom and bride are pulled across the threshold inside the groom's parents' house by the groom's mother or his *hili* (eBW) is referred to as *tiril-tarob*
tulsi	basil; its leaves have sacred connotations; *tulsi* and leaves of the mango tree (*uli daru**) are put in water during any ritual thus purifying it; the objects (sacrificial sites, sacrificial animals, stones, roofs/houses) sprinkled with purified water become purified as a result

tunki	a medium size basket. From fieldwork: a newly bought *tunki* containing paddy seeds is used for the first sowing; kept in *adin**; it is decorated with scented white flowers for this purpose
tupu	to dip (e. g. *baba** in water)
umbul ader	rite at death to accompany the soul of a dead from grave to house and call the *rowa** inside the *adin**
uli daru	mango tree; its leaves are assigned sacred qualities; see also *tulsi**
undi	younger 'brother'; HyZH
undi-boya	children of the same parents (also *boko-boya**)
undi-kui	younger 'sister'; HyBW
unupud	fermentation
upud	of rice-beer: to ferment
uri:	cattle (cows, oxen, buffaloes, bullocks)
uri: ar	cattle for ploughing (oxen, bullocks, buffaloes); *ar* – yoke
uri: bonga	cattle sacrifice; from fieldwork: ritual performed by Santal community once every five years; presided over by Santal ritual guide (*naeke*); one cow, one ox sacrificed at night; *maran buru** and *jayer ayo* (the Ho equivalent is *jayer buri**) called upon to safeguard well-being of villagers, keep away epilepsy and chicken-pox; cow's meat and meat of the ox distributed separately as *kui jilu* (female meat) and *kowa jilu* (male meat) in equal shares to 98 households within the Santal hamlet in the research area
Waran Chiti	devised in the early 1950s by Lako Bodra as a distinctive indigenous script of the Ho language and promoted by Ho intelligentsia in the Chaibasa area/Jharkhand and in Mayurbhanj/Odisha (Anderson 2008: 195). Deeney (1978, 2005) makes use of a Romanized and Hindi-based Devanagari transcription instead in his Ho – English Dictionary.

Lists of Plates, Figures, and Maps

Collages

Plates

Figures

https://doi.org/10.1515/9783110666199-015

Maps

References

Allen, Nicholas A. 1985. The category of the person: a reading of Mauss's last essay. In Carrithers, Michael; Collins, Steven and Steven Lukes (eds.). *The category of the person. Anthropology, philosophy, history.* Cambridge: Cambridge University Press: 26–46.

Anderson, Gregory D.S. (ed.) 2008. *The Munda Languages.* Abingdon, New York: Routledge.

Anderson, Gregory D.S.; Osada, Toshiki and K. David Harrison 2008. Ho and the other Kherwarian Languages. In Anderson, Gregory D. S.(ed.). *The Munda Languages.* Abingdon: 195–255.

Areeparampil, Mathew 2002. *Struggle for Swaraj. A History of Adivasi Movements in Jharkhand (from the earliest times to the present day).* Lupungutu, Chaibasa: Tribal Research and Training Centre.

Assmann, Jan 2007 [1992]. *Das kulturelle Gedächtnis. Schrift, Erinnerung und politische Identität in frühen Hochkulturen.* München: C.H. Beck.

Bailey, Frederic G. 1961. "Tribe" and "Caste" in India. *Contributions to Indian Sociology* 5: 7–19.

Barnard, Alan and Anthony Good 1984. *Research Practices in the Study of Kinship.* London: Academic Press.

Barnard, Alan 2003. *History And Theory In Anthropology.* Cambridge: Cambridge University Press.

Barnard, Alan and Jonathan Spencer (eds.) 2007 [1996]. *Encyclopaedia Of Social And Cultural Anthropology.* London, New York: Routledge.

Barnes, John Arundel 2007 [1961]. African Models in the New Guinea Highlands. In Parkin, Robert and Linda Stone (eds.). *Kinship and Family. An Anthropological Reader.* Malden: Blackwell Publishing: 97–104.

Barraud, Cécile 2015. Kinship, equality, and hierarchy. Sex distinction and values in comparative perspective. *HAU: Journal of Ethnographic Theory* 5(1): 227–250.

Beer, Bettina 2001. Friendship, Anthropology of. In Smelser, Neil and Paul Bates (eds.). *International Encyclopaedia of the Social and Behavioral Sciences.* Oxford: Elsevier Science: 5805–5808.

Bell, Sandra and Simon Coleman (eds.) 1999. *The Anthropology of Friendship.* Oxford: Berg.

Benteler, Miriam 2014. Shared Values. Hierarchy and Affinity in a Latin Catholic Community of South India. New Delhi: Manohar.

Benthall, Jonathan 1992. A Late Developer? The Ethnography of Children. *Anthropology Today,* 8 (2): 1.

Bera, G.K. (ed.) 2008. *The Unrest Axle. Ethno-social movements in Eastern India.* New Delhi: Mittal Publications: 183–210.

Berger, Peter 2002. The Gadaba and the "non-ST" Desia of Koraput, Orissa. In Pfeffer, Georg and Deepak Kumar Behera (eds.). *Contemporary Society: Tribal Studies.* Vol. V. *The Concept of Tribal Society.* New Delhi: Concept Publishing: 57–90.

Berger, Peter 2007. *Füttern, Speisen Und Verschlingen. Ritual und Gesellschaft im Hochland von Orissa, Indien.* Berlin: LIT.

Berger, Peter et.al. (eds.) 2009. Fieldwork. Social Realities in Anthropological Perspectives. *Berliner Beiträge zur Ethnologie.* Band 15. Berlin: Weißensee Verlag.

Berger, Peter et.al. (eds.) 2010. *The Anthropology of Values. Essays in Honour of Georg Pfeffer.* Delhi: Pearson.

https://doi.org/10.1515/9783110666199-016

Berger, Peter 2015 [German 2007]. *Feeding, Sharing, and Devouring: Ritual and Society in Highland Odisha, India*. Boston, Berlin: De Gruyter.

Berreman, Gerald D. 1974 [1963]. *Hindus of the Himalayas. Ethnography and Change*. Berkeley, Los Angeles, London: University of California Press.

Béteille, André 1974.Tribe and Peasantry. In *Six Essays in Comparative Sociology*. Delhi: Oxford University Press.

Béteille, André 1998. The Idea of Indigenous People. *Current Anthropology* 39 (2): 187–91.

Bloch, Maurice and Jonathan Parry 1982. Introduction: Death and the regeneration of life. In Bloch, M. and J. Parry (eds.). *Death and the regeneration of life*. Cambridge: Cambridge University Press.

Bloch, Maurice 1982. Death, women and power. In Bloch, M. and Jonathan Parry (eds.). *Death and the regeneration of life*. Cambridge: Cambridge University Press: 211–230.

Bloch, Maurice 1988. Introduction. Death and the Concept of a Person. In Cederroth, S.; Corlin, C. and J. Lindström (eds.). *On the Meaning of Death: Essays on Mortuary Rituals and Eschatological Beliefs*. Uppsala: 11–30.

Bloch, Maurice 2013. *In And Out Of Each Other's Bodies. Theory of Mind, Evolution, Truth, and the Nature of the Social*. London: Paradigm Publishers.

Bluebond-Langner, Myra and Jill E. Korbin 2007. Challenges and Opportunities in the Anthropology of Childhoods: An Introduction to Children, Childhoods, and Childhood Studies. *American Anthropologist* 109 (2): 241–246.

Boas, Franz 1974 [1911]. The Instability of Human Types. In Stocking, G.W. (ed.). *The Shaping of American Anthropology 1883–1911. A Franz Boas Reader*. New York: Basic Books: 214–218.

Boas, Franz 1966 [1940]. *Race, language and culture*. New York: Free Press.

Bodding, P.O. 1932–1936. *A Santal Dictionary*. 7 parts in 5 volumes. New Delhi: Gyan Publishing House.

Borutta, Helmuth (n.d.). *Erinnerungen. Zehn Jahre Missionsarbeit unter den Hos in Singbhum/ Bihar Indien 1949–1958*. Published by author.

Bouez, Serge 1979. Sens et répétition dans le rite: la cérémonie de mariage des Ho (Inde). *L'Ethnographie* 80 (1979-II): 85–107.

Bouez, Serge 1985. *Réciprocité et Hiérarchie. L'Alliance Chez Les Ho Et Les Santal De L'Inde*. Paris: Société d' Ethnographie.

Bouez, Serge 1990. L'Alliance classificatoire chez les Ho. Préférence ou prescription. In Franoise Héritier-Augé and Elisabeth Copet-Rougier (eds.), *Les complexités de l'alliance. Les systèmes semi-complexes*. Montreux: Gordon and Breach Science Publishers: 1–23.

Bradley-Birt, Frances Bradley 1905. *The Story of an Indian Upland*. Whitefish: Kessinger Publishings Legacy Reprint Series.

Carrithers, Michael; Collins, Steven and Steven Lukes 2004 [1985] (eds.). *The category of the person. Anthropology, philosophy, history*. Cambridge: Cambridge University Press.

Carsten, Janet 2000 (ed.). *Cultures of Relatedness: New Approaches to the Study of Kinship*. Cambridge: Cambridge University Press.

Census Atlas 1988. Part XII. Distribution of Population by Language mainly spoken in the Household 1981. Map 66, Series 4. Bihar: *Census of India*.

Chandramonti, C. 2013. Ministry of Home Affairs. *Census of India 2011. Release of Primary Census Abstract. Data Highlights*. 3–12.

Charnov, Eric 2001. Evolution of Mammal Life Histories. *Evolutionary Ecology Research* 3: 371–383.

Craven, J.A. 1898. *Final Report on the Settlement of the Kolhan Government Estate in District Singhbhum of the year 1897*. Calcutta: Bengal Secretariat Press.

Crowther, Jonathan 1995. *Oxford Advanced Learner's Dictionary of Current English*. Oxford: Oxford University Press. [reference in this book: ALD]

Dalton, Edward T. 1868. The "Kols" of Chota-Nagpore. *Transactions of the Ethnological Society of London*. Vol.6: 1–41.

Dalton, Edward T. 1973 [1872]. *Descriptive Ethnology of Bengal*. Reprint. Calcutta: Indian Studies Past and Present.

Das Gupta, Sanjukta 2003. Women in the Traditional World of the Singhbhum Hos. In *Bengal Past and Present*. Vol. 122 (234–35), parts I-II: 56–67.

Das Gupta, Sanjukta 2006. The Changing World of the Singhbhum Hos. 1820 – 1932. *Indian Historical Review*. Vol. 23 (1): 76–98.

Das Gupta, Sanjukta 2011. *Adivasis and the Raj. Socio-economic Transition of the Hos, 1820–1932*. New Delhi: Orient Blackswan.

Dawkins, Richard 1989. *The Selfish Gene*. New York: Oxford University Press.

Deeney, John S.J. 1991. *Introduction to the Ho Language*. Chaibasa: Xavier Ho Publications.

Deeney, John S.J. 2002 [1975]. *Ho Grammar and Vocabulary*. Lupungutu: Xavier Ho Publications.

Deeney, John S.J. 2005 [1978]. *Ho – English Dictionary*. New edition – revised and enlarged. 1 volume. Ranchi: Xavier Publications.

Deeney, John S.J. 2008. *The Spirit World of the Ho Tribals. And other glimpses into the Ho world*. Ranchi: Xavier Publications.

de Maaker, Erik 2006. *Negotiating Life: Garo Death Rituals and the Transformation of Society*. Doctoral Thesis. Publ. by Research School CNWS: Leiden University.

Desai, Amit 2010. A Matter of Affection: Ritual Friendship in Central India. In Desai, A. and Evan Killick (eds.). *The Ways of Friendship. Anthropological Perspectives*. New York, Oxford: Berghahn Books: 114–133.

Desai, Amit and Evan Killick (eds.) 2010. *The Ways of Friendship. Anthropological Perspectives*. New York, Oxford: Berghahn.

Deshpande, Satish and Nandini Sundar 1998. Caste and the Census. Implications for Society and the Social Sciences. In *Economic and Political Weekly*: 2157–2159.

Deutsches Ärzteblatt. Die Zeitschrift der Ärzteschaft 2013. Adoleszenz. Hirnentwicklung und psychische Störungen. Ausgabe C, Heft 25. June 21st: author unknown.

Dhan, Rekha O. 1961. The Hos of Saranda: An Ethnographic Study. In N. Prasad (ed.). *Bulletin of the Bihar Tribal Research Institute*. Vol. 3 (1). Ranchi: 37–114.

Dhan, Rekha O. 1962. The Religion of the Hos of Saranda. In Sachchidananda (ed.). *Bulletin of the Bihar Tribal Research Institute*. Vol. 4 (1). Ranchi: 17–35.

Dhir, Anil 2012. Man with a Mission. *Uday India*. Vol. III (38), September 01, 2012. Delhi: 36–49.

Dumont, Louis 1962. "Tribe" and "Caste" in India. *Contributions to Indian Sociology* VI: 120–124.

Dumont, Louis 1970 [1966]. *Homo Hierarchicus. The Caste System and Its Implications*. London: Weidenfeld and Nicolson.

Dumont, Louis 1983. *Affinity as a Value. Marriage Alliance in South India, with Comparative Essays on Australia*. Chicago, London: The University of Chicago Press.

Durkheim, David Émile 1976 [1895]. *Die Regeln der soziologischen Methode*. Darmstadt, Neuwied: Luchterhand.

Eggan, Fred 1970 [1937]. The Cheyenne and Arapaho Kinship System. In Eggan, Fred (ed.). *Social Anthropology of North American Tribes*. Chicago: The University of Chicago Press: 35–98.

Ethnologue: Languages of the World 2017. In Simon, Gray F. and Charles D. Fennig (eds.). *Ethnologue: Languages of the World*. Dallas, Texas: SIL International, United States. 20th edition. Web edition.

Evans-Pritchard, Edward Evan 1969 [1940]. *The Nuer. A Description of the Modes of Livelihood and Political Institutions of a Nilotic People*. New York and Oxford: Oxford University Press.

Firth, Raymond William 1967 [1936]. Bond Friendship. In Firth, R. (ed.). *Tikopia Ritual and Belief*. London: Allen &Unwin: 108–115.

Firth, Raymond William 1999. Preface. In Bell, Sandra and Simon Coleman (eds.). *The Anthropology of Friendship*. Oxford: Berg: VIII-XV.

Froerer, Peggy 2010. Close Friends: The Importance of Proximity in Children's Peer Relations in Chhattisgarh, Central India. In Desai, Amit and Evan Killick (eds.). *The Ways of Friendship. Anthropological Perspectives*. New York, Oxford: Berghahn Books: 133–154.

Fuhrmann, Berit 2013. *Die Menschen des Mutterhauses. Soziale Beziehungen, rituelle Prozesse und lokales Christentum bei den Karow in Meghalaya, Indien*. University of Münster: online-publication.

Gatzlaff-Hälsig, Margot (ed.) 2002. *Handwörterbuch Hindi – Deutsch*. Hamburg: Buske.

Godelier, Maurice; Trautmann, Thomas R. and Franklin E. Tjon Sie Fat (eds.) 1998. *Transformations of Kinship*. Washington: Smithsonian Institution Press.

Goody, Jack 1983. *The development of the family and marriage in Europe*. Cambridge, New York: Cambridge University Press.

Gregory, Christopher A. 1982. *Gifts and Commodities*. London: Academic Press.

Gregory, Christopher A. 1983. Kula gift exchange and capitalist commodity exchange: a comparison. In Leach, J. and Edmund Leach (eds.). *The Kula: New Perspectives on Massim Exchange*. Cambridge: Cambridge University Press: 103–117.

Gregory, Christopher A. 2009. Brotherhood and Otherhood in Bastar: On the Social Specificity of "Dual Organization" in Aboriginal India. In Pfeffer, Georg and Deepak K. Behera (eds.). *Contemporary Society: Tribal Studies*. Vol. 8: 67–83.

Hall, Granville Stanley 1904. *Adolescence: Its Psychology and Its Relations to Physiology, Anthropology, Sociology, Sex, Crime, Religion, and Education*. New York: Appleton.

Hardenberg, Roland 2005. *Children of the Earth Goddess: Society, Marriage and Sacrifice in the Highlands of Orissa*. Münster: Habilitationsschrift (unpubl.)

Hardenberg, Roland 2018. *Children of the Earth Goddess: Society, Marriage and Sacrifice in the Highlands of Odisha*. Berlin, Boston: de Gruyter.

Hardiman, David 1987. *The Coming of the Devi: Adivasi Assertion in Western India*. New Delhi: Oxford University Press.

Hebbar, Ritambhara 2003. Eternal and Ephemeral. The Significance of Myth and Ritual among the Ho. In Sen, Padmaja (ed.). *Changing Tribal Life: A Socio-Philosophical Perspective*. New Delhi: Concept Publishers: 40 – 49.

Hertz, Robert 1960 [1907]. A Contribution to the Study of the Collective Representation of Death. In Needham, Rodney and Claudia Needham (tr.). *Death and the Right Hand*. Aberdeen: Cohen & West: 27–86.

Hirschfeld, Lawrence 2002. Why Don't Anthropologists Like Children? *American Anthropologist. New Series* 104 (2): 611–627.

Hirschfeld, Lawrence 1999. L'enfant terrible: Anthropology and its Aversion to Children. *Etnofoor* (Kids and Culture) 12 (1): 5–26.

Hoffman, John and A. van Emelen 1990 [1950]. *Encyclopaedia Mundarica*. 16 volumes. New Delhi: Gian Publishing House.

Hoffman, John 2005 [1950]. *The World of the Mundas*. New Delhi: Critical Quest: 1–40.

Homans, G.C. and Schneider, David M. 1955. *Marriage, Authority and Final Causes: A Study of Unilateral Cross-Cousin Marriage*. Glencoe: Free Press.

Hubert, Henri and Marcel Mauss 1981 [1964]. *Sacrifice. Its Nature and Functions*. The University of Chicago Press: Midway Reprint.

Jai Jharkhand 1999. Sarini Occasional Papers 2. Sarini and Birsa-Johar (eds.). Chaibasa, Bhubaneswar.

James, Allison 2007. Giving Voice to Children's Voices: Practices and Problems, Pitfalls and Potentials. *American Anthropologist*, 109 (2): 261–272.

Jay, E.J. 1973. Bridging the Gap between Castes; Ceremonial Friendship in Chhattisgarh. *Contributions to Indian Sociology* 7: 144–58.

Jaoul, Nicolas and Naike Desquesnes 2011. Operation Green Hunt. *Le Monde Diplomatique*. November 11th, 2011: 15.

Killick, Evan and Amit Desai 2010. Introduction: Valuing Friendship. In Desai, A. and E. Killick (eds.). *The Ways of Friendship. Anthropological Perspectives*. New York, Oxford: Berghahn Books.

Lancy, David F. 2008. *The Anthropology of Childhood. Cherubs, Chattel, Changelings*. New York: Cambridge University Press.

Lancy, David F. 2012.Unmasking Children's Agency. Retrieved November 15th from www.usu. edu/anthro/davidlancyspages/blog

Leach, Edmund R. 1951. The Structural Implications of Matrilateral Cross-Cousin Marriage. In Leach, E.R. 1971 [1961]. *Rethinking Anthropology*. New York: The Athlone Press: 54–105.

Leach, Edmund R. 1968. *A Runaway world?* Oxford: Oxford University Press.

Leach, Edmund R. 1971 [1961]. *Rethinking Anthropology*. London: The Athlone Press.

Leach, Edmund R. 1977 [1954]. *Political Systems of Highland Burma. A Study of Kachin Social Structure*. London and New York: Continuum.

Leach, Edmund R. 1990. Aryan Invasions over Four Millenia. In Ohnuki-Tierney, Emiko (ed.). *Culture Through Time. Anthropological Approaches*. Stanford: Stanford University Press: 227–245.

Leach, Edmund R. 1991 [1970]. *Claude Lévi-Strauss zur Einführung*. Hamburg: Junius Verlag.

LeVine, Robert A. 2007. Ethnographic Studies of Childhood: A Historical Overview. *American Anthropologist*, 109 (2): 247–260.

Lévi-Strauss, Claude 1953. Social Structure. In Kroeber, Alfred L. (ed.). *Anthropology Today. An Encyclopaedic Inventory*. Chicago: The University of Chicago Press: 524–53.

Lévi-Strauss, Claude 1968 [1962]. *Das Ende des Totemismus*. Frankfurt am Main: Suhrkamp Verlag. edition suhrkamp 128.

Lévi-Strauss, Claude 1969 [French 1949]. *The Elementary Structures of Kinship* (2nd edn). London: Eyre and Spottiswoode.

Lewis, M. Paul (ed.) 2009. *Ethnologue. Languages of the World.* Dallas: SIL International. Print version.

Lourdusamy, Stan 1999. On the altar of India's nuclear weapons programme. In Sarini and BIRSA-JOHAR (ed.). *Jai Jharkhand. Occasional Papers* 2: 105–115.

MacPherson, T.S. 1972 [1930]. Differences in Custom between the Hos and the Mundas in the Singbhum District. Reprint. In Sarat Ch. Roy (ed.). *Man in India.* Vol. 10: 167–8.

Majumdar, Dhirendra Nath 1924. The traditional origin of the Hos; together with a brief description of the Chief Bongas (or Gods) of the Hos. Calcutta: *Journal and proceedings of the Asiatic Society of Bengal* (XX): 193–197.

Majumdar, Dhirendra Nath 1950. *The Affairs of a Tribe. A Study In Tribal Dynamics.* The Mall, Lucknow: Universal Publishers.

Malinowski, Bronislaw 1927. *Sex and Repression in Savage Society.* London: Paul, Trench, Trubner.

Mallebrein, Cornelia 2008. Orissa brennt. Erneute hindunationalistische Pogrome in Indien. *Suedasien.info:* September 12th.

Mauss, Marcel 1985 [1938]. A category of the human mind: the notion of person; the notion of self. In Carrithers, Michael, Steven Collins, Steven Lukes (eds.) 1985. *The category of the person. Anthropology, philosophy, history.* Cambridge: Cambridge University Press: 1–26.

Mauss, Marcel 1990 [1925]. *The Gift. The form and reason for exchange in archaic societies.* London: Routledge.

McDougal, Charles W. 1963. *The Social Structure of the Hill Juang.* The University of New Mexico, Ann Arbor. PhD Dissertation: University Microfilms.

McGregor, R.S. (ed.) 2011 [1993]. *Oxford Hindi-English Dictionary.* New Delhi: Oxford University Press.

Mead, Margaret 1928a. *Coming of Age in Samoa.* New York: William Morrow.

Mead, Margaret 1928b. Samoan Children at Work and Play. *Natural History* 28: 626–636.

Mohanty, Uma Charan 1973–4. Bond-Friendship Among the Gadaba. *Man in Society* I: 130–55.

Moharana, Khirod Chandra 2012. *Mental Illness among the Hos of Odisha: An Ethnographic Study.* Delhi: Indian Institute of Technology. Unpublished Dissertation.

Montgomery, Heather 2009. *An Introduction to Childhood. Anthropological Perspectives on Children's Lives.* Chichester: Wiley-Blackwell.

Morgan, Lewis Henry 1871. *Systems of Consanguinity and Affinity of the Human Family.* Washington D.C.: Smithonian Institution.

Munda, Ram Dayal 2014 [2000]. *Adi-dharam. Religious beliefs of the Adivasis of India.* Kolkata: sarini, Birsa & adivani.

Mundu, John B. 2003. *The Ho Christian community. Towards a new self-understanding as communion.* Delhi: Media House.

Mundu, John B. 2012. Tribal and Indigenous Peoples in India. In Thomas &. John Desrochers D'Sa: Centre for Social Action. Bangalore: *An NBCLC Series on Current Issues* no 9: 7–17.

Nathan, Dev and Virginius Xaxa 2012. *Social exclusion and adverse inclusion. Development and deprivation of Adivasis in India.* New Delhi: Oxford University Press.

Needham, Rodney 1962. *Structure and Sentiment.* Chicago: University of Chicago Press.

Needham, Rodney 1973. Prescription. *Oceania* 42: 166–181.

Niggemeyer, Hermann 1964. Kuttia Kond und Pano. Zur Stellung der verachteten Klassen in Indien. In Haberland, Eike; Schuster, Meinhard; Straube, Helmut (eds.). *Festschrift für A. E. Jensen.* Teil II. München: Klaus Renner: 407–413.

Otten, Tina 2006. *Heilung durch Rituale. Vom Umgang mit Krankheit bei den Rona im Hochland Orissas.* Berlin: LIT Verlag.

Paine, R. 1969. In Search of Friendship: An Exploratory Analysis in 'Middle-Class' Culture. *Man* 4(4): 505–524.

Parkin, Robert 1992. *The Munda of Central India. An Account of their Social Organization.* Delhi: Oxford University Press.

Parkin, Robert 2000: Proving Indigeneity, Exploiting Modernity. Modalities of Identity Construction in Middle India. *Anthropos* vol. 95 (1): 49–63.

Parry, Jonathan P. 1986.The Gift, the 'Indian' Gift, and the 'Indian Gift'. *Man* (n.s.) 21 (3): 453–73.

Parry, Jonathan P. 1994. *Death in Banares.* The Lewis Henry Morgan Lectures 1988. Cambridge: Cambridge University Press.

Perry-Castaneda Map Collection. *India and Pakistan AMS Topographic Maps.* Sheet NF 45–6: *Jamshedpur.* Series U502. University of Texas Library Online: The University of Texas at Austin. (Retrieved: 5.02.2018).

Petermann, Werner 2004. *Die Geschichte der Ethnologie.* Wuppertal: Peter Hammer Verlag. Edition Trickster.

Pfeffer, Georg 1982. Status And Affinity In Middle India. *Beiträge zur Südasienforschung.* Südasien-Institut Universität Heidelberg. Band 76. Wiesbaden: Franz Steiner Verlag.

Pfeffer, Georg 1997. The Scheduled Tribes of Middle India as a Unit: Problems of Internal und External Comparison. In Pfeffer, Georg and Deepak Behera (eds.). *Contemporary Society: Tribal Studies.* Volume One. *Structure and Process.* New Delhi: Concept Publishers: 3–27.

Pfeffer, Georg 2001. A ritual of Revival Among the Gadaba of Koraput. In Kulke, Hermann and Burkhard Schnepel (eds.). *Jagannath Revisited: Studying Society, Religion and the State in Orissa.* New Delhi: Manohar: 99–125.

Pfeffer, Georg and Burkhard Schnepel (eds.). *Jagannath Revisited: Studying Society, Religion and the State in Orissa.* New Delhi: Manohar: 99–125.

Pfeffer, Georg 2002. The Structure of Middle Indian Tribal Society Compared. In Pfeffer, Georg and Deepak Behera 2002 (eds.), *Contemporary Society. Tribal studies.* Volume Five. *Concept of Tribal Society.* New Delhi: Concept: 9–31; 208–229.

Pfeffer, Georg 2003. Hunters, Tribes, Peasants: Cultural Crisis and Comparison. *The Dr. Ambedkar Memorial Lecture Series.* Bhubaneswar: NISWASS.

Pfeffer, Georg 2004. Order in Tribal Middle Indian 'Kinship'. *Anthropos* 99.2004: 381–409.

Pfeffer, Georg 2014. Ethnographies of States and Tribes in Highland Odisha. *Asian Ethnology.* Vol. 73 (1–2): 259–279.

Pfeffer, Georg 2016. Verwandtschaft als Verfassung. Unbürokratische Muster öffentlicher Ordnung. Baden-Baden: Nomos Verlagsgesellschaft.

Pfeffer, Georg 2017. Tribal Social Structure in Odisha. In Skoda, Uwe and Biswamoy Pati (eds.). *Highland Odisha. Life and Society Beyond the Coastal World.* Delhi: Primus: 49–71.

Pfeffer, Georg 2019. *Lewis Henry Morgan's Comparisons. Reassessing Terminology, Anarchy and Worldview in Indigenous Societies of America, Australia and Highland Middle India.* New York, Oxford: Berghahn.

Pöhl, Friedrich and Bernhard Tilg (eds.) 2011. Einleitung. In *Franz Boas. Kultur, Sprache, Rasse. Wege einer antirassistischen Anthropologie.* LIT-Verlag Wien, Berlin. Bd. 19: 14.

Pucilowski, Anna 2013. *Topics In Ho Morphophonology And Morphosyntax.* Oregon: Unpublished Dissertation.

Purty, Dhanur Singh 1978–1982. *Ho Disum Ho Honko.* 7 volumes. Chaibasa: Xavier Ho Publications.

Raza, M. and A. Ahmad 1990. *An atlas of tribal India.* New Delhi: Concept Publishers.

Reich, David et al. 2009. Reconstructing Indian population history. *Nature. The International Weekly Journal of Science.* Vol. 461: 489–494. September 24th.

Reichel, Eva 2009. *Notions of Life in Death and Dying. The Dead in Tribal Middle India.* New Delhi: Manohar.

Reichel, Eva 2014a. Concepts of Children and Childhood in Anthropology and in a Tribal Community of Middle India. *The Oriental Anthropologist.* Vol. 14 (2): 189–201.

Reichel, Eva 2014b. Exploring Illness: Notes from recent fieldwork among the Ho. In Behera, Deepak Kumar (ed.). *Contemporary Society: Tribal Studies.* Vol. 9. New Delhi: Concept Publishing: 32–46.

Reichel, Eva 2014c. *Gift Exchanges between the Living and the Dead.* Unpublished manuscript of lecture held at panel 046: S233 at EASA congress in Tallinn on August 2nd, 2014.

Reichel, Eva 2017. On Death and the Ho's Relationship with their Dead. In Skoda, Uwe and Biswmoy Pati (eds.). *Highland Odisha. Life and Society Beyond the Coastal World.* Delhi: Primus Books: 107–135.

Reichel, Eva 2018. Scholarly Commitment: John Deeney and the Ho of Kolhan. In Pfeffer, Georg and Nibedita Nath (eds.). *Empirical Anthropology. Issues of Academic Friends and Friends in the Field.* New Delhi: Concept Publishing Company: 194–204.

Risley, Herbert Hope 1891. *People of India, 1901. The Tribes and Castes of Bengal.* 4 volumes. Calcutta. (reference in Majumdar 1950:362).

Rothermund, Dietmar 1978. *Government, landlord, and peasant in India. Agrarian relations under British rule: 1865–1935.* Wiesbaden: Steiner.

Rothermund, Dietmar 1989 [1976]. *Indische Geschichte in Grundzügen.* Darmstadt: Wissenschaftliche Buchgesellschaft.

Rothermund, Dietmar 2001. *The Rural Roots Of Jharkhand.* Manuscript: 1–12.

Rothermund, Dietmar 2013. The Rural Roots of Jharkhand. Essay No 6. In Rothermund, D. *Empires in Indian History and Other Essays.* New Delhi: Manohar.

Roy, Arundhati 2012. *Walking with the Comrades.* New York: Penguin Books.

Roy, Sarat Chandra 1970 [1912]. *The Mundas and Their Country.* London: Asia Publishing House.

Sahlins, Marshall David 1968. *Tribesmen.* Eaglewood Cliffs. Prentice Hall.

Sahlins, Marshall David 1994 [1976]. *Kultur und praktische Vernunft.* Frankfurt am Main: Suhrkamp Verlag. Suhrkamp Taschenbuch Wissenschaft 1139.

Sahlins, Marshall David 2000 [1999]. What is Anthropological Enlightenment? Some Lessons of the Twentieth Century. In *Culture in Practice. Selected Essays.* New York: Zone Books: 501–526.

Sahlins, Marshall David 2008. *The Western illusion of human nature. With reflections on the long history of hierarchy, equality and the sublimation of anarchy in the West, and comparative notes on other conceptions of the human condition.* Paradigm 32. Chicago: Prickly Paradigm Press.

Sapir, Edward 1993. *The Psychology of Culture. A Course of Lectures.* Reconstructed and edited by Judith Irvine. The Hague: Mouton de Gruyter.

Schulte-Droesch, Lea 2018. *Making Place through Ritual. Land, Environment and Region among the Santal of Central India.* Berlin, Boston: De Gruyter.

Sen, Asoka Kumar 2012. *From village elder to British judge. Custom, customary law and tribal society.* New Delhi: Orient Blackswan.

Sen, Padmaja (ed.) 2003. *Changing Tribal Life. A Socio-Philosophical Perspective.* New Delhi: Concept.

Sen, Padmaja 2006. Understanding Tribal Cosmology and the Creation Myths of the Adivasis of Jharkhand. In Surendra Gopal (ed.). *Colonial India. Research Publication series* 4. Arrah: Veer Kunwar Singh University: 310–320.

Sen, Padmaja (forthcoming). Socio-religious movements and the evolution of religious identity among the *Adivasis* of Jharkhand. In Mishra., A. and C.K. Paty (eds.). *Tribal Movement in Jharkhand 1857–2007.* New Delhi: Concept: 1–15.

Shah, Alpa 2003. *Understanding the State: An Anthropological Study of Rural Jharkhand, India.* London: London School of Economics. Unpublished dissertation.

Shah, Alpa 2010. *In the shadows of the state. Indigenous politics, environmentalism, and insurgency in Jharkhand, India.* Durham, NC: Duke University Press.

Shah, Alpa 2013. The tensions over liberal citizenship in a Marxist revolutionary situation: The Maoists in India. *Critique of Anthropology* 33 (1): 91–109.

Simon, Gray F. and Charles D. Fennig (eds.) 2017. *Ethnologue: Languages of the World.* 20th edition. Dallas, Texas: SIL International. web edition.

Singh, C.P 1978. *The Ho Tribe of Singhbhum.* New Delhi: Classical Publications.

Singh, K. Suresh 1966. *The Dust-Storm and the Hanging Mist. A study of Birsa Munda and his movement in Chhotanagpur (1874–1901).* Calcutta: K.L. Mukhopadhyay.

Singh, K. Suresh 1982. Transformation of Tribal Society. Integration vs Assimilation. *Economic and Political Weekly.* Vol.17 (33): 1318–1325.

Singh, K. Suresh 1997. *The Scheduled Tribes. People of India.* Oxford University Press. National Series. Volume 3.

Skoda, Uwe 2004. Ritual Friendship in a Converging Tribal and Caste Society. *Journal of Social Sciences* 8(2): 167–177.

Skoda, Uwe 2005. The Aghria. A Peasant Caste on a Tribal Frontier. New Delhi: Manohar.

Skoda, Uwe and Biswamoy Pati (eds.) 2017. *Highland Odisha. Life and Society Beyond the Coastal World.* Delhi: Primus Books.

Spencer, F.C. 1899. *Education of the Pueblo Child: A Study in Arrested Development.* New York.

Strathern, Marilyn 1972. *Women in Between. Female Roles in a Male World: Mount Hagen, New Guinea.* London and New York: Seminar Press.

Strathern, Marilyn 1988. *The Gender of the Gift.* Berkeley: University of California Press.

Streumer, Paul 2012. Changes and Chances in a Long View. The Ho people of West Singhbhum and the Challenges of Rapid Economic Growth. In Nathan, Dev and Virginius

Xaxa (eds.). *Social Exclusion and Adverse Inclusion. Development and Deprivation of Adivasis in India*. New Delhi: Oxford University Press: 261–271.

Streumer, Paul 2016. *A Land of their Own. Samuel Richard Tickell and the Formation of the Autonomous Ho Country in Jharkhand, 1818 – 1842*. The historians' edition. The Netherlands: Houten.

südasien.info: das Informationsportal zu Südasien. Web edition. Berlin: Südasien-Informationsnetz e.V. (Herausgeber). www.südasien.info

Tickell, S. R. 1840. Memoir on the Hodesum (Improperly Called the Kolehan). *Journal of the Asiatic Society of Bengal, Vol. 9* (2): 694–710, 783–808.

Tjon Sie Fat, Franklin E. 1998. On the Formal Analysis of 'Dravidian', 'Iroquois', and 'Generational' Varieties as Nearly Associative Combinations. In Godelier, M., T.R. Trautmann, F.Tjon Sie Fat (eds.). *Transformations of Kinship*. Washington: Smithsonian Institution Press: 59–94.

Trautmann, Thomas R. 1981. *Dravidian Kinship*. Cambridge: Cambridge University Press.

Trautmann, Thomas R. 2000. India and the Study of Kinship Terminologies. *L'Homme* 154–5: 559–572.

Trautmann, Thomas R. and Peter Whiteley (eds.) 2012. *Crow-Omaha. New Light on a Classic Problem of Kinship Analysis*. Tucso i: The University of Arizona Press.

Trawick, Margaret 2012. Position Paper for the 2012 Inter-Congress of the IUAES Commission on Children, Childhood and Youth. Bhubaneswar, India.

Tripathi, Amish 2015. Are You An Aryan Invader? Colonial views on fair-skinned Aryans vs dark-skinned Dravidians have wide political currency today. *The Times of India, GOA:* December 17th.

Tuckey, A.D. 1920. *Final Report on the Resettlement of the Kolhan Government Estate*. Patna.

Vansina, Jan M. 1985. *Oral Tradition as History*. Madison: University of Wisconsin Press.

Verardo, Barbara 2003a. Forest People, Modern People: Modernity and Social Change among the Ho and Munda People of Jharkhand. In Sen, Padmaja (ed.). *Changing Tribal Life. A Socio-Philosophical Perspective*. Delhi: Concept Publishing House: 81–94.

Verardo, Barbara 2003b. *Rebels and Devotees of Jharkhand. Social, Religious and Political Transformations among the Adivasis of Northern India*. Ph.D. thesis (unpublished). London: University of London.

Verma, S.K., R.N. Sahai 2010 [2003] (eds.). *Oxford English-Hindi Dictionary*. New Delhi: Oxford University Press.

Vitebsky, Piers 1993. *Dialogues with the Dead. The discussion of mortality among the Sora of eastern India*. Cambridge: Cambridge University Press.

Vitebsky, Piers 2008. Loving and Forgetting. Moments of Inarticulacy in Tribal India. *Journal of the Royal Anthropological Institute*. (N.S.) 14: 2434 – 261.

Vitebsky, Piers 2012. Repeated Returns and Special Friends. From Mythic Encounter to Shared History. In Howell, Signe and Aud Talle (eds.) *Returns To The Field. Multitemporal Research and Contemporary Anthropology*. Bloomington and Indianapolis: Indiana University Press: 180–202.

Vitebsky, Piers 2017. *Living Without The Dead. Loss And Redemption In A Jungle Cosmos*. Chicago and London: The University Of Chicago Press.

Weber, Max 1976 [1922]. *Wirtschaft und Gesellschaft*. Tübingen: Mohr.

Whiteley, Peter 2016. *Why Do Crow/Omaha Kinship Systems Exist?* Contribution to the workshop on Kinship, Cognition and Practice (14 – 16 September 2016). Unpublished manuscript. Halle/Saale: Max Planck-Institute for Social Anthropology.

Whiting, Beatrice and C.P. Edwards 1988. *Children of Different Worlds: The Formation of Social Behaviour.* Cambridge: Harvard University Press.

Whiting, Beatrice 1963. *Six Cultures. Studies of Child Rearing.* New York: Wiley.

Wittgenstein, Ludwig 2003 [1921]. *Tractatus Logico-Philosophicus.* Frankfurt a.M.: Suhrkamp: 5.6.

Yorke, Michael P. 1976. *Decisions And Analogy: Political Structure and Discourse among the Ho Tribals of India.* SOAS: University of London. Unpublished Dissertation.

Internet Sources

Census of India Website: Office of the Registrar General and Census Commissioner, India. www.censusindia.gov.in/2011-common/map.html; www.censusindia.gov.in/2011-com mon/census data2011.html

Ethnologue: Languages of the World. 2017: 20th edition. Online version: https://www.ethno logue.com/

Index